Introduction to

PHILOSOPHY OF EDUCATION

By STELLA VAN PETTEN HENDERSON

Introduction to

PHILOSOPHY

of

EDUCATION

THE UNIVERSITY OF CHICAGO PRESS

CHICAGO & LONDON

THE UNIVERSITY OF CHICAGO PRESS, CHICAGO & LONDON
The University of Toronto Press, Toronto 5, Canada

DEDICATED TO
THE MEMORY OF MY FATHER
EDWIN MALANEY VAN PETTEN

PREFACE

THIS textbook was written to assist the undergraduate student who is preparing to teach in formulating a philosophy of education. Teaching is a profession the importance and dignity of which cannot be overestimated. This was never truer than in the troubled modern world. Teachers cannot assume the entire responsibility for making the decision as to how the social changes necessary for a better world will be brought about. Such changes may come only through man's suffering and bitter experience. Or they may come as the result of man's growth in intelligence, good will, and ability to use his imagination in foreseeing the consequences of his behavior. It is, therefore, certain that the better teachers do their work, the more speedily and effectively will men work cooperatively and intelligently to promote human welfare. If teachers do not see how their work is related to the problem of social progress, man's suffering is sure to be greater than it need be and his advance slower than it could be. To help teachers see this major responsibility and understand the implications of such a concept is the purpose of the author.

Philosophers have always been concerned not only with attempts to understand the world as it is, but also with discovering how life should be lived, what man should strive for, and how he can improve his social organization. Philosophers have also understood the importance of education in promoting this better world. If teachers are to be successful in furthering human welfare, they need to study philosophy in order to apply it to the study of educational problems. Education cannot be understood apart from life itself, for the ends and objectives of living determine educational aims. The connection between philosophy, philosophy of education, and the work of a teacher has not always been recognized. One of the most hopeful signs, however, in the field of education today, is the growing conviction that every teacher needs a carefully formulated and intelligently criticized philosophy of education and that this philosophy of education must be rooted in philosophy itself.[1] In a recent book written by Brand Blanshard and his associates after an investigation into the relation of philosophy to the educational and social scene, there is a severe criticism of philosophy of education as it is taught in many schools. The writer quotes John H. Randall, who condemned "that complacent acceptance of a gospel that marks too many a student of 'the philosophy of education' in these United States." The author continues, "And it may seem obvious that the road to improvement lies . . . . in putting more philosophy into philosophy of education."[2] That, the writer of this text intended to do from the inception of the book.

Philosophy has been applied to the study of every problem introduced. While every philosopher worthy of the name has something of insight and wisdom to contribute to the solution of human problems, the author has cited Plato, Aristotle, and Kant more frequently than others. Kant has been said to combine the idealism of Plato with the hardheadedness and practicality of Aristotle. While a modern student of philosophy would find it impossible to agree with everything that Kant wrote, his fundamental positions in epistemology, ethics, and aesthetics seem sound to the writer. Certainly no one has formulated better the basic principle upon which true democratic thought and practice are founded: the principle of respect for human personality.

Kant was a great synthesizer. He could see the strengths and weaknesses in two opposing views and was able to integrate the truth in each into a unified concept. Such an operation is needed badly today in educational theory. There is a growing uneasiness with and distrust of many practices in modern education. In some communities there has even been a demand that everything known as Progressive education be abolished and the older type of school procedure restored. To do this would often mean a backward step. Modern Progressive education has grown out of the philosophies of Rousseau

1. See report of Committee on Teaching Philosophy, "Philosophy and Philosophy of Education," *Journal of Philosophy*, XXXIX (April 9, 1942), 205–12; also articles by H. A. Larrabee and A. G. A. Balz, *School and Society*, LVI (July 4, 1942), 4–9; and C. D. Champlin, *School and Society*, LVI (September 19, 1942), 231–34.

2. Brand Blanshard and Others, *Philosophy in American Education*, p. 243.

and John Dewey. That which seems objectionable in the philosophy of this movement stems from Rousseau's extreme individualism and from Dewey's pragmatism. There is more in Rousseau than individualism and more in John Dewey than pragmatism. To dismiss all educational theory and practice from these sources would be to "throw out the baby with the bath."[3]

True, Progressive education unfortunately has advocated some questionable practices. But it has also advocated and put into practice reforms long overdue in the schools. These reforms were suggested before the days of the Progressive Education Association; they are time-tested and were advocated by educational reformers who were defenders neither of extreme individualism nor of modern pragmatism. All teachers should be progressives in the sense that they should work for social progress and for the kind of education which will promote human welfare. Many sound and promising practices will be found in Progressive education. Study, in the light of philosophy, should enable students of education to separate the wheat from the chaff.

A philosophy of education should answer three questions: What is education; what ought education to accomplish; and by what means can this be done? To answer these questions, it is necessary to inquire into the nature of man and also into the problem of how man may live his life to the fullest. Only then can the what, the why, and the how of education be defined. Chapter i of this text is an introduction. Chapters ii and iii deal with the what of education. Chapters iv through xii are concerned with understanding what education should accomplish; they deal with the why of the educative process. Chapters xiii through xvi are concerned with the how of education, i.e., how we can realize the aims implicit in the educative process. It is, of course, impossible to discuss any one of these without reference to the others. For example, as Aristotle pointed out, one cannot understand the what of anything without reference to the why. But attention has at least been centered on attempting to answer each of these questions in turn.

This text has been used in manuscript form for five years in the philosophy of education classes at Illinois State Normal University

3. See chap. xii.

and was revised in the light of the experiences of the teachers of the course.

There is for every chapter, first, an outline of the contents of the chapter. Then comes the exposition. After that there is a summary, followed by questions which the student may use to check his understanding. Each chapter ends with a bibliography for supplementary reading.

There has been no attempt to give an exhaustive bibliography for each chapter. Each bibliography is, rather, a selective one. Most of the references have been tried and tested in use. Materials of all grades of difficulty and of differing points of view have been included.

The Glossary of Philosophical Terms at the end of the book can be used as a dictionary, but students should be encouraged to consult an encyclopedia, particularly the *Britannica*, for more extended discussions of the meanings of the terms.

The author is deeply indebted, for more things than could be enumerated, to Dean Emeritus H. H. Schroeder. Without his help and encouragement this book would not have been written. He not only introduced the author to the study of philosophy, and particularly the Kantian philosophy, but read and criticized this entire manuscript. From those criticisms the author profited greatly. He was also kind enough to furnish translations for some passages in Kant's work for which translations either are not available or are unsatisfactory.

The author also owes a debt of gratitude to Professor William Heard Kilpatrick. He is a great teacher. During a year of stimulating and challenging study with him, Professor Kilpatrick never failed in kindly and friendly interest, even where there was disagreement on basic, philosophic issues.

Professor Newton Edwards of the University of Chicago read the manuscript and offered valuable suggestions and materials.

The author is also indebted to certain of her colleagues who were kind enough to read the manuscript and to give her the benefit of their suggestions. Dr. Gerda Okerlund read and criticized the entire manuscript. Differing from the writer as she does on many philosophical questions, her criticisms were particularly helpful. The book is better for her comments, and to her the author gratefully acknowledges deep obligations. Dr. Bertha Royce, Dr. John Kinneman, and Dean Chris De Young read portions of the manuscript and criticized what they read most helpfully.

It was a student, Miss Alma Uphoff, who suggested that a list of novels with philosophical implications be included. She had read Tolstoy's *Anna Karenina* and Somerset Maugham's *Of Human Bondage* during the Christmas vacation of the semester in which she was studying philosophy of education and had found to her delight that the books meant so much more to her than they could have meant before any acquaintance with philosophical terms or concepts.

In the hope that other students may be tempted to repeat her experience, a list of such novels is included. Although the writer, in making the list, has had the assistance of several of her colleagues in the English department, there is no intent to suggest that this is an authoritative and inclusive list of all such books.

TABLE OF CONTENTS

CHAPTER I

PHILOSOPHY, SCIENCE, AND PHILOSOPHY
OF EDUCATION

The origins of Western philosophy—The meaning and function of philosophy: (1) Philosophy defined; (2) The question with which philosophy deals—The relation between philosophy and science: (1) Comparison as to (a) history, (b) content, (c) method, (d) purpose; (2) Need for both philosophy and science in solving life's problems—The relation between philosophy and philosophy of education—The relation between philosophy of education and the science of education: (1) The function of philosophy of education; (2) The function of science of education; (3) Their complementary nature— The teacher's imperative need for philosophy of education

---

THE sixth century before Christ was an amazing one in the history of human thought. About 604 B.C., in China, Lao-tse, the father of Taoism, was born. In 551 B.C., in that same country, Kung-fu-tse, whom we know by his Latinized name, Confucius, first saw the light of day. In 560 B.C., in India, Gautama, who became the Enlightened One, the Buddha, gladdened the heart of his mother, Māyā. Persian tradition says that it was during the sixth century that Zoroaster lived and taught in ancient Iran. And most important for us of the Western world, Thales, the father of Greek philosophy "flourished" in the early years of the century.[1]

Said to have been born in 640 B.C., Thales was a citizen of Miletus with the reputation of being the wisest of the Greeks. Legend relates that it was he who said that the hardest task for a man was to know himself; the easiest, to give advice to another. When asked what was most pleasant for man, he is said to have replied "success," and to the question what was the strangest thing he had ever seen, he an-

---

1. Thales (fl. *ca.* 585 B.C., the date of the eclipse), in Diogenes Laërtius *Lives of Eminent Philosophers* 23.

swered "an aged tyrant." A statement which modern man would
hopefully applaud. Again, when people inquired how they could best
bear adversity, he said, according to the tale, "By seeing your enemies
in a worse plight."[2]

But Thales' reputation for wisdom does not rest upon his repartee,
however discerning a knowledge of human nature it reveals. Rightly
or wrongly, he received credit for having begun in our Western
world that search for wisdom which we call philosophy, to which the
Greeks gave such impetus and for which they are so justly honored.

In China, Lao-tse and Confucius were studying, editing, rearrang-
ing, and expounding ancient wisdom. In India, Gautama was re-
belling against the Hindu conception of the world and, with Buddhism, setting his disciples upon another path. In Palestine, Jeremiah
and Ezekiel were thundering at their people to return to those moral
standards, the origin of which probably lies in the hoary civilization
of ancient Egypt where Breasted says the conscience of man had its
dawn.[3] In Iran, Zoroaster taught his people a dualistic philosophy
of the good and evil forces which he thought lay at the basis of this
world. It was during this age, as stated before, that Greek philosophy
was born.

These remarkable currents of thought showed astonishing similarities for a world in which travel was so dangerous and so difficult.
That they were somehow connected seems possible. Tradition pointing in that direction has in recent years been confirmed by some
oriental scholars.[4] It may be that the Greeks served as transmitters
rather than as originators of what we call early Greek philosophy.
Certainly it was in the eastern colonies of Greece that their philosophy began. It was the Ionian speculative thinkers who introduced
philosophy into other parts of Greece. Moreover, Greek traditions
refer to the influence of Egyptian teachers upon Thales and other
early savants. Oriental philosophy may have influenced the development of Greek thought.

Wherever it originated, Greek philosophy has been for us of the
greatest significance. It has been Greek thought, combined with
Hebrew-Christian doctrines, which has molded the Western mind.

2. *Ibid.* 37–39.
3. James H. Breasted, *The Dawn of Conscience*, chap. xvii.
4. *Ibid.*, Foreword.

It is in these systems that we find the germs of all the philosophies which have followed. It was the Greeks' insatiable curiosity, their passion for the truth, their respect for clear logical thinking, which enabled them to make the remarkable start in both science and philosophy for which they are justly honored. And Thales is remembered because, so far as we know, he was the first of these Greek thinkers.

PHILOSOPHY AND ITS FUNCTION

Philosophy is an attempt to understand all that comes within the range of human experience. It is a "search for a comprehensive view of nature, an attempt at a universal explanation of the nature of things."[5] It is only in the light of such a search that man can hope to understand himself and to obtain some glimmer of light on his relation to the rest of the universe. The word "philosophy" meant originally "the love of wisdom." And that is not a bad interpretation of its present meaning, if the word "wisdom" is rightly understood and if one is convinced that the only lovers of wisdom are those who continually seek it.

Wisdom is more than knowledge. It presupposes knowledge but goes beyond knowledge to find relationships and to discover implications. There is discernment and depth in wisdom. Speculation is usually an essential part of philosophy, particularly in that branch known as "metaphysics," but it is a rigorously disciplined speculation, not that resulting from armchair dreaming.

There is much misunderstanding on the part of the general public as to the meaning of the word philosophy. It is used commonly to mean anyone's belief or point of view concerning purposes or values. A student in one of the author's classes, in a paper on the curriculum, once discussed the "philosophy of the notebook." Such an expression is pretentious and inexact. It would have been better to have spoken of the value or the purpose of the notebook.

It is also common to speak of anyone's ideas about life's values or purposes as his "philosophy of life." Commenting on this, one writer says:

There is indeed a sort of philosophy untouched by any conscious acquaintance with scientific lore. . . . . The only philosophy ultimately worthy

5. Alfred Weber, *History of Philosophy*, p. 1.

of acceptance is that which is built on the foundations laid by the best
thought and experience of the race. . . . . In short we must pass from the
philosophy of common sense, with which we begin, to philosophy as a
reasoned discipline. Otherwise, we remain in bondage to largely untutored
prejudices.[6]

Actually, philosophy is a rigorous, disciplined, guarded analysis of
some of the most difficult problems which man has ever faced, not
just anyone's point of view. It requires the best thought of which man
is capable. Philosophers are men of great intelligence and remarkable
insight who have been able to see the significance of the discrete
events in human experience and, to use Plato's term, take a synoptic
view of them.[7] Philosophers have asked and tried to answer such
questions as the following:

How does it happen that mankind is here? What is life for? What
is right for man to do? What is wrong? How can man live a life that
is worth while and satisfying? Is there any intelligent purpose back
of the fact of this world and its phenomena? What can man hope for
after this life? What sort of world is this in its essence? Is there any
one substance out of which everything is composed? Or, are
there two or more substances? What is the nature of the substance
or substances? What does it mean "to be"? Is man's mind capable of
answering these and many other questions? How do we get the
knowledge we think we have? How valid is this knowledge or supposed knowledge?

Philosophers differ in their answers to these questions. The beginning student is often confused and troubled because he can find so
few answers which he can be certain are true. So eminent a philosopher as John Dewey thinks that it is foolish to attempt to discover the
answers to most of these questions and that philosophers should
turn their attention to solving social problems.[8]

Another famous modern philosopher has this to say on the study of
unanswerable questions:

Philosophy is to be studied not for the sake of any definite answers to
its questions, ... but rather for the sake of the questions themselves;

6. G. W. Cunningham, *Problems of Philosophy*, pp. 31–32.
7. Plato *Republic* 537C.
8. See esp. John Dewey, *Problems of Men*, Introd.

because these questions enlarge our conception of what is possible, enrich our intellectual imagination and diminish the dogmatic assurance which closes the mind against speculation; but above all because through the greatness of the universe which philosophy contemplates, the mind also is rendered great and becomes capable of that union with the universe which constitutes its highest good.[9]

But the student should not jump to the conclusion that there is no knowledge to be derived from philosophy. It is possible to achieve certainty on many important questions, although there are other questions which cannot be answered with any certitude.

The word "synoptic," used in the previous section, gives us a clue not only to the meaning of philosophy but to an important difference between philosophy and science. The scientist, of course, attempts to understand our environment, but the philosopher views the universe as a whole. Science divides and analyzes. Each science concerns itself with one field of human knowledge: mathematics, astronomy, geology, physics, chemistry, biology, or psychology—to name some of the most important—each has a fairly well-recognized and delimited area. The philosopher learns all that he can from the various sciences and, in the light of all the knowledge he is able to obtain from them, attempts to see the universe as a whole and to understand man's place in it. Wholes have characteristics that their parts do not have, and what these characteristics are is philosophy's deepest concern.[10]

There is a sense in which philosophy is the mother of science. In the ancient world all known science was a part of philosophy. Thales was primarily interested in trying to discover some fundamental, underlying substance, the combinations and variations of which make up the infinite variety of individual things in the world. This same problem was the principal one of his immediate successors. Aristotle was a very remarkable scientist, who observed, classified, investigated, and generalized about the phenomena of physics, zoölogy, psychology, politics, and cosmology. He might have been distressed

9. Bertrand Russell, *The Problems of Philosophy*, pp. 249–50.

10. Edgar Brightman, *An Introduction to Philosophy*, p. 10.

at some of the very unscientific uses to which the results of his investigations were put all through the medieval age.

Mathematics was the first science to become independent of Mother Philosophy; astronomy followed next. Then, as man learned not only to observe and to generalize from his observations but to devise instruments which would help him in his observations, as well as to experiment under controlled conditions, other sciences developed and became independent. Men found it advisable to specialize, to study more and more deeply into a particular field. Physics, chemistry, biology, psychology, and finally sociology stood each on its own feet. Then philosophers put together and studied as a whole the knowledge discovered by specialists working in these different fields.

Indeed, many modern philosophers as well as the ancients were scientists first. Descartes and Leibnitz would have been remembered for their contributions to mathematics if they had never become interested in philosophy. Kant was an expert in geography and a physicist, antedating Laplace with his nebular hypothesis. Because of the intimate connection between science and philosophy, philosophy is sometimes called the science of sciences.[11]

But there are other differences between science and philosophy. The scientist is primarily interested in obtaining facts about things as they are. He wants to know what *is*. He does not concern himself as a scientist about what *ought to be*. If he discovers how to split the atom, he does not tell us as a condition for sharing his knowledge whether it should be used to destroy man or to make life easier for him. He may be and often is concerned as a citizen. Men of science have written and spoken much on the subject of man's individual and social welfare. But in doing so they speak as citizens. The modern physical scientist, for example, appalled at the use to which man may put the discovery of the release of atomic energy, is using both the radio and the press to urge wise controls. But scientists make it clear that they speak as citizens and that as scientists it is their business to discover facts, to invent techniques, to devise means. In contrast, it is the business of philosophy, as it is of religion, to help mankind to decide how such discoveries should be used, indeed, to decide upon those ends toward the realization of which all scientific

11. Robert Flint, *Philosophy as Scientia scientiarum*, p. 3.

facts and knowledge of techniques ought to be used as means, for philosophy does concern itself with values and with what ought to be as well as with what is.

Again, the scientist starts with assumptions. So do most of us. It does not occur to the average citizen to question whether there are such things as cause and effect, time, space, or matter. He assumes that the way things seem to him is the way they are. Science, too, starts with such assumptions, although the world which the scientist investigates is not the world as it appears to our senses. For example, the scientist assumes that matter is real. Reasoning from such an assumption, observing and experimenting, he arrives at the atomic theory and later at a theory of electrons. Philosophy, too, has its assumptions, but questions them, accepting nothing without critical examination.

There is also a difference in the method used by these agencies. The most important advances have been made in science since men have learned to use the controlled experiment. It is true that many of the sciences called "social" can use this method only to a limited degree. To control all factors, to have but one variable, is well-nigh impossible wherever human beings are concerned. It is even more difficult, if not impossible, to reach conclusions about the characteristics of wholes, about values, or about ends, by means of experiment. To be sure, conclusions may be and should be tested through the experience of man. Philosophers certainly have to begin with man's experience. That is where all knowledge begins. But philosophers use not only experience but reason in arriving at their conclusions. So, of course, do scientists. Galileo, for example, arrived at his conclusions concerning falling bodies by mathematics rather than by empirical evidence.[12] But he did test his reasoning by experience, if only to demonstrate the truth of his conclusions to his opponents. Since philosophers are concerned with many problems which cannot be immediately verified in experience, reason is depended on to an even greater degree for reaching conclusions. In fact, some philosophical problems are of such a nature that man may never find a solution. The central and most important problem of all, answers to which in the judgment of many philosophers affect answers given to almost

12. E. A. Burtt, *The Metaphysical Foundations of Modern Physical Science,* p. 65.

all other questions, is that concerning the nature of ultimate reality. Is there some one substance which lies at the basis of the infinite variety of objects which we experience? Or is there more than one substance? And what is the nature of this substance or these substances? That, as has been pointed out, was the problem of Thales and his successors. It is one to which there is as yet no answer that can be confirmed by experience. The truth of the matter may never be discovered by man.

Because this is true of many philosophical problems, some thinkers have declared that philosophy cannot arrive at truth. If science has established a truth, it was done through empirical evidence. And that is the only way, say they, that truth can be established. Supposed knowledge is not knowledge unless it has been so verified. Positivism is the name given to this position. While the term "positivism" is applied to any philosophy which confines itself to the knowledge gained and verified through sense-experience, it is most commonly applied to the school of thought founded by the French sociologist, Auguste Comte (1798–1857). Impressed by the success of the physical or positive sciences, Comte proposed to introduce the same scientific methods into the study of society. He thought it would be possible to discover general laws operating in social phenomena if sociologists would examine the actual facts of social existence and forget about causes of social relationships or ideal arrangements for society. In other words, he taught that whatever is given through sense-experience constitutes the only objects of knowledge, as well as being the supreme standard for judging the validity of human knowledge.

This idea has been widely taught and is generally accepted in this scientific age. It helps to account for the high respect in which science and scientists are held. The scientist alone, by the scientific method, can reach truth. Through scientific research he has learned a great deal which has helped us to control our environment. Life has been lengthened and made easier and more comfortable. No longer need disease, famine, or backbreaking labor harry man. Science has shown us the way to control disease, to produce all the food we need, to do much of our work by machine. Our homes are more comfortable and our lives easier than those even of the most fortunate few several generations ago. Science has shown us how to produce more and more with less and less effort. All hail to science! It alone can be depended on to give us the truth about our world on which to build that good life for man which has been the dream of the race.

While science was growing in the estimation of man, philosophy and even religion were losing in prestige. It is unfortunately true that, as far as regards educated people, the influence of the church has been waning during the last one hundred years or more. It is likewise true that, at least until quite recently, the standing of philosophy had sustained a similar loss both as a study in college and as a guiding influence in men's lives.

Within the last decade—preceded by some few hardy voices crying in the wilderness—there has been growing uneasiness about this one-sided view; occasionally there is evidenced an actual distrust and even condemnation of science. We hear that, although science has given us lives more free from disease, from famine, and from hard labor, she has given us death-dealing instruments as well. Scientists have helped us to learn how to produce wealth but not how to distribute it. While some nations already wealthy became richer, other countries where poverty was stalking became poorer. Economic disparities became more apparent within nations. Some persons grew very wealthy; others sank into the depths of destitution. And this occurred in the midst of an actual or potential plenty. The world shrank in size because of improved transportation and communication, but people did not get along any better in the family of nations suddenly brought so much closer to each other. In short, we have become aware that in spite of our scientific advances our civilization is confronted by grave difficulties. Some persons would make of science a whipping-boy, for, say they, our difficulties grow out of our scientific advances.

But it would be a mistake to blame science or scientists for this condition or to believe that we would be better off if the sciences had not made possible the Industrial Revolution and all its attendant changes. Our difficulties have been caused by our own selfishness and blindness. As citizens, scientists have shared in these mistakes, but we can scarcely blame them as scientists. As has been said, it is the province of science to discover the facts about this world—to find out what is. These facts then, may be applied in such a way as to furnish man with tools, with instruments, with means for living. It is not the province of science to decide on the ends toward which these means should be used. To reiterate, it is the task of religion and philosophy to help us understand the meaning of life, the ends toward which we should direct our efforts, the kind of life which it is good for man to live. Too much has been expected of science, perhaps because we have forgotten that it takes more than material goods, important as they are, for the good life. Let us have all that science can discover for us, but let us not neglect the study of how this knowledge should be used, what the ends of living are, what the good life means. Else we shall destroy ourselves with the instruments which we have devised. That there is a growing realization of this need is apparent from many sources. In a recent book we read:

> The world is probably closer to disintegration now than at any time since the fall of the Roman Empire. . . . . Our country has long been afflicted with problems which, though apparently insoluble, must be solved if this nation is to be preserved or to be worth preserving. These problems are not material problems. . . . . No, our problems are moral, intellectual, and spiritual. The paradox of starvation in the midst of plenty illustrates the nature of our difficulties. This paradox will not be resolved by technical skill or scientific data. It will be resolved, if it is resolved at all, by wisdom and goodness.[13]

From Chancellor Hutchins of the University of Chicago has come for some years trenchant criticism of the college education which neglects the study of philosophy; and from Mortimer Adler, a member of the faculty of the same institution, has come an equally severe indictment of the philosophy known as positivism. He believes that positivism has been the source of our civilization's sickness, for it has led people to believe only in science and to think of religion and philosophy as superstition or vain speculation.[14] However people may disagree with the specific curriculum which Chancellor Hutchins would substitute for the present one and however one may regret the somewhat dogmatic assertions of Mortimer Adler, the conviction is growing that these men have an important case to state.

There are problems with which philosophy deals that we may never solve. But there are others, solved by reason, which could not have been solved in any other way. And there are still other truths

13. Robert Maynard Hutchins, *Education for Freedom*, p. 23.

14. Mortimer Adler, "This Pre-war Generation," *Harper's*, CLXXXI (October, 1940), 524–34.

which in time perhaps can be verified through experience as well as by reason. To illustrate a truth which cannot be established except through reason, we have only to mention a basic belief on which our whole Western civilization has been founded—that of the infinite value of the individual. This is not a mere hypothesis or the result of wishful thinking but a certainty which can be proved by reason.[15] Experience with man as an individual could hardly lead one to such a conclusion unless it were aided by reason. No experiment could be tried which would result in establishing such a truth. But it is a truth nevertheless.

Illustrative of a truth which may some day be proved by experience as well as through reason is the answer to that problem so vital today: What is the best form of social organization for man? It can be proved by reason that democracy is the best form. But it has not yet been tried and proved through experience. What we call democracy is far from being real democracy. Perhaps in time we shall achieve a social organization which deserves that name but only if we can be certain that it is the best form of social organization for man.

Of course all these proofs begin with experience. All knowledge, let us repeat, is rooted in experience. But while knowledge starts with sense-experience, it has never been proved that knowledge cannot be obtained where sense-experience cannot be used. Man can think and achieve certainty in the solution of some problems which are beyond the reach of empirical verification. Neither do we have to depend on experimental science for all our truths. We can, through the study of philosophy and the use of our own minds, achieve certainty about right and wrong, about the necessary requirements of the good life for man, about the best form of social organization for man. For this we shall use all of man's past experience. But we shall also need the insights of those most blessed with that best of man's possessions, the power to reason. And we shall need to use our own reason to the best of our ability. In short, we shall attempt to discover through our study of philosophy the goals toward which man should direct his efforts. Then science can help us with the tools which will aid us in reaching those goals. Philosophy and science are comple-

15. See W. T. Stace, *The Destiny of Western Man*, chap. vi, for a logical demonstration.

mentary, and we need both for solving life's problems. We can, for example, be certain, through the study of philosophy, that democracy is the best form of social organization for man. Then science can help in deciding how to achieve democracy. Scientists can furnish the knowledge, the tools, the techniques, for achieving our ideals. But science, as usually understood, can provide neither the ideals nor the proofs that those ideals are worthy of man's endeavor. Science cannot furnish that wisdom, the love and pursuit of which has been the distinguishing characteristic of the philosopher, so sorely needed by man that he may survive in the atomic age. As a distinguished modern philosopher says: "Science is like art in this, that though both are good in themselves man can put them to bad uses and bad purposes; while in so far as man uses wisdom—and the same is true of virtue—he can only use it for good purposes."[16]

PHILOSOPHY AND PHILOSOPHY OF EDUCATION

What does all this have to do with the work of the school and with philosophy of education? Philosophy of education is the application of philosophy to the study of the problems of education. One cannot apply that which he does not know. It is imperative for a teacher to know some philosophy. He needs it as a person. He needs it as a teacher. The purposes of education are always relative to the ends of living nor can they be understood apart from life itself. An adequate philosophy of life is a prerequisite for a sound philosophy of education. Philosophers have always known this. As we have seen, philosophy concerns itself with interpreting all that comes within the range of man's experience. One of philosophy's most important tasks has been, from the days of Greek philosophy to this, to formulate the objectives and content of a satisfying life. It is the task of education to guide the growth and development of boys and girls so that they will become competent and social-minded citizens of our commonwealth; so that they will work for the common welfare, not just for their own narrow ends; and so that they will be a more intelligent and altruistic generation than previous ones. So may mankind come a little closer to the realization of the goals which philosophers have formulated as worthy of man's endeavor.

16. Jacques Maritain, *Science and Wisdom*, p. 32.

It is only those teachers who have assimilated the contributions of great thinkers to the study of these problems and who have on the basis of this knowledge done their own thinking about the problems of living and of learning who have any right to speak of their philosophy of life or of their philosophy of education. Either is an applied philosophy and presupposes some knowledge of philosophy to use in studying the problems of living or of education. This is true of any applied philosophy, be it the ones already mentioned or a philosophy of law, of history, or of economics.

PHILOSOPHY OF EDUCATION AND SCIENCE OF EDUCATION

There is probably no worker whose practice is more affected by his philosophy or lack of philosophy than is a teacher. Too many teachers teach as they were taught. Others have acquired from reading or from observation certain ideas as to what they should do. So long as they may stay on a beaten path they get along fairly well. But teachers cannot remain on a familiar road. They meet new problems. They must help children who have diverse personalities and backgrounds. They must select experiences and subject matter for these children. They must know what constitutes desirable conduct for children and why. They must decide on methods to use, emphases to make, values to prefer, conditions to strive for, changes to advocate. Human nature is so complex, human problems so many, that it is impossible to give prospective teachers a bag of tricks or even to help them learn a set of habits which they may use in every situation in which they find themselves. One cannot write recipes for successful teaching as one writes recipes for successful cooking. It is not so simple as that.

Certainly science can help the teacher solve many problems. There is a science of education with which we should all be familiar and the results of which we should be able to use. But just as we have expected too much of science in our daily living, so we have expected too much of the science of education. Some great universities during the early part of this century devoted much of the time of their most brilliant men to scientific experimentation in education. This was a good thing so far as it went. For at least ten years, however, more and more educators have been realizing that it did not go far enough. Thorndike's famous dictum, "Everything that exists, exists in some quantity and can be measured," belongs to this early period when we experimented, measured, counted, and classified with commendable zeal but thought little about the ends toward which all this scientific endeavor was to be used.

Consider the question: Shall homogeneous grouping be used in our schools? By homogeneous grouping was usually meant a grouping on the basis of ability to do school work as indicated by intelligence tests and, sometimes, achievement tests. There are numerous accounts in educational literature of experiments which have been tried in order to solve this problem. Children were grouped homogeneously, then heterogeneously, taught the same subjects by the same teacher or by teachers of like competence. As nearly as it is possible in dealing with human beings, all conditions but the one of grouping were held constant. That was the only variable intended although there always were others. Then the children were tested for the amount learned. Results were confusing. Sometimes homogeneous grouping seemed to give the better results, sometimes heterogeneous grouping. It was the rare voice, however, which was raised to ask, "better for what?"

To solve with any degree of success the constant succession of problems which a teacher meets, these fundamental questions must be answered: What am I trying to accomplish? For what were schools established? This child being what he is and the demands of society being what they are, how can I best guide his growth so as to realize the purposes of education? The answers to these questions constitute the framework for a philosophy of education. And they can be answered only with reference to what is most worth while in life. A science of education can assist with means, with tools, with techniques, once we have settled upon our ends and our objectives. But for those we need philosophy. Just as science and philosophy are complementary in all phases of life, so are they complementary in education.

The science of education will contribute knowledge gained through experimentation, through analyzing, measuring, counting, classifying, and comparing. Philosophy of education will aid in the discovery of the goals toward which all this effort should be expended. The question, Shall homogeneous grouping be used in our schools? must be answered not alone by a science of education but by a philosophy of education, also. Will grouping children according to their ability to do school work contribute to the realization of the purpose of education? How can one know? What is the purpose of education? To teach children a certain amount of subject matter? Is that all?

One author puts it: "The answer to every educational question is ultimately influenced by our philosophy of life. Although few formulate it, every system of education must have an aim and the aim of education is relative to the aim of life."[17] There is nothing easy about deciding on these ends or on how to achieve them. Indeed, the task of guiding the development of boys and girls is one of the most difficult, if most rewarding, which man may set himself. Teaching is not work which can or should be done by just anyone. It needs the finest personality, the highest intelligence, the greatest knowledge. Any real teacher always feels humble before the demands of his task.

Civilization is, indeed, as H. G. Wells has remarked, a race between education and catastrophe. Perhaps catastrophe is so close upon us because we have done so poorly this greatest of human tasks. We spend in this country great amounts of money on schools and equipment, but we have not yet attracted to teaching a large enough number of our most intelligent and social-minded young people nor have we equipped them with an understanding of children and the learning process, with a knowledge of the results of scientific research in education, with an adequate philosophy of education, and with the kind of education for themselves which will make of them cultured, informed, intelligent, altruistic human beings.

In *Alice in Wonderland,* the heroine asked the Cheshire Cat: "Would you tell me please which way I ought to go from here?"

"That depends a good deal on where you want to get to," said the Cat.

"I don't much care where—" said Alice.

"Then it doesn't matter which way you go," said the Cat.

"—so long as I get *somewhere,*" Alice added as an explanation.

"Oh, you're sure to do that," said the Cat, "if you only walk long enough."

We teachers need to know where we want to get to." Otherwise we may walk a long way, get *very* tired, and accomplish practically nothing.

17. R. R. Rusk, *Philosophical Bases of Education,* p. 15.

SUMMARY

I. MEANING OF THE TERM "PHILOSOPHY"

1. The word "philosophy" means literally "the love of wisdom."

2. According to informed usage today, philosophy means the attempt to conceive and present an inclusive and systematic view of the universe and man's place in it. A science deals with a portion of the field of knowledge; philosophy is an attempt to understand the whole.

3. Applied philosophy, such as philosophy of education, of history, of law, or of religion, is an application of philosophy to the study of problems in the respective fields.

4. Popularly, philosophy means one's general view of life, of men, of ideals, and of values. In this sense everyone has a philosophy of life and every teacher a philosophy of education. Unless one has consciously criticized his views in the light of the best human thought, such a use of the term is rather pretentious and unwise.

II. PRINCIPAL RELATIONSHIPS BETWEEN SCIENCE AND PHILOSOPHY

SCIENCE	PHILOSOPHY
1. Originally, the child of philosophy.	1. Mother of knowledge.
2. Analytic; examines all phenomena minutely so as to describe them in terms of their constituent parts.	2. Synoptic; views the world, and even the universe, as a whole so as to explain, interpret, and, if possible, understand the whole.
3. Concerned with facts, with describing things as they are; tries to abstract from human desires and wants.	3. Concerned not only with things as they are but also with the way they ought to be. Human desires and human values are an important factor.
4. Begins with assumptions.	4. Examines and questions all assumptions.
5. Uses the controlled experiment as its most important and characteristic method; verifies by means of sense-experience.	5. Uses all pertinent findings of science; verifies through reason based on human experience.

III. THE NEED FOR PHILOSOPHY AND SCIENCE IN EDUCATION

1. Teachers need to study philosophy so that they may apply it to the study of vital educational problems. Basic to the solution of all educational problems are the answers given to such questions as: What am I trying to accomplish? What is education for? Educational aims cannot be determined apart from the ends and aims of life itself, for educational aims grow

out of life's aims. To determine what constitutes a life worth living has been one of the chief tasks of philosophy.

2. Philosophy of education and science of education supplement one another. Teachers need both. Science of education is needed to discover the best means and techniques for achieving the goals which philosophy of education has helped us to see as our objective.

QUESTIONS TO AID STUDY

1. What is the derivation and the present meaning of the word "philosophy"? Who was the father of Western philosophy? Why is he given that credit?
2. What is it to take a synoptic view of things? Compare philosophy and science as to the way in which each views the universe.
3. How are philosophy and science related? In what ways are they different?
4. What is meant by the word "positivism"? How do some writers criticize this theory? Do you agree or disagree? Why?
5. Do you agree or disagree with the statement that science can solve all the human problems that are solvable? Explain.
6. Why do teachers need to study philosophy and philosophy of education?
7. Compare the contribution of educational science toward the solution of educational problems with that of educational philosophy.
8. Select a specific controversial problem from your own teaching field, the solution of which seems important to you; it should be one which needs both science and philosophy for its solution. Indicate what science could contribute to its solution and for what philosophy would be needed.

SUGGESTED REFERENCES

ADLER, MORTIMER. "This Pre-war Generation," *Harper's*, CLXXXI (October, 1940), 524–34.

BREED, FREDERICK S. *Education and the New Realism* (New York: Macmillan Co., 1939), chap. i.

BRIGHTMAN, EDGAR. *An Introduction to Philosophy* (New York: Henry Holt & Co., 1925), chap. i.

DEMIASHKEVICH, MICHAEL J. *An Introduction to the Philosophy of Education* (New York: American Book Co., 1935), chap. i.

HOCKING, WILLIAM E. *Science and the Idea of God* (Chapel Hill: University of North Carolina Press, 1944), chap. i.

KNODE, JAY CARROLL, and ASSOCIATES. *Foundations of an American Philosophy of Education* (New York: D. Van Nostrand Co., 1942), Introd.

KÖHLER, WOLFGANG. *The Place of Value in a World of Facts* (New York: H. Liveright, 1938), chap. i.

18   *Philosophy of Education*

LEPLEY, RAY. *Dependability in Philosophy of Education* (New York: Bureau of Publications, Columbia University, 1931), chap. i.
MARITAIN, JACQUES. *Science and Wisdom.* London: G. Bles, Centenary Press, 1940.
MARTZ, V. "Philosophy and Science," *Encyclopedia of Educational Research* (New York: Macmillan Co., 1941), pp. 795–97.
MONTAGUE, WILLIAM P. *The Ways of Things* (New York: Prentice-Hall, Inc., 1940), pp. 3–17.
NAKOSTEEN, MEHDI. *A Three-Fold Philosophy of Education* (Denver, Colo.: Charles Mapes Pub. Co., 1943), chap. i.
PATRICK, G. T. W. *Introduction to Philosophy* (rev. ed.; New York: Houghton Mifflin Co., 1935), chaps. i and ii.
REDDEN, JOHN D., and RYAN, FRANCIS A. *A Catholic Philosophy of Education* (Milwaukee: Bruce Pub. Co., 1942), chaps. i and ii.
THOMAS, FRANK W., and LANG, ALBERT R. *Principles of Modern Education* (New York: Houghton Mifflin Co., 1937), chap. i.
WAHLQUIST, J. T. *The Philosophy of American Education* (New York: Ronald Press, 1942), chap. i.

CHAPTER II
THE NATURE OF THE EDUCATIVE PROCESS
EDUCATION AND THE INDIVIDUAL

Ancient controversy over the nature of education: (1) Handing on the social heritage; (2) Growth and development of the individual— Resolving the controversy through the study of man's nature and his relation to the rest of the living world—Mystery of life; theories as to its origin and nature: (1) Mechanism and vitalism; (2) Emergent evolution; (3) Insights from the new physics—Familiar concepts concerning biological characteristics of man: (1) Man as an animal; his ancestry; (2) His distinguishing biological characteristics; (3) Man as the highest animal; (4) Heredity and variation—Less familiar concepts concerning likenesses between man and other living creatures: (1) Urge to live; purposive and purposeful behavior; (2) Unity of an organism; organismic concept; (3) Dependence of an organism upon its environment; basic unchanging factors in human nature; human development and the environment; (4) Man's dependence upon a social as well as a physical environment; (5) Ability to grow and change; interaction; learning—Leaders in emphasizing education as growth: (1) Jean Jacques Rousseau; (2) Johann Basedow; (3) Johann Pestalozzi; (4) Friedrich Froebel; (5) John Dewey—The social nature of man

O NE of the oldest controversies in the educational world is over the nature of education. *What* is it? How is it to be defined? Is it a handing-on of the social heritage or is it the growth and development of the individual? Is the school an institution for giving authoritative information or a place where creative powers are developed? Should the pupil be relatively passive and docile or active and aggressive? Is the school to be subject-centered or child-centered? Ought the school to encourage conformity or freedom to act? Shall we have a prescribed curriculum or free electives? How much of

19

20   Philosophy of Education

schooling shall be general and required of all, and how much may be specialized along individual lines? How can we distinguish between educational needs and educational wants? What relative emphasis shall we place on each?

This controversy is not only a very old one, but it still rages today. It is one of the chief points of difference between the group of teachers who call themselves Progressives and those who are called Traditionalists.[1]

When, over a period of many years, intelligent people of good will take opposing points of view on a question, it is possible that not all the truth lies with one or the other but that there may be some truth in each. If the apparent opposites were seen in their context as parts of a larger whole they might be reconciled. It is quite possible that education is neither merely a handing-on of the social heritage nor just individual growth but that it is something of each. Education may have a twofold nature. Perhaps if we study man and his development, we can understand how this can be.

We really know very little about man. Medical science is still in its infancy. Endocrinology, for instance, dawned only recently. Psychology and sociology are the youngest of the sciences. Anthropology is relatively new. Biology itself is far from being one of the older sciences. Socrates, with other ancients, proclaimed that the "proper study of mankind is man." But it took man a long time to learn much about himself.

So long as man considered himself to be a creature apart from the rest of living things, a "fallen angel" and a sojourner here rather than a product of nature, so long he failed in even beginning to understand himself. We can begin to comprehend man only as we study him in the context of the living world as well as see him as a creature unique and different. All scientifically educated people accept as truth that man evolved from lower forms of animal life. The evidence seems indubitable. Such a view of man helps to explain much about him. But that does not mean that man is only an animal. There are wide differences between man and the highest of the other animals.[2]

1. See, e.g., the recently published Harvard report, General Education in a Free Society. Compare this with the Educational Policies Commission's publication, Education for All American Youth.

2. See chap. iv.

If man, as seems certain, had an animal ancestry, he must have taken a Gargantuan leap by the time his earliest direct ancestor appeared on the family tree.

To recognize that we live in a cosmos of which we are an integral part is to heighten our respect for nature and its mysteries. What is nature? What is this material world which surrounds us? What is life? Where did the first living cell come from? Or has life always existed? What is the connection, if any, between living and nonliving material? What happens when a cell dies? How account for the fact that, so far as we know, only living cells can produce living cells? How explain that like produces like? Or the strange phenomenon of embryology described by Jennings and which might be summarized somewhat as follows:

During the early embryological period what will be produced from the cells in the usual course of events can be predicted with certainty. Some will produce eyes, others the spinal cord, others skin, etc. If, however, in the early stages, from the region that is to produce the skin a portion is removed and transplanted to the region which is to produce the brain, then the fate of the transplanted cells is changed; then they become part of the brain. The reverse is also true. What the cell becomes depends not only upon what it is itself, but upon what its neighboring cells are becoming. Jennings says that there is some organizing influence of an unknown nature passing from cell to cell, causing each one to alter internally through the interaction of the genes and cytoplasm. In fact, the genes alter their action on the cytoplasm as the surroundings of the cell containing them change. The fate of cells in these early stages depends not on different genes nor on diverse cytoplasm but on conditions surrounding each cell. In time, of course, definite cytoplasmic structure is produced; then the cells can no longer be changed.[3]

To the questions we ask about these mysteries there are as yet no answers. Perhaps in time science may solve some of these problems; others may never be solved. So far as the mystery of life is concerned, biologists seem equally dissatisfied with the old mechanistic view of living material, which attempted to explain life in terms of the current physics and chemistry, and with vitalism, which postulates

3. H. S. Jennings, *The Biological Basis of Human Nature*, pp. 88–100.

the presence of a vital principle, an entelechy or *élan vital*, as the difference between living and nonliving material.

The mechanist believes that the only essential difference between a living organism and nonliving material lies in the fact that the organism is a more complex arrangement of the elements. He explains all the actions and functions of life in terms of physics and chemistry. Life, to the mechanist, is reducible to simpler terms and can be explained by the same laws which govern the nonliving. The mechanist says that it is conceivable that man some day will be able to combine the necessary elements in such a way as to make a living cell; the only cause of his inability to do so now lies in his ignorance of the conditions under which the organization will take place.

The vitalist, on the other hand, says that living material, be it a plant or animal cell, contains a vital principle, an immaterial entity, which distinguishes it from inanimate matter. Science, says the vitalist, will never bridge the gap between the living and the nonliving. It takes protoplasm to make protoplasm and it always will.

Some philosophically inclined biologists, Jennings among them, find in emergent evolution the most satisfying theory. This theory "asserts that the appearance of new things possessing new properties is due in all cases to the formation of new combinations, new arrangements, new organizations of already existing things."[4] But this appearance is not the mechanical product of the simpler antecedent phase of evolution. For example, say some, when sodium and chlorine combine to form sodium chloride, common table salt, one could not possibly have foretold the nature or properties of sodium chloride from a knowledge of the nature and properties of sodium and chlorine. Sodium chloride is unique, with characteristics of its own. In the same way, the living cell, while formed from what was already existing, is unique and cannot be explained in terms of the nonliving or through laws of physics or chemistry. It simply "emerged" when a certain complexity of physical and chemical conditions arose.[5]

Other biologists, also philosophically inclined, see in the new physics a gradual approach to an understanding of the relation between the living and the nonliving. As the new physics has aban-

4. David R. Major, *An Introduction to Philosophy*, p. 93.
5. J. S. Haldane, *The Philosophy of a Biologist*, p. 73.

doned the old distinction between matter and energy and the concept
of energy as an attribute of matter and has replaced it by a theory in
which matter itself is thought to be an expression of energy, so life is
regarded as an energy phenomenon, and the old gap between the
living and the nonliving seems less wide. The eminent British biologist, Haldane, says on this point:

> When we examine more completely what we at present call the inorganic
> world we shall find in it phenomena which are the same as those of life.
> Until about twenty-five years ago this conclusion seemed inconsistent
> with current physical and chemical conceptions. It was only a philo-
> sophical faith such as I had myself at that time expressed. But recent ad-
> vances in physics have brought us much nearer to such a conclusion. An
> atom, or even an electron, or light-quantum, is for recent physics some-
> thing of which the existence, like that of a living organism, is an expression
> of ceaseless co-ordinated activity, incapable of being interpreted in mechan-
> ical terms as that of a mere particle in the old sense.[6]

Haldane himself is careful to say that biologists are still "a long
way from being able to identify life definitely in the mere details of
what we commonly designate as inorganic phenomena"[7] and that
when we study *man* as a part of the biological world we must not
forget that "conscious behavior is much more than.... mere life."[8]
Much scientific research is still needed, and there may be problems
here which, as has been said, we shall never solve. Also, it would be
a mistake to think of man merely in terms of biological concepts. But
there are characteristics which he shares with other animals, and an
understanding of this fact helps us better to understand him.

   The teacher needs to understand and keep in mind as a minimum,
the following biological concepts, undisputed and accepted in the
scientific world:

   1. Man is an animal; he is the product of evolutionary forces working, we know not how, in this world out of which the first manlike
creature came, perhaps a million years ago.[9]

   2. Man has certain distinguishing biological characteristics: (*a*)
He walks erect. (*b*) He has an opposable thumb; this makes it possible
for him to use tools. (*c*) He has a more highly developed brain than

6. *Ibid.,* pp. 70–71.

7. *Ibid.,* p. 71.   8. *Ibid.,* p. 43.

9. T. W. Wallbank and A. M. Taylor, *Civilization—Past and Present,* pp. 7–12.

any other animal. *(d)* He is equipped with vocal organs which make it possible for him to speak. *(e)* His young remain relatively helpless for a long period of time; they do not have at birth many specific reflexive or instinctive abilities but rather highly plastic and adaptable potentialities.

3. Man is biologically the most highly developed of the animals. Progress is measured biologically by the degree in which the organism exercises control over the environment and lives in some independence of it. The idea of progress, says Julian Huxley, the eminent British biologist, is not a mere anthropomorphism. "Man possesses greater power of control over and lives in greater independence of his environment than any monkey."[10]

4. The process of biological heredity is basically the same in man and other living creatures. Human variations have their physical basis in this process.

These ideas are familiar to all persons who have studied a minimum of biology in high school and college. But there are other concepts concerning the relation of man to the rest of the living world not so apparent to the beginner. All living things seem to be characterized by the following:

1. *An urge or a will to live.*—All living things act *as if* they were the bearers of a purposive force or agency whose one aim is to achieve and continue life.

2. *A unity which pervades the activities of the various parts.*— All the parts and activities of a biological organism seem to be arranged so as to further either the interests of the organism as a whole or those of the species to which it belongs.

3. *A dependence of the organism upon the environment which makes them one.*—"Just as the parts and activities of the organism are one, in the sense that though we can distinguish them, we cannot separate them unaltered, and consequently cannot understand or investigate one apart from the rest,"[11] so is it true that the organism and environment are one.

4. *An ability to grow and to change.*—This growth may be promoted or retarded by the interaction of the organism with its environment.

10. Julian Huxley, *Evolution, the Modern Synthesis*, p. 565.
11. J. S. Haldane, *Organism and Environment*, p. 99.

Education and the Individual 25

In man these characteristics exhibit themselves and have implications for an understanding of his nature, as follows:

1. All man's behavior is purposive or purposeful, that is, it is directed, unconsciously or consciously, toward satisfying his wants. Breathing is usually purposive behavior unless interfered with. Then it becomes purposeful. Man's wants may be needs, or they may be other than needs. He wants food; that, he needs. He may want an automobile and direct effort toward obtaining it, whether or not he needs it. But all his behavior is goal-seeking, effort directed toward achieving his purposes, either recognized or unrecognized. Basically these efforts are to continue the life of the individual and the species. Man has many wants beyond biological ones,[12] but the latter are fundamental.

2. Philosophers and psychologists have not always seen man as a unified creature. The relation of his mind to his body is one that has puzzled thinkers for hundreds of years.[13] It is because man has a mind that Haldane reminded his readers that "conscious behavior is much more .... than mere life." Whether the mind is a spiritual entity, of different substance from the body, whether it and the body are appearances of some common underlying reality, whether the mind is a mere epiphenomenon, or whether it is something still different, certain it is that, in life, man's mind and body are so closely interwoven that one cannot be separated from or understood apart from the other.

It is the realization of this fact that prompts writers on child psychology to emphasize repeatedly that it is the "whole child" for whose development we are responsible. We are not teaching disembodied minds. That an organism is a whole, and a whole which is more than the sum of its parts, is known as the organismic concept.

3. Just as we cannot separate a human being into a mind and a body, neither can we separate a human being from his environment. What he is and what he becomes not only depend upon his biological equipment but have from the moment of conception depended also upon his environment. This environment is not only the physical one but a social environment, with its accumulation of knowledge, skills, art, ideals, language, customs, religion, buildings, machines, etc., both immaterial and material in nature. Upon other human be-

12. See chaps. iv and v.   13. See chap. x.

ings and the social heritage into which he is born, man is dependent for becoming, first, what we call "human," and, second, to a large degree, the kind of human being that he is.

The new-born babe is not really a human being; he is a candidate for humanity. He has a fundamental instinctive equipment not greatly different from that of the lower animals, but he has also the capacity so to react to social stimuli that he will develop human habits. But he cannot develop the human habits without the social stimuli. This is the difference between the human infant and the young of lower animals. The new-born pup is a real dog, equipped with the tendencies to act which belong to his species. These will develop apart from contact with any other canine being. He will be truly a dog when he is grown whether he has ever lived with other dogs or not. Entirely different is the human child. He will never become human except through the stimuli of human society. He will never know himself as a self, except through interaction with other selves.[14]

This dependence of man upon his culture is what Immanuel Kant had in mind when he said: "Man can become man through education only. He is what education makes him."[15]

Of course, the kind of person this candidate for humanity becomes is also dependent upon his original equipment. If a baby did not have a potential ability to understand the discriminate use of language, he could not be educated. Man is born a biological organism with a basis for the development of various potentialities. His physical equipment probably determines the limits within which this development takes place. A child born with so defective a brain as to prevent the development of normal intelligence can never, so far as we know, have that defect remedied by any environment. But scientific experiments seem to show that a child born with the possibility for the development of normal intelligence may, by the environment, be so inhibited in growth as to appear feeble-minded.

As regards emotional development and character growth, the influence of the environment is of even greater importance. People are not born co-operative or competitive. They have the possibility for the development of either, or both to a degree. People are not born either good or bad, kindly or cruel, sympathetic or callous, unselfish or selfish. Human nature at birth is most accurately described as a

14. Theodore G. Soares, *Religious Education*, pp. 17–18.
15. *The Educational Theory of Immanuel Kant* (trans. and ed. Edward Franklin Buchner), p. 107.

bundle of potentialities, differing of course with different individuals but dependent upon the environment for development. There is almost infinite capacity for the development of different characteristics and patterns of behavior.

Let us suppose for illustrative purposes a situation which is most unlikely, that two children are born into two different families with practically the same potentialities. John was welcomed and loved, fed an adequate diet with regularity, managed with affectionate firmness; he learned very early that it did no good to yell and stamp his feet in an endeavor to get his own way yet, on the other hand, had every opportunity to satisfy his needs and legitimate wants. He was talked to, read to, played with. He heard music, poetry, the children's classics. He was taken to stores, to the park, to the zoo. His questions, when not merely aimed at getting attention, were intelligently answered. He had apparatus to climb on, tools to work with. He was encouraged, not frustrated, in pursuing his goals, unless those goals interfered with his own safety, his best development, or the rights of others.

He learned to pick up and put away his own toys, to "take turns" with playmates, to take care of a pet, to dry the dishes for mother, to weed the garden with father, to fight his own battles with the neighborhood bully, to watch over his younger sister, to play games fairly and to be a "good sport," whether he won or lost, and to take responsibility and be dependable.

Billy, too, was welcomed and loved. But he was fed whenever he cried, given whatever he wanted. He learned very early that it did pay to howl for what he wanted; he got it. His parents found it too much trouble to teach him what he could have and do and what he could not have and do. They were too busy to talk to him, to read to him, or to help him get acquainted with the world in which he was living. Billy was left with a maid who sometimes indulged and sometimes punished him. There was no security in his life. He got the idea that to satisfy his wants he had to get the best of people. He became sly, plausible, untruthful. Because he had no responsibility in his home, he cared little for that home.

When he started to school, his teacher found little readiness for learning to read because his experiences had been neither rich nor wide. He could not get along with other children. He was a most unhappy child; and, unless his teachers could work a miracle in his parents, as well as change the direction of his growth, he was destined for an unhappy life, because his best potentialities had not been developed and his worst were growing lustily.

John was a happy, manly youngster on his way to becoming a useful citizen. Billy was a confused, spoiled, unhappy child on his way to becoming a poor citizen. Both started, by definition, with the same potentialities. Experiments seem to have shown that identical twins, who apparently have the same biological equipment, if brought up in widely different environments, develop very differently, one from the other.[16] No person is born with the self which he becomes fatalistically predetermined. That self was at birth merely a potential self. The development might have been different had early influences been different. The self develops, says a modern sociologist, as "we are met and answered, opposed and blamed, praised and encouraged."[17] It is in the development of a self that man differs from other animals. "A human being," says the same authority, "is a being which has a self. No other animals have selves. A self is a subject which is its own object."[18] To understand how the self is developed is exceedingly important for all parents, teachers, or other students of human nature.

The question "Does human nature change?" is often raised. Many people insist that we shall never get rid of war, poverty, cruelty, injustice—in short, that we cannot hope for progress in human relationships, because these evils grow out of human nature itself and human nature does not change. It is true that such evils do come from human nature—human nature in a particular kind of environment. In its basic constitution, human nature probably does remain the same. John Dewey says in a recent publication:

I do not think it can be shown that the innate needs of men have changed since man became man or that there is any evidence that they will change as long as man is on the earth.

By "needs" I mean the inherent demands that men make because of their constitution. Needs for food and drink and for moving about, for

16. H. D. Carter, "Ten Years of Research on Twins," *Thirty-ninth Yearbook of National Society for the Study of Education,* Part V, p. 240.

17. Ellsworth Faris, *The Nature of Human Nature,* p. 7.

18. *Ibid.,* p. 3.

example, are so much a part of our being that we cannot imagine any condition under which they would cease to be. There are other things not so directly physical that seem to me equally ingrained in human nature. I would mention as examples the need for some kind of companionship; the need for exhibiting energy, for bringing one's powers to bear upon surrounding conditions; the need for both cooperation with and emulation of one's fellows for mutual aid and combat alike; the need for some sort of aesthetic expression and satisfaction; the need to lead and to follow, etc.

Whether my particular examples are well chosen or not does not matter so much as does recognition of the fact that there are some tendencies so integral a part of human nature that the latter would not be human nature if they changed.

Where we are likely to go wrong, after the fact is recognized that there is something unchangeable in the structure of human nature, is the inference we draw from it. We suppose that the manifestation of these needs is also unalterable.[19]

Human nature contains many potentialities. Sympathy is as much a part of human nature as is selfishness. Human nature is plastic and may develop many different patterns of behavior. The prying curiosity of the neighborhood gossip and the investigations of the scientist both spring from a common factor in human nature. "The pattern of the personality of the individual is not an inborn latency which merely requires time to unfold and mature."[20]

4. It is a characteristic of human beings to grow: to grow physically, intellectually, emotionally, socially, spiritually. While we may talk of these types of growth as if distinct, they are actually inseparable. One depends upon and continues with the others.

Looked at biologically, man's life is a constant interaction between a human organism and an environment. Action is directed toward satisfying wants. Because man is able to connect what he does with what happens to him in this interaction, we speak of human life as a constant succession of experiences. As a result of these experiences, human beings are changed. Some of their potentialities are developed, others inhibited. They have to adjust themselves to the world they are in, but they also can utilize and change parts of this world to their purposes. The changes in human beings resulting from their experiences we call "learning." The entire process of growth and

19. John Dewey, *The Problems of Men*, pp. 184–85.
20. Staff of Teachers College, Columbia University, *Readings in the Foundations of Education*, I, 127.

development in which this learning takes place we call "education."
If there has been no change, there has been no learning. As Henry
Morrison says:

All down through the ages, from Greek times at least and probably
earlier, the one consistent meaning found in the writings of those who
have been and are trying to think straight about the matter is the notion
that *learning is becoming* and that the product is a new birth in the individual, a changed point of view, a new taste or set of values, a new
ability.[21]

It would seem, then, that those who insist that education is growth
have a sound biological basis upon which to make such an assertion.
This is what John Dewey seems to say in such statements as the following: "Since growth is the characteristic of life, education is all one
with growing; it has no end beyond itself."[22] "Since in reality there
is nothing to which growth is relative save more growth, there is nothing to which education is subordinate save more education."[23]

Dewey, however, has always realized that this growth takes place
in society and that the social heritage is of importance to human
growth. Many of his followers have been far more individualistic
than he. In this, the movement known as Progressive education really follows Rousseau rather than Dewey, although it is unfortunately
true that many of Dewey's statements, including the two above quotations, lend themselves to the interpretation of excessive individualism.

Jean Jacques Rousseau (1712–78) was a French philosopher whose
book *Émile* profoundly influenced the history of education. The key
to his belief is to be found in the opening sentence of that classic. It is
usually translated something like this: "Everything is good as it
comes from the hands of the Author of Nature; but everything de-
generates in the hands of man."[24] And, further on, speaking of man
himself, he says: "Let us lay it down as an incontrovertible rule that
the first impulses of nature are always right; there is no original sin in
the human heart; the how and why of the entrance of every vice can
be traced."[25]

21. H. C. Morrison, *Basic Principles in Education*, p. 38.
22. John Dewey, *Democracy and Education*, p. 62.
23. *Ibid.*, p. 60.
24. Jean Jacques Rousseau, *Émile*, p. 4.   25. *Ibid.*, p. 56.

Rousseau found society evil; he would educate each child apart from the group, under the pretext of following nature. He is not very specific as to what he means by nature, but it seems to be the material world apart from what man has made of it. Émile is to have a tutor, but no family life after early infancy; he is to take his lessons from nature, not from man. He is to learn through his own personal experiences, not through the study of man's organized experience which we call subject matter. He is to be a discoverer, not an imitator; his creative powers are to be aroused, not his memory relied upon. He must learn to depend upon himself, not upon others; he must have a great deal of freedom to act. "Let his unreasonable wishes meet with physical obstacles only or the punishment which results from his own actions."[26] He is not to be treated as if he were a miniature man, but as a child, and his education must always be suited to the level of his ability. Physical education and vigorous exercise must be an important part of his life. And, above all, the *desire* to learn must be cultivated; the teacher must not depend upon extrinsic motivation. True education, taught Rousseau, is something that happens from within the individual; it is an unfolding of his own latent powers.

Rousseau contented himself with theorizing; he was unwilling even to bring up his own children. But his writing had a deep influence upon three men who did popularize his method. Johann Basedow, a German theologian, in 1774 founded a school at Dessau, which he called the Philanthropinum, in which he tried to make study pleasant and easy. The child-centered school is nothing new. The Philanthropinum was child-centered to perhaps an absurd degree.

Johann Pestalozzi (1746–1827), a Swiss, and Friedrich Froebel (1782–1852), a German, were men whose memories are revered in the educational world. Taking some of Rousseau's theories, chiefly, that children are children, not miniature adults, the importance of personal experience in learning, and education as the development of inborn powers, these two men effected important changes in the schools of Europe and eventually, here.

As a whole, Rousseau's ideas were completely impracticable. He did have some important insights into child nature and the educative process. But to believe that education can be carried on apart

26. *Ibid.*, p. 49.

from society or that child nature, left to itself, will automatically develop into goodness shows a serious lack of insight into human nature.

Man is fundamentally a social being; he becomes a self and the kind of self he is as he interacts with other human beings. He is born neither bad nor good but with propensities for both. If the society in which he lives is evil, the growth of evil in his nature is encouraged. If the society with which he interacts is good, the growth of good in his nature is stimulated. No human being ever approaches human excellence by living to himself alone. It is basic in human nature to be selfish and self-centered. When the philosopher Kant spoke of the "unsocial sociability of man," he recognized a paradox in human beings. We are individuals and we want what we want when we want it; but our individual welfare, even our becoming human rather than animal, depends upon others. The individual and society are inextricably interwoven.

Many of Rousseau's followers recognized this fact. Neither Pestalozzi nor Froebel accepted Rousseau's extreme individualism; but with the present century we have seen a revival of individualistic educational practice, reaching its crest during the 1920's, sponsored by Progressive education. This movement seems to be waning, and there is some danger that we may go too far to the opposite extreme, losing sight of the individual through social pressures.

To achieve a happy balance between extreme individualism and social conformity is one of the most pressing of modern social problems. It has its repercussions not only in the educational world but in all phases of social organization. In achieving this balance, as in any progressive step, our social heritage has an important role.

SUMMARY

Men have argued for many years over whether education can best be understood as a handing-on of the social heritage or as human growth and development. It is probably something of each. A study of man may help us to know where to put the emphasis and how to reconcile the apparent conflict.

Man has a nature which is basically animal, and he cannot be understood apart from the natural world out of which he has come. But he is also different from other living creatures.

Life is a constant interaction between a living organism and an environment, inextricably interwoven. Man acts to satisfy his wants. He is able to connect what he does with what happens to him and to direct much of his activity toward goals which he sets in accord with his purposes. As he does this, conduct is modified; attitudes and understandings are changed; skills are developed. Such changes we call "learning"; if there has been no change, there has been no learning.

No one is born with the self he becomes already predetermined. He is at birth a bundle of potentialities. Interaction with the physical and social environment promotes the growth of some of these potentialities and inhibits the development of others. Because a human being is so dependent upon society for his development, individual welfare and social welfare are interdependent. Since man's nature is fundamentally social, it would seem to be a mistake to think of education exclusively in terms of individual growth without reference to society and social needs.

QUESTIONS TO AID STUDY

1. Supposing that by some strange accident you had been exchanged at birth with a child from the Solomon Islands; you grew up there and he grew up here. Would you or the changeling be more like what you now are? How would you be different and how like what you now are? Who would be more like the natives of the Solomons—you or the changeling?
2. Does human nature change? Explain.
3. Is your theory as to the origin of life of any importance? Explain.
4. Explain vitalism, mechanism, and emergent evolution as explanations of the relation between the living and the nonliving.
5. Does the belief that man is the result of an evolutionary process remove the necessity for a belief in God? Explain.
6. What distinguishing characteristics does man have as an animal?
7. What characteristics that all living things show seem to have particular significance for understanding man? Show how.
8. What is the organismic concept? How does it apply in the educative process?
9. What is meant by saying that no baby is born a self? How does the self develop? When is this development complete?
10. Look up in any history of education the lives and deeds of Rousseau, Basedow, Pestalozzi, Froebel. How do you think that each one of these men would answer the questions at the beginning of the chapter? How would you answer the same questions?
11. Read chapter iv in Dewey's *Democracy and Education.* How do you think that he would answer each question?
12. Upon what fact does the contention that extreme individualism is a mistake rest? Explain.

34   *Philosophy of Education*

SUGGESTED REFERENCES

ANDREWS, ROY CHAPMAN. *Meet Your Ancestors* (New York: Viking Press, 1945), chaps. i–ii.

BAGLEY, WILLIAM C. *Education and Emergent Man* (New York: T. Nelson & Sons, 1934), chaps. i–ii.

CHILDS, JOHN LAURENCE. *Education and the Philosophy of Experimentalism* (New York: Century Co., 1931), pp. 69–87.

DEWEY, JOHN. *Democracy and Education* (rev. ed.; New York: Macmillan Co., 1931), chap. iv.

——. *The Problems of Men* (New York: Philosophical Library, 1946), pp. 184–92.

DOUGHTON, ISAAC. *Modern Public Education* (New York: D. Appleton–Century Co., 1935), chaps. iii and iv.

EATON, THEODORE HILDRETH. *An Approach to a Philosophy of Education* (New York: J. Wiley & Sons, 1938), chap. i.

GRUENBERG, BENJAMIN CHARLES. *The Story of Evolution.* New York: D. Van Nostrand Co., 1929.

HALDANE, JOHN SCOTT. *The Philosophy of a Biologist* (Oxford: Clarendon Press, 1935), chap. ii.

JENNINGS, HERBERT SPENCER. *The Biological Basis of Human Nature* (New York: W. W. Norton & Co., 1930), chap. xvi.

KILPATRICK, WILLIAM HEARD. *Self-hood and Civilization* (New York: Macmillan Co., 1941), chap. i.

KNODE, JAY CARROLL, and ASSOCIATES. *Foundations of an American Philosophy of Education* (New York: D. Van Nostrand Co., 1942), chap. ii.

LECOMTE DU NOÜY, PIERRE. *Human Destiny.* New York: Longmans, Green & Co., 1947.

LILLIE, RALPH STAYNER. *General Biology and the Philosophy of Organism* (Chicago: University of Chicago Press, 1945), chaps. i and xiv.

MORRISON, HENRY CLINTON. *Basic Principles in Education* (New York: Houghton Mifflin Co., 1934), chap. iv.

OVERSTREET, HARRY. *The Enduring Quest* (New York: W. W. Norton & Co., 1931), chap. iv.

RALL, HARRIS FRANKLIN. *Christianity* (New York: Charles Scribner's Sons, 1940), chap vi.

THOMAS, FRANK W., and LANG, ALBERT R. *Principles of Modern Education* (New York: Houghton Mifflin Co., 1937), chaps. iv–v.

THORNDIKE, EDWARD L. *Man and His Works* (Cambridge, Mass.: Harvard University Press, 1943), chap. i.

WALLBANK, T. WALTER, and TAYLOR, ALASTAIR M. *Civilization—Past and Present* (Chicago: Scott, Foresman & Co., 1942), pp. 7–12.

YOUNG, CLARENCE, and OTHERS. *The Human Organism and the World of Life* (New York: Harper & Bros., 1938), chaps. xiii, xiv, and xvii.

CHAPTER III
THE NATURE OF THE EDUCATIVE PROCESS
EDUCATION AND THE SOCIAL HERITAGE

Man's ability to profit from the experience of others in satisfying his wants—Formal and informal education: (1) Formal, where there is intent to teach; (2) Informal, through watching, imitating, participating in living with persons who are not intent on teaching—Education and social progress: (1) Impossibility of understanding the what of education apart from the why; (2) Idea of progress in human history; (3) The measurement of progress; (4) Evidence for the possibility of progress; its dependence upon man's intelligent effort; (5) The attainment of further progress (a) positive means: education (b) negative means: suffering—The twofold nature of the educative process—Three aspects of education: training, instruction, inspiration

---

IT IS not only civilized man to whom education has been and is of importance. Man has always, unconsciously and then consciously, educated his young. If it were not the nature of man to learn from the experience of others as well as from his own, we should be more like the primitive ape men than we are. There have been some organic changes in man since the most ancient near-human creatures known roamed Asia and the neighboring islands. Biologically Cro-Magnon man was an improvement over *Pithecanthropus erectus*. Modern man's improvement over Cro-Magnon man has not been a biological one. Physically there have been few changes in man for at least thirty thousand years. But culturally there have been tremendous changes and, most of us believe, some improvement; this progress would have been impossible without the cumulative effect of human experience.

When the bright eyes of a small son and daughter watched the laborious work of their mother as she prepared crude clothing from the skin of the animal which the father had captured; when they followed the father as he fashioned rude weapons from stone; when these children in their play or work imitated the actions of their parents; when the mother or father showed the children how to perform the skills they themselves had stumbled upon, devised, or learned from others, those children were being educated. Their intelligence—the ability to recognize and solve successfully the problems of living—was being developed. What the previous generations had learned about satisfying human wants was being passed on to the new generation.

As mentioned in the previous chapter, psychologists tell us that all man's conduct springs from attempts to satisfy his wants. With primitive man and, basically, with modern man, these wants were and are on an animal level. To remain alive and to continue the life of the species engaged most of early man's endeavor. Through accident, through trial and error, and, much later, through deliberate and controlled experimentation, man discovered more and better ways to satisfy his wants. As basic wants were cared for, he discovered that he had wants beyond those of the animals. Because man is endowed with memory, he was able to recall and use again these discoveries and inventions. Furthermore, other men who may not have been so fortunate or so intelligent, could imitate these pioneers. So could the rising generation. Thus, fortunate contrivances were passed on, becoming cumulative in their effect.

As this cultural heritage became more extensive, it contained more information about the skills and techniques to be used in gaining protection from enemies and in the obtaining of food. It also included the socially approved way to do things, to placate the gods, and to behave upon all occasions. Parents did not have time to instruct their offspring in all these matters. The old men and women, no longer able to contribute to the protection and support of the group, took over the task of instructing the younger members. Later, as specialization was found advantageous in the life of the group, teaching came to be done by the younger adults who were assigned to that responsibility or who assumed it.

Children, of course, watched and imitated their parents and other adults as they do today. Parents as today also taught their offspring much that they knew. The parent was then, as he is now, the child's first and most important teacher. A child's education begins in his home. As he watches, imitates, participates, in the activities of living, he is being informally educated. When he is being consciously and intentionally taught, that is formal education.

FORMAL AND INFORMAL EDUCATION

Much of formal education—and some informal education, too—is given in the institution organized originally by society for the express purpose of transmitting the social heritage. Schools are more than that today, although to transmit our cultural heritage is still a most important function and one which we neglect to our peril. The distinction between formal and informal education has its roots in the prehistoric past, perhaps even further back than that. Animals seem consciously to teach their young some things, while other things are learned through imitation. So far as man is concerned, formal education began when the adults of a group made conscious provision for introducing the young to their social heritage. The school is one of the social forms or institutions through which society makes this introduction. It is, in fact, next to the home in importance for this transmission.

Education is far wider and more inclusive than schooling, important though that be. It begins soon after birth and continues until senescence or death. It is a concomitant of living, an inevitable and necessary outgrowth from the nature of man and of his group life. It is because man is able to assimilate the results of his experience and that of others in attempting to satisfy human wants and to profit thereby that he is different from Cro-Magnon man of yesterday. The school, where much of the systematic, planned, and guided instruction which we call "formal" education has been given, has played an important part in bringing about these differences.

It is this role of education in the continuing life of the group of which John Dewey was thinking when he wrote his first chapter in *Democracy and Education*. Professor Horne has summarized Dewey's views in these words:

The means whereby a social group continues itself, renews itself, maintains its ideals, is, in the broadest sense of the term, education. Unless there were education in this sense, the characteristic life of the group would cease with the death of the elders. The young must be preserved physically and initiated socially, learning the ways of the elders, if the life of the group is to continue. . . . . As biological life maintains and transmits itself by nutrition and reproduction, so social life transmits itself by education.[1]

This does not sound as though Dewey fails to see the importance of transmitting the social heritage. True, he would use organized subject matter differently from the way in which it is used in the traditional school.[2] But he recognizes its value in stimulating the growth of the individual. The chief fault to be found with his conception of education is that he fails to define the ends toward which that growth should be directed. Growth for the sake of more growth, education for more education, is not enough. Certainly human beings should continue to grow; education is a process which goes on throughout life. But toward what? As Aristotle pointed out, it seems impossible to understand the what of anything apart from the why. We cannot understand what education is, apart from the study of why education is necessary and what it should accomplish.

Though he frequently slips backward, modern man has made a beginning toward bringing about the conditions on this earth which would make it possible for all mankind to live in accordance with human ideals. As was pointed out in chapter i, man has the knowledge gained through scientific research which makes it possible to provide all kinds of material goods. He has gone far toward controlling and using the physical environment for his purposes. He has embodied beauty in what we call "the arts." He has a religion based on something other than fear. He has ideals and aspirations toward the realization of which he stumbles forward. And, most difficult accomplishment of all, as old Thales understood, he seems to have made some progress toward understanding human nature. And now modern man wants a world in which human needs can be satisfied more fully. He is not content merely to transmit the social heritage. He wishes to improve upon it as well as to preserve it.

EDUCATION AND SOCIAL PROGRESS

Just when this idea of progress entered into the thinking of man is difficult to determine. That there has been improvement in the condition of man since prehistoric days and that there will be continued

1. H. H. Horne, *The Democratic Philosophy of Education*, p. 7.
2. See John Dewey, *Experience and Education*, chap. vii; also chaps. xii–xiii in this text.

improvement is an idea so common among us that it is difficult for us to believe that there were centuries in which man seems neither to have conceived such a notion nor to have particularly desired such a process. Certainly with primitive man the chief endeavor was to preserve intact the "cake of custom."

It is doubtful whether any of the ancient thinkers imagined that the world we live in might be made a progressively better place for man. So far as we know, the Greek philosophy of history was either a cyclic one or one of degeneration from a past golden age or a combination of the two. Such tales as that of Prometheus do tell a story of man's ascent from barbarism to civilization, but this improvement in man's lot seems to have been interpreted as a mere phase of one cycle. In the eighth book of the *Republic*, Plato discusses his perfect state in relation to the cyclic theory of history. An ideal state, he thought, could not last forever. After its establishment by philosophers who were kings, any change would prove disastrous.[3] Interestingly enough, the cyclic theory has been revived in modern times by Nietzsche and by Oswald Spengler.

During the Middle Ages the intellectual climate was set by Christianity as interpreted by Augustine and others of the early Fathers. With their doctrines of the fall of man, and of the resulting natural and total depravity with which each is born, and their belief that this world is a mere place of preparation for a future life the notion of progress as we conceive it was not compatible.

Bury, a student of the idea of social progress, says that it was not until the latter part of the sixteenth century and the early part of the seventeenth, that men first began to look upon history as the story of man's progress and to postulate the possibility of its continuance.[4] Bury gives to Bodin, a French historian, the credit for being the first writer to enunciate the view that human history is not the story of degeneration from a past golden age but is the recital of progress. To the French philosopher Abbé de Saint-Pierre belongs the credit for teaching that man can, by concerted effort, create a markedly better world.[5]

3. See also Plato's *Timaeus* 22C and the *Laws* iii. 677 for references to the cyclic theory.

4. J. B. Bury, *The Idea of Progress*, pp. 33 and 35.

5. *Ibid.*, pp. 37–41.

Some students have found in the writings of the Roman Stoic philosopher Seneca the notion of progress; others, the same idea in the writings of the Epicureans, particularly in Lucretius' *De rerum natura*. But, as Bury points out, Stoicism and Epicureanism were both philosophies of resignation; and, looked at in their context, the reflections of these writers do not contain the notion of the possibility of man's advancement to progressively better conditions.[6]

Beginning with the seventeenth century the idea of progress gradually became a commonplace. Some thinkers were overoptimistic. Condorcet, in his *Sketch of a Historical Picture of the Progress of the Human Mind*, seemed to believe that progress was inevitable, a law of the universe. Comte was almost as optimistic. To many, Darwin's theory of evolution appeared to lend support to such a doctrine. Herbert Spencer was one philosopher who so interpreted man's history.

The idea of attainable improvement entered as a general "article of faith" into the thinking of most educated people during the latter part of the nineteenth century and the early part of the twentieth. There was an attitude of optimism among the majority of thinking persons. Today we find this optimism questioned and a growth of pessimism toward the possibility of improving the lot of man on earth. Spengler has his disciples. His book, *The Decline of the West*, is a scholarly and convincing presentation of the cyclic theory. Nations do rise, become static, then decline and decay. We see about us old civilizations crumbling, new types of social organization rising, a recrudescence of cruelty and suffering in the world, global depressions and wars the order of the day. No wonder individuals are suspicious of the easy optimism of fifty years ago.

Thoughtful and troubled people are again asking: Is progress possible? What do we mean by progress? What are its components? Is it to be measured by the fact that we can produce more goods with less effort? That we live longer? How, if at all, can we insure progress?

To answer these questions, we must be clear on (1) what constitutes progress for man, (2) what scientific evidence there is that we may hope for continued progress, and (3) how further progress may be secured.

6. *Ibid.*, p. 128.

1. *What constitutes progress for man?*—Thoughtful consideration of the problem would seem to lead to the conclusion that man progresses as more and more human beings are able to live a life that is satisfying for man to live, a life which provides for every facet of his nature in such a way that he becomes the best human being he could become.

Material advances would seem to be an essential factor in progress. Advances in medical science likewise are a part of it. But, taken alone, no one of these factors constitutes progress. We do make more goods with less effort; and many of the great cities of the world lie in ruins. Medical science saves lives, particularly the lives of babies, but to preserve the lives of infants merely to have them lost later on the battlefield seems wasteful. And simply to prolong life is a doubtful criterion for progress. What kind of life is worth prolonging? Any kind? Is life more satisfying and worth while than it used to be? Statistics on suicide and insanity make one wonder.

It is to man's total nature that we must go to find what he must have in order to lead a life that is good to live. Only as we attempt to understand human nature in its entirety, only as we make provision for *all* man's needs as we discover what they are, can we attain and measure progress. It is from the study of man's nature, as well as from his history, that we get some evidence that the hope for continued progress is not a vain and chimerical dream of man.

2. *What evidence is there for the reality of progress?*—Whether thinkers are justified in conceiving progress as inevitable for man depends upon what is meant by such a statement. If they intend to take responsibility for intelligent and socially directed effort off man's shoulders and to say that, no matter what man does, progress will surely come because it is the law of the universe, they are probably making a serious mistake. Historians do not teach that man's course has always been one that brought improvement nor that we can be certain that the future will bring advances toward the good life for all. No scientist interprets evolution to mean that change has always brought progress in the biological world.

But if they mean that it seems to be man's nature to struggle, often unconscious of the goal, toward making a world in which man can live as man, then history, biology, psychology, and sociology unite in giving us hope that such may be the case. It seems as if the progress that has been attained has come as a result of man's attempts to achieve a satisfying life; that it has been cyclic in the sense that there have been regressions as well as advances but that the general trend has been slowly and painfully upward; that man's nature contains the potentialities for the development of better human beings; and that, while man cannot be certain that progress will continue, a study of man's nature and history gives us that hope and some evidence on which to base such hope.[7]

That man has made less progress than we might wish for is not surprising and should not discourage us. Until material advances which would allow a decent standard of living for everyone were made, we could not expect much social progress. Civilization is relatively young in the history of mankind. Franz Werfel says in a recent book that one hundred thousand years from now man will look upon this age as part of a primitive age.[8]

Let us recall what was said in the previous chapter about the development of human personality. Criminals were not born to be criminals. Antisocial individuals were not predetermined in their attitudes toward their fellow human beings. Man is not born to become with fatalistic certainty the self he becomes. He is born with many potential selves. He becomes the self he is through interaction with his physical and social environment. If we could improve the influences that play upon him, we could improve the result of such interaction. Not only could man's attitudes toward his fellow-man be improved, but there is some evidence that what we call "intelligence" can be developed in a favorable environment beyond the amount of effective intelligence in the world today.[9] Opportunity for improved physical and social conditions of living brings improvement in men. Not that men will ever be perfect! We must not forget that men are basically animals, and we can never make them angels in this world.

If this be true—and biology, psychology, and sociology unite in offering supporting evidence—then those of us fortunate enough to have lived under the conditions which made it possible to develop social attitudes and some intelligence have a responsibility for work-

7. See Arnold Toynbee's *A Study of History* for an elaboration of this point of view.

8. Franz Werfel, *Star of the Unborn*, p. 46, for example.

9. See chap. xiii.

ing together to improve the conditions under which all men live. Man has probably never stood in graver danger than he does today. The scientists responsible for the release of atomic energy are calling our attention to the fact that, if we go one way, mankind will commit suicide. If we go another, we can build a world in which all mankind can live a life which is good to live.

We should now be able to see what evidence there is for faith in continued progress, not only from a study of man's history but from an investigation of his nature. It looks as if there were hope based on scientific evidence that man could advance in the future as he seems to have done in the past. But there is no certainty that he will. It depends upon *him*. Will we use whatever intelligence is now available in that direction?

3. *How may further progress be secured?*—Parents and teachers know that children learn the lessons of life in one of two ways. On the one hand, they learn through example set before them, through persuasion, through reasoning with them. On the other hand, that is not always sufficient to teach children what they must know for their own good. So punishment has to be used. If used wisely, children become better, making progress toward successful adulthood.

Adults, like children, learn in either of two ways. They may learn by studying man's history, and the consequences have been serious for those who refused so to learn. "Those who forget history seem doomed to repeat it." They may learn by applying their reason to the solution of life's problems in the light of the knowledge and ideals mankind has discovered. They may learn by heeding their own best nature. But, like children, adults will not learn all life's lessons in these ways. Wrong acts eventually bring their own punishment, often very severe punishment—retribution which strikes the innocent as well as the guilty. It seems as though man learns many of his lessons only through severe suffering.

If we could, through education, direct the growth of boys and girls so that their best potentialities were developed, thus helping them to become men and women who would work intelligently toward promoting human progress, mankind would suffer less. Surely it is better to work toward man's improvement through education than to have him suffer the pain that inevitably follows if he fails to profit from what is known of man's nature and of his history here.

44 Philosophy of Education

Education cannot stop with schooling boys and girls. Even formal education should continue throughout adult life. It must so continue if man is to learn in time to use wisely the awesome knowledge which science is giving him. But the work of the majority of teachers still lies with the immature. And it is becoming more and more apparent that education is the necessary and inevitable result of society's need to guide the growth and development of its younger members in order to produce an improved generation. In earlier pages, education was said to be a necessary and inevitable result of society's need for handing on the social heritage. There is no necessary conflict between these two statements.

THE TWOFOLD NATURE OF THE EDUCATIVE PROCESS

To concentrate merely upon passing on the social heritage is to make education serve only as a recapitulation of the past, to attempt to secure stability, and to preserve the status quo in a world which refuses to remain stable and to keep the status quo. It is to refuse the better and the surer method for achieving progress; it is to impede and even to check possible progress; it is to invite disaster.

To concentrate merely on the growth and development of children is to make the mistake which John Dewey says too many of the so-called "progressives" have made: to neglect the social heritage, proceeding as if the past had no contribution to make to the present.[10] We shall lose, as perhaps we have already lost, much of the result of man's experience and thought if we continue along such a path. That, too, is to invite disaster.

But to see education as a process of growth and development—taking place as a result of the interaction of an individual with his environment, both physical and social, beginning at birth and lasting as long as life itself—a process in which the social heritage as a part of the social environment becomes a tool to be used toward the development of the best and most intelligent persons possible, men and women who will promote human welfare, that is to see the educative process as philosophers and educational reformers conceived it. It is certainly the way that Kant, Pestalozzi, Froebel, Herbart, Herbert Spencer, G. Stanley Hall, and William James understood it. And, in spite of his concept of education as growth with no goal but

10. John Dewey, *op. cit.*, pp. 2–3.

further growth, it is probably the way that John Dewey sees it. It is always implicit in his writings and sometimes explicit. For example, he wrote that "the function of education is to help the growing of a helpless young animal into a happy, moral, and efficient human being."[11]

During the twelfth century, Bernard de Chartres is said to have remarked: "We are dwarfs standing on the shoulders of giants." Occasionally during the history of man there have been born individuals of unusual intelligence and insight, giants in comparison with most of us, who have contributed to man's welfare in science, industry, art, philosophy, and religion. One of the fortunate characteristics of man is his ability to assimilate and profit by the insights of the geniuses among us. We can profit from their labors by assimilating the results of their efforts, by climbing to their shoulders. But to climb is not easy. It takes hard, concentrated effort. Too many people stop at the giant's knees or even below the knees. If a person continues to the shoulders, it is possible that, though he be but a dwarf, he may see further than did the giants. But if we bring up a generation unacquainted with the accomplishment of the giants of human thought, the perspective obtainable from their shoulders will be lost and progress immeasurably slowed.

To progress, we must have more and more knowledge of man and this universe. We must have more ethical insights and more of a disposition to act upon time-tested ideals of conduct. To forget what man has already worked out in these fields is to slip backward. Nicholas Murray Butler says:

> Only the scholar can realize how little that is being said and thought in the modern world is in any sense new. It was the colossal triumph of the ancient Greeks and Romans and of the great thinkers of the Middle Ages to sound the depths of almost every problem which human nature has to offer, and to interpret human thought and human aspiration with astounding profundity and insight. Unhappily, these deep-lying facts which should be controlling in the life of a civilized people with a historic background are known only to the few, while the many grasp, now at ancient and well-demonstrated falsehood and now at old and well-proved truth, as if each had all the attraction of novelty.[12]

11. John Dewey and Evelyn Dewey, *Schools of Tomorrow*, p. 136.

12. Introd. to a recent edition of the 1796 translation of Kant, *Perpetual Peace*, p. vii.

It is the business of teachers, engaged as we are in furthering the educative process, to see that these "old and well-proved truths" become more widely disseminated and that "ancient and well-demonstrated falsehoods" are recognized as such. Education for progress implies preservation as well as change.

Change is, of course, necessary in order to bring about progress. But not all change is progress. Too many people believe that anything that is old is thereby bad and anything that is new is thereby good. Customs, mores, and institutions have grown out of man's needs. Certainly when they no longer serve a need, they should be changed. But we should be certain that they do no longer serve a need. To be constantly changing without getting closer to a worthwhile goal is to be in the same predicament as that in which Lewis Carroll's Alice found herself when she went through the looking-glass:

"Well, in *our* country," said Alice, still panting a little, "you'd generally get to somewhere else—if you ran very fast for a long time as we've been doing."

"A slow sort of country," said the Queen. "Now *here*, you see, it takes all the running you can do, to keep in the same place."

Before we can be in any position to decide on changes which will promote progress rather than keep us running in the same place, we should learn what has been already discovered about the life that is good for man to live and what needs to be done in order to promote his welfare.

This is the meaning of the educative process, particularly of formal education. In order to guide the growth of boys and girls toward the development of human excellence necessary for social progress, they must have *training, instruction,* and *inspiration.* Training aims at habit formation. The more useful habits we can help children form, the better equipped for life they are. But training is not enough. It will suffice for animals but not for human beings. Through training we get desirable overt activity. But children need to know the reason why, as well as to act in an acceptable fashion. They must be equipped to solve novel problems as well as to act in routine matters. Instruction aims at helping pupils to gain knowledge and so to develop their own intelligence. The social heritage must be transmitted in such a way as to stimulate intellectual growth. But habit formation and instruction are still not in themselves enough. Dispositions to use one's intelligence and ability for the welfare of all must be developed. Therefore, inspiration is a necessary part of education. Our emotions are the basis for our behavior, and their proper development is an important part of education. Children must grow into adults who *want* the welfare of others as well as their own if social progress through concerted effort is to become a reality.

It has been said that education must be directed toward attaining social progress and that social progress can be measured only by the quality of human life. Man progresses as more and more human beings are able to live the kind of life which promotes human excellence. This would indicate that the goals of education cannot be determined apart from the goals of life itself. What constitutes the good life? How can man find out? What end must man serve? To investigate these problems is the purpose of the following eight chapters.

SUMMARY

Education both formal and informal is used by society for preserving the values of the past. But we wish to progress as well as to preserve. We progress when the quality of living is such as to encourage the development of a greater amount of human excellence in the world. There is some evidence from history that man has started on this road. There is more evidence from those sciences which study the nature of man and society that he can hope for further progress if he will intelligently direct his efforts toward improving the social conditions under which men live and toward using the social heritage as a tool for promoting the best growth of the rising generation. There is no real conflict between the conception of education as individual growth and as social maintenance, for the self and society are interdependent and man needs for his proper growth the results of man's previous experience. The meaning of proper growth can be determined only through an examination of the meaning of human excellence.

QUESTIONS TO AID STUDY

1. Distinguish between formal and informal education; between education and schooling.
2. Do you think formal or informal education has been the more important in your development? Explain.
3. In what sense was formal education a natural and inevitable development in man's history?
4. Argue for or against the following: Man never does anything he does not want to do. Connect this statement with what psychology teaches

us concerning the motive back of all man's conduct. What problem does this pose?

5. By what criterion could progress be measured? In what respect and to what degree has man made progress?
6. Are there arguments against the possibility of man's progress? State and discuss any that you can find.
7. What danger is there in being too optimistic concerning the possibility of human progress? Too pessimistic?
8. What evidence is there for the possibility of social progress? How, if at all, will further progress be obtained?
9. If human nature does not change, how can man progress?
10. What is meant by the social heritage?
11. How may the social heritage be used to further human progress? What is the relation of subject matter as used in the school to the social heritage?
12. Can you illustrate change which has not been progress?
13. What three divisions are there to the educative process?
14. Explain what is meant by the twofold aspect of education.
15. Would you answer any of the questions at the beginning of chapter ii differently now? Discuss.
16. Define education in your own words.
17. Criticize the following definitions of education: (a) Education is the getting and giving of knowledge so as to pass on our culture from one generation to the next. (b) Education is the process by which a person is adjusted to those elements of his environment which are of concern in modern life so as to prepare him for successful adult living. (c) Education is "that reconstruction or reorganization of experience which adds to the meaning of experience and which increases ability to direct the course of subsequent experience."[13] (d) Education is the process by which the individual is taught loyalty and conformity to the group and to social institutions. (e) Education is the process by which the human mind is disciplined and developed. (f) Education is a process of growth in which the individual is helped to develop his powers, his talents, his abilities, and his interests.

SUGGESTED REFERENCES

Bury, John Bagnell. *The Idea of Progress* (New York: Macmillan Co., 1932), pp. 1–36 and 334–49.
Cooley, Charles Horton. *Social Organization* (New York: Charles Scribner's Sons, 1929), chaps. i and ii.
Demiashkevich, Michael J. *An Introduction to the Philosophy of Education* (New York: American Book Co., 1935), chap. vii.

13. John Dewey, *Democracy and Education*, pp. 89–90.

DEWEY, JOHN. *Democracy and Education* (rev. ed.; New York: Macmillan Co., 1931), chaps. i and ii.

FARIS, ELLSWORTH. *The Nature of Human Nature* (New York: McGraw-Hill Book Co., 1937), chap. ii.

HORNE, HERMANN HARRELL. *The Democratic Philosophy of Education* (New York: Macmillan Co., 1932), chaps. i and ii.

JEANS, SIR JAMES. *The Universe around Us* (4th ed.; Cambridge: University Press, 1944), Introd. and pp. 276–89.

KNIGHT, EDGAR WALLACE. *Progress and Educational Perspective.* New York: Macmillan Co., 1942.

MEAD, MARGARET. *Sex and Temperament in Three Primitive Societies.* New York: W. Morrow & Co., 1935.

MORRISON, HENRY CLINTON. *Basic Principles in Education* (New York: Houghton Mifflin Co., 1934), chap. v.

OVERSTREET, HARRY. *The Enduring Quest* (New York: W. W. Norton & Co., 1931), chap. v.

THOMAS, FRANK W., and LANG, ALBERT R. *Principles of Modern Education* (New York: Houghton Mifflin Co., 1937), chap. viii.

CHAPTER IV
THE CHIEF END OF MAN

Interpretations of the meaning of life: (1) *Teleological interpretations;* (2) *Nonteleological interpretations;* (3) *Ultimate destiny of man unknowable through use of human powers;* (4) *Chief end in this world might be established deductively—The nature of man as man:* (1) *Importance of determining distinctive characteristics;* (2) *Use of language as symbols as the human characteristic* (a) *relation of this ability to formation of the self,* (b) *relation of this ability to human reason,* (c) *relation of this ability to creative imagination,* (d) *relation of this ability to making moral distinctions—A conception of the chief end of man:* (1) *The attainment of human excellence* (a) *argument from man's nature,* (b) *argument from religion;* (2) *The relation between the general welfare and individual welfare;* (3) *The social nature of self-realization—Historic conceptions of the highest good:* (1) *Happiness as life's aim* (a) *Aristotle's doctrine of the mean,* (b) *Epicureanism,* (c) *hedonism,* (d) *utilitarianism;* (2) *Stoic tranquillity; harmony with things as they are;* (3) *Puritanism;* (4) *Happiness as a by-product of self-realization—Realizing man's chief end:* (1) *Necessity for intelligent action;* (2) *Responsibilities of teachers*

WHAT thoughtful person does not understand the feelings of the young man of whom the poet Heinrich Heine wrote:

> By the sea, by the waste, nocturnal sea,
> Stands a youthful man,
> His breast full of sadness, his head full of doubt,
> And with mournful lips
> Does he ask the billows:

> "Oh, solve me the riddle of life,
> The agonizing, world-old riddle,
> Upon which so many heads have pondered,
> Heads in hieroglyphic caps,

Heads in turbans, and in black biretta,
Heads in perukes and a thousand other
Poor, perspiring human heads—
Tell me, of what significance is man?
Whence does he come? Whither does he go?
Who dwells up there on golden stars?"

The billows murmur their eternal murmur,
The wind doth blow, the clouds pass by,
The stars twinkle indifferent and cold,
And foolish the man that awaits reply.

Foolish indeed the man who awaits a reply from the billows!
Answers to such questions can be obtained, if at all, only through the
use of man's reason and faith. Such answers have metaphysical and
religious implications. Men have always differed and probably always will differ in their beliefs. We cannot *know* the answers in the
sense that science knows about many of the things in the world in
which we live. Metaphysics and religion have answers, but there is
no general agreement among even the wisest of men to such questions as the following: Why am I here? Why is there a world? A universe? Is there some Divine Purpose back of it all? Or is it all the
result of blind chance? What does life mean, if anything? Is there a
Friend to man and his endeavors in the universe? Is man of any cosmic importance? Or is the universe and all in it indifferent to man
and his struggles? Does life have meaning? What is it? How can I
find out? What should I do with my life? What values are worth pursuing? Is there anything beyond this life?

To seek the meaning of life has been the eternal quest of man.
Great literature has often dealt with the problem. Philosophers have
treated it as one of the most important realms for their inquiry. That
life does have a meaning has seemed to most men indubitable. True,
at times, life may appear to be "a tale told by an idiot, full of sound
and fury, signifying nothing." But for hundreds of years an over-
whelming majority of people have believed that there is an order in
the universe which has meaning for human beings, a God who cares
about human lives and gives them, and all events, their direction.
In such a faith millions have found and still find the meaning of life.
Such an interpretation is called "teleological," that is, it sees purpose
back of human life. Tolstoy, in *War and Peace,* has Pierre, the hero of

the tale, come to this conclusion after his capture by the French. It was while Pierre was a prisoner that he came under the influence of Karataev, a man of noble character who was an earnest Christian. Tolstoy says of Pierre:

> The very question that had formerly tormented him, the thing he had continually sought to find—the aim of life—no longer existed for him now. That search for the aim of life had not merely disappeared temporarily— he felt that it no longer existed for him and could not present itself again. .... That search for an aim had been simply a search for God, and suddenly in his captivity he had learned not by words or reasoning but by direct feeling what his nurse had told him long ago: that God is here and everywhere..... He felt like a man who after straining his eyes to see into the far distance finds what he sought at his very feet. All his life he had looked over the heads of the men around him, when he should have merely looked in front of him without straining his eyes.[1]

That there is purpose back of the universe and human life and that man has cosmic significance cannot, of course, be proved. Many thoughtful people have believed that the scientific investigations of the past few hundred years have thrown considerable doubt upon any teleological interpretation of our lives. The more we learn of ourselves and of the universe, say they, the more doubt there is of any "divinity that shapes our ends, rough-hew them how we will." Such doubts have bred extreme pessimism and the belief that life has no meaning. Thomas Hardy expresses this view when he writes:

> O Immanence, That reasonest not
> In putting forth all things begot,
> Thou buildst Thy house in space—for what?
> O Loveless, Hateless!—past the sense
> Of kindly eyed benevolence,
> To what tune danceth this Immense?
> For one, I cannot answer. But I know
> 'Tis handsome of our Pities so to sing
> The praises of the dreaming, dark, dumb Thing
> That turns the handle of this idle Show.[2]

There are, however, many intelligent men and women, well versed in modern science and philosophy, who do not share this pessimism. It is sometimes a little knowledge which is a dangerous thing. As

1. Leo Tolstoy, *War and Peace*, Book XV, p. 1226.
2. Thomas Hardy, *The Dynasts*, p. 353.

Kant pointed out, it is quite as impossible to disprove the existence of God and of man's immortality as to prove it. While few educated people today believe that the Almighty assumes a direct personal control over events in this world or over human conduct, there are many who believe that there is a divine purpose working in the world through man himself. Usually they have come to this conclusion through a study of man's nature. Here is a being, the product of evolutionary forces working in the universe, a creature who clearly bears the marks of his animal ancestry and yet who exhibits qualities which are unique and which in their perfection man links with the divine.

DISTINCTIVE CHARACTERISTICS OF MAN AS MAN

Man has characteristics which create a deep chasm between him and the highest of the other animals. It is important to investigate and understand these differences as well as to recognize man's likenesses to the animal world. In fact, basic to any adequate philosophy of life or of education is an understanding, so far as possible, of the total nature of man. We probably could not agree upon any answers concerning man's ultimate destiny. We might be able to agree upon those things which human observation and experience as well as scientific investigations have taught us about human nature. On the basis of that study perhaps we can reach some conclusions concerning what man should do with his life, in this world at least.

Perhaps the most important question with which to begin is this: What does it mean to be *human?* Is there a distinctly *human* quality common to all men and distinguishing man from animal? Or "is he only a highly developed beast who will develop beastliness to ever higher forms?"[3]

Since ancient times it has been customary to designate man as the "rational animal," that is, to point out the fact that man can reason, that he can think in logical form, "connecting ideas consciously, coherently, and purposively." Reasoning "is the process of passing from certain propositions already known or assumed to be true, to another truth distinct from them but following from them."[4] It is

3. Erich R. Kahler, *Man the Measure*, p. 6.

4. Thomas Greenwood, *The Dictionary of Philosophy* (ed. D. D. Runes), p. 264.

because man has this ability, in addition to others, that he has been able to discover whatever truth about this universe and himself he now possesses. It is the highest factor in what we call "intelligence."

True it is that man often fails to use his reason. He is a creature of emotion as well as of reason and too seldom is guided in his actions by reason. "Certainly," says the psychologist Thorndike, "the passion of the logician for consistency is one of the rarer human passions."[5] Perhaps it would be more exact to say that man is capable of reason.

But is the ability to reason an exclusively human characteristic? Recent investigations have found that some of the other higher animals exhibit behavior which indicates the possession of reason on a most elementary plane.[6] It does not seem to be an exclusive property of man. This, in view of our animal ancestry, should not surprise us. However, reasoning among even the highest of the other animals seems to be on a very much lower plane than it is in man. We know that men differ among themselves in their possession of this ability. But even the least intelligent of those whom we call normal human beings are better able to draw inferences from premises than are any other animals. The difference between reason in man and in lower animals seems to be in the fact that it is possible for human beings to use language as symbols to designate or describe objects and ideas.[7] As one writer puts it: "While man shares insight and ability to use tools with the apes, he alone communicates with his fellows by means of language. No other living creature has learned to use words as symbols of objects, situations, or acts. . . . . With the aid of language, written as well as spoken, he has entered into the realm of ideas, a realm probably closed to most animals."[8]

It is difficult indeed to obtain any evidence for the presence of ideas in animals lower than man. Cassirer says that the sounds made by animals are used to express emotion but never to designate or describe objects, much less ideas.[9] Perhaps, suggests Cassirer, instead of defining man as an *animal rationale*, we should define him

5. E. L. Thorndike, *Man and His Works*, p. 54.

6. See Wolfgang Köhler, *Mentality of Apes*, and Robert Yerkes, *The Great Apes*.

7. See Ernst Cassirer, *An Essay on Man*, for a scholarly discussion.

8. Ruth Crosby Noble, *The Nature of the Beast*, p. 63.

9. Cassirer, *op. cit.*. p. 29.

as an *animal symbolicum*.[10] The ability to use symbols to express thought does seem to be man's unique possession.

Not only does this possession help to account for the difference between reason in animals and in man, but it also makes for differences between animal society and human society. Man has been called a social being, but he is not the only social animal. Bees and ants, for example, exhibit a highly developed social organization. Among them there is a high degree of specialization of function and division of labor. Men, too, have a highly developed social organization with specialization and division of labor. In addition, because man is a social being who uses symbols to communicate thought, man "has a society not only of action but of thought and feeling."[11] Moreover, "man cannot find himself, he cannot become aware of his individuality, save through the medium of social life."[12] It is this "society of thought and feeling" for the formation of which the use of symbols is necessary which makes human society different from animal society.

This, then, is man's supreme and unique ability. It is because man can use symbols to express ideas and ideals rather than for the expression of feeling alone that he has been able to think and to communicate on a human level. What one man discovers, he can pass on. The insights of genius can become the property of all. Science, art, industry, ethics, philosophy, and religion have become possible for man. Through the use of symbols man can reason on a much higher level than can any other animal. And not only does he draw inferences, but he is conscious of a self who is drawing inferences.

But this ability to reason is not all that comes from the ability to use symbols. Man also has what we call "imagination." The reproductive phase of imagination, better called "imagery," is probably present in other animals. But if animals have anything which might be called a productive or creative imagination, it is not of the human type.[13] Only man has an imagination which uses symbols in its operation. Only man is able to combine elements which have been separately perceived in sensory experience or, perhaps, never experienced through the senses, in such a way as to produce a *Paradise Lost*, a "Last Supper," a *Fifth Symphony*, or a *Gulliver's Travels*. Bees construct hives, beavers build dams, but only man erects a Cologne

10. *Ibid.*, p. 26.   11. *Ibid.*, p. 223.   12. *Ibid.*   13. *Ibid.*, p. 33.

Cathedral, a Taj Mahal, or the Pyramids of Egypt. The ape may be able to solve the problem of obtaining a banana out of his reach, but only man can solve the problem of sowing, reaping, and marketing. Guided by reason and checked by sense-experience, imagination has played an important part in scientific discovery, in mathematical history, in the practical arts, in architecture and the fine arts, and in the formulation of the ideals which are man's guiding star.

The word "creative" is used very loosely today, so loosely that it has almost lost any real meaning. Too often writers and speakers talk of "creating" when they should say "discovering." But there is a sense in which man creates; not that he makes something out of nothing but that he can bring into being new syntheses and new unifications of already existing elements. He can and does embody and appreciate beauty in what we call "art." In all this, symbolic imagination plays a large part.

Again, man is a creature who makes moral distinctions. This animals do not seem to do. Only human beings question whether an act is morally right or wrong. Only human beings do what they themselves condemn as wrong. Aldous Huxley says in *Ends and Means:* "The craving for righteousness seems to be as universal a human characteristic as the craving for understanding." So far as we know, man has always been concerned with right and wrong, however dimly he perceived them. Students of primitive man are impressed by his solicitude for what he conceived to be moral. Such a book as W. I. Thomas' *Primitive Behavior,* among others, makes this clear. There have been few, if any, human societies that have not had their codes of ethics. There are few, if any, human beings not interested in distinctions between right and wrong. In almost any group a warm and interested discussion on ethical questions can be generated easily.

This is not to say that men agree, have agreed, or will surely come to agree on what is right and what is wrong. It is to say that man is discovering painfully and slowly the basic principles on which it seems that he must act if he is to live a satisfying life, that is, one in harmony with the needs of his total nature.

These, then, are man's *human* characteristics: he is conscious of himself as a person; he uses symbols to express thought; through the use of symbols he can reason, create, and express moral distinctions.

This description does not explain what there is in man which enables him to have these abilities. It does not describe the element in his nature which forms the basis for such characteristics. Can they be explained on the basis of a superior brain alone? Or must one postulate a mind which is a spiritual entity in order to understand such abilities?[14] These are questions on which there is no general agreement. There is general agreement upon man's distinguishing characteristics. When he is exhibiting these characteristics, he is being human.

It is unfortunately true that many human beings frequently use these human qualities on a very low plane. This will not surprise us if we remember what psychology and sociology teach us about human development. Who among us always lives up to the best of which he is capable? But the pursuit of truth, beauty, and goodness seems to be eternal in human life. Oliver Wendell Holmes once said: "I find the great thing in this world is not so much where we stand as in what direction we are moving."

Who are the great in human history? Whom do we honor? Whose fame goes down through the centuries? Is it not those most successful in the pursuit of truth, beauty, or goodness? Is it not those who have used their abilities to reason, to create, or to make moral distinctions on a high level?

It is easy to become discouraged over human nature and human society in these troubled times. But there has been an Aristotle, a Thomas Aquinas, a Leonardo da Vinci, a Beethoven, a Shakespeare, a Goethe, a Keats, an Ehrlich, a Pasteur, an Einstein. There has been a Socrates drinking hemlock with calmness and fortitude, a Bruno dying at the stake, a Joan of Arc perishing in the flames, a Jane Addams devoting her life to the underprivileged, a Pastor Niemöller living in a German concentration camp, a Jawaharlal Nehru spending many of his mature years in British jails in India, as well as countless men and women living their undistinguished lives with quiet courage and idealism, seeking not for happiness but that "they might be worthy of happiness." It is this ability of man, man as a product of the evolutionary forces of the universe, to formulate and cherish ideals, to suffer the loss of all else he holds dear, even life itself, rather than to relinquish those ideals, which inspires us with respect for our

14. See chap. x for a further discussion of this problem.

58   *Philosophy of Education*

species. In commenting on this, Kant wrote: "For there is something in us that we can never cease admiring once we have contemplated it, and this is also that which elevates mankind *in idea* to a dignity which one would hardly expect to find in men as an object of experience."[15] Wise Kant. Certainly most of our experiences with man could easily lead to cynicism concerning human nature. And then we meet some bit of heroism, of courage, of unselfishness, and take heart again.

History and literature are full of instances of the operation of the highest and best in man. Who can read the *Phaedo* unmoved? Here is a picture of a man about to die, a man who has spurned opportunities for flight, surrounded by friends who are much more in need of comfort than he who is facing his fate with humor, courage, and serenity. Socrates discussed the immortality of the soul with his companions. And then we see him die. And we realize that Socrates is immortal with a kind of immortality against which the cup of hemlock was impotent. His soul is with us still, saying to us that it is the way we live that is important. Socrates is remembered and revered today because we believe he lived for his ideals—and died for them.

Whether all persons possess this quality in the same degree, even as a potentiality, is doubtful. But it can scarcely be denied that all men formulate and cherish ideals in some realm of life, though their ideals may lack nobility and though their lives may be sordid and depraved. Socrates tells us that wickedness and wrongdoing are caused chiefly by lack of knowledge of anything better, but that, perhaps, is open to question. It seems certain, however, as pointed out in chapter ii, that if social influences and arrangements were improved, if homes were more wholesome, if education did its work more effectively, these finer aspects of mankind would develop to a higher degree and we might see them manifested by a larger proportion of our population.

This mixture of good and bad and of sympathy and selfishness that is man has been the subject of thoughtful scrutiny for thousands of years. In ancient China, Confucius assumed that man is good by

15. Immanuel Kant, *Streit der Fakultäten*, Part I (ed. J. H. v. Kirchmann), V, 92. Wherever in this book the citation from Kant is not from a recognized English translation of his works, the translation was furnished by Dean Emeritus H. H. Schroeder from unpublished material which he uses in his classes in philosophy and ethics at Illinois State Normal University.

nature. His followers for centuries explored and debated the implications of such a belief. Mencius (372–289 B.C.), the greatest of the Confucianists, declared that man was originally and essentially good.[16] A contemporary, Kao by name, disputed this contention, saying that man is neither good nor bad by nature but that his nature was without "bias" in itself. Like water which may be deflected to the east or to the west, human nature may be bent and trained toward the good or toward the evil.

The Western world, with a few exceptions, has not been historically so charitable in its view of man. Augustine is generally credited with having formulated the doctrine that Adam's fall imposed evil upon man's nature and that every child born into this world from that time to this has borne the impress of original sin. The Council of Trent declared that man by the prevarication of Adam had lost his primeval innocence. This doctrine was generally accepted and was taught by Luther and Calvin. In reaction against such a belief Rousseau was much too optimistic about man's original nature. He taught, it will be remembered, as had Confucius and Mencius, that man is by nature good and becomes corrupted by society.

We know today that Kao came nearer the truth than did Augustine or Rousseau. The scientific view today seems to be that human nature is plastic and highly modifiable. Its growth and development could be guided and directed in such a way that man could make faster progress toward that better world of which men have dreamed and toward which too few have worked intelligently and consistently. As one writer puts it: "The theological doctrine of man's essentially evil nature metaphorically expresses the truth that he is always limited, always tempted, and never free from his animal origins. . . . . He is neither one [evil] nor the other [good] but he becomes good or evil depending upon his society, his habits, and his intelligence."[17]

THE CHIEF END OF MAN

On the basis of this study of man's nature could we come to any conclusions concerning the purpose of human life? Does it seem probable that human life has meaning and that man is here for some purpose?

16. Mencius, Book XI; also Book VI, Parts I, II, III. (See any translation.)
17. Y. H. Krikorian, *Naturalism and the Human Spirit*, p. 62.

Is it not possible that man's nature points to this, that the ideals which he formulates are evidence of this divine purpose? Natural law governs the universe, and its Author does not seem to interfere. But he has given man unique abilities by the use of which he may discover the laws of the universe, both physical and moral. Man himself shares, at least in potentiality, in those qualities and in that nature which we call "divine." He is capable of noble conduct. Perhaps God has given him this nature, his reason, imagination, and the potential ability to make moral distinctions and then given him the opportunity to use them in order to grow to his full stature, to make of himself a creature more nearly approaching the ideal man. In philosophy this concept of man's chief end is usually called that of "self-realization." What man's ultimate destiny is we cannot know; that, each man will have to decide, if at all, through faith—a part of man's nature which theologians and some philosophers place above reason in importance. But his destiny on earth seems clear. On this, a student and teacher of philosophy says: "But every man, whatever his intellectual beliefs, who lives in the modern world, has been influenced by one fundamental notion: whatever may be man's ultimate destiny, his life is to be lived and his salvation worked out in this life and this world, and with the materials it places at his disposal."[18]

Christianity has taught through the ages that man is here to achieve as high a degree of human excellence as he possibly can. Philosophy would teach the same and would insist that, whether this is for a future life or only for this life, it is still man's chief end. It is only thus that he can realize the totality of his nature; only so can he be really human. This is what Kant had in mind when he wrote: "The greatest concern of man is to know how he may properly fulfil his place in creation and rightly to understand what one must be to be a man."

Christianity also has taught that man liveth not to himself alone; psychology and sociology prove convincingly that man and society are interdependent and that the only way man can become human is through the society with which he interacts. It follows, then, that the achievement of self-realization is not an individualistic affair but a co-operative one. One achieves full development of one's powers not in isolation but as one works for the common welfare. Perhaps

18. J. H. Randall, *The Making of the Modern Mind*, p. 563.

it would be wise, then, to speak of "co-operative self-realization" as man's chief end.

Erich Kahler in a recent book interprets the whole of human history as "an evolution leading from the preindividual community to post-individual community through the development and completion of the individual."[19] He sees man's essential quality as the ability to go beyond himself, to transcend the limits of his own being, to take the role of another, and to establish a new and conscious relationship with others. Man is forever reaching beyond what he is—the "sting that bids nor sit nor stand, but go"—toward what he may become. His salvation in this world depends upon his using this self-transcending quality to build a universal kingdom of man.

From the days of the ancients, man has dreamed of the Kingdom of God on earth. He has had a vision of a world in which it would be good to live, in which injustice and exploitation would no longer reign, in which every human being might live fully and completely, managing his life and affairs in such a way as to benefit himself and others. Many of these dreams have been embodied in books such as Plato's *Republic*, Bacon's *New Atlantis*, Campanella's *City of the Sun*, Sir Thomas More's *Utopia*, and Bellamy's *Looking Backward*.

But these utopian visions share a common fault. They were not based on a realistic understanding of human nature. Societies were conceived which could not succeed because they expected the impossible of the individuals composing them. We can never expect this world to be a perfect world, any more than we can expect human beings to become perfect.

But to promote what Kant called "world welfare," to bring the day closer when all men can live in such a way as to encourage the development of the best in their natures, to contribute to the development of a better race and the building of a better world, that surely is a goal worthy of man's endeavors. Examined in the light of what we know of man's nature, it seems attainable. Man probably is not perfectible; but he is improvable. It is only as we work together in common endeavor to make better the conditions under which man lives that he will be improved. To engage in such a common enterprise brings out the best in all of us.

19. *Op. cit.,* p. 21.

It has been pointed out that man acts to satisfy his wants. Anything which satisfies a human want becomes thereby a value. To say, then, that our conduct is motivated by our values is another way of saying that we act to satisfy our wants. Since wants are for both material and nonmaterial goods, values are both material and nonmaterial in nature. We want food, clothing, shelter; we value them because they satisfy wants. These goods are material in nature. Many men want and therefore attach value to beauty, truth, and goodness. These are nonmaterial values. That which we value, we work to obtain. It is our convictions, either consciously or unconsciously held, concerning that which is most worth while in life which motivate our conduct. It is only as man comes to value the goal here presented as man's chief end that he will seek the means which will be used to achieve the purpose of man's endeavor.

Thomas Aquinas, one of the keenest thinkers mankind has known, said: "First one must consider the final end of human life, and then those things through which man may attain this end, or deviate from it. For one must accept from an end the rationale of those things which are ordained to that end."

It is quite likely that few men consciously value the attainment of human excellence as the highest good. It is happiness that mankind desires. The majority of people, if asked what they want above everything else, would reply "happiness" or perhaps they would name something which they think they want because they believe it will make them happy.

Many thinkers, too, have said that happiness is the supreme value. Aristotle was one of these. He wrote:

Now that which is pursued as an end in itself is more final than that which is pursued as a means to something else, and that which is never chosen as means than that which is chosen both as an end in itself and as means, and that is strictly final which is always chosen as an end in itself and never as means. Happiness seems more than anything else to answer this description; for we always choose it for itself, and never for the sake of something else.[20]

Aristotle thought it perfectly apparent that happiness is the *summum bonum* of life, but he realized that it is very difficult so to order

20. Aristotle *Nicomachean Ethics* Book i.

one's life that happiness would be attained. He wrote his *Nicomachean Ethics* in order to help a young man reach that end. His words of advice have doubtless influenced the lives of thousands of men, and, while there is much common sense in them, there is little concern with the world that ought to be rather than the world that is. His doctrine of the mean, of prudent living, is one of the best examples in human thought of egoistic eudaemonism, that is, of the belief that personal happiness is the supreme value and that one should so order his life as to work toward that end.

Aristotle wrote that in order to be happy one must be virtuous. Virtue is attained through following the mean between two extremes. Vice and virtue are not opposites, but virtue is found between two errors—those of excess, on one hand, and of deficiency, on the other. For example, liberality is a virtue between two vices, those of prodigality (too much) and stinginess (too little). Courage is a virtue; recklessness and cowardice are the vices. Wit is a virtue; buffoonery and boorishness are the two extremes and therefore vices. And so on through a long list of virtues and vices, some of which he has difficulty in fitting to this pattern.

But, said Aristotle, man's greatest happiness comes from the exercise of his most characteristically human possession—his reason. Aristotle also taught that man is a social being and that each man is a friend and relation to everyone else.[21] This did not keep Aristotle, however, from justifying slavery.

Epicurus (341–270 B.C.) was another Greek philosopher who believed that happiness was life's *summum bonum*, but his advice on how to attain it was somewhat different from that of Aristotle. Epicurus taught that the way to be happy was to avoid anything that might bring pain. Pleasure was to be welcomed but regulated and never abused.

Consider this quotation from Epicurus: "I can find no meaning which I can attach to what is termed good if I take away from it the pleasures obtained by taste, the pleasures which come from listening to music, the charm derived by the eyes from the sight of figures in movement, or other pleasures produced by any of the senses in the whole man."[22]

21. *Ibid.* Book viii.
22. Quoted from Epicurus by Cicero *Tusculanarum disputationum* iii. 18.

If Epicurus meant by this that life would indeed be drab and lacking in what we call the "good" if man were deprived of the pleasures of the senses, then we could all agree with him. But, if he meant that the gratification of the senses is *all* that is meant by the good, then we must say that such a teaching shows a serious lack of understanding of the totality of man's nature. Sense pleasure is a part of life and a legitimate part, so long as it does not interfere with man's chief end, but contributes toward it, as it may if properly used. The Epicureans at least did not go so far in a frank advocacy of sensual pleasure as did the Hedonists, with whom their teachings are often confused. Moderation in sense gratification, the Epicureans taught, was necessary in order to avoid pain. It is the Hedonist who advises us "to eat, drink, and be merry, because tomorrow we die."

Epicurus himself led a model life and was said to have been loved and respected by all who knew him. His philosophy is often called "the philosophy of the Garden." He gathered his followers about him in his garden where they enjoyed the pleasures of friendship, of beauty, of conversation, and of other aesthetic gratifications. But Epicurus advised his followers to avoid concern with public life or the common good. To participate would certainly bring pain—and so it might! Avoid the evils of the world, taught this philosophy, by withdrawing into a garden. Make yourself an oasis of beauty and peace and let the rest of the world go by. But be moderate in all things. If you want but little, you will not be so likely to be disappointed, and as a consequence, to suffer pain. Contentment comes through a wise regulation of pleasure and from independence of external conditions. This all sounds completely egoistic, although it is a civilized, urbane concern with self.

Not all eudaemonists have been so egoistic. In modern times a group of philosophers in England who were called Utilitarians, were altruistic eudaemonists. These nineteenth-century Utilitarians taught that the greatest good consisted in general happiness; that man should not direct his efforts toward obtaining his own personal, individual happiness alone but should so conduct his life as to add to the general happiness. For them an action was moral which added to or did not subtract from the sum total of happiness in the world; it was immoral if it did subtract from that happiness. The happiness of the few or of the individual was less important than the happiness of the many. A woman who wishes to divorce the husband she has ceased to love in order to marry a new love has no right to do that, according to the Utilitarian, if, by so doing, she makes unhappy not only the discarded husband, but her children, her family, and her friends, to say nothing of setting a bad example for the entire community.

Jeremy Bentham, James Mill, and John Stuart Mill were the chief spokesmen for the Utilitarians. They were all interested in social reform in an England which badly needed reforms and were indignant over conditions which brought misery, squalor, and despair to thousands of human beings.

Whether happiness is the supreme value or not, it is earnestly desired by man. We are driven by our very natures to prize it. A completely unhappy man or woman is seldom a useful one. On the other hand, the individual whose constant aim is to achieve happiness is seldom a useful one. Furthermore he is not likely to achieve happiness by aiming at it. Happiness may be an end we all desire, but as an aim it will defeat itself. The happiest people are those who forget about happiness as an aim and instead seek to "make themselves worthy of happiness," as mankind was advised to do by the philosopher Immanuel Kant.

Nicolai Hartmann, a respected modern writer in the field of ethics, emphasizes these same points. He says: "It is in the very nature of happiness to tease man and to mock him as long as he lives: to lure him on, to mislead him and to leave him standing with empty hands."[23]

Happiness, says Hartmann, is a genuine, indisputable value. We all feel that, and there is no need to argue it. Pleasure also is a value. But neither is the highest value. Not all striving is toward attaining happiness, nor should it be. Happiness comes to him who sets his gaze upon the primary values. It is an *accompanying* phenomenon.[24]

Another writer says: "The real question cannot be simply, am I happy or unhappy, but rather, is it well that I am thus happy or unhappy."[25]

One of the unfortunate results of the belief that happiness is the

23. Nicolai Hartmann, *Ethics*, I, 149.
24. *Ibid.*, pp. 146–51.
25. Tsanoff Radoslav, *Moral Ideals of Our Civilization*, p. 601.

highest value, and therefore to be aimed for, is the feeling that life has cheated you when unhappiness comes, as it does to every one. Then one is likely to lament with Bacchylides:

> Never to have seen the light, never to
> have been born,
> That would be best; for no mortal man
> remains happy to the end.

The Stoics were a group of philosophers who taught that man could not expect to be happy. This school of thought was developing at about the same time as Epicureanism, and it, too, was a philosophy which tried to help men live with some tranquillity in an evil world. Instead of withdrawing from the world into a garden, the Stoics preached a kind of withdrawal into one's self. Nothing can really hurt you if you do not let it. And, instead of teaching that one could obtain happiness through avoiding pain and regulating pleasure, they advised repressing the desire for pleasure or for happiness.

They taught that the chief good lies in living in agreement and harmony with nature. "Seek not that things which happen should happen as you wish, but wish the things which happen to be as they are and you will have a tranquil flow of life. . . . . This is your duty—to act well the part that is given you; but to select the part belongs to another."[26] They were usually fatalists and quietists, as the foregoing quotations would indicate.

Though the Stoic philosophy was in many respects a somewhat self-centered one in its warnings against letting one's self be disturbed by anything which happens, even the loss of loved ones, or the sorrow of a friend,[27] there was probably more genuine happiness attained through its practice than through the practice of any eudaemonistic philosophy. The Stoics' insistence upon the self-forgetfulness of duty, upon the essential brotherhood of man, upon the spiritual dignity of man, not only gave them an effective armor against what seemed an evil world but furnished a foundation for

26. Epictetus *Discourses*.

27. E.g., from the *Discourses:* "If you see a man sorrowing be kind to him; sympathize outwardly but do not enter into his trouble inwardly so as to disturb your own tranquillity."

that formulation of the natural rights of man on which democracy came to be built.[28]

There have been some interpretations of Christianity which taught not only that happiness is not life's highest value but that it was not a value at all. We should not expect or desire to be happy in this world, according to this belief. We still sing hymns in our churches which reflect this point of view. The world is evil, man is a worm, we are here to suffer so that we may thereby be prepared for the next world. Whether we are happy here or not is immaterial. Our Puritan forefathers connected joy with sin and suspected any desire for happiness as a device of the devil.

Modern Christianity is wiser, we believe. This world has evil in it, but it is our business to make evil a less potent factor. Man is not a worm. He has an animal nature, but there is a spark of the divine there too, though it may be buried deeply in too many of us. Sorrow in this life is not only inevitable but may be necessary and ennobling. Life has tragedy in it, but it is not all tragedy. There is no reason why man should not prize happiness if he does not set it up as the supreme value for which he should always strive. Happiness is not the *summum bonum* of life; it is the accompaniment of a life nobly lived.

Happiness can be achieved, if at all, by living fully and completely: by feeling needed and useful, by having friendships with others because one is a friend, through using all one's powers not *just* for one's self but for the common good as well as for self, by developing many and varied interests, through setting one's self challenging tasks, "through experiencing and realizing as many of the creative potentialities of the universe as our individual natures allow."[29]

It is only as man's reason, his imagination, and his moral idealism are developed that he is lifted above the animal level. Without the first, man would be helpless in this world; like the rest of the animal world and all of the plant world he would perish where he was not adapted to the environment. Without the second, man's creative life would come to an end. And without the third, man would be merely an advanced simian, a creature in whom might made right, with no

28. Robert M. Wenley, *Stoicism and Its Influence*, p. 132.
29. Robert Ulich, *Fundamentals of Democratic Education*, p. 139.

more concern for his fellow-man than was demanded by an enlightened self-interest.

It is too true that in many men this self-interest is the chief motivating factor. But it need not be. Man has the capacity for acting for the general good. Parents and teachers should do all in their power to develop it. And the most effective way to teach is through personal example.

To think not only of our individual welfare but also of the general welfare; not only to assume responsibility for ourselves and our families but also to feel a responsibility for all mankind, really to believe and act upon the belief that our own weal or woe is irrevocably bound up with that of all other human beings—this is to put our lives to good use so far as this world is concerned and probably to make the best possible preparation for any conceivable future life. If happiness comes as a by-product, well and good. And where the search for happiness does not jeopardize the development of intelligence and of moral idealism in man, there is no reason why we should not seek it. Let us have all the happiness we can, so long as it does not interfere with our chief end. In fact, happiness is a means toward the development of the finest personalities, particularly in childhood.

REALIZING MAN'S CHIEF END

This development of the best in himself is not something which the individual can do alone. The most important years are the early years of life. Not until adolescence can the individual himself take a significant part in directing his own higher development. And for many it is then too late, since their aims and habits will have been pointed for too long a time in the wrong direction. Only as we work together can we create the conditions which make it possible for man to realize his best and for more of us to live the good life and thereby promote human progress.

It would seem that this is indeed the next step necessary for human progress. Most of the advances we have made in the long slow climb from primitive life have been the result of man's more or less blind efforts to survive and to expend less effort for mere survival. Conflicts and competition, wars and strife, have accompanied these efforts. Man has stumbled upon improved ways of satisfying his basic wants; he has acquired new wants; he has, sometimes blindly, sometimes intelligently, undertaken to find the means for their gratification. He has invented marvelous machines and through their use has tried to conquer the earth and his fellow-man. He has unlocked the secret of the release of atomic energy. He has piled up wealth and learned to produce more and more goods to satisfy more and more wants.

All through history, from Plato through Kant to the thinkers of today, great minds have seen that this blind striving of man can never really achieve the good life for all humanity. So our thinkers have concerned themselves more and more with what would be necessary to bring about the welfare of the whole human family. They have reminded man that to forget that he is more than an animal and that he has human dignity proceeding from a rational, creative, and moral nature is just as unwise and mistaken as to forget man's animal ancestry and to regard him as a fallen angel. To attach value only to those things which will satisfy material wants is just as foolish as to attach value only to ascetic ideals. Every facet of man's nature must be taken care of in such a way as to promote the best possible development.

For teachers this means that we will lend our influence to every movement designed to promote the welfare of all men rather than to those movements that are concerned only with the welfare of a small and selfish group. It means that we will act with good will toward all men. It means that we will work with other responsible, intelligent adults to improve the conditions under which human beings live. It means that we will direct our teaching and the whole life of the school toward developing the finest possible boys and girls, young people who are as intelligent as it is possible for them to become and who are as sensitive as possible to the demands of morality. It means that we will realize and act upon the realization that our chief vocation on this earth is to live up to the best that is in us and to work with other human beings to bring about conditions which will make it possible for all men to do likewise. This would bring progress, the good life for more and more men.

SUMMARY

It seems impossible to know with any certainty man's ultimate destiny or the meaning of life in any cosmic sense through the use of man's natural powers. But we might discover what man should do with his life in this world through a study of his distinctive and unique characteristics, thus learning what it would mean to live as *man*.

Man is the only creature who uses the symbol to express more than feeling. The ability to do this has made it possible for him to reason, to be creative, and to express moral distinctions. The ability to use symbols also plays an important part in the development of self-consciousness. It would seem that to live a human life would mean the development of all these powers and abilities to as high a degree as his individual possession of them would allow. This achievement is called "self-realization."

Because this self is formed only in a social situation, self-realization is not an individualistic enterprise. It is co-operative. A human being realizes his own highest development only when he takes some responsibility for the common welfare as well as for his own individual welfare. Co-operative self-realization, then, seems to be man's chief end in this life.

Although happiness is desired by all men and has been considered life's highest value by some of mankind's most profound thinkers, it is probably a mistake for any person to make the attainment of happiness his chief aim. Happiness is an accompaniment of a life lived fully and completely; it is better to aim at being worthy of happiness than at happiness itself.

The fact that the attainment of human excellence is so dependent upon the society with which the individual interacts makes it necessary for teachers to work with other adults of intelligence and good will to improve social conditions. Teachers cannot do their work in the schoolroom alone. Social progress demands more intelligent action toward the kind of society that will encourage human excellence.

QUESTIONS TO AID STUDY

1. Does it seem to you that human life has cosmic meaning? Why or why not?
2. What is meant by a teleological view of the universe and of man?
3. What is a utopia? Have you ever read any description of a utopia? What do you think of it?
4. Does man have any characteristics not found in the rest of the animal world? Explain.
5. Upon what ability do all man's *human* characteristics seem to rest? Show how.
6. How could we proceed in order to discover the answer to the problem of man's chief end? What is your opinion of the author's view concerning man's chief end?
7. What is meant by saying that there seems to be a divine purpose in the world working through man himself? Is there any evidence for such a view? Explain.
8. How do you account for the fact that many human beings show little evidence of the development of the human characteristics?

9. What is the relation between the use of symbolism and the self-transcending quality of man emphasized by Kahler?
10. What seems to be true concerning good and evil in man's nature?
11. How do Christianity and the philosophy here presented agree as to man's chief end? How might there be a difference in emphasis?
12. Discuss self-realization and individualism.
13. Show how the attainment of human excellence and the working for a better society are practically synonymous in meaning.
14. Summarize the principal historic views concerning the *summum bonum* of life.
15. What do you think of service as man's chief end? Why?
16. What do you think it would take to make you happy? With which historic view are you most in accord? Why?
17. How can man's chief end be realized? In this an easy task? Explain.
18. What is the relation between self-realization, as philosophers use the term, and social progress?

SUGGESTED REFERENCES

ARISTOTLE. *Nicomachean Ethics* Book i (any translation).
———. "Pleasure and Happiness," *Readings in Philosophy*, edited by J. H. RANDALL, JUSTUS BUCHLER, and EVELYN SHIRK (New York: Barnes & Noble, 1946), pp. 356–68.
AURELIUS, MARCUS. *Meditations* (any translation).
CASSIRER, ERNST. *An Essay on Man* (New Haven: Yale University Press, 1944), especially chaps. ii and iii.
DUVALL, T. G. *Great Thinkers: The Quest of Life for Its Meaning* (New York: Oxford University Press, 1937), pp. 81–89 and chap. vii.
EINSTEIN, ALBERT; DEWEY, JOHN; and OTHERS. *Living Philosophies*. New York: Simon & Schuster, 1931 (read according to interest).
EPICTETUS. *Discourses* (any translation).
FICHTE, JOHANN G. *Vocation of Man*. Translated by WILLIAM SMITH. La Salle, Ill.: Open Court Pub. Co., 1940 (or any other translation).
FULLER, BENJAMIN A. G. *History of Philosophy* (New York: Henry Holt & Co., 1938), pp. 193–98, 205–9, and 510–11.
HARTMANN, NICOLAI. *Ethics* (New York: Macmillan Co., 1932), Vol. I, pp. 146–51.
HICKS, R. D. *Stoic and Epicurean*. New York: Charles Scribner's Sons, 1910.
HYDE, WILLIAM DEWITT. *Five Great Philosophies of Life* (New York: Macmillan Co., 1928), chaps. i, ii, and iv.
JOAD, C. E. M. "The Values of Civilization," *Britain Today*, No. 68 (Dec. 12, 1941), pp. 8–12.

72   *Philosophy of Education*

KAHLER, ERICH. *Man the Measure* (New York: Pantheon Books, 1943), Introd.

KILPATRICK, WILLIAM HEARD. *Selfhood and Civilization* (New York: Macmillan Co., 1941), chap. iii.

LIPPMANN, WALTER. *A Preface to Morals* (New York: Macmillan Co., 1929), chaps. i and ix.

ORCHARD, W. E. *Humanity: What? Whence? Whither* (Milwaukee: Bruce Pub. Co., 1944), chaps. ii and iii.

OVERSTREET, HARRY. *The Enduring Quest* (New York: W. W. Norton & Co., 1931), chaps. vi and xvi.

RANDALL, JOHN HERMAN. *The Making of the Modern Mind* (rev. ed.; New York: Houghton Mifflin Co., 1940), chaps. xxi–xxii.

RANDALL, JOHN HERMAN, and BUCHLER, JUSTUS. *Philosophy: An Introduction* (New York: Barnes & Noble, 1942), pp. 255–62.

REDDEN, JOHN D., and RYAN, FRANCIS A. *A Catholic Philosophy of Education* (Milwaukee: Bruce Pub. Co., 1942), pp. 49–50 and 143–46.

ROGERS, A. K. *Student's History of Philosophy* (rev. ed.; New York: Macmillan Co., 1935), pp. 109–15 and 122–29.

RUSSELL, BERTRAND. *The Conquest of Happiness* (New York: H. Liveright, 1930), especially chap. xvii.

———. *A History of Western Philosophy.* New York: Simon & Schuster, 1945 (use index for references to different schools of thought).

SPINOZA, BENEDICT. "Reflections on the Good of Man," *Readings in Philosophy,* edited by J. H. RANDALL, JUSTUS BUCHLER, and EVELYN SHIRK (New York: Barnes & Noble, 1946), pp. 225–62.

THORNDIKE, EDWARD L. *Man and His Works* (Cambridge, Mass.: Harvard University Press, 1943), chap. iv.

TITUS, HAROLD HOPPER. *Ethics for Today* (New York: American Book Co., 1936), chaps. iv and vi.

WENLEY, ROBERT MARK. *Stoicism and Its Influence.* Boston: Marshall Jones Co., 1924.

WHEELWRIGHT, PHILIP E. *Critical Introduction to Ethics* (Garden City, N.Y.: Doubleday, Doran & Co., 1935), pp. 67–100 and 164–73.

CHAPTER V
COMPONENTS OF THE GOOD LIFE

Principle on the basis of which we can decide on the components of the good life—The needs of man: (1) *Food, shelter, clothing;* (2) *Satisfying social relationships;* (3) *Work and leisure;* (4) *Struggle; success and failure;* (5) *Freedom to manage his own affairs in harmony with common welfare;* (6) *Opportunity to develop special talents;* (7) *Intellectual and aesthetic interests;* (8) *Religion and a philosophy of life—The importance of this analysis to the teacher:* (1) *In his personal and social life;* (2) *In his relations to his pupils and in classroom management;* (3) *In curriculum development*

IF TEACHERS are to work with other responsible and intelligent adults toward making the good life possible for more and more people and if they are intelligently to direct the development of boys and girls so that they, when grown, will be able and willing to further this most worth-while work of mankind, then teachers must have as clear an understanding as is now possible of the kind of life which is good for man to live. What must man have and be to live a truly human life?

THE BASIS FOR DECIDING ON THE COMPONENTS OF THE GOOD LIFE

It has already been pointed out that the answer is to be found from a study of his nature. Every aspect of that nature must be provided for in such a way as to allow for man's highest development. Man is an animal, and his animal needs are basic and imperative. But these animal needs should be met in such a way as to make it possible for him to be a man and not just an animal.

In fact it is only as biological needs are satisfactorily met that man can rise above the animal. A hungry man is not likely to be much concerned with spiritual values. He wants food, and the drive toward self-preservation which he shares with all living things leads

73

him to forget all else in order to get it. This fundamental truth points out our paramount social problem, suggests the imperative need for giving thought to the steps that must be taken if man's progress is to continue, and should make it apparent that all other efforts to make this a better world will be futile if this problem is ignored.

There is nothing new about the search for the good life. Sages have expounded it; religious leaders have discussed it. It is the motivating force back of the average man's more or less blind efforts. In recent years educators have taken an increasing interest in the question. Edward Thorndike, in a book published in 1940, has drawn from his knowledge of human nature a list of twenty-six requirements for human welfare.[1] A book on the curriculum by Franklin Bobbitt devotes the first chapter to a discussion of man's needs, though the author uses fewer items than did Thorndike and makes statements which are more general in nature.[2]

THE NEEDS OF MAN

With the principle referred to in the previous section in mind, the needs of man would seem to be the following:

1. Man should have enough of the physical necessities of life to insure abounding health and, if possible, a margin of this world's goods above this minimum.

2. Man should be able to satisfy his social needs: his need for human society, for friends, for a mate and children. It is through association with human beings that man becomes human and is enabled to satisfy those deep emotional needs which all of us have for security, for recognition, for status in a group, for friendship, and for love.

3. Man needs work which he feels is of importance in this world. He also needs leisure in which he may play and rest.

4. Man needs the necessity for struggle; he needs to succeed, and he needs to fail. He should know the joy which comes from achieving one's purposes in the face of uncertainty and discouragement, as well as the lessons which can be learned from frustration and from disappointment.

5. Man needs freedom: freedom of mind to seek the truth wher-

1. Edward L. Thorndike, *Human Nature and the Social Order*, pp. 403–18.
2. Franklin Bobbitt, *The Curriculum of Modern Education*, chap. i.

ever it may lie, and freedom of body to live life as a human being should live.

6. Man needs opportunity to develop any talents or special gifts and abilities he may have.

7. Man needs to develop and enjoy intellectual and aesthetic interests. The wider and deeper these interests, the more worth while his life.

8. Man needs a religion. He needs a philosophy of life based on a thoughtful study of man and his social heritage. These should furnish conviction concerning life's purposes, as well as give meaning and unity to all his experience.

Undoubtedly, there is some overlapping in these statements regarding human needs. Man is a unified creature, and his needs are interwoven and difficult to state separately. Individuals will feel the pull of these needs differently and will certainly find different ways of satisfying them. It is also true that we by no means know all that there is to know about human nature, and it is most likely that further research will make necessary some revision in any analysis of this kind. It may be possible to live a satisfying life without meeting every one of the needs listed. Man compensates for a lack of opportunity in one field by a concentration on others. But, in the light of human experience and present insight, the foregoing enumeration does seem to indicate the needs common to our basic human nature. Perhaps it is necessary to examine further and elaborate upon each.

EXPOSITION OF EACH OF MAN'S NEEDS

1. As has been repeatedly stated, basic to all else must be provisions for meeting man's physical necessities and legitimate wants. Man needs food—not a mere subsistence diet but food that is pleasant to the taste as well as nourishing. Meat, eggs, milk, fresh vegetables, and fruits should be available to all. Man needs clothing, not only to keep him warm but to adorn his body. Man needs shelter, a place of warmth, comfort, beauty, and privacy. He needs a home, with all which that word implies. Man needs medical and dental services. He needs fresh air and sunshine. He needs all the material things necessary to maintain abounding health. He should be able to get these things through his own efforts in a way compatible with human dignity, and he should not have to spend every waking moment in such

endeavors. Man is not merely an animal to spend most of his time and every ounce of available energy in the struggle to survive. Wherever and whenever this *is* man's sole concern, he remains perilously close to the brute existence out of which man evolved. It makes of him a brutish man.

Fichte wrote:

It is not only a devout wish for man but it is the absolutely necessary demand of his rights and of his destiny that he should live as easily, as freely, as much in control of nature, as truly humanly as is ever possible. Man should work but not like a beast of burden that sinks into sleep under its load and, after the scantiest recuperation of its exhausted strength, is again aroused to the resumption of the self-same burden. He should work fearlessly, with joy and with pleasure, and have enough leisure to lift his soul and his eyes to heaven, to the contemplation of which he has been created.[3]

It is, of course, a mistake to identify the good life with wealth or even with a continually rising standard of living. A large amount of this world's goods is not necessary in order to lead a complete and satisfying life. The story is told that Socrates, when looking on at auctions, often would say, "How many things there are which I do not need!"[4]

But certainly, as a minimum, enough wealth to provide for maintaining the body in health and decency with some margin above for gracious living is desirable if not imperative.

Men of science know, even if the general public has not yet learned, that there are no naturally superior and inferior peoples. There are only advanced and backward peoples. This means that some members of the human race have lived under conditions which have brought out the qualities necessary for building civilizations; others have not. There are neither races nor nations naturally over-aggressive and war-loving, nor are there other races and nations naturally democratic and peace-loving. Competitive behavior and co-operative behavior each develop in human beings in response to the conditions under which they live. We may be certain that man will always become aggressive when repeatedly frustrated in attempts to satisfy his basic needs. That is human nature.

3. J. G. Fichte, *Der geschlossene Handelsstaat* (ed. Fritz Medicus), III, 422–23.

4. Diogenes Laërtius *Lives of the Philosophers*, "Socrates," p. 10.

If we want people to develop the finest characteristics in them, we shall have to make it possible for them to live in such a way that the best can grow. While a solution to our economic problems would not automatically produce ideal human beings, that is certainly the first step which we must take if this is ever to be a better world and if the dream of human progress is to be more than wishful thinking.

The American standard of living is the highest in the world, but it falls far short of what is needed. We have become increasingly conscious during the last fifteen years of that third of the nation, ill-fed, ill-clothed, ill-housed, of which President Roosevelt so often spoke. Such books as *The Grapes of Wrath* and *Native Son,* such plays as *Tobacco Road* and *Dead End,* have awakened social consciences as never before.

In 1938 the National Resources Committee reported that in the year 1935–36, a year which was one neither of serious depression nor of great prosperity, one-third of all our people had an income of $780 or less per spending unit of four and that the lowest two-thirds of the population had incomes amounting to $1,450 or less per spending unit of four.[5] It was only the top third, with incomes ranging from $1,450 to over a million, averaging about $3,000, who really had enough to meet the standard outlined here. These figures do not represent money income alone but include the value in money of food raised, rent where the home is owned, and all income of any sort.

Such a situation would be bad enough if necessary, but it is not. Authorities in the field of political science and economics are of the opinion that for the first time in the world's history we know how to produce enough so that every human being could live as a human being should. Herein we have made real progress. But we have not yet learned how to distribute what we can produce in such a way that every man can, through his own efforts, obtain what he and his family should have. The very conservative Brookings Institution has said that every family of four could have in real wages as a minimum income what in 1929 was represented by an income of $2,500, and that without taking from those whose income was at that time higher.

It is of course understood that incomes will never be equal. That is neither necessary nor desirable. Individual differences are real,

5. National Resources Committee report, "Consumer Income in the United States—Their Distribution in 1935–36."

and the value of people's service to society will always vary. Their return in terms of money and goods will and should vary. But there is a minimum which is today possible for every person which would provide the goods and services necessary to develop and maintain health and give a comfortable margin beyond.

As has been stated before, this is the most important social problem in the world today. The existence of democracy, the only form of social organization in which human dignity is really possible, depends upon its solution, for democracy does not and cannot exist where great disparities of wealth are found. The forms of totalitarianism rife in the modern world arose out of attempts to solve economic problems. Basic to the wars of this century has been and is the attempt on the part of millions of people to get by force that which has been denied them through peaceful means: access to raw materials and to markets by which they can have a decent standard of living. Those who have this decent standard of living do not like such aggression, any more than we approve of thieves who break into our homes and steal our hard-earned possessions. But we might just as well realize that, while we may have to meet such aggression with force at the moment, that force will not remove the causes of the aggression, whether the aggressor be a nation or an individual.

Aristotle showed a keen understanding of human nature when he said that conditions are ripe for revolution when people who consider themselves the equals of others more fortunately situated must live on a much lower social and economic plane. "It is inequality, as we have seen, that is everywhere the cause of sedition."[6] Until this condition is on its way to a solution, we will never have peace in this war-torn world or the good life possible for its harried, distressed, and suffering inhabitants.

2. Man needs human society. He is, we say, a gregarious creature. The causes of this gregariousness lie in the nature of man himself. As has been pointed out, our human potentialities develop as a result of human associations. Literally, man cannot live to himself alone. He is dependent for protection and security upon association with others. The role of the mother in reproduction and the helplessness of infancy made some kind of group life an inevitable development.

6. Aristotle *Politics* (trans. J. E. C. Welldon), p. 341.

The groups in which primitive man lived were small and built primarily upon the family.

Today the truly civilized man identifies himself and his welfare with that of all mankind. He realizes that his welfare is bound up with theirs. "World welfare" is of real importance to such a person. There are comparatively few human beings who have as yet reached such a high state of human development. The group with which men identify themselves is usually much smaller, although it has been growing steadily larger as civilization has progressed. The family, the tribe, the city, the nation, must give way in time to the world group if man's welfare is ever to be attained.

But even those who realize that they are members of a society which is world-wide in scope need, in addition, a smaller group to which to belong, a group which knows its members "face-to-face," a group in which to find acquaintances and friends, a group with which to work in closer association, a group in which each has status and a measure of recognition, the love of which is so basic a human motivating force.

And within this group we need a still smaller group in which the bonds of friendship are closer and the association is more intimate. Family life furnishes the ideal for this closest of all human association. The majority of people find in their parents and brothers and sisters, then in mate and children, the most basic and satisfying of all human companionships. There is no comradeship so complete or so rewarding as that which develops between husband and wife, well mated. Unless marriage does furnish this highest possible friendship, it has failed to reach its finest potentialities. It is, of course, possible to live a rich and satisfying life without marriage, but it is not easy. Not that it is easy to live happily and successfully within marriage. Many a human being has found only misery and unhappiness in the marital tie, and many an unmarried person is happier and more useful than he would be if married. Marriage must be worked at if it is to succeed, and it is so delicate a relationship that it takes more care to make it succeed than is the case with most human associations.

Young people need a great deal of help in learning how to meet their social needs. How to be popular with one's own and with the opposite sex is a problem engaging a great deal of the attention of adolescents and young adults. To come to a mature understanding of the qualities which earn the respect and affection of others, of what one must do and be to deserve friendship, is an important part of human development. It is only as young people are helped to be the kind of human beings who will have friends and who will have the opportunity to marry and establish a home that the majority of them will be able to identify themselves with an ever widening circle. For the majority of people the natural, normal relationships of family and intimate friends are necessary as a foundation for concern with the welfare of other human beings.

This is not true, of course, of all. There seem to be some persons, women particularly, single by choice, in whom the passion for human service is so strong that they are able to compensate thereby for the family ties desired by most people. Jane Addams, Florence Nightingale, Lillian Wald, Susan B. Anthony, and Clara Barton were great and useful women. There have been others in convents, in schools, and in social centers. The clergy of the Roman Catholic church live lives of usefulness and happiness without marriage.

Many of the greatest thinkers either never married or were notoriously unsuccessful family men. One cannot help but have some sympathy for Xanthippe when we read that, in a fit of abstraction, Socrates would stand in a portico or on the street, hours on end, forgetting any appointments or obligations. Such is the tyranny of a great intellect. Immanuel Kant never married. Neither did Isaac Newton. Not only did Schopenhauer never marry, but he was a misogynist.

It is probably a fortunate thing for mankind that there have been individuals who have forgone marriage in order to concentrate on thought, on art, on religion, and on service to others and that there continue to be such people in the world. More than one teacher has spent his life trying to rectify the mistakes made by well-meaning but ignorant parents in bringing up their children. It would not be difficult to decide whether such teachers had lived a worth-while life.

Certainly there is no guaranty that marriage and parenthood will produce wider sympathies and greater wisdom in a person. The opposite is often true. Nevertheless, family life can and does contribute to full and complete living. Man's nature, moreover, usually drives him to desire this finest of human relationships.

3. One of the most unfortunate delusions under which man suffers is the belief that work is a misfortune. Many a person has thought that he would be completely happy if only he had no work to do, if only he could play all the time in some Cockaigne or Lubberland.

The classic distinction between work and play has been that work is activity directed toward the attainment of some end not contained within that activity. Work is a means toward an end. Play is activity engaged in for the sake of the activity itself. It *is* an end. When the small boy cleans the snow from the sidewalk, it is not done in order to enjoy cleaning the snow from the walk. He may enjoy it if the task is not beyond his powers, if he sees why he does it, and if he does not want too badly to be doing something else. But he does it to please mother, to save father the task, to earn money, or because it is his job and thereby his contribution to the family life. Now watch him as he and his gang construct a snowman. That is play. They are doing it for the fun of constructing the snowman. That is not a means to an end but an end in itself.

Work has earned the bad reputation it' has with many people for several reasons. There may be too much of it, or it may be beyond the worker's strength. The end toward which it is directed may not be of the worker's choosing. Plato said that to labor to accomplish another's ends is slavery. The world of work still has many slaves within it. Much work is onerous in itself and has been in the past even more difficult. The machine has lifted much of the burden of backbreaking physical labor from the shoulders of perspiring mankind. Man did not admit the immorality of slavery until after the machine was invented. We remember that even Aristotle accepted slavery as proper. Even with the machine there will probably always be hard work to do, and, perhaps, because of the machine, there will in all likelihood always be some uninteresting, monotonous work to do.

Nevertheless, work is a blessing—not too difficult work, or too much of it, or work that one does not himself choose, but work which is of importance in this world in contributing to human welfare. It has not been where nature has provided an easy living for man that industry, science, and philosophy have flourished. It has been where he has had to struggle for a living, where life has not been easy. But neither has it been where life is a constant and unremitting struggle merely to stay alive. Some measure of leisure is necessary. The birth of our civilization and the direction of its spread depended upon conditions which made it imperative for man to work, which called upon him to exercise his intelligence and ingenuity and which rewarded him with enough time to ponder upon his accomplishments, upon the environment in which he found himself, and the uses to which he might put that which he discovered. Thus he grew.

And so grows the individual man or woman. Not by mere play. That has its place. We all need time to follow our own bents and to engage in activity for its own sake. Such activity can contribute to individual development. Adults need leisure for their physical and mental health. Children need time to play. Psychologists tell us that play is children's serious business; in a sense it is their work.

It is only through hard and serious work that we grow. This work may be mental as well as physical; each of us needs some of both. It should be the kind of work through which we can best contribute to our own individual development and to that end which is the proper end of man—the welfare of all.

The plumber who takes pride in his work; the machinist to whom the whir of his machine is sweeter music than Beethoven's *Seventh Symphony;* the factory worker who does a competent piece of work without constant oversight; the salesman whose motto is not *caveat emptor;* the teacher whose constant concern is the best possible growth of his pupils; the politician who, with all the compromises he makes, tries honestly to serve those who elected him; the businessman who serves his community; the mother who devotes herself to the welfare of her family—each of these is in his own way serving the interests of all as well as his own.

4. Even if a man did not need to work in order to earn a living, he would need to work in order to live. A playboy knows nothing about life's realities and life's possibilities. One cannot become a strong man or woman without struggle, without the joy which comes from succeeding in carrying out one's purposes, without the lessons one can learn from failure. It is only through struggle and effort that man develops his best talents, his finest potentialities. Ortega y Gasset, the Spanish philosopher, says in his *Revolt of the Masses:*

> There is no doubt that the most radical division that it is possible to make of humanity is that which splits it into two classes of creatures: those who make great demands on themselves, piling up difficulties and duties; and

those who demand nothing special of themselves, but for whom to live is to be every moment what they already are, without imposing on themselves any effort towards perfection; mere buoys that float on the waves.[7]

For me, then, nobility is synonymous with a life of effort, ever set on excelling oneself, in passing beyond what one is, to what one sets up as a duty and an obligation.[8]

People who accept such ideals were not born with them. They adopted them as a result of their experiences in living a life not of ease and play but of labor, of effort, of threatened frustration. Of course we must not constantly meet frustration. But some frustration is good for all of us. We are quite likely in this world to be threatened with frustration often, if not actually to meet it. Life should not be too easy if we are to grow to full stature. It is through meeting difficulties, overcoming them, facing our own assets and liabilities as they are, and learning to utilize the talents we have that we gain self-confidence and self-reliance out of which grow the feeling of security and competence.

A recent book on great teachers, written by their students, says that all those great teachers made their students want to reach beyond their present attainments.[9] No teacher can be considered even superior who does not stimulate his pupils to think, who does not set his standards high and fire his students with a desire to scale the heights.

Parents and teachers who make things too easy for children are doing them a grave injustice. They are really stunting their growth. Children need to learn to do hard things, to experience the joy of accomplishment, to have success as a result of their own hard work, and to face failure courageously. Of course, it is cruel to expect children to accomplish what is beyond their ability to do. That is too often the case in the school. But let us not go to the opposite extreme and make school merely a place for play. Little children need much play and, as they grow older, a gradually increasing amount of work. Adults need some play and much work, work suited to their

7. José Ortega y Gasset, *Revolt of the Masses*, p. 15.

8. *Ibid.*, p. 71.

9. Houston Peterson (ed.), *Great Teachers, Portrayed by Those Who Studied under Them*, "Epilogue."

abilities and interests and directed toward goals which they. themselves set.

5. Freedom is necessary for man's best development. Its necessity comes from the fact that man is the kind of creature that he is. It is not a gift, to be bestowed on him by a beneficent and kindly authority, or taken from him by those who consider themselves able to control and manage "the masses." It is a "natural right," that is, a right growing out of the necessities of his nature, belonging to man because he is man. Like all rights, it carries with it an attendant responsibility for its proper use. No child is born knowing how to use it. That he must learn as he is educated. Without the gradual assumption of self-direction and self-control, man never can grow to his full stature.[10]

6. All normal human beings have some capacity, some strength, which they need to learn to exercise. Some individuals are more talented than are others. It is one of the functions of education, both informal and formal, to discover these potential abilities and to help children develop and use them.

Whether it be a talent for music; for painting; for modeling; for organizing; for research; for making, repairing, or running machinery; for writing; for cooking; for leadership; for teaching; for gardening; or for anything else, human beings need to be helped to discover, to develop, and to learn to use such abilities for their own pleasure and for the profit of all.

7. Man needs intellectual and aesthetic interests in order to live completely. He has intellect, imagination, love of beauty. If his basic biological needs are properly met from infancy on, if he need not spend his entire adult life in the effort to satisfy these basic drives, it will be possible to develop these interests in the greater part of the population.

Every normal person has the possibility of developing to some degree intellectual interests, interests in ideas. Some people become much more interested in ideas than do others. Not everyone could become a scientist, a poet, a novelist, a philosopher, a theologian. The power for original thought is not given to all human beings. But the great majority of mankind can assimilate and utilize the thought

10. See chaps. vii and viii for further discussion.

of others. This has probably been the greatest factor in man's progress.

There is no good reason why boys and girls who expect to earn their living in factories and on farms should not study and come to love Shakespeare, Plato, Goethe, and Dostoevski. Many of us have believed that much of our cultural heritage belongs only to those who are to enter the professions. "If we send everyone to high school and so many to college," say some of our citizens, "who is to do the practical machine-tending and hand-labor work which we so need to have done?" Why not high-school and college graduates? Too long have we labored under the delusion that white-collar jobs and the professions were more respectable than overall jobs and work with machines. A strange development in a democracy! Too long have people sent their children to college in order to insure that they will not have to earn their living by manual labor. As a result we have a tragic shortage in our civilization of mechanical experts and an equally tragic oversupply of white-collar workers. Perhaps the war, with its emphasis on technical expertness, will have helped to change this. Helping young people learn how to earn a living is only part of the function of education. Its total function is to help them to the best all-round living. Life is richer and more meaningful for those who have assimilated at least part of our cultural heritage. Good teachers can awaken interest in the study of ideas. Lawyers, doctors, teachers, accountants, businessmen, do not have a monopoly on brains. Machinists, farmers, carpenters, plumbers, waiters, have ability, too. Adult-education programs show that men from all walks of life can be interested in ideas and that intellectual interests develop as their pertinence to life becomes apparent to the students. The notion that all men and women who graduate from high school and particularly those who go to college must earn their living by mental rather than by manual labor and that intellectual interests belong only to professional men and women is false. Such interests can be awakened in the vast majority of people.

The love of beauty is also an important part of man's nature. Whether it is expressed by the presence of a cheap lithograph on a wall, a bright geranium in a slum window, a struggling petunia in a dust-bowl farmyard, or by the attendance of a sophisticated audience at Carnegie Hall, at the Metropolitan Museum of Art, or at the Civic Opera House, the source is the same. This source is man's hunger for loveliness. We may differ in what seems beautiful to us. Philosophers have argued as to whether there are absolute standards for beauty or whether beauty is relative to man's likes and dislikes. The fact that sensitive and intelligent persons who thoughtfully study the problem of what constitutes beauty come to a measure of agreement on the standards and principles by which beauty may be judged points to the probability that aesthetic values are the same for all men because they have their source in our common humanity. Further than that we cannot know. Children need to become acquainted with as many forms of beauty as can be introduced to them. It is well to start with those things which seem lovely to them and then gradually to raise their level of taste by exposing them to the same kind of pictures, music, and literature which they admire but which are a little better than those they themselves would pick.

They also need to learn to make beautiful things as well as to enjoy what others have created. Recent experiments show that most children have an astonishing ability to design, model, paint, write poetry, music, and prose if properly encouraged. Their imaginations are active and creative. Even though few of them ever develop great genius, at least the adult level of appreciation of beauty can be raised, and perhaps more talent for creating it can be developed. Certainly more people will understand and put into practice the contributions that such interests make toward the good life.

8. There are similarities and mutual interests between religion and philosophy. There are differences as well. Philosophy will go no further in its assertions than reason will sanction. If a proposition cannot be proved through empirical means or through reason, the philosopher says: "We do not know." Religion asserts the priority of faith over reason: "We may not know, but we believe."

The religion of the Western world, no matter what the creed, is based on faith in the fatherhood of God and the brotherhood of man. This means that man has, as the essence of his nature, something of the divine. From this follows the religious belief in the inherent dignity and worth of every human being, the cornerstone of democratic theory.

Religion must do two things for man. It must help him feel at home in the universe, to achieve a faith concerning man's relation to the cosmos. It is this aspect of religion which has been emphasized historically. It was this of which McTaggart was thinking when he defined religion as "an emotion resting on a conviction of a harmony between ourselves and the universe at large." The same idea is to be found in the definition given by L. de Grandmaison. "Religion is the sum total of beliefs, sentiments and practices, individual and social, which have for their object a power which man recognizes as supreme, on which he depends and with which he can enter (or has entered) into relation."

But religion is more than this. It helps us arrive at convictions concerning our relations with one another and on what constitutes proper conduct to one another, as well as to a Supreme Being. It was this aspect of religion of which Kant was thinking when he wrote that "religion is the recognition of all duties as divine commands" and of which Matthew Arnold was conscious when he said, "religion is morality touched by emotions." Alfred North Whitehead, the noted modern philosopher, seems to have both these aspects of religion in mind when he writes:

The religious insight is the grasp of this truth: that the order of the world, the depth of reality of the world, the value of the world in its whole and in its parts, the beauty of the world, the zest of life, and the mastery of evil, are all bound together—not accidentally but by reason of this truth: that the universe exhibits a creativity with infinite freedom, and a realm of forms with infinite possibilities; but that this creativity and these forms are together impotent to achieve actuality apart from the completed ideal harmony, which is God.[11]

The need for religion is as fundamental to man's nature as is the need for food. Religion is found universally among all human beings, and beginning students of comparative religion are often astonished at the similarities among the great religions of mankind. Some writers held the view that the source of religion is man's fear of the unknown and of that which he cannot explain. This seems to be a very superficial view. It is true that with primitive man fear was and still is an important motivating force in his religion. But with less fear and more

11. A. N. Whitehead, *Religion in the Making*, pp. 119–20.

knowledge, religion has not disappeared. Instead, religion has been changed, ennobled, and made less anthropomorphic.

The men of science who know the most about the universe are often the most religious. They do not fear the forces of our cosmos. They do look upon the universe with an awe and wonder which does not decrease with increasing knowledge. Many of them believe that man and nature are equally unexplainable without God. With Kant they would say: "Two things fill the mind with ever new and increasing admiration and awe, the oftener and the more steadily we reflect upon them: *the starry heavens above and the moral law within.*"[12]

One of the most important functions of education is to assist young people in their search for a philosophy of life. It is during adolescence and young adulthood that life's controlling ideals are usually aroused and developed. The school has an opportunity and an obligation to assist young people in their questioning and searching. While our public schools cannot teach sectarian religion, they can inculcate respect for it and instruct in its history and literature. By precept and example, our students should remain or become convinced that lives without religion are lacking in an important respect, that man has spiritual needs and that any adequate philosophy of life does not ignore religion.

Our students need to know what men with rare insight into life and its problems have believed. It is on the basis of such knowledge that they can think adequately for themselves on life's problems. They should be helped to see that the fundamental cornerstone of any desirable philosophy of life is a conviction that man, because he is man, has worth; they should learn of the source of human worth and dignity and why there seem to be so many people who ordinarily give so little evidence of human excellence; they should see what this means for an understanding of morality, or moral conduct, and for social organization. On such a foundation there can be built a philosophy of life that will become an effective motivating force toward human progress.

Not that perfection will ever be reached or an ideal life be fully attained. It is a journey with a destination conceived by man's mind

12. Kant, *Methodology of Pure Practical Reason* (trans. T. K. Abbott), p. 260.

as an ideal. To live fully, man needs ideals and loyalties. He needs to lose himself in a cause greater than his individual concerns. His life gains meaning as he works with others toward the realization of man's mutual enterprise—the building of a better world. But he can never expect a perfect world:

Mathematical ideals are never realized in the concrete world of existence. We find various curves, but we do not find straight lines or perfect circles. For the mind which has grasped the ideal, the lines which we draw are approximations and symbols, but the ideals must be grasped by creative intelligence; they cannot be perceived by sense. The same holds of the good and beautiful. The good life is not completely realized in existent society or in existent individuals. . . . . It must, like the mathematical ideals, be grasped by creative intelligence. Its significance does not derive from the varying existent lives, but these owe their significance to their approximation to the perfect.[13]

THE COMPONENTS OF THE GOOD LIFE AND THE WORK OF THE SCHOOL

Several suggestions have been made as to the importance of this analysis to the teacher. It has been said that the teacher needs to know the components of the good life so that he may direct his own living more intelligently; as a citizen he needs this information so that he may work with other adults more effectively toward conditions under which all may have a more abundant life; as a teacher he must help boys and girls become aware of their needs, their capacities, and their interests and learn how to satisfy and develop them in a legitimate way. As Briggs puts it in his classic statement: "The first duty of the school is to teach pupils to do better the desirable things that they are likely to do anyway."[14] And the second is "to reveal higher activities and to make them both desired and to a maximum extent possible."[15] For this task a teacher needs a clear idea of what is desirable and of what activities are higher and why. The teacher has a responsibility for assisting his pupils through example, through his teaching, and through his classroom management in their search for a philosophy of life.

But, important though they be, these suggestions do not exhaust

13. John Boodin, *Three Interpretations of the Universe*, p. 278.
14. Thomas H. Briggs, *Secondary Education*, p. 258.
15. *Ibid.*, p. 263.

the connections between an analysis of the needs of man for abundant living and the school. Such an analysis has important implications for curriculum development. It was mentioned earlier that
Franklin Bobbitt, a pioneer in curriculum revision, begins a book on
the curriculum with a list of the components of the good life.

Authorities in the field of curriculum development generally agree
that the curriculum should be made on the basis of human needs.
Authorities do not always agree on what these needs are, on the relation of wants to needs, or on whether the emphasis is to be placed on
individual needs or social needs, on present needs or future needs,
on child needs or adult needs. But an analysis of our common human
needs in terms of the components of a life good to live would seem
to be basic to any decisions concerning curriculum content. As we
continue our study of how man may live fully and completely, perhaps the answers to these questions may become more apparent.[16]

SUMMARY

While we cannot be certain that anyone is wise enough to prescribe all
the components of the life which it would be good to live, we can be fairly certain that such a list must provide for the development of every facet
of man's nature in such a way as to promote the full and harmonious
working-together of all his powers—to use an Aristotelian phrase—in unity.

Because man is an animal, he must have his biological needs for food,
shelter, and clothing met first. These are basic. Because he is a social animal, he has need for adequate relationships with other human beings in
both small and large groups through which he may obtain affection, recognition, and status in the group. He needs work through which he may feel
useful; he needs leisure in which to play. He needs struggle through which
he may grow. He should have the opportunity to develop any special talents he may have; he needs intellectual and aesthetic interests. He should
be free to manage his own affairs and to participate in the management of
the common welfare, always accepting the responsibilities which accompany this freedom. He needs religion and a philosophy of life which will
give direction to his life and help him to see himself and his responsibilities in relation to the "Power, not ourselves, which makes for righteousness."

Such an analysis is of importance to the teacher in his personal and
social life, in his relations with his pupils in his classroom management,
and in his development of the curriculum for the school.

16. See chaps. xii, xiii, and xvi for further discussions of this problem.

QUESTIONS TO AID STUDY

1. Before you do any reading, make a list of what you believe to be the requisites for the kind of life you would like to lead.
2. Compare the lists given by Thorndike, Bobbitt, Johnson, and this text with each other and with yours. What likenesses and what differences do you find?
3. Is there a principle which may be used in deciding on such a list? If so, what is it?
4. Are there superior and inferior racial stocks? How do you account for backward peoples? For warlike peoples? For peace-loving peoples? For depraved and brutal peoples?
5. What seems to be the world's paramount social problem? Do you think it can be solved?
6. Is work a good or an evil? How about meaningful work versus meaningless work?
7. In which of Ortega y Gasset's two groups do you think you belong? Why?
8. Do you believe marriage is necessary for a satisfying life? Why or why not?
9. Do you think that boys and girls who are going to be farmers, factory workers, or housewives should study Shakespeare or others of the great in literature? Why or why not? Is there a better basis than that of prospective occupation for deciding such a question?
10. How is struggle related to the good life? Frustration? Success?
11. State the basic philosophy on which Western civilization is built. Is such an idea universally accepted? Is there any foundation for such a belief?
12. Can man expect ever to reach perfection and to establish a utopia on earth? What can he reasonably expect to accomplish?

SUGGESTED REFERENCES

BOBBITT, FRANKLIN. *The Curriculum of Modern Education* (New York: McGraw-Hill Book Co., 1941), chap. i, especially pp. 3–12, 17–29.

BOWER, WILLIAM CLAYTON. *Religion and the Good Life* (New York: Abingdon Press, 1933), especially chap. ii.

DEWEY, JOHN. *A Common Faith.* New Haven: Yale University Press, 1934.

EDMAN, IRWIN. *Human Traits and Their Social Significance.* New York: Arbor Press, 1919.

EMERSON, RALPH WALDO. *The Conduct of Life.* Rev. ed. New York: Houghton Mifflin Co., 1891.

JAMES, WILLIAM. *Varieties of Religious Experience* (New York: Longmans, Green & Co., 1903), especially chap. xx.

JOHNSON, FREDERICK ERNEST. *Economics and the Good Life* (New York: Association Press, 1934), chap. i.

RUSSELL, BERTRAND. *Education and the Good Life.* New York: A. and C. Boni, 1926.

SANTAYANA, GEORGE. "Ultimate Religion," *Readings in Philosophy,* edited by J. H. RANDALL, JUSTUS BUCHLER, and EVELYN SHIRK (New York: Barnes & Noble, 1946), pp. 368–77.

SENECA, LUCIUS ANNAEUS. *Seneca's Letters to Lucilius.* Translated by E. PHILLIPS BARKER. Oxford: Clarendon Press, 1932. (Use any translation.)

THORNDIKE, EDWARD L. "Goal of Social Effort," *Educational Record,* XVII (April, 1936), 153–68.

———. *Human Nature and the Social Order* (New York: Macmillan Co., 1940), chap. xvi.

WOODWARD, HUGH McCURDY. *Humanity's Greatest Need: The Common Message of the World's Great Teachers* (New York: G. P. Putnam's Sons, 1932), chaps. vi and xv.

CHAPTER VI
MORALITY AND MORAL CONDUCT

Source of morality: (1) Sociological theory; (2) Morality as foreign to man (a) imposed by God, (b) imposed by man on man; (3) Morality as immanent in man's nature (a) relation to mores, (b) relation to religious views—Nature of morality: (1) Man-made; changing; no universally valid moral principles (moral relativity); (2) Man-discovered; universally valid and natural moral law (moral objectivity)— Basic principle of moral conduct: (1) Golden Rule; (2) Practical imperative; (3) Source of the validity of any statement—Difficulty in living by moral principle: (1) Difficulties arising from the lack of admirable personalities in others; (2) Complexity of human life; conflicting values; (3) Human selfishness—Human motives: (1) Self-regard; (2) Regard for others; (3) Regard for right; sense of duty

---

WE CAN sometimes learn something of the history of human thought through studying the derivation of words in common use. The word "moral" and all its derivatives come from the Latin *mos*, which means "manner, custom, habit." The nominative plural of *mos* is *mores*, a word used commonly in modern sociology. According to *Webster's New International Dictionary*, it means "fixed customs or folkways imbued with an ethical significance." The word "ethical" from the Greek *ethos*, has a similar derivation. *Ethos* means "custom" or "usage." Today ethics refers to the basic principles of morally right action.

That seems to imply that the Romans and the Greeks, as well as our own ancestors, took for granted that those attitudes and acts sanctioned by custom because they seemed to promote individual or group welfare were the attitudes and acts which were right. One of the greatest of modern sociologists, William G. Sumner, says of the origin of morality:

93

The operation by which folkways are produced consists in the frequent repetition of petty acts, often by great numbers acting in concert or, at least, acting in the same way when face to face with the same need. The immediate motive is interest. It produces habit in the individual and custom in the group. It is, therefore, in the highest degree original and primitive. Out of the unconscious experiment which every repetition of the ways includes there issues pleasure or pain, and then, so far as the men are capable of reflection, convictions that the ways are conducive to social welfare. When this conviction as to the relation to welfare is added to the folkways, they are converted into mores, and, by virtue of the philosophical and ethical element added to them, they win utility and importance and become the source of the science and art of living.[1]

Here is explicitly stated the theory that morality is man-made; that it has had an evolutionary history; that it arose, first, out of man's attempt to procure pleasure and avoid pain and, second, from convictions about conduct needed to secure social welfare. Such a theory, of course, is not the only one concerning the nature and source of morality. That is a problem on which thinkers have differed and still differ. The principal questions seem to be, first, what is the source of morality? Has it been imposed on man from an outside source or is it in some way an outgrowth of his own nature? Second, are there any ethical principles which always have been and always will be universally valid and true?

In Plato's *Euthyphro*, Socrates asks "whether the pious or holy is beloved by the gods because it is holy or holy because it is beloved by the gods."[2]

In the same vein, men have asked for centuries whether a thing is right because it is required of them or required of them because it is right.

The Hebrew prophets taught their people that moral principles were commandments which came from Jehovah. Many thoughtful and intelligent people believe today that morality is imposed on man from on high. "God does not require actions because they are right,

1. William G. Sumner, *Folkways*, pp. 3–4.
2. (Trans. Benjamin Jowett) 7.

but they are right because He requires them, just as others are evil because He forbids them."³

Another belief, often argued, is that moral standards were and are imposed upon the weak by the strong in order to achieve their purposes. "Might makes right." In Plato's *Republic*, Thrasymachus proclaims to Socrates that "justice is nothing else than the interest of the stronger."⁴ Good and evil are good and evil because the rulers say so. However, in Plato's *Gorgias*, Callicles, a politician and friend of Gorgias, the famous Sophist, argues that virtue is a mere convention intended by the weak to shackle the strong and that this is unnatural and to be treated with contempt. He insists that the strong man is happy so long as he is prosperous in his career of crime. "Nature herself intimates that it is just for the better to have more than the worse, the more powerful than the weaker."

These quotations remind us of the modern Nietzsche, who says that there are two kinds of morality; morality may be either that of the powerful or that of the weak. When it is the first, the rulers "determine the conception 'good' " and that, while one has duties to one's equals, "one may act towards beings of a lower rank . . . . just as seems good to one, or 'as the heart desires,' and in any case, 'beyond good and evil. . . . .' "

It is otherwise with the second type of morality, slave-morality. . . . . Those qualities which serve to alleviate the existence of sufferers are brought into prominence and flooded with light; it is here that sympathy, the kind, helping hand, the warm heart, patience, diligence, humility, and friendliness attain to honor; for here these are the most useful qualities, and almost the only means of supporting the burden of existence.⁵

In other words, Nietzsche believed that the morality of kindness, helpfulness, and humility came into being because such rules of conduct made life supportable for slaves. Christianity, he said, was a slave morality.

But strong men can make their own morality. They are beyond good and evil and may impose their will upon those weaker than they.

3. Durant Drake, *The New Morality*, p. 5.
4. i. 339A.
5. Friedrich Nietzsche, *Beyond Good and Evil*, pp. 201-3.

Thus Nietzsche, Callicles, and Thrasymachus represent all who have believed and still believe that morality is an invention of man imposed upon other men in order to gain their own ends. For them morality is a purely human device, with a human origin, used to achieve human purposes. Worse, their notion as to what is human seems very limited. Man, to them, is merely an intelligent animal, justified in following the law of the jungle. It is the doctrine of the "survival of the fittest" carried to its logical conclusion, if by fittest one means strongest.

Such a view of human nature seems superficial. As pointed out in previous chapters, man is not merely an intelligent animal. He has a nature which demands that he make moral distinctions, a conscience which says, "you ought." According to history and anthropology, man has always been concerned with problems of right and wrong. He has often been mistaken about what he thought was right; he has often done the wrong instead of the right; but among all peoples and at all times, so far as we know, he has made moral distinctions. And he has not, by any means, always believed or acted upon the belief that that was right which gave him the advantage over other men or even that merely the expedient or the prudent was the right. Nor has his criterion continued to be that of procuring pleasure and avoiding pain, whatever it may have been with primitive man. To say that man's motives are merely those of an intelligent animal is to do him considerable injustice.

MORALITY AS IMMANENT

Many thinkers, including the ancient Confucius and Buddha, as well as Plato and others of the Greeks, have taught that man is by nature either essentially or potentially good and that morality is an expression of this good in his nature. How else, say they, can we account for man's rise from savagery to ethical insight and behavior? How else could we understand the noble behavior and the selflessness for which all human beings seem to have the capacity?

The modern philosopher who made this conception of human nature his central doctrine was Kant. It is implicit in his entire ethical system. A careful and scholarly student of this great thinker says of Kant: "He is likewise conscious of the way in which the moral law is an outgrowth of man's own nature: 'The *moral* personality is then nothing other than the freedom of a rational being under moral laws. . . . ; whence it follows that a person is subject only to those laws which he (either alone, or at least jointly with others) gives to himself!' "⁶

Many other quotations from Kant might be used to illustrate his position on this problem. In speaking of man's reason, he says: "It [reason] must regard itself as the author of its principles independent of foreign influences."⁷

Kant, of course, is not the only philosopher to teach that morality is the outgrowth of man's nature. The Greeks were the progenitors of this idea in the Western world, and few of them were as superficial in their analysis of the theory as Thrasymachus and Callicles were represented to be. While there are many ideas as to the origin of morality to be found in Plato's writings, both he and Aristotle seem to have believed that morality is immanent in human nature and arises as an expression of man's fundamental being.

When we say this, we do not mean that morality arises spontaneously as far as *what* man conceives right and wrong to be. He may be interested in right and wrong as spontaneously as he is interested in finding out about the world he lives in. But no man's conscience tells him infallibly what is right or wrong. For that we need the insight of our keenest thinkers, those who have learned the most about human nature and needs. Human thought, human experience, human suffering—sometimes bitter indeed—help us learn what is the right.

THE NATURE OF MORALITY

The solution of the second problem, that dealing with the universality of morality—its truth for all men in all times and at all places—depends upon the answer given to the first problem, the source of morality. A person who believes that morals are imposed on man by God would probably believe in their absolute nature, that is, that moral principles are universally valid. If, however, morality has been invented by man, if it is nothing more than the mores of the group, something that changes with changes in society, then there can be nothing universally valid about moral principles.

6. H. H. Schroeder, "Some Common Misinterpretations of the Kantian Ethics," *Philosophical Review*, XLIX (July, 1940), 445–46.
7. Immanuel Kant, *Metaphysic of Morals* (trans. T. K. Abbott), p. 67.

This is a very common doctrine in the modern world. Sociologists have pointed out how the mores came to be. They are different at different times and among different peoples. There is scarcely any practice which we believe to be wrong but that some people at some time have practiced it, believing it morally right. The Chinese revere their aged. Filial piety has been and is one of their chief virtues. Sons and daughters obey the family's oldest members and tenderly care for them. On the other hand, among many primitive people the old were killed when they could no longer contribute to the support and protection of the group. Life was so precarious that only the helpless young, never the helpless old, must burden active adults. For the Chinese it is morally right that they cherish the aged; for primitive people whose life is harsh and uncertain it is morally right that they deprive their old of a life which is only a burden to the group. Morality is only the mores, customs on the preservation of which people believe their welfare depends. Slavery was once right; now it is wrong. Smoking was once wrong for women; in many groups it is no longer wrong. Morality changes. So it is said, according to this point of view, there is nothing universally valid in what we call "ethical" principles.

Positivism is one of the philosophical schools which has come to this same conclusion, although on different grounds. As pointed out in chapter i, positivism asserts that only empirical evidence can establish truth. Ethical principles do not refer to objective facts, so it is meaningless to discuss them in relation to truth. To say that a thing is right or wrong is simply to say that "I like this" or "I do not like that." It means no more than to say that "I like ice cream" and "I do not like parsnips." One is thereby expressing mere emotional predilections. Morality changes, say they, just as other likes and dislikes change. There are people who do not like ice cream. There are persons who do like parsnips. Likes and dislikes change, not only from time to time and people to people but in an individual. Children may dislike oatmeal, but as adults they enjoy it. So with likes and dislikes for moral standards. Since morality is nothing but an expression of these changing emotional predilections, there can be no universal validity for ethical principles.

Some students of the problem, however, convinced that morality is an expression of man's fundamental nature and that mankind gives himself his own laws, ask whether it is not likely that in our common humanity, our basic human nature, may be found the foundation for those ethical principles which are true and universally valid, whether man knows of them or not.

A careful study of man's nature and of his history seems to point to the truth of this view. Moral idealism is an expression of a potentiality of man's nature, just as are art, music, literature, just as is the hunger for knowledge. This concept does not deny that God is the source of morality. It does dispute the idea that God uses morality for man as a gardener uses an espalier for a tree: to make him develop in a way foreign to his nature. It does maintain that man has something in his own nature that aspires toward the good, that he has been endowed with reason and with the power to recognize moral principles, and that it is his responsibility to discover what morality really is.

Many intelligent and scholarly individuals believe that man has been aided in this search by direct revelations from God to some persons particularly sensitive to the spiritual; others believe that man must search aided only by his own natural gifts. Both these groups unite in insisting that morality is far more than just the mores. The mores represent merely a group's convictions about morality. They may contain much that is genuine morality; they may contain many false ideas, as well.

MORALITY AND THE GOOD LIFE

We have already spoken of the truth that man, consciously or unconsciously, has always been searching for the life which is good for him to live. Such a life must be one that provides for every aspect of his nature in such a way as to promote the full and harmonious working-together of all his powers. This is a co-operative endeavor; its realization depends upon our relations with other human beings. Because of man's social nature, his best development is dependent upon the welfare of others. To live the good life, so far as our knowledge of its essential characteristics goes, it is necessary that our conduct be in harmony with its demands. Morality consists of the sum total of the principles we must follow in our relations with others and in the development of our own selves if we are to live the good life. Man discovers these principles through his experiences in living and through studying human nature—what it is and what it needs in order to realize its best potentialities, that is, those potentialities which will make it possible for man to live the good life.

There seem to be such rules of conduct. They have been discovered again and again by mankind. It is not easy to apply them in our daily lives. Human nature has in it conflicting elements. In addition to man's "unsocial sociability," life is so complex that even with the best will in the world it is difficult to know just how to apply the ethical principle which we earnestly desire to follow. But to say that there are no ethical principles of universal validity is to deny our common human nature, to deny that there is a way of living, binding upon all men, which will allow for the best development of this human nature. It is to deny the possibility for arriving at any knowledge about the life which is good for man to live on this earth. We may not yet know all that we should know about human nature and our needs, but that does not mean that there are no universally valid rules of conduct.

Let us use an analogy for illustrative purposes. Man has always been concerned with his health. Primitive man had his medicine man. Many customs and even superstitions concerning the maintenance of health and the cure of disease had an element of truth in them along with much of error. Man still does not know all that there is to know concerning the health of his body; medical science is yet in its infancy. But whether men knew of them or not, whether man today has discovered all the truth or not, there are things we should do and other things we should not do if we wish to maintain our health. These principles of health are universally binding upon all men: Chinese, Americans, Russians, Italians.

So, too, with the development of human personality. In philosophy and ethics, the word "person" has been used to apply to man as distinguished from animals. Personality is the result of the development of that distinguishing nature. There are things that man must do if this personality is to be developed in him and in others. The fact that he may be mistaken in what he believes his conduct should be, that his knowledge of what constitutes or helps develop a fine personality may be deficient, does not change the fact that here, too, we have a common humanity and that there are principles to be discovered which, if put into effect, help or hinder its best development.

This is not to deny individual differences. The pigmentation of the skin of Mongolians is different from that of Caucasians. But every individual of either race has a skin which performs much the same function. And in spite of individual differences, we are, in all races, more alike than different in our psychological, as well as in our physical, nature.

As we have a common nature and common needs, so are there common principles of conduct which we must follow if our needs are to be met in such a way as to develop human personality as it should develop. The denial that moral principles are valid and true would probably, if adopted and acted upon by any considerable number of people, make it impossible to continue human progress. It would seem to mean that our whole way of life and all our ideals would be in danger.

Many modern scholars have expressed their concern over the prevalence of the idea in the world today that there is nothing objective and therefore universally binding about ethical principles.

The late J. H. Breasted in his book *The Dawn of Conscience* expressed his concern over the swing from the idea of morality as revelation from above to that of mere man-made custom.[8] He wrote this book in order to show by historical evidence that the nature of man demands that he act in accord with certain principles, that human beings began discovering what these ethical principles were in the dim past, that we have a rich moral heritage from this past which man should examine, criticize, and keep.

John Dewey in his new book, *Problems of Men*, inveighs with equal vigor against the philosophical movement which holds that "what is good and evil is wholly a matter of sheer likes and dislikes."[9]

Arthur Murphy[10] and W. T. Stace,[11] among others, have discussed the problem in recent publications. While there are differences among these men as to the exact nature of morality, they all agree that there is danger to civilization in many of the current views of morality and that, in some sense, morality is objective, not subjective, in its nature.

It would seem to the author that morality is inherent in the nature and needs of man, both individual and social; that, as pointed out by

8. Esp. Introd. 9. P. 9.
10. *The Uses of Reason*, pp. 97–180.
11. *The Destiny of Western Man*, chaps. ii and iii.

Kant, it is no more man-made than is the law of gravity; that, like the law of gravity, it inheres in the nature of things as they are and is to be discovered by man through reasoning about human experience and human needs.

Man's search for a principle of conduct from which he could derive ideas as to what is right and what is wrong for him to do has had repeatedly the same result: the formulation of a principle stating or implying that there is in some way and in spite of apparent differences a moral equality among men, that every individual is important, and that each person should treat human beings, himself as well as others, with respect.

This spirit is embodied in the Golden Rule: Do unto others as you would they should do unto you, or, as it is often put, do as you would be done by. If this rule is intelligently used, it will usually result in moral conduct. However, as stated, it has two serious defects. In the first place, one cannot be certain that it will promote the well-being of other people to have done to them precisely and literally what one himself would like.

Suppose that an individual likes jazz music. He can imagine nothing that would make him happier than to have someone treat him to a good jazz band concert. So he treats others, whose pet aversion is jazz, to the experience that he would like to have them provide for him. Of course what the Golden Rule means as a guide in this situation is this: Since each person enjoys having his inclinations indulged and his aversions avoided by others, do the same to them. But it is not always so interpreted by well-meaning but insensitive individuals.

The second defect is that it says nothing about the way one should treat one's self, or expect to be treated, for each person has a moral responsibility for conduct to himself as well as to others.

No man has stated better the basic guide to right conduct than did Immanuel Kant in what he called the practical—by which he meant moral—imperative: "So act as to treat humanity, whether in thine own person or in that of any other, in every case as an end withal, never as means only."[12]

12. Kant, *Theory of Ethics* (trans. Abbott; 6th ed.), p. 47.

Every human being looks upon himself as an end, that is, of value in and of himself. He is not, in his own eyes, valuable only as a means to something else. He has value, infinite value, as a human being. Faust discovered that to exchange the world for his own soul is a poor bargain, indeed, a bargain impossible to keep. Pity the man who no longer has his self-respect, whose worth in his own eyes is gone. If there be such persons who can find nothing in themselves to respect, then nothing in the world can have value.

THE WORTH OF MAN

Why is every human being an end, a creature of infinite value? The reply might be made in several different ways. Religion tells us that it is because man is the son of God, with an immortal soul, the object of God's infinite care and tenderness.

The answer might be put in humanistic terms. Stace does this when he says:

> The natural man can place everything in the world outside himself in a scale of values; and every such thing will have a finite value in that scale. But himself, the satisfaction of himself, the satisfaction of his personality, cannot be placed in that or any other scale. . . . . It is for him infinite. . . . . It is no more than what is expressed in the question: "What shall it profit a man if he gain the whole world and lose his own soul?" This means that the value of his own soul to him is more than the value of the whole world, and this is another way of saying that its value for him is infinite. For it cannot be measured on the scale of values, which he applies to all other things in the world.[13]

Another way of answering the question is to say with Kant that the individual is of infinite value because he is a *person*, that is, a responsible being.

> Man in the system of nature is a being of slight importance, and has, along with the other animals as a product of the soil, a common value. . . . . But man considered as a *person*, i.e., as a subject of moral-practical reason, is elevated above all price; for as such he is to be valued not merely as a means to the ends of others, yes not even as means to his own ends. but as an end in itself, i.e., he possesses a dignity and a worth (an absolute inner value) through which he commands the respect of all other rational beings with others of the same kind and can appraise himself on the basis of equality.[14]

13. Stace, *op. cit.*, p. 133.
14. Kant, *Tugendlehre* (ed. J. H. Kirchmann), IV, 279.

All these answers agree that man's worth inheres in his essential nature. He recognizes that every human being, not just he himself, has infinite worth and must be treated as an end.

This is what is meant by saying that morality is an expression of man's nature. As a rational creature he can understand something of human nature and see that there are things that he must do and other things that he must not do if he is to live in harmony with his own essential nature. Basic to all right conduct is the idea of man as an end.

Kant said that an end is something to be promoted so that it may be fulfilled. This means that in every man are potentialities, "dispositions toward greater perfection," and that it is our business to conduct ourselves so that these potentialities may be developed and the progress of man toward world welfare promoted.[15]

It is easy to think of one's self as an end, but it is difficult to treat everyone else as an end and not merely as a means. We use everything else than man merely as means to our own ends. We kill animals and use them for food. We use trees for lumber to build our houses and our furniture. We use metals for machines of all kinds and descriptions. What more natural than that we should often use human beings to satisfy our wants. And we do, every day. There is nothing wrong about that if there is a reciprocal relation in the situation so that we are not using people *merely* as means. Students use their teachers to help them get the education they need. Teachers make their living thereby and, if they are genuine teachers, get a great deal more than that from it. They would say with William Lyon Phelps: "The excitement of teaching comes from the fact that one is teaching a subject one loves to individuals who are worth more than all the money in the world." Under such circumstances, there is, then, no using of human beings merely as means. There is a reciprocal relationship by which each profits.

But slavery is wrong. It has always been wrong, whether man knew it or not. We cannot condemn men for not knowing, any more than we can condemn them for not knowing about vitamins. But it always was, is, and will be wrong to use human beings as a mere tool to the comfort and profit of the owner. Slaves were kept by their servitude from developing the full potentialities of their manhood and woman-

15. Kant, *Metaphysic of Morals*, p. 48.

hood. They could not become persons. In the same way, many economic practices of the present day are wrong. Whenever and wherever a human being takes advantage of another, using him as a means to his own ends without reference to the purposes, the welfare, and the best development of his fellow-man, that is immoral and a violation of this basic principle.

Moreover, man must not allow himself to be used by others merely as a means to their ends. If he did, he would be dishonoring humanity in his own person. We have the right, for example, of self-defense. It is, in fact, from our nature, because we are the kind of creatures that we are, that all our natural rights arise. We cannot allow them to be violated. Nor must we violate these rights possessed by all men as well as by ourselves. That which any one claims as a right based upon his essential nature as man, he must concede to every other human being.

In this equality of rights based on man's essential nature lies the equality of man. It is a moral equality. We all recognize that some human beings are potentially and actually more intelligent than others. We possess differing capacities and abilities. But we are the same in our common humanity, in our essential human nature, and thus in those rights which are ours because we are human beings.

It should now be clear why we have a right to speak of human dignity and human worth. Respect for human personality because of its essential value is the cornerstone of morality, the foundation for the good life, the essence of true democracy. No thinker ever saw this more clearly or argued it more convincingly than did Kant.

DIFFICULTY IN LIVING BY THE PRACTICAL IMPERATIVE

It is true that it is not easy to live up to this ideal of treating all human beings as ends, never merely as means. In the first place, there are so many human beings who dishonor humanity in their own being. It is sometimes difficult to remember that the wicked and the depraved, the selfish and the cruel, have a right to be treated with respect. This, of course, does not mean that they should be allowed to continue in antisocial conduct. They may have to be restrained. But nothing that is done to them should result in a further loss of self-respect and human decency either on their part or on the part of those who seek to restrain them. Everything should be done to develop the latent manhood within them. If we remember how the personality of human beings becomes what it does, we will understand that only through treating these unfortunates as men can they ever become men. Kant saw this clearly when he wrote:

> To despise (*contemnere*) others, i.e., to withhold from them the respect that is due to all human beings, is in all cases a violation of duty, for they are human beings. It is true that at times it is unavoidable in making comparisons with others to feel contempt (*despicatui habere*) for them, but the external manifestation of contempt is nothing short of an insult. . . . . I cannot deny even the depraved man as a human being all respect, which may not be withheld from him in the quality of a human being, even though he makes himself unworthy of the same through his behavior. So there can be disgraceful punishments dishonoring mankind itself . . . . which are not only more painful to the one punished . . . . because of the disgrace, than the loss of property and of life, but also bring the blush of shame to the spectator at the thought of his belonging to a race that can be treated in such a manner.[16]

In the second place, this principle is not easy to apply. Human life is exceedingly complex. Our conduct touches many people. With the best intentions possible we may not do the thing which results in promoting the interests of all mankind, in treating others as ends. It takes intelligence as well as good will to do the right thing. There is no list of commandments which can be given for him to follow blindly and without thought. We may be convinced that it is always right to treat man as an end and always wrong to treat him merely as a means, but unless we use our best intelligence to apply such a formula, we shall make serious mistakes in our behavior. There is no rule which can be used automatically, absolving man from the necessity of using his reason. Moral problems are usually very difficult to solve. Conflicting values so often enter in. To illustrate:

A physician finds a woman suffering from an incurable disease. To tell her the truth would hasten her end and increase her mental suffering. She asks the physician point-blank: "What is my illness? What are my chances?" Shall he tell her? Must he lie? Is lying ever justifiable?

A brilliant student knows that a mediocre student has copied and handed in as his own some material worked out by the former. Ought he to tell? Should a student report cheating? If ever, when?

16. Kant, *Tugendlehre, op. cit.*, p. 315.

Is it ever right to kill another human being? How about self-defense? How about war and one's duty to country? Equally conscientious people come to differing conclusions.

Because moral problems are difficult and people come to differing conclusions on the questions involved, many people have come to the conclusion, as previously mentioned, that there is no one right way to solve them. That does not follow. There may be a right solution even though we do not readily discover it. Usually, if we ask ourselves, intelligently and honestly: "How shall I act in this situation so as to treat others as end, not *merely* as means to my ends?" we can find the answer. Sometimes it seems impossible to do the right thing in this imperfect world, and we have to choose the lesser of two evils.

HUMAN MOTIVES

But the chief difficulty in doing right does not lie in the fact that others seem not worthy of such treatment or even in the difficulty of determining the right thing to do but in the psychology of our own conduct. It is so easy to deceive ourselves. Human motives are many, and the natural man in us is strong. We have an animal nature as well as a spark of the divine. We are a product of a natural world in which the struggle for existence is keen, in which every living thing acts as if it were the bearer of a purposive force whose one aim seems to be to achieve and continue life. Every child begins life as an egocentric creature who acts only in his own interests. The motive of self-regard is primary and always potent. True, regard for others develops very early if the child is lovingly treated. He comes to identify himself with the mother or the nurse who cares for his needs and helps him satisfy them. He is endowed with a capacity which we call "sympathy," because of which he responds to others and, as his imagination develops, comes to understand that they feel as he feels. Sympathy can also be seen operating among the animals other than man. Psychologists say that it is a highly generalized psychophysiological property of living matter and is the passive, receptive side of the phenomenon which, on the active, motor side, we call "imitation."[17] This may describe sympathy but does not explain it. We know that man can, through the joint operation of his emotions and

17. Thomas Ribot, *The Psychology of the Emotions*, p. 230.

his imagination, share the emotions of others. Henri Bergson defines sympathy as "the infectious character of feelings and emotions."[18]

Both self-regard and regard for others are powerful and valuable human motives. Because man is always interested in that which concerns himself, such valuable qualities as initiative, ambition, thrift, and concern for health have developed and operate in determining his conduct. On the whole, society is better off because each man has a healthy self-regard. Each man should, so far as possible, take care of his own needs. Self-respect grows from competent and worthwhile self-regard. The love of recognition and the desire for security are outgrowths of self-regard. We know what powerful determiners of human conduct they are and that they can be and have been used to promote the good life for man.

So powerful, in fact, is self-regard in determining action that many people believe it is, in the last analysis, the only motive. Introspection leads many people to believe that there is no such thing as unselfishness. They argue: Everything that we do of our own volition is done to satisfy our wants. We never do anything that does not satisfy a want. The martyr who gives up his life for an ideal is doing the thing that, under the circumstances, gives him the most satisfaction. Any act we perform, for others as well as for ourselves, gives *us* satisfaction. There are established psychological principles, and they cannot be disputed. But that is not all that needs to be considered: "Is the agent, or is he not, *aiming* at satisfaction to be derived from the act? It is true that all of us do those things from which we would ordinarily derive most satisfaction, but this is by no means saying that we do all of those things *in order* to derive such satisfaction. Some of our actions are no doubt prompted by the thought of deriving satisfaction from them; but by no means all of them, or even a majority of them."[19]

If man does aim at such satisfaction, his act is self-regarding; if it be one that involves a disregard of others, then it is selfish. In either case there is no unselfishness there. But if he performs the act without any thought of the satisfaction he will get, considering the happiness of others as an end in itself and getting his satisfaction from their

18. Quoted by Stace, *op. cit.*, p. 109.

19. H. H. Schroeder, *The Psychology of Conduct*, p. 40.

happiness, then the act was not prompted by self-regard, although of course the agent obtains satisfaction. Man does have the ability to treat others, their desires and needs, as ends in themselves. He is capable of unselfish behavior.

Suppose that a child is absent from school for some time because of illness. He needs help if he is to go on with the group. His family is a humble one, his father a tenant farmer or an unskilled worker. His teacher thinks to herself: "I am not going to spend my precious time after school helping him. I'm tired after a day's work; what good will it do me to spend extra time with him? His family has no influence." That is selfishness; she is ignoring her responsibility to this child; she is not treating him as an end. Suppose that she says: "I'll help him. And I'll take care that the principal knows about it. I'll tell my landlady, too—I can let it drop in a casual way. She's quite a talker. It will get around that I am spending extra time on this poor child." That is self-regarding. She helps the child. Her conduct is in harmony with the demands of moral principles. But she is aiming at the satisfaction which she will get from the praise of others or from thinking to herself how noble she is. But if she thinks: "This child needs help, I must give it to him," with never a thought of how well she is behaving and never a word to others about it, then her act is not prompted by self-regard but is inspired by another motive. It certainly is unselfish.

Regard for others as well as self-regard often prompts man to conduct which is in harmony with moral principles. Love for family, consideration for friends, sympathy for humanity in general—all are conducive to treating others as ends. But the difficulty here is that we do not have the same regard for everyone. It is easy to treat as ends those whom we love. But it is impossible to love everyone, to feel for all human bings that warm affection which we feel for family and intimate friends. And just as it is natural to favor our own ends, so is it natural to show preference in our conduct for those for whom we feel this affection. Neither self-regard nor love for others will always motivate man to conduct in harmony with the moral imperative.

Psychologists know that it is our emotions which prompt action. But emotions are many and varied. They need guidance. Without reason to guide them, right conduct would be fitful indeed. Love is an emotion leading to action. But we cannot love everyone. Love for some may cause us to act unjustly to others. If someone objects to this, saying that the Bible commands us to love everyone, we need to remember that Christian love is *benevolencia,* the good-will attitude, not "love" as we usually use the term. It is, of course, humanly possible, though not easy, to develop the good-will attitude toward everyone. But love which is discriminating might lead us to act unjustly to those whom we do not love. Fear is an emotion felt when life or that which we hold as dear as life is threatened. All these emotions are useful and, if properly directed, conducive to promoting the good life. But they do not, undirected and unguided, issue in conduct promoting man's welfare.

Sympathy alone cannot be depended upon. In the first place, it operates effectively only in face-to-face relations. If my neighbor's home burns down, my sympathy is easily aroused and I hasten to assist. But if Shanghai is bombed or if Greek children are hungry, it is difficult to feel the urgency and to make the effort that was natural in the other situation. Even in situations close at hand sympathy does not always produce right behavior. Sometimes one's emotions roused in sympathy at other's sufferings are so painful that it is easy to succumb to the temptation to pass by on the "other side of the street." Did not Dives turn away during life from the beggar Lazarus who lay at his door?

Useful as they are, proper in their place as they may be, neither self-regard nor regard for others can be depended upon always to motivate a person to right conduct. Some other motive must operate. If man is to live the good life, he will have to do the right thing because it is the right thing to do. The sense of duty, latent in all of us, must be developed.

"Duty" is not a pleasant word. That is easily understood. We prefer to act from inclination, disregarding or overriding those human beings whose interests conflict with our interests. The prayer of the old man, "Dear God, bless me and my wife, my son John and his wife, us four and no more," is a common, if sometimes subconscious, petition. Duty often demands that we forget such preferences and treat *all* men as ends, whether we like them or not, whether such conduct brings happiness to us and to those we love or not. The "stern Daughter of the Voice of God" is a difficult and harsh taskmistress. But duty is the only motive which can be depended upon always to induce conduct which will promote the good life for man or to further his progress with a minimum of suffering.

The concept of duty has fallen somewhat into disrepute in this and the preceding generation. It is not only that we find it unpleasant to do our duty and that the modern world is one that has followed too much the dictates of hedonism. There is no doubt but that the idea has been abused. Around it clings the aura of Puritanism. Puritanism made duty seem even harsher than it is. In addition, hypocrites have too often prated of duty and acted otherwise. Individuals with a martyr complex have piously announced their devotion to duty. Then, too, we all know that the sense of duty, improperly and unintelligently guided, has done a great deal of harm in the world. Much of "man's inhumanity to man" has been prompted by a misguided sense of duty. But mankind should know better than to abandon a valuable concept simply because it has been misused. No abuse is sufficient cause for discarding duty as a human motive. The cure lies in guiding it by the practical imperative, as well as in developing it.

The Stoics and perhaps their predecessors, the Cynics, were the only groups among ancient Greek and Roman philosophers who understood the importance of this noblest of human motives. No modern philosopher has been so clearheaded and so outspoken on this subject as has Kant. He has also been much misunderstood. Some writers have even gone so far as to insist that Kant taught that one must do everything from a sense of duty and that any act from any other motive than duty was immoral. Kant taught nothing of the kind.[20] He was far too intelligent a person.

The "inclinations," that is, the motives of self-regard and regard for others, are good according to Kant as long as they prompt one to act in conformance with the moral law. It would be absurd and even monstrous to do everything from a sense of duty. Who would present a gift to his beloved because he is prompted by a sense of duty? On the other hand, if there were not in man this capacity to act from a sense of duty, to do the right just because it is right, there would be in man no nobility: no power to live, to fight, and to die for principles. No Latimer burning at the stake in Oxford would have said to his

20. See Schroeder, "Some Common Misinterpretations," *op. cit.*, p. 424.

fellow-victim, "Be of good comfort, Master Ridley, and play the man. We shall this day light such a candle by God's grace in England as I trust shall never be put out."

If man could not act from motives other than those springing from self-regard or from love and sympathy for others, his entire history would have been different. He would never have conceived ideals or held to them whatever happened to him. There would have been little heroism, nobility, self-sacrifice, or human dignity. Man's chief end, then, could not be the attainment of world welfare, the achieving of personality worthy of happiness. The good life for him would be very different from what it is.

It was this inherent nobility of man of which Walter Lippmann was thinking when he wrote of the defenders of Bataan:

> So they fought knowing that they themselves had no hope. This is the very heart of courage transcending all other acts of which men are capable, and the surest proof that man is more than his flesh, his blood, his bones and his appetites. On this proof as on a rock, that there is in all men a capacity to live and a willingness to die for things which they themselves can never hope to enjoy, there rests the whole of man's dignity and the title to all his rights. Were man not the kind of creature who can pursue more than his own happiness, he would never have imagined his freedom, much less have sought it.

THE TEACHER AND THE PRACTICAL IMPERATIVE

For the teacher there is no more helpful guide to be found than in the idea of respect for human personality. The teacher as well as the layman will find the concept helpful in all his relationships. It is particularly useful in giving him the key to successful teacher-pupil relationships.

The essence of it, of course, is this: It is the business of the teacher to do all in his power to promote the best development of each and every one of his pupils. Not just the children of the school-board members or of prominent citizens, but of *all* the children. If the teacher respects their personalities, he will challenge their abilities but never, of course, expect the impossible. He will study each child to discover his strengths, his abilities, his weaknesses. The adult must be kind, but firm, for children are not wise enough to understand what they need to do in order to become intelligent, socially responsible, mature human beings. Teachers must never use sarcasm; that hurts and never helps. They must not "use" children nor their efforts merely to obtain honor or preferment for themselves. Always the adult must think about what is best for the pupils in the light of their needs as nearly as these needs can be determined. When a child does wrong—as all children do—he should be set right, but never with contempt. No child should ever be treated in such a way as to lose self-respect, or, if possible, the respect of his peers. If this has happened, he should be helped to regain this respect.

In other words, treat children as if they were important. *They are.* But remember that this importance lies in the fact that they have potentialities for becoming intelligent, creative, moral human beings. It is not acting with respect for human personality to treat them in any way which does not encourage the development of these human characteristics. They have a right to the wise guidance of adults toward the achievement of that end.

SUMMARY

To summarize, then, the discussion of the nature of morality and moral conduct as comprehended here: Morality indicates the conduct toward himself and others necessary for achieving man's chief end and, thereby, the good life. It grows out of and expresses his own essential nature—a nature fundamentally social. Man discovers ethical principles of universal validity because there are ways man must behave toward himself and others to achieve the good life; this is true because man's fundamental nature and needs are unchanging.

The best statement of a guide to moral behavior is Kant's practical imperative: So act as to treat humanity, whether in thine own person or in that of any other, not merely as a means, but also always as an end. To treat one's self or others as an end is to promote the development of the best possible personality. This is not a formula which can be applied without thought. It takes intelligent and conscientious study of a situation to determine what is right to do. Any of the various motives which move man will prompt him to action in accord with the moral law at times; when other motives fail, the motive which, if properly developed and intelligently guided, will *always* prompt him to such action is the regard for duty. Therefore, we must see to it that such a regard, potential in all men, is developed in ourselves and in the children for whom we are responsible.

Not all students of the problem would agree on all these points. With those persons whose religion would lead them to state basic beliefs differently, there should be no quarrel but open-minded and respectful consideration. The view which seems dangerous for human welfare is that of

114   *Philosophy of Education*

moral skepticism. There can be no rational proof either for or against God as a source of morality, except as we conceive the ways in which man differs from animals as indications of a divine nature and as having their source in God. But there can be rational proof against moral skepticism.[21] That is fortunate, for man's individual and social welfare depend upon the truth of the opposite view. There is a growing realization of this truth among writers in ethics. In a recent number of the *Philosophical Review*, Professor Hudson wrote: "The imperative of teleological obligation tends to be based upon the authority of our fundamental and permanent desires over our merely passing and superficial wants; these fundamental desires being regarded as expressions of our fundamental capacities and powers, whose total realization is our highest good."[22] And elsewhere in the article he said: "Virtues are of worth because they lead to acts for the best interests or for the welfare of all sentient beings."[23]

In other words, we can find the basis for morality in our own natures, in the conduct necessary to realize our best potentialities and the kind of society in which man could live as man. This implies respect for human personality. Teachers should study with careful attention the problem of what it means to treat their pupils as ends, with respect for their growing, developing personalities. Teachers should seek to understand each pupil so that he may be helped to develop to the utmost his human powers and capacities.

QUESTIONS TO AID STUDY

1. What does it mean to say that morality is immanent in man, not imposed upon him? Do you agree or disagree? Why?
2. Are there ethical principles which always have been and always will be true? Can you illustrate? What is moral skepticism?
3. What is meant by a moral absolute? Can you understand why many people dislike to use the term?
4. How do you account for the fact that most sociologists use the terms "mores" and "morality" synonymously? What other interpretation of the relation between the mores and morality might be made?
5. What is the relation of positivism to the problem of determining right from wrong? Why does the positivist take that position?
6. What is the relation of morality to the good life?
7. What arguments are there for the reality of moral law? How do people who accept this view account for the changes in moral standards and beliefs?

21. See Stace, *op. cit.*, for an extended and convincing argument.

22. J. W. Hudson, "Teleology in Ethics," *Philosophical Review*, XLIX (March, 1940), 110.

23. *Ibid.*, p. 109.

8. From what motives do men act? Does man always act from self-regard, or even from selfishness? Explain.
9. What does the phrase "respect for human personality" mean? On what basis does man deserve respect? How can we respect the personality of the mean, the wicked, the depraved? What is it to treat a person merely as a means? As an end?
10. How important is it to develop a sense of duty in human beings? Is there any other motive which could take its place?
11. By what principle should the sense of duty always be guided?
12. Write a short paper in which you state a moral problem which a college student might face and show how the practical imperative could be applied in its solution.
13. Do you think that the use of coercion is in harmony with the principle of respect for human personality? Explain why or why not. How about exploitation?
14. How do you treat your pupils if you respect their personalities? What will you refrain from doing?
15. Can you apply the practical imperative to problems that often arise in connection with contests at school? School exhibits? "Apple-polishing"? Showing favoritism? Snobbishness?

SUGGESTED REFERENCES

AQUINAS, THOMAS. "Faith and Reason," *Readings in Philosophy*, edited by J. H. RANDALL, JUSTUS BUCHLER, and EVELYN SHIRK (New York: Barnes & Noble, 1946), pp. 263–75.

BREASTED, JAMES HENRY. *The Dawn of Conscience* (New York: Charles S. Scribner's Sons, 1933), especially Introd.

DEWEY, JOHN. *Democracy and Education* (rev. ed.; New York: Macmillan Co., 1931), chap. xxvi.

———. *Human Nature and Conduct* (New York: Henry Holt & Co., 1922), pp. 210–23 and 295–302.

———. *Problems of Men* (New York: Philosophical Library, 1946), Introd.

EBY, LOUISE SAXE. *Quest for Moral Law* (New York: Columbia University Press, 1944), especially chap. i.

HORNE, HERMAN HARRELL. *Democratic Philosophy of Education* (New York: Macmillan Co., 1932), chap. xxvi.

KANT, IMMANUEL. Excerpts from his *Metaphysic of Morals* in EDMAN, IRWIN, and SCHNEIDER, H. W., *Landmarks for Beginners in Philosophy* (New York: Reynal & Hitchcock, 1941), pp. 574–645; and in SMITH, THOMAS, and GRENE, MARJORIE, *From Descartes to Kant* (Chicago: University of Chicago Press, 1940), pp. 886–99.

LINK, HENRY C. *The Rediscovery of Morals*. New York: E. P. Dutton Co., 1947.

MELVIN, A. GORDON. *The New Culture* (New York: Reynal & Hitchcock, 1937), chap. iv.

MURPHY, ARTHUR. *The Uses of Reason* (New York: Macmillan Co., 1943), pp. 97–180.

NIETZSCHE, FRIEDRICH. *Beyond Good and Evil* (any translation).

PLATO. *Dialogues; Euthyphro; Republic* Book i; *Gorgias* (any translation).

SCHROEDER, HERMAN HENRY. *The Psychology of Conduct* (Chicago: Row, Peterson & Co., 1911), chaps. iii and vii.

———. "Some Common Misinterpretations of the Kantian Ethics," *Philosophical Review*, XLIX (July, 1940), 425–46.

STACE, W. T. *The Destiny of Western Man* (New York: Reynal & Hitchcock, 1942), chaps. ii and iii.

SUMNER, WILLIAM GRAHAM. *Folkways* (Boston: Ginn & Co., 1906), chap. i.

TITUS, HAROLD HOPPER. *Ethics for Today* (New York: American Book Co., 1936), pp. 153–65.

———. *What Is a Mature Morality?* (New York: Macmillan Co., 1943), chap. ii.

WHEELWRIGHT, PHILIP. *Critical Introduction to Ethics* (Garden City, N.Y.: Doubleday Doran & Co., 1935), pp. 173–86.

WRIGHT, WILLIAM KELLEY. *General Introduction to Ethics* (New York: Macmillan Co., 1929), chap. xii.

CHAPTER VII
FREEDOM: MORAL AND SOCIAL

IN DOSTOEVSKI'S remarkable book *Crime and Punishment* is told the story of Raskolnikov, a college student who murdered a rich old pawnbroker, Alyona Ivanovna, and her much-abused sister, Lizaveta, and of the retribution which followed this crime. Poverty-stricken, Raskolnikov pawned "to an awful old harpy" his dead father's silver watch and a gold ring his sister had given him. He felt an immediate repulsion when he first saw the old pawnbroker and later became certain that such a terrible old woman had no business being alive.

In his hot attic he had for some time been brooding over theories of human conduct and thought that he had discovered a philosophical justification for crime. He felt that many peculiar circumstances and coincidences influenced him strangely, causing him to kill the old women. After the crime, he was so tortured mentally that he could not endure it. To his beloved, Sonia, he confessed but tried to excuse himself:

"I've only killed a louse, Sonia, a useless, loathsome, harmful creature."

"A human being—a louse!"

"I, too, know it wasn't a louse; I've been talking nonsense a long time."

Within two weeks, although in no danger of arrest, he reported his deed to the authorities.

This novel, certainly one of the greatest ever written, could be read merely as a detective story. Actually, it is a drama of sin and retribution in which can be found much of psychological and philosophical significance.

Could Raskolnikov, being the sort of person that he was and circumstances being as they were, have done otherwise than he did? Was he influenced by outside factors which made his crime inevitable? Under the same circumstances could he have chosen *not* to kill Alyona Ivanovna? Was he responsible for the choice he made? In what sense? Why did he feel such terrible remorse? Should he be punished? Why? How free is man in making his choices? Is his conduct caused by factors outside his control, or is he free to choose any of several courses of action?

Such questions occur not only to one reading *Crime and Punishment* or some other book on this same problem but to every thoughtful person as he faces his own moral dilemmas or sees other human beings struggling with ethical questions. It is of particular importance to teachers, not only for their own peace of mind, but because they must guide the moral development of children. The problem of man's moral freedom has been one of the most important philosophical questions for centuries.

THE PROBLEM OF MORAL FREEDOM

It must be admitted to begin with that there is no way to prove that man is free or not free to make any one of several different choices. We *feel* free, but that may be because, as Spinoza put it, "Men are conscious of their own desires but are ignorant of the causes whereby that desire has been determined."[1] After we have made a choice and acted upon it, there is no possible way by which we may undo what we have done, make another choice, and prove thereby

1. Baruch de Spinoza, *The Philosophy of Spinoza* (ed. Joseph Ratner), p. 204.

that one would have been as possible as the other. We may insist that we know through intuition, but that does not prove the point.

Students of ethical problems generally would agree that if a man is sane and not acting under compulsion, he is morally responsible for his conduct. Moral responsibility implies a kind of freedom: freedom from coercion, but not necessarily freedom from causation. Any choice a man makes is his choice whether or not he could have chosen differently. Raskolnikov was morally responsible for his conduct. He felt himself so, otherwise he would not have suffered remorse; likewise, he was held responsible by society. The cynic might say that it was because he was held responsible by society that he held himself responsible. Dostoevski does not so understand human nature; but the kind of freedom implied by moral responsibility is a problem on which thinkers have ever differed and on which they differ today.

The two principal points of view on this question are known as "determinism" and "indeterminism." The determinist insists that man's choices are antecedently determined by preceding events in such a way that, being the kind of person he is and circumstances being as they are, he could not have chosen differently from the way in which he did choose. The indeterminist says that man is able to transcend the ordinary chain of cause and effect in such a way as to make either one of several alternative choices. Some indeterminists even insist that man may act without any motive. In any case they hold that heredity and environment do not inevitably determine his choices.

We distinguish between two kinds of determinism: physical determinism and psychical determinism. Physical determinism is a part of that interpretation of the world and man which is known as "mechanistic." The word mechanistic is used to describe the kind of physics and world view which reduces everything to a few simple laws of motion. It was the kind of physics which pervaded the thinking of men when Descartes wrote: "Give me matter and give me motion and I will make a universe." The mechanistic point of view includes an assumption that the complex is to be understood in terms of the parts which compose it and that it is no more than the sum of its parts.

PHYSICAL DETERMINISM

The physical determinist argues that this is a world of cause and effect, that the same cause always brings identical results, and that nothing happens in this world unless the causes are of such a kind as to produce the event. Since man is an integral part of this world, he, too, is determined by laws. Some of these laws we have discovered, others we shall discover. It is only because of our ignorance that we are unable to predict all of man's behavior, for it follows from causes quite as inevitably as does the action of sticks and stones. "Free will" is an illusion, for we are all constrained to act as we do. Each part of this universe, including man, is irrevocably determined by laws which govern the whole. Nature is an unbroken continuity of cause and effect.

Baruch de Spinoza (1632–77), the great Jewish thinker, put the implications of this doctrine into a noble and enduring form. The central controlling idea of his philosophy is that all things are necessarily determined in nature, which he conceives to be an absolutely unified and uniform order.[2] And, again, Spinoza's metaphysics makes man's body consubstantial with the infinite attribute of matter and his mind consubstantial with the infinite attribute of thought which is the mind of nature or God. Man, as a "mode" of extension and thought is necessarily subject to the laws of these two attributes of which he is compounded.[3]

Spinoza himself wrote in his *Ethics:*

The mind . . . . cannot be the free cause of its own actions, or have an absolute faculty of willing or not willing, but must be determined to this or that volition by a cause which is also determined by another cause, and this again by another, and so on *ad infinitum.*[4]

And, again:

The madman, the chatterer, the boy, and others of the same kind, all believe that they speak by a free command of the mind, whilst in truth, they have no power to restrain the impulse which they have to speak, so that experience itself, no less than reason, clearly teaches that men believe themselves to be free simply because they are conscious of their own actions, knowing nothing of the causes by which they are determined.[5]

2. *Ibid.*, p. xxxiii.   4. *Ibid.*, p. 191.

3. *Ibid.*, p. xliv.   5. *Ibid.*, p. 204.

This seems to have been the view of Schopenhauer when he wrote:

Everyone believes himself *a priori* to be perfectly free, even in his individual actions, and thinks that at any moment he can commence another manner of life, which just means that he can become another person. But *a posteriori* through experience, he finds to his astonishment that he is not free, but subjected to necessity; that in spite of all his resolutions and reflections he does not change his conduct, and that from the beginning of his life to the end of it he must carry out the very character which he himself condemns and, as it were, play the part which he has undertaken to the very end.[6]

It was not until scientists adopted the view of the universe as an unbroken continuity of cause and effect that man made much advance in explaining and controlling his environment. By the eighteenth century this view had grown to include man as a part of the universe; this was the accepted view of many scientific men. Together with Darwin's theory of evolution, it constituted the bone of contention between science and religion during the latter part of the nineteenth century.

With new developments in physics, many scientists now hold such a view of physical determinism inadequate. With the advent of the quantum theory and Heisenberg's "principle of uncertainty," there has been on the part of many scientists a radical change in attitude. Dr. Arthur H. Compton, eminent in physics and a Nobel prize winner for experiments with cosmic rays, said in a recent address at the University of Chicago:

Natural phenomena do not obey exact laws. This statement marks perhaps the most significant revolution in the history of scientific thought. For faith in the reliability of nature is the bedrock upon which the structure of science is built. It has nearly always been assumed that this reliability implies the exactness of nature's laws. . . . . The new quantum mechanics is not deterministic, in that it leaves open a range of possibilities within which the actual event may occur. . . . . It is no longer justifiable to use physical law as evidence against human freedom.[7]

Not all scientists would agree with Dr. Compton. Max Planck, for example, insists that in time quantum phenomena will eventually,

6. Arthur Schopenhauer, *The World as Will and Idea*, I, 147.
7. For a more complete discussion see Arthur Compton, *Freedom of Man*.

when we know more, be brought under a causal scheme. But it cannot be denied that the theory of physical determinism has declined in influence.

PSYCHICAL DETERMINISM

Psychical determinism emphasizes self-determination: Being the kind of creature that one is, with the desires, impulses, drives, and values that one has, one's actions are as they are. Man's nature determines his behavior. Since man's nature is determined by environmental as well as by hereditary influences, his conduct derives from outside factors as well as inner; but it is *his* character, or lack of it; *his* purposes, whatever their origin; *his* nature, however it was formed, which causes his behavior. Because man is not an entirely independent creature, he cannot be the sole cause of his activity in any ultimate sense. But, being the self he is, he does as he does and could not do otherwise. As usually interpreted, psychical determinism rejects a mechanistic view of man, interpreting life and mind as something different from matter. According to psychical determinists, selfhood and personality cannot be accounted for or given their just due in a mechanistic scheme.

Although the problem as here stated probably did not occur to Aristotle, there are passages in his *Nicomachean Ethics* that seem to indicate that he believed man's conduct to be determined by his nature: "Now some may say that all men desire the apparent good, but have no control over the appearance, but the end appears to each man in a form answering to his character. We reply that if each man is somehow responsible for his state of mind, he will also be somehow responsible for the appearance."[8]

This quotation needs to be read in its context really to be understood, but it seems clear that Aristotle taught that our character determines our behavior quite irrevocably.

FATALISM

Determinism, however interpreted, must be distinguished from fatalism and its theological counterpart, predestination. Fatalism assumes some arbiter of destiny, a providence or a fate which predetermines or foredooms all that happens. Marcus Aurelius expressed it

8. Aristotle *Nicomachean Ethics* iii. 5. 1114.

when he said, "Whatever may befall thee, it was pre-ordained thee from everlasting."[9] Determinism sees orderly sequences of cause and effect, in which man's desires and decisions are part of the causal chain. In fatalism man's purposes do not figure as effective.

Oriental philosophies are usually fatalistic. In India all forms of Hinduism assume a determiner of destiny. One of the principal tenets of Hinduism is that of karma: that the life man leads determines the nature of his next reincarnation, not because of any divine judgment, but because such is an impersonal law of nature. Buddhism adopted this doctrine, and it is an essential part of the modern point of view in China and Japan. Taoism in China is also a fatalistic philosophy. Mohammedanism, with its principle of kismet, contains much the same teaching.

Wherever there is wretchedness and suffering in social conditions, there is fertile ground for a belief in a destiny against which man struggles in vain. The Stoic philosophy, more nearly one of fatalism than any other of the Greek systems, grew out of calamitous social conditions and appealed always to those individuals who could do nothing about the situation in which they lived. A slave and an emperor were two of the most noted Stoics.

Predestination is the theological aspect that fatalism took in early Christianity. Augustine seems to have worked it out on the basis of some of Paul's teachings, and John Calvin adopted it from this source. The American theologian, Jonathan Edwards, a remarkable thinker and able logician, argued for the doctrine. Predestination teaches that all the events of man's life, including "election" to eternal happiness or damnation to eternal punishment, have been determined beforehand by Deity. In his *Confessions*, Augustine says:

And I directed my attention to discern what I now heard, that free will was the cause of our doing evil, and Thy righteous judgment of our suffering it. But I was unable clearly to discern it. So, then trying to draw the eye of my mind from that pit, I was plunged again therein, and trying often, was as often plunged back again. But this raised me towards Thy light, that I knew as well that I had a will as that I had life; when therefore, I was willing or unwilling to do anything I was most certain that it was none but myself that was willing and unwilling; and immediately I persuaded myself that there was the cause of my sin. But what I did against my will I saw that I suffered rather than did, and that judged I not to be

9. *Meditations* A. 5.

my fault but my punishment; whereby believing Thee to be most just, I quickly confessed myself to be not unjustly punished. But again I said, Who made me? Did not my God, who is not only good but goodness itself? Whence then came I to will to do evil and to be unwilling to do good, that there might be cause for my just punishment? Who was it that put this in me, and implanted into me this root of bitterness, seeing that I was altogether made by my most sweet God? If the devil were the author, whence is that devil? And if he also by his own perverse will, of good angel became a devil, whence also was the evil will in him whereby he became a devil, seeing that the angel was made altogether good by that most good Creator?[10]

Augustine—not then a saint, nor even a convert—thus saw and stated the problem of evil in the world as men have agonized over it for centuries. One is reminded of the naïve and mildly blasphemous proposal of the old man who said that if he had been God, he would have killed the devil long ago. William James stated this dilemma in succinct and concise form when he said: "If God be good, how came he to create—or if he did not create, how comes he to permit—the devil?"[11] Can God be both all good and all powerful? How can the kind of world we live in with all its evil and suffering be the creation of a benevolent and omnipotent God?

Augustine resolved his predicament through the formulation of the doctrine of predeterminism: man through the fall of Adam became sinful and incapable of good save through the grace of God; God has predestined some men to be saved by his grace, others to be damned. That this will happen, God foreknows, but his foreknowledge is not that which renders it necessary. Necessity lay in man's own wayward will.

Jonathan Edwards, in a famous and closely argued *Inquiry into the Freedom of the Will,* came to the conclusion that man's conduct is necessarily caused:

Having thus explained what I mean by Cause, I assert that nothing ever comes to pass without a Cause. What is self-existent must be from eternity, and must be unchangeable; but as to all things that begin to be, they are not self-existent and therefore must have some foundation of their existence without themselves. That whosoever begins to be, which before was not, must have a Cause why it begins to exist, seems to be the first dictate of

10. Augustine *Confessions* vii. 3. par. 5.
11. William James, *The Will To Believe,* p. 167.

the common and natural sense which God hath implanted in the minds of all mankind, and the main foundation of all our reasonings about the existence of things, past, present, or to come.[12]

How God's foreknowledge and man's moral responsibility could be reconciled posed a theological question which was argued down the centuries and is still heard in modified form in the modern world.

Although fatalism and determinism are not identical, they are often confused. This is particularly true of physical determinism, which William James, the most eloquent defender of indeterminism in modern times, called *hard* determinism.

<h3 style="text-align:center">INDETERMINISM</h3>

Indeterminism holds that when a volition has occurred, "another volition might have occurred in its place"; not just *any* volition, says James.[13] "Free-will does not say that everything that is physically conceivable is also morally possible. It merely says that of alternatives that really tempt our will more than one is really possible.[14]

James admits that indeterminism means that chance plays a real part in the universe. Until very recently scientists have denied the possibility of any happenings in the universe which might be described as according to chance. Now there seems to be some difference of opinion among them. James held that chance merely meant that "no part of the world, however big can claim to control absolutely the destinies of the whole,"[15] and the only reason for our thinking that there is no such thing as chance in this sense is that we see events "after the fact."[16] Then, of course, the process cannot be reversed and another event substituted for the occurrence.[17]

When applied to the realm of morals, indeterminacy has usually been interpreted to mean either that man is himself an originating source of energy, which enables him to transcend the ordinary cause-effect relationship by modifying the stream of causation which plays upon him, or that he has the power to choose any of several alternatives and *can* act from an initially weaker motive. To say that one or

12. Jonathan Edwards, *An Inquiry into the Freedom of the Will*, p. 51.

13. James, *op. cit.*, p. 151.

14. *Ibid.*, p. 157 n.   16. *Ibid.*, p. 156.

15. *Ibid.*, p. 159.   17. *Ibid.*, pp. 155–56.

the other of these statements is true is not to prove it. In fact, as was said earlier, it seems impossible to prove or, on the other hand, to disprove that at the moment of choice man could, under the same circumstances, have chosen another course of action.

Some scientists, Eddington and Jeans, as well as Compton, insist that the new physics banishes determinism. "The revolution of theory which has expelled determinism from present-day physics has therefore the important consequence that it is no longer necessary to suppose that human actions are completely pre-determined."[18]

Eddington's concept of determinism is one of predeterminism, a strict physical determinism that approaches fatalism. He quotes as a definition of determinism the verse of Omar Khayyám:

> With Earth's first Clay They did the Last Man's Knead,
> And then of the Last Harvest sow'd the seed:
> Yea, the first Morning of Creation wrote
> What the Last Dawn of Reckoning shall read.[19]

That is fatalism. Determinism merely assumes the regularity of cause and effect in nature and not that man is a mere puppet. His desire and actions are recognized as part of the causal nexus.

As has been pointed out, other scientists believe that more knowledge of the quantum mechanics will show that cause and effect operate in the subatomic world as in the rest of nature.

Other students insist that if the principle of indeterminacy were established, it would be irrelevant to the problem. Even if true, say they, it would not account for the large amount of unpredictability that the indeterminist believes that man exhibits.[20] One writer puts it thus:

> But it does not in the least follow from the Indeterminacy Principle, if we understand it, that such large amounts of unpredictability in human behavior exist. It does follow, of course, that there will be some indeterminacy. But for large numbers of particles, say those composing a billiard ball, this indeterminacy may be minute. Now the human body is a system composed of an enormous number of particles and, though the behavior of such a system will be slightly indeterministic, it cannot be inferred that this indeterminacy will be anything like the amount which would satisfy the libertarian's requirements. . . . .

18. Sir Arthur Eddington, *New Pathways in Science,* p. 87.

19. *Ibid.,* p. 75.   20. See *ibid.,* pp. 87–88.

The point is that it is still an open question and that it does not follow from the indeterminacy of sub-atomic phenomena that the behavior of gross bodies is predictable with small accuracy.[21]

THE NATURE OF MORAL FREEDOM

The problem of human freedom is really the problem of the nature of the self, of human personality. That, like the problem of life itself, is one of the puzzling mysteries which scientists and philosophers have tried to solve, with little success. We know that man is a product of nature and that, at least so far as his body is concerned, he is subject to the laws that operate with all material substance. Gravitation acts on men, as well as on Newton's apple. The self is not material in nature, but it is dependent for its development upon a body, with which it is so intimately connected that they cannot be separated in life. The self is merely a potentiality at birth, becoming what it does as a result of the interaction with a physical and social environment. It is a commonplace with psychologists, teachers, and informed adults everywhere that to understand human behavior we must look for its causes. This indicates that there might be some truth in psychical determinism, that is, in the belief that our choices are caused by our own nature.

Neither determinism nor indeterminism is a very satisfactory explanation of the nature of freedom, and which of them is a true explanation no one can say. As Wright puts it:

The determinist finds it difficult to show that the self-determination of which he speaks affords the individual any real choice at all. Is he not the slave of his own self? Could he possibly have done otherwise than he did; and if not is he really free? On the other hand, the indeterminist finds some difficulty in meeting the charge of believing in chance. If a person's decisions are not determined by his character, what does govern his choice? Himself? If so, indeterminism becomes determinism. If not, then the decisions are effected by some alien and contingent force which is not the person's own impulses, sentiments, and character, and over which it is hard to see that the man has any real control.[22]

Kant said that a belief in freedom of choice was something which, like the existence of God and the immortality of the soul, must be

21. W. T. Jones, *Morality and Freedom in the Philosophy of Immanuel Kant,* pp. 144–45.

22. W. K. Wright, *General Introduction to Ethics,* pp. 277–78.

taken on faith, for no one could either prove or disprove the truth of such a belief by reason. But of what use would it be for man to feel that he ought to follow a certain course of action if he could not do it? "Thou can'st, because thou oughtst." Because the moral law is a categorical imperative, human freedom seems to be implied thereby.

In fact, Kant believed us to be free because we are determined by the moral law. "A free will and a will subject to the moral law are one and the same."[23] This may sound very strange, but if we remember that Kant taught that man gives himself his own laws of conduct and that morality grows out of and expresses his own nature, we can see what he meant. Freedom is autonomy. "What else then can freedom of the will be but autonomy?"[24]

Man desires to be the determiner of his own conduct, to feel that his behavior issues from his own purposes and that it has not been compelled by any extraneous force. It is only if this be actually true that we are morally responsible.

Since man's chief end, the various aspects of the good life, and the rules of conduct for achieving his aims grow out of his nature and can be discovered only by studying that nature, it follows that man is free when he is obeying the law which he gives himself in order to achieve this.

Suppose that a student asked his householder to call him at seven in the morning so that he could make an eight o'clock class. He would be foolish to refuse to rise when called and to say instead, "You cannot tell me what to do." Any sensible person would recognize that in rising he was obeying his own will, doing what was necessary in order to achieve his own ends.

In the same way we are free when we do the things which allow us to reach the ends demanded by our own nature, those things which help our personality become what it should become. This is what Kant meant; we are free when what moves us to action is "our recognition of the worth human personality has in itself."[25]

Notice that this is not saying that everyone *can* always do this. That is the problem about which thinkers disagree and which was discussed in the first part of the chapter. But when we do so act, then we are free.

23. Immanuel Kant, *Metaphysic of Morals*, p. 66.

24. *Ibid.*, p. 65.   25. Jones, *op. cit.*, p. 107.

Whether we call this psychical determinism or freedom does not much matter. To recognize that our conduct comes from and is determined by our nature is not disturbing to human dignity or to moral responsibility if we take cognizance of the totality of our nature. We are not sticks and stones, nor are we merely animals. We have the ability to reason and to make moral distinctions, to love truth, and to create beauty. To cultivate these aspects of our nature so that our conduct issues from the highest and best in us is to act with recognition of the worth which personality has in itself and is to be free. "A *person* is that being that is responsible for his acts. So the moral personality is nothing other than the freedom of a rational being under moral laws . . . . ; from which it follows that a person is not subject to any other laws than those he gives himself, (either alone, or at least in conjunction with others)."[26]

Those people who say that to be determined by our own nature makes us the slaves of our desires are taking what seems to be a superficial and incomplete view of our nature instead of seeing it in its totality. A man who is ruled by his emotions, his desires only, is governed by only a part of his nature, not by its totality, and is not free. True, our emotions are an important part of human nature. All our activity issues therefrom. But our emotions, as pointed out earlier, need guidance. That guidance our reason must give.

There have been philosophers who made the mistake of believing that man's reason is merely the instrument of his desires, instead of their guide, that our conduct is determined by our irrational nature, and that the role of reason is merely to find the way to gratify our basic urges. The unfortunate Nietzsche taught that doctrine. Some psychologists so interpret the truth that man always acts to satisfy his wants. To act as the instrument of our volitional life is undoubtedly one function of man's reason. Man desires food; this is a biological need which man's nature drives him to satisfy. He does use his intelligence to find the means for satisfying this need. So with all man's basic needs. It is because this is indubitably true that man should not have to spend all his time and effort on mere survival. If these basic wants are supplied, then and not until then can man turn his reason to the discovery of other needs of his nature. It is through the use of his reason that man has found other ends toward which to direct his

26. Immanuel Kant, *Jurisprudence*, Introd., pp. 23–24.

activity. Civilization would never have developed if man had not, through reason, learned that his nature had needs other than those on the animal level. "The unexamined life is not worth living"[27] is a discovery that many men have made, both before and after the days of Plato. To live merely on the affective level of existence is not to live the life of a *man*. Through the use of reason, man becomes aware of the totality of his nature, of the worth of human personality, of the moral law. He controls the emotional life and turns his activity toward achieving the goals revealed to him as worthy by his reason.

Thomas Aquinas recognized the importance of reason in man's life. "The whole root of freedom lies in reason,"[28] he wrote. Maritain, an eminent modern Thomist, emphasizes the same idea repeatedly in a recent publication. "To be free," he writes, "is of the essence of every intellectual being."[29] We act freely, he says, "if we act in the character of men, that is to say, under the direction of reason."[30] And he continues, "Every time a man pulls himself together in order to think out his last end and to decide his destiny"[31] he is acting freely.

John Dewey, too, emphasizes the importance of human intelligence when he says: "The only freedom that is of enduring importance is freedom of intelligence, that is to say, freedom of observation and of judgment exercised in behalf of purposes that are intrinsically worth while."[32]

The point was made in a previous chapter that much can be learned about human thought from the derivation of words. Consider the phrase, "a liberal education." The word "liberal" comes from the Latin *liber*, which means "free." A liberal education is one that frees man. It frees him by developing his intelligence, by helping him to assimilate our social heritage, by releasing him from the bondage of superstition and the fear that is caused by ignorance, by aiding him to achieve the stature of a *man* who understands the totality of his nature and then acts upon the moral principles which will allow him to achieve his chief end. Epictetus made a profound observation

27. Plato *Apology*, p. 38.
28. Thomas Aquinas *De veritate*, Q. 24, art. 2.
29. Jacques Maritain, *Freedom in the Modern World*, p. 6.
30. *Ibid.*, p. 15.
31. *Ibid.*, p. 16.
32. John Dewey, *Experience and Education*, p. 69.

when he said: "The State has said that only freemen shall be educated, but God says only educated men shall be free."

Man is free in the sense that he need not be determined by anything beyond his own nature or being. He is not born already free; he is born to become free through an innate potentiality for such an achievement. This is a mutual enterprise, something at which man must work in community. We each have an individual responsibility for continuing our own development along these lines and for making it possible for other human beings to do the same. That is something every college student and prospective teacher is able to do; his intelligence and character have already been started along the line of self-realization so that he himself can continue their advancement; otherwise he would not be in college or interested in teaching.

SOCIAL FREEDOM AND MORAL FREEDOM

It can readily be understood that social freedom, freedom from compulsion by his fellow-man, is related to the foregoing. Man feels that he is free so long as he is not frustrated and hampered in effecting his choices, whether or not he possesses what theologians have called a "free will." This desire for liberty is a basic one, growing out of our very nature. Man does not want to be interfered with. He wants to live his own life in his own way without external restrictions. He wants political freedom, economic freedom, intellectual freedom.

Not that freedom can ever be absolute. We do not live in isolation from one another, and no man can be free from the restraints of group life and group pressures. But each man should have a voice in determining the policies which are to control him. Free men can and do and should restrict their own freedom. It is the freedom to manage their individual affairs and their common affairs for the welfare of all that men want and have a right to expect.

This is not a mere wish or whim. It is a real need. It should be apparent from the foregoing why this is true. Intelligence must be free in order to grow. Shackling the mind results in the worst kind of slavery. Much of the progress man has made in this world has been won through his struggle for the right to seek the truth wherever it is to be found, no matter how it may contradict accepted dogma and established prejudices. Those acquainted with man's history know at what a price this right has been achieved and the cost in suffering which men of intellectual integrity have paid. Man must be as free from outer compulsion as is compatible with human welfare if he is to be free intellectually and morally.

If man is not allowed independence but is kept in shackles; if he is not allowed to control himself and his own affairs but is dictated to either by a group of the "élite" or by an individual, he remains a child except in body. Parents who refuse to let their children become independent, who fail to free them gradually from parental control, who do not wean them psychologically, do those children a wrong. The results may be most tragic. The children must either rebel or never become effective adults.

It is only through exercising our intelligence that it develops. It is only through gradual assumption of responsibility with attendant consequences that we learn self-control. Notice that the word "gradual" was used. Children cannot be given freedom to control themselves and make their own decisions before they have the knowledge and the maturity to do it wisely. But such knowledge and maturity do not develop overnight before the twenty-first birthday. From childhood on, young people need to learn to choose wisely. That calls for patient guidance by adults. Young people must learn to use physical freedom so as to become intellectually and morally free.

Freedom is a natural right growing out of the nature of man because he cannot become truly man without it, but that does not mean that children should be given unrestricted freedom from birth. The right to life itself is also a natural right. But we do not expect infants and children to assume the responsibility for the preservation of their own lives. Neither should we expect them to be able to exercise properly their natural right to freedom. They must be taught.

If we remember that freedom to control and manage one's self is a natural right because it is necessary for the development of intellectual and moral freedom and that *that* is necessary for the development of human personality with all which is thereby implied, if we will also remember that we are not born full-fledged personalities but must develop into such a state, we shall then begin to have an adequate understanding of the meaning and use of freedom.

Many men abuse liberty because of the inherent selfishness of human beings. Too much must not be expected of man, so little removed from savage ancestors. Our highly competitive society is not conducive to the development of unselfishness. One is reminded of Cervantes: "Every man is as Heaven made him, and sometimes a great deal worse."

CONDITIONS UNDER WHICH MAN CAN BE FREE

But very often men do not understand the meaning of the term "liberty." Too many in this so-called "land of the free" think that liberty means that they may do as they please. It does not and never did mean that. If freedom from restraint, that which we call liberty, is claimed by man because it is a necessary factor for achieving the best growth in human personality, it follows that we must concede to every other man what we demand for ourselves because of our essential human nature and that we must use it so as to develop the best in us. Any other use is an abuse and indicates a need for education.

Rousseau wrote: "To renounce one's liberty is to renounce one's quality as a man, the rights and also the duties of humanity. For him who renounces everything there is no possible compensation. Such a renunciation is incompatible with man's nature, for to take away all freedom from his will is to take all morality from his actions."[33]

All man's experience corroborates this declaration. But there are circumstances under which, of his own volition, man will surrender his independence and submit his will to that of another. Most men regret such surrender sooner or later, but so long as human nature remains as it is and so long as conditions arise which cause such yielding of precious rights, so long will man continue to do what he later regrets.

Edmund Burke said that "people never give up their liberties but under some delusion." If this is so, a large number of the people of the modern world were greatly deluded. The conditions under which people have always been willing to surrender their freedom are those which threaten survival. When the problem of maintaining life seems impossible for individuals to solve in the accustomed way, they turn to a "leader," a strong man, for help. We ourselves do this in time of war. Economic stress beyond endurance brings the same result. If there is any lesson which modern history teaches, it is that, as John Dewey says, "if we want individuals to be free we must see to it that suitable conditions exist."[34] Those conditions must be those in which

33. Rousseau, *Social Contract*, chap. iv.   34. *Freedom and Culture*, p. 34.

man's passion for self-realization can be satisfied, those in which justice is possible. "Whenever a separation is made between liberty and justice," said Edmund Burke, "neither is safe."[35]

Harold Laski writes:

Generally it may be argued that the existence of liberty depends upon our willingness to build the foundations of society upon a basis of rational justice and to adjust them to changing conditions in terms of reasoned discussion and not of violence. But if that be the case, the existence of liberty depends upon the attainment of a society in which men are recognized to have an equal claim upon the results of social effort and the general admission that if differences are to obtain these must be proved desirable in terms of rational justice also.[36]

There is no doubt that the decision as to what constitutes justice in our complex world is a tremendously difficult one to make, but until we turn to its rational determination, our liberty is in grave danger. Until then the four freedoms of the Atlantic Charter—freedom from want, freedom from fear, freedom of religious worship, and freedom of speech and expression—are empty words. As has been previously said, the determination of economic justice is today our paramount social problem. Daniel Webster doubtless was right when he said: "Justice, sir, is the great interest of man on earth." And until every man can, through his own efforts, obtain an adequate livelihood, he will not feel that justice is being done; and if he is frustrated severely in obtaining the necessities for survival, he will rebel. From such treatment are criminals born; out of such widespread conditions revolutions spring and wars grow.

Rights belong to man, as Locke saw, because of his nature. That nature is a social nature. It is impossible for him to become man unless he enters into social relations. It is a mistake to interpret the doctrine of natural rights as meaning extreme individualism. That mistake was made by the laissez faire economists. Wherever there are rights, there are obligations. What I claim as my right, I am obliged to concede to others. Equality as to rights there certainly is in the nature of things. If freedom of thought is a natural right necessary to the realization of man's best potentialities, by claiming that

35. From a letter by Albert Harno to the law alumni of the University of Illinois, April, 1942.

36. Harold Laski, "Liberty," *Encyclopaedia of the Social Sciences*, V (1937), 446.

right I put myself under the obligation to use it for that purpose. I also must concede it to every other man to use for that purpose. Voltaire is said to have written to Madame du Deffand, "I disapprove of what you say, but I will defend to the death your right to say it." The doctrine of natural rights always means the doctrine of the common good. Too often, as Laski points out, liberty has been evoked "as the rallying cry of a selfish interest intent upon privilege for itself."[37] It means the common good because, by nature, man is a social creature and can achieve personality only through mutual relations, correlative duties and rights.

It would, of course, be a mistake to believe that the general welfare could be tested in any other way than as Hobhouse puts it, "by its bearing on the actual lives of men and women."

What is sound in the collective life is that which completes the personal and carries it on to a higher harmony of wider sweep. What is unsound is that which, pretending superiority to the pettiness of personal life, is in reality moved by the pettier personal motives, such as those of ambition, egoism, love of domination and the rest, and, by infusing these toxins into the spirit of community corrupts the best influences that might regenerate human life.[38]

If man could, on earth, become an angel, if he really were perfectible, we might hope that eventually he would work for the common good without any coercion. In the light of all that we know of human nature, this seems quite unlikely. "Liberty within the law," a law which moves closer and closer toward a realization of the ideal of justice, is probably the only solution. It must be law which embodies justice; it should be enacted by men who are representative of and accountable to those who are to live by it; it must be obeyed by all whom it concerns and changed when outmoded or when more insight into the demands of justice so indicate. Else hollow, indeed, are the great words of the Declaration of Independence: "We hold these truths to be self-evident; that all men are created equal; that they are endowed by their Creator with certain inalienable Rights; that among these are Life, Liberty, and the pursuit of Happiness."

37. *Op. cit.*, p. 442.

38. L. T. Hobhouse, *The Elements of Social Justice*, p. 25.

EDUCATION AND THE PROBLEM OF FREEDOM

This discussion has important implications for teachers. It should make us more understanding and tolerant of other human beings to realize that it is quite possible that, being what they are, in the circumstances in which they live, perhaps they could not have chosen other than they did. Of course, it is important that we do all we can to help them choose more wisely next time. As John Dewey says, society says to the wrongdoer: "We do not care a fig whether you did this deliberately or not. We intend that you *shall* deliberate before you do it again, and that if possible your deliberation shall prevent a repetition of this act we object to. . . . . The individual is held responsible for what he *has* done in order that he may be responsive in what he is *going* to do."[39]

It was just that Raskolnikov should be punished, whether or not he could have chosen to do other than he did do. The punishment he endured from his own remorse was more severe than that which society inflicted. He violated, and knew that he had violated, the dictates of his own best nature. That there were causes for his so doing did not constitute any excuse. It is only when punishment does bring remorse and the determination not to repeat the wrongdoing that it is effective. For that reason punishment should never be administered as retribution; it should be used as a deterrent to repetition.

As Socrates pointed out, probably no one deliberately chooses to be bad because he prefers badness. There is a cause for a child's misbehavior which should be ascertained and, if possible, removed. The difficulty is not an "evil will" that needs to be extirpated. Children have to learn the lessons of self-control in the interests of all. This means that discipline will have to be exercised by the adults responsible for their development. Discipline should be used in such a way as to result finally in self-discipline, in the proper assumption of freedom, by the young person. This does not just happen. Self-control follows from wise control from without; self-discipline develops through firm but kind discipline from others, with the opportunity for gradual assumption of responsibility for one's own behavior.

The natural consequence of one's own behavior is the best form of punishment for wrongdoing. But sometimes natural consequences are too severe. No child should ever be made to feel that by his behavior he has forfeited the good will of his teacher or the love of

39. John Dewey, *Human Nature and Conduct*, pp. 315–16.

his parents. His behavior can and should be condemned. He, as a person, is still respected and loved. He is expected to do better. That will help him to do better. If toward our children we take the attitude of the physician toward his patient, we shall better understand them and their wrongdoing.

To make men free is the work of education. Rousseau was mistaken in those opening words of *The Social Contract*, "Man is born free." Man is born to become free. He becomes free through the process of education. It was of this that Chancellor Hutchins of the University of Chicago was thinking when in an address on "The Free Mind" he said:

When we say we want free minds, we mean that we want minds able to operate well. The free mind is first of all the disciplined mind. The first step in education is to give the mind good habits. The next step in the education of free minds is the understanding of what is good. The mind cannot be free if it is a slave to what is bad. . . . . We have been concerned with the transitory and the superficial instead of the enduring and basic problems of life and of society.

SUMMARY

Whether man, having chosen, could have chosen differently, is a question that cannot be answered with certainty. Man is free in the sense that morality grows out of and expresses the totality of his nature; in that sense he gives himself his own laws; he is therefore autonomous. Man recognizes these laws through his reason; the more use he makes of his reason in discovering and applying these laws of his nature, the freer he becomes. Because, to realize his best self, man must live in harmonious social relations, his natural rights involve duties to others as well as to himself. The doctrine of natural rights means the promotion of the common welfare, not the doctrine of laissez faire.

Social freedom, the right to manage our own affairs, is necessary for the best development of man. The ability to use it for our best development is a gradual growth in human beings and a difficult attainment. Its proper use depends upon the voluntary assumption by man of the responsibilities that accompany rights. If men are to be free, we must co-operatively see that they live under the conditions in which they can be free; liberty and justice are inseparable.

To help young people to develop into free men is the work of education. Young people need the kind of education which will free them from ignorance, which will make them progressively better able to manage their own individual and the common affairs, which will make them more morally sensitive and socially responsible, and which will make them able to participate on a higher level of creative appreciations and activities.

Teachers should find the study of the problems of man's moral and social freedom helpful for understanding children and the kind of education they need.

QUESTIONS TO AID STUDY

1. Do you think that Raskolnikov *could* have chosen not to kill the old pawnbroker? What is the connection between moral responsibility and moral freedom?
2. Summarize the points of view of determinism, indeterminism, and fatalism toward the problem of moral freedom. Distinguish between two kinds of determinism. Can man's moral freedom be proved?
3. What is Heisenberg's principle of uncertainty? What connection, if any, does it have with the problem of man's moral freedom?
4. What is meant by saying that man is free when he obeys his own best nature? Summarize Kant's position on the problem of moral freedom.
5. What does human reason have to do with man's moral freedom?
6. Why is social freedom one of man's needs?
7. Does this mean complete freedom? What is meant by "liberty within the law"? Illustrate.
8. What did Rousseau mean when he said "Man is born free and everywhere he is in chains"?
9. How much freedom should children have?
10. Are there any natural restraints upon individual freedom? Explain.
11. Under what circumstances will men renounce their liberty? What must be done by society if men are to be free?
12. Show the connection between rights and obligations.
13. How can the disciplined mind be the free mind?
14. Of what use to teachers is a study of the problems of moral and social freedom?

SUGGESTED REFERENCES

ANSHEN, RUTH NANDA (ed.). *Freedom: Its Meaning.* New York: Harcourt Brace & Co., 1940.

BRENNAN, ROBERT EDWARD. *Thomistic Psychology: A Philosophic Analysis of the Nature of Man* (New York: Macmillan Co., 1941), pp. 217–31.

COMPTON, ARTHUR HOLLY. *The Freedom of Man* (New Haven: Yale University Press, 1935), especially chap. ii.

DEWEY, JOHN. *Freedom and Culture* (New York: G. P. Putnam's Sons, 1939), especially chaps. i and v.

DEWEY, JOHN, and TUFTS, JAMES H. *Ethics* (rev. ed.; New York: Henry Holt & Co., 1932), chap. xv.

EDDINGTON, ARTHUR STANLEY. *Nature of the Physical World* (Cambridge: University Press, 1929), pp. 220–29 and chap. xiv.

———. *New Pathways in Science* (New York: Macmillan Co., 1935), chaps. iv–v.

EDWARDS, JONATHAN. "Freedom of the Will," *Representative Selections.*

edited by CLARENCE FAUST and THOMAS H. JOHNSON (New York: American Book Co., 1935), pp. 263–309.

FIELD, MARSHALL. *Freedom Is More than a Word* (Chicago: University of Chicago Press, 1945), especially pp. 3–63.

FRANK, JEROME. *Fate and Freedom* (New York: Simon & Schuster, 1945), chaps. xii–xiii and xv–xvi.

HARKNESS, GEORGIA. *Conflicts in Religious Thought* (New York: Henry Holt & Co., 1929), pp. 233–39.

HERRICK, CHARLES JUDSON. *Fatalism or Freedom: A Biologist's Answer.* New York: W. W. Norton & Co., 1926.

JAMES, WILLIAM. "The Dilemma of Determinism" in *The Will To Believe.* New York: Longmans, Green & Co., 1897.

JOAD, CYRIL E. M. *God and Evil.* New York: Harper & Bros., 1943.

JONES, WILLIAM THOMAS. *Morality and Freedom in the Philosophy of Immanuel Kant.* London: Oxford University Press, 1940.

KALLEN, HORACE MEYER (ed.). *Freedom in the Modern World.* New York: Coward-McCann, 1928.

LASKI, HAROLD. "Liberty," *Encyclopaedia of the Social Sciences,* V (New York: Macmillan Co., 1937), 446.

MARITAIN, JACQUES. *Freedom in the Modern World.* New York: Charles Scribner's Sons, 1936.

MARSHALL, JAMES. *The Freedom To Be Free* (New York: John Day Co., 1943), especially chaps. i–ii, vi, and ix.

MILL, JOHN STUART. "Free Will, Man and History," *Readings in Philosophy,* edited by J. H. RANDALL, JUSTUS BUCHLER, and EVELYN SHIRK (New York: Barnes & Noble, 1946), pp. 197–218.

OVERSTREET, BONARO W. *Freedom's People: How We Qualify for a Democratic Society* (New York: Harper & Bros., 1945), especially chaps. i–ii and x–xi.

OVERSTREET, HARRY. *Our Free Minds* (New York: W. W. Norton & Co., 1941), chap. i.

PARRINGTON, VERNON LOUIS. *Main Currents in American Thought* (New York: Harcourt, Brace & Co., 1930), Vol. III, chap. i.

PERRY, RALPH BARTON. *Puritanism and Democracy* (New York: Vanguard Press, 1944), pp. 417 and 446–50.

SCHOPENHAUER, ARTHUR. *On Human Nature,* selected and translated by T. BAILEY SAUNDERS (New York: Macmillan Co., 1897), chap. iii (use any translation).

STACE, WILLIAM T. *The Destiny of Western Man* (New York: Reynal & Hitchcock, 1942), chaps. viii and xi.

TITUS, HAROLD H. *Ethics for Today* (New York: American Book Co., 1936), chap. ix, pp. 138–49.

ULICH, ROBERT. *Fundamentals of Democratic Education* (New York: American Book Co., 1940), pp. 279–94.

WRIGHT, WILLIAM KELLEY. *General Introduction to Ethics* (New York: Macmillan Co., 1929), pp. 275–80.

CHAPTER VIII
DEMOCRACY AND ITS FOUNDATIONS

---

*Causes of modern uncertainty concerning adequacy of democracy:
(1) Identification of democracy with political democracy alone; (2)
Lack of conviction concerning religious basis of democracy; (3)
Ignorance of philosophical bases of democracy; (4) Devotion to pragmatic conception of truth—Nature of democracy: (1) Two assumptions upon which it is based; (2) Provisions of a society organized on
such assumptions; (3) Philosophical basis for faith in democracy;
(4) Religious basis for faith in democracy; connection with Christianity—History of the idea of democracy: (1) Relation of this idea to
history of civilization; (2) Presence of the idea in the Orient; (3)
Greek city-state and democracy; Greek thinkers and democracy; (4)
Contribution of the church during the Dark Ages; (5) Advances
during Middle Ages and early modern times; (6) Doctrine of the
rights of man; revolt of the masses; (7) Democracy and the American dream—Operation of democracy in all areas of life: (1) Political
democracy; why men want it; (2) Economic democracy; (3) Social
democracy; (4) Necessity for discovering means for making democratic ideals more effective—Democracy and totalitarianism—Conditions necessary for the success of democracy—The teacher's responsibilities: (1) With organizations for human betterment; (2) Individually (a) as a citizen, (b) as a teacher*

TO SAY that democracy has been under fire in this generation is a
commonplace. Teachers and parents are fully aware that young
people, and some not so young, are questioning today what a generation ago was taken for granted. Then democracy was accepted as, of
course, the only kind of political organization worth having. It probably was not understood any better than it is today, but the majority
of people in many countries of the Western world looked forward con-
fidently to the day when political democracy, at least, should be established over the entire face of the earth. Not so in these days.

In many groups, when discussing democracy and its problems, thoughtful people will say: "But perhaps in our world today democracy is *not* the best form of social organization for man." Asked whether political democracy is better than totalitarianism, the majority of people would say that democracy is preferable, but, if pressed for a reason, few could give one. Usually they will say that they prefer it, perhaps because they have grown up with the idea that democracy is superior to anything else. Ask them whether it can be proved that democracy is the best form of social organization for men, and the answer is: "Of course not."

But there are incontrovertible arguments for democracy as the best kind of social organization for man, arguments based on the nature of man himself. It is the only arrangement for group living in which man can be man. Totalitarianism or any form of despotism can never be lasting, for men will rebel against continuing to live in such a system. It is contrary to the needs and demands of human nature.

There are several reasons why few persons in a nation which calls itself a democracy know these arguments. Basic to all, is the fact that people generally are not aware of all the meaning back of the term "democracy" and so confuse it with one of its aspects: political democracy. This is probably the case because what lies back of the people's desire to rule themselves is imperfectly understood. Second, although there is a religious argument for democracy, it carries too little conviction; people may do lip service to the idea of the fatherhood of God and the brotherhood of man, but they act in a way totally opposite to the principle. Third, the philosophical foundations for democracy have been forgotten or even, in the minds of some, discredited. And, fourth, there is a widespread belief in the modern world, as previously pointed out, that truth can be established by pragmatic proof alone: If a thing works in experience, that makes it true. And what people take to be democracy does not seem to work; the 1930's convinced many of that.

THE NATURE OF DEMOCRACY

Democracy is an ideal, toward the understanding of which man has been struggling since the dawn of history. He is still far from understanding all its implications and certainly a long way from its realization. Democracy is based on two assumptions: the infinite value and worth of human personality and the belief that men are capable of managing their own affairs in such a way as to promote the welfare of all and that, therefore, they should have the freedom to do so. A democratic society is one so organized as to:

1. Recognize the essential moral equality of men; their equality as *ends*, with all which that implies. This means that society provides equal rights for all: the rights necessary for achieving human personality; this includes, as a requisite, participation in making the major decisions which affect one, as well as the possession of civil rights.
2. Provide for the assumption of the duties which accompany these rights, for it is only as each person assumes social responsibility that the welfare of all will be promoted.
3. Provide for settling controversial matters by the use of reason; force is to be used only as the last resort when the general welfare makes it imperative.

It is apparent that such an organization of society includes much more than political factors. Its conception came from a study of human nature and faith in it. Out of this grew a political doctrine. To confuse mere political democracy with democracy itself may well be a serious matter for the dreams of man. Along this same line, Walter Lippmann writes:

The institutions of the Western world were formed by men who learned to regard themselves as inviolable persons because they were rational and free. They meant by rational that they were capable of comprehending the moral order of the universe and their place in this moral order. They meant when they regarded themselves as free that within that order they had a personal moral responsibility to perform their duties and to exercise their corresponding rights. From this conception of the unity of mankind in a rational order the Western world has derived its conception of law— which is that all men and all communities of men and all authority among men are subject to law, and that the character of all particular laws is to be judged by whether they conform to or violate, approach or depart from the rational order of the universe and of man's nature. From this conception of law was derived the idea of constitutional government and of the consent of the governed and of civil liberty. Upon this conception of law our own institutions were founded.[1]

1. Walter Lippmann, "Education vs. Western Civilization," *American Scholar,* X (spring, 1941), 184.

PHILOSOPHICAL BASIS OF DEMOCRACY

The thoughtful reader will perceive that the philosophical basis for faith in these principles has been laid in the preceding chapters. To recapitulate the essential points:

1. Man has the ability to use symbols in such a way as to enable him to reason, to create, and to express moral distinctions.

2. It is through the exercise of these abilities that man lifts himself above the plane of the animal and commands the respect of rational beings.

3. All normal men have these abilities in potentiality, at least in some degree.

4. The best kind of social organization is the kind which allows for the growth and development of these peculiarly human potentialities.

5. These abilities must be exercised in order to develop. Therefore, man must have the equal rights with their attendant responsibilities which are necessary in order to realize his best potentialities. A society organized to make this possible in all areas of living is a democratic society.

Democracy has a religious as well as a philosophical basis. The belief that man is the son of God, that he has an immortal soul, that all men are brothers, and that social arrangements should be such as to provide for the dignity and worth attaching to man is the essence of the Christian faith. It is unfortunately true that such a belief is more honored in the breach than in the observance.

HISTORY OF THE IDEA OF DEMOCRACY

In a sense, the history of democracy is the history of civilization. So far as we know the record of man's activity, it has been an attempt on the part of men, as Laski puts it, "to affirm their own essence and to remove all barriers to that affirmation."[2] This meant first that the basis for political power had to be widened. So, to have a voice in the government, to establish political democracy, seems to have been the earliest goal of man's effort toward this affirmation.

2. Harold Laski, "Democracy," *Encyclopaedia of the Social Sciences*, III (1937), 76.

This was as true of the Orient as of the Occident. Many Hindu writers upheld such democratic institutions as popular assemblies, community undertakings, and personal liberty. The ideal of human brotherhood and personal equality was often expressed.[3] Buddha's teachings breathed this spirit. He taught his people that their prosperity depended upon the maintenance of popular local assemblies.

The Chinese, like the Hindu, expressed the same idea in their philosophy in spite of their failure to practice it. Mencius wrote, "The most important element in a state is the people . . . . and the least in importance is the king." To the Chinese the saying *vox populi, vox Dei* would have been a truism.[4]

It was in the Greek city-state, however, that we find the ideas of democracy embodied in the earliest effective organization of which we know. Today we would scarcely call those Greek political arrangements democratic, for the large majority of the people were slaves. But the citizen minority did, for that period in their history known as the Periclean, conduct a brilliant experiment in self-rule. The funeral oration of Pericles may still be read with profit for the meaning of the term "democracy."

Not all Greek thinkers approved of democracy. Plato certainly did not, perhaps because he saw so clearly how it could and did degenerate. Aristotle accepted the idea with reservations. He held that "man is by nature a political animal."[5] If this is true, man to be man must participate in the management of the state. He admired what he called "polity," by which he meant that form of government in which the sovereignty is the entire body of citizens and the government is managed for the welfare of all. We should call this democracy. He called it constitutional government and a fusion of oligarchy and democracy.[6]

It was from the Greek Stoic, Zeno, that the strain of thought came, which, when it met Christianity, gave impetus to the growth of democratic thought. The Roman Stoics, particularly Seneca and Cicero, showed their approval of democratic ideals. In their philosophy all men were equal in that they were able to distinguish between good

3. R. G. Gettell, *History of Political Thought*, p. 27.
4. *Ibid.*, pp. 28–29.
5. Aristotle *Politics* Book i. 2. par. 9.
6. *Ibid.* Book iv. 7. par. 3.

and evil, the base and the honorable. Therefore, every man had dignity and was entitled to respect. This, for the Stoics, was in accord with natural law, in harmony with which they believed man should live. The practical result of this teaching was the injunction to be humane rather than democratic as we understand the terms, but it was a step in the direction of democratic thought.

Democracy in Rome was never really effective. In its early history the assembly provided a democratic element. At various times the masses had a vote but often no bread. Their protests were quieted by the distribution of grain, gladitorial exhibitions, and other such pacifiers.

When the Teutons appeared upon the scene of history, they, too, had a contribution to make to democratic thought. They put a high value upon personal independence and emphasized the importance of the individual in relation to his government. The popular assembly had long been one of their institutions.[7]

The Dark Ages contributed little to the development of the brotherhood of man. It was an age of social anarchy, controlled for a short time in central Europe by Charlemagne. With him, however, began the recognition by the church of the divine right of kings. It was the church itself that during these years kept alive the ideas that had produced earlier civilizations. It emphasized then, as it always has, the moral worth of the individual and the equality of all souls in the eyes of God.

In the Middle Ages, several important advances were made. Out of feudalism came the contract with the idea that both parties had duties to perform. The idea of representation seems to have originated during the thirteenth century. Magna Charta laid the foundations for constitutional government. It was during these years that a bourgeois class emerged, many members of which carried on the struggle for liberty.

Other members of the *bourgeoisie,* after their own rights were recognized, were so anxious that order be maintained so that business could go on that they were reactionary in their influence. By the sixteenth century absolute monarchy was, as a consequence, common on the Continent. Hobbes (1588–1679), the English philosopher, wrote in his *The Great Leviathan* the most famous justification for

7. Gettell, *op. cit.,* p. 91.

absolutism that philosophy has known. There was little alleviation for the masses until after the French Revolution, although some few carried on the fight for freedom.

Milton's *Areopagitica*, written to defend the right of unlicensed printing, is one of the most eloquent pleas for freedom of thought in the history of man: "As good almost kill a man as kill a good book; who kills a man kills a reasonable creature, God's image; but he who destroys a good book, kills reason itself. . . . . Though all the winds of doctrine were let loose to play upon the earth, so Truth be in the field, we do ingloriously, by licensing and prohibiting, to misdoubt her strength. Let her and Falsehood grapple; who ever knew Truth put to the worse in a free and open encounter?"

Even during the sixteenth century, as since, little Switzerland, a loose federation of independent republics, was able to maintain democratic theory and practice. Holland managed to shake off the rule of the Spaniards and became a refuge for the persecuted. Here lived Descartes and Spinoza, whose philosophical doctrines had made trouble for them at home.

The seventeenth century saw the revolutions of 1642 and 1688 in England, through which parliamentary government was safely established. This also was the century of John Locke, whose *Treatise on Civil Government* was a philosophical defense of the Revolution of 1688, designed to weaken the belief in the divine right of kings. As a counterargument he used the doctrine of the natural rights of man. Not only the doctrine but many of the phrases in his *True End of Government* are to be found in the American Declaration of Independence.

This doctrine of the natural rights of man has been so important in modern democratic thought that it should be clearly understood. Succinctly stated in the Preamble to the Declaration of Independence, it was the direct descendant of the Stoic law of nature, the form which that concept took in the modern world. Its essence was that respect and regard for *human* nature is the basis for all our social arrangements. It is true that in its formulation there was often evinced an incomplete understanding of the relation between the individual and society. Insight into man's actual rights, those which can be claimed on the basis of his nature, was not always profound. With the rise of social science in this and the past century, some students of society and its problems insisted that natural rights did not grow out of man's nature but simply expressed some of the values he believed important because of the culture in which he lived; in other words, that there is no such thing as a natural right.

Such a conclusion was in harmony with the spirit of the age: an age of materialism, of the machine, of faith in science, an age in which philosophy and religion lost prestige, an age of "debunking." Recently there have been signs that men are again ready to listen to those who have always considered man more than an animal, a creature whose nature demands suitable conditions for realizing his best potentialities. Of these three periods John Dewey is speaking when he describes them as a drama in three acts:

> The first act, as far as it is possible to tell its condensed story, is that of a one-sided simplification of human nature which was used to promote and justify the new political movement. The second act is that of the reaction against the theory and the practices connected with it, on the ground that it was the forerunner of moral and social anarchy, the cause of dissolution of the ties of cohesion that bind human beings together in organic union. The third act, now playing, is that of recovery of the moral significance of the connection of human nature and democracy, now stated in concrete terms of existing conditions and freed from the one-sided exaggerations of the earlier statement.[8]

The first act of this drama was played during the seventeenth and eighteenth centuries. The eighteenth century was the age of Rousseau and Voltaire in France, of Kant in Germany, of Thomas Paine, Thomas Jefferson, and the American Revolution, and, finally, of the French Revolution. It was the age when the common man made his voice heard; it was the beginning of what Ortega y Gasset calls "the revolt of the masses."[9]

The nineteenth century found much of Europe astir with this ferment. France had its lesser revolutions of 1830 and 1848. Germany, weary of the disunity which had made her the prey and the battleground for Europe for hundreds of years, after the final defeat of Napoleon set up the German Confederation with the liberal as well as the nationalistic teachings of Fichte and Ranke in the background. The government became more conservative and gradually sup-

8. John Dewey, *Freedom and Culture*, p. 104.
9. See his book by that name.

148   *Philosophy of Education*

pressed the liberal movement until the year 1848 saw the unsuccessful revolution against the conservative government which sent to America so many German revolutionaries.

Labor unionization and social legislation began during this century in England, Germany, and other European countries as well as in the United States. De Tocqueville, in his *Democracy in America*, described what he had seen, predicting that eventually democracy would prevail over the civilized world. America freed her slaves and, much later, enfranchised women.

America itself has been a haven for the oppressed. Pioneer life and the necessity for common endeavor emphasized the innate equality of man. A man could hold his head high when he owned a piece of ground and when he helped to determine the conditions under which he lived and worked. Thomas Paine wrote: "Here the value and quality of liberty, the nature of government, and the dignity of man, were known and understood, and the attachment of the Americans to these principles produced the Revolution as a natural and unavoidable consequence."[10]

This has been the American dream. Our nation was definitely founded upon these democratic principles. That they have not yet been realized should surprise no one. The Industrial Revolution has created within our country and within a growingly interdependent world many complex problems, tremendous in their scope. Human nature itself is so peculiar a paradox that progress toward ideals comes slowly.

There can be no doubt but that democracy, understood in its wider meaning, is the best form of social organization for man. It is the only one in which he can realize his best self. But it makes great demands upon him and is certainly the most arduous form of social organization. Rousseau wrote, "If there were a nation of gods, it would be governed democratically."[11] Men are not gods. They can be described as Arthur Compton puts it when he said: "Man is a creature with animal limitations but with Godlike powers, sharing with his Creator the responsibilities for making this world a fit place for life."[12]

Democracy presupposes a lower and a higher self in man, an em-

10. Quoted by Albert J. Snyder in *America's Purpose*, p. 28.
11. Jean Jacques Rousseau, *The Social Contract*, Book III, chap. xxi.
12. Arthur Compton, *Vital Speeches*, VI (November 15, 1939), 72.

pirical and an ideal person, and a conviction that all normal individuals can and will subject their lower to their higher powers when summoned thereto by the public interest.[13]

THE OPERATION OF DEMOCRACY IN ALL AREAS IN LIFE

It can readily be seen what a mistake it is to identify the spirit of democracy with political democracy alone. That spirit must permeate all areas of living—the economic and social as well as political. In fact, political democracy is of little use unless it promotes favorable conditions in the economic and social phases of life. The purpose of good government has always been to "establish justice, insure domestic tranquillity, provide for the common defense, promote the general welfare." Political democracy was fought and died for because men believed that, if they could be free to govern themselves, they could secure economic and social democracy. Our forefathers took such a principle for granted.

It seemed to them that men could take care of their own welfare if the government left them free in the economic and social world. If they controlled the government themselves, this would be insured. This creed was well stated by James Parton, the biographer of Andrew Jackson: "The office of government is solely to maintain justice between nation and other nations. It should have nothing to do with carrying letters, supporting schools, digging canals, constructing railroads, or establishing scientific institutions. Its business is simply to suppress villains, foreign and domestic. The people are to be left absolutely free to work out their welfare in their own way."[14]

Such a policy might have worked fairly well in a pioneer agricultural society. Our forefathers could not foresee the Industrial Revolution and the ensuing problems. In so extreme a form as here stated, this theory of government was early abandoned, but there are still too many people in this country who resent as undemocratic any interference with individual enterprise on the part of the government. This, of course, demonstrates that they do not comprehend the meaning of the words "democratic" and "undemocratic."

To resolve the conflict between liberty and social control, between

13. J. A. Leighton, *Social Philosophies in Conflict*, p. 358.

14. Quoted by Charles Beard, *The Unique Function of Education in American Democracy*, a publication of the Educational Policies Commission.

freedom and government, is a major problem today in democracy. Speaking of this difficulty, a distinguished writer in political economy writes that we must always "consciously keep before us" as the goal of political civilization "the reconciliation of Government with Liberty, so that, however, the latter shall be seen to be the more ultimate; that it shall be seen to be both end and means, while the former is only means."[15]

Democratic principles must operate not only in the political field but in economic and social areas as well. That is what is meant by the common modern expression, "Democracy is a way of life." Boyd Bode says that a way of life means "a determining influence in every major area of life."[16]

Political democracy means, in this country, that through their representatives, the people will provide the measures necessary to insure the welfare of all. It means government of the people, by the people, for the people. It means rule by the majority with full recognition of the rights of minorities. It means the guaranty of civil rights to every citizen. It means that government is the servant of the governed, responsible to them for achieving conditions conducive to the welfare of all.

Economic democracy, by reference to the underlying assumptions of democracy, means that everyone must have the opportunity to obtain through his own efforts the material goods necessary for maintaining life at its best. It means that every human being shall have the opportunity to become competent in the economic world; and that if through some misfortune a man becomes or has been born incompetent, he will be cared for by society. It means that each worker will have a voice in determining the conditions under which he works and that he will receive a fair share of the wealth he helps to produce. The worker is never to be treated merely as a means for the accumulation of wealth by others but is to be recognized as himself an end and is to be so treated.

Social democracy means, by the same standard, that there are no special privileges, restrictions, or oppressions because of race, class, color, or creed. It means equalization, but not identity, of educational opportunity. It means the doing-away with intolerance, with unfair

15. J. W. Burgess, *The Reconciliation of Government with Liberty*, p. 383.
16. *Democracy as a Way of Life*, p. 4.

discrimination, with race arrogance, with injustice in its every form. It means that every man shall have the opportunity to become the best human being *he* can become. It means a better life for all.

The practical arrangements necessary for putting such principles into practice in this complex society are far from being understood, let alone achieved. It is easy to become discouraged when contemplating the immensity of the task. Historical perspective is needed. If we can remember that man's life on earth in proportion to the age of the earth itself has been very short and that the period of man's civilized life constitutes a very small portion of his entire existence on this globe, we may obtain a more optimistic attitude toward our upward struggle. Sir James Jeans suggests that we imagine a postage stamp stuck on top of a penny, which is then placed on top of Cleopatra's Needle. The height of the whole structure may be taken to represent the time that has elapsed since the earth was born. The thickness of the penny and the postage stamp together represents the time that man has lived on earth; the thickness of the postage stamp represents the time that he has been civilized and the thickness of the penny, the time that he lived in an uncivilized state.[17] We must not expect too much of man, so lately sprung from an animal ancestry.

Pertinent to the situation is a story told of Socrates:

Once upon a time there came down from the Thessalian Plains, southward to the city of Athens, a man dissatisfied. He entered the Agora and there came upon Socrates.

"Sir," he cried, "I am a very miserable fool."

"The thing is possible," said Socrates.

"For here have I," went on the discontented one, "been striving these thirty years to build in Thessaly a Parthenon. And, lo, I can only manage a mud hut."

"Take heart, my friend," cried Socrates, "for you are in better case than most. For there are few enough of men who try to build a Parthenon and of the few, the most part build themselves a mud hut and take it for a Parthenon."[18]

We are at least attempting to build a Parthenon, a temple to the finest in man. That it is so far but a mud hut should not discourage

17. Sir James Jeans, *The Universe around Us*, p. 339.

18. Related in Mann, Sievers, and Cox, *The Real Democracy*, p. 1.

us. On the other hand, we must not take our mud hut for the Parthenon. It is merely one step toward our ideal.

It would be most unwise indeed to join those who have abandoned the building of a Parthenon. Perhaps they are scarcely to blame because they cannot see the outlines of a noble Parthenon emerging from the mud hut. If we persist and if we see that they have the materials, in time they will surely join us. To believe otherwise would be to misunderstand man's nature.

We are well aware of the totalitarian states of this century and of the gibes, unfortunately sometimes deserved, of their leaders at the so-called "democracies." These totalitarian states were not organized on a consciously held basis. Mussolini himself said that totalitarianism was born out of the need for action, not out of a doctrine drafted at a desk.[19] We also know that C. B. Hoover was right when he wrote: "Dictatorships emerge when either economic depression or political or social chaos exists and the parliamentary regime does not or cannot restore tolerable conditions."[20]

But totalitarian states do have an ideology. Writers have attempted to justify the regime after the act. The two principal tenets of their philosophy seem to be, first, that there are permanently superior men and permanently inferior men, those fit to rule and those who must be ruled. We find the idea usually coupled with the notion that the individual is merely a means to the ends of the state or of the party, not an end in himself. Second, most of them teach that reason is merely a tool for man to use to achieve his purposes rather than the crown and ruler of his nature.

One of the most interesting expositions of the theory of totalitarianism was that given by Alfredo Rocco, the minister of justice under Mussolini, in an address delivered at Perugia on August 30, 1925. This address was given Mussolini's enthusiastic indorsement. Rocco compared fascism with liberalism and democracy, saying: "For Liberalism, the individual is the end and society the means; nor is it conceivable that the individual, considered in the dignity of an ultimate finality, be lowered to mere instrumentality. For Fascism, society is

19. See his *Doctrine of Fascism*, pp. 25–26.
20. *Dictators and Democracies*, p. 13.

the end, individuals the means, and its whole life consists in using individuals as instruments for its social ends."[21] Rocco also condemns Kant who, he says, "was without doubt the most powerful and thorough philosopher of Liberalism.[22]

When the leaders of the totalitarian states spoke of "the new order," they meant just that. They had a totally different conception of the good life, of morality, and of human nature. Their conception seems shocking to us as well as erroneous.

The war ended in the destruction of the power of several of the totalitarian states. We need to remember, however, that we have not killed ideas by killing men. When we were attacked at Pearl Harbor, there was nothing else to do but to go to war. But winning the war did not establish democratic principles over the world. The use of force does not change men's minds or disabuse them of mistaken ideas. If we wish democracy to spread, we shall have to see that people have a chance to see it in action and to experience it in their living. Our own conduct, both in managing our own affairs and in our actions toward conquered peoples, has not always been such as to engender confidence in the ideals which we say we hold.

CONDITIONS NECESSARY FOR THE SUCCESS OF DEMOCRACY

Democracy will not and cannot succeed unless there is a possibility in the situation for some measure of economic well-being. Men cannot eat votes. As stated in the previous chapter, men will give up political freedom when political freedom does not help them obtain jobs, goods, and services. This is true all over the world of every people in every country. It would seem, then, that if we desire to spread democracy, we must make it possible for men to eat. They must have access to raw materials and to the channels of trade. And who now would say that this is none of our concern! In a world in which we are more interdependent and much closer together than formerly, the success of our own democracy depends not only upon our internal arrangements but also upon our willingness to assume responsibility for furthering justice in the family of nations. Isolationism is both selfish and shortsighted.

To further the cause of democracy, which after all is the cause

21. Alfredo Rocco, *The Political Doctrine of Fascism*, p. 19.
22. *Ibid.*, p. 12.

of human progress, teachers should do two things. First, with other adults, they must follow the advice of John Dewey: "Find out how all the constituents of our existing culture are operating and then see to it that whenever and wherever needed they be modified in order that their working may release and fulfill the possibilities of human nature."[23]

In the second place, teachers must educate boys and girls for active participation in the improvement of democracy. The two go hand in hand. The question has been raised: "Can the school build a new social order?" Not alone. In the first place, teachers do not have the wisdom; in the second place, they do not have entire control over the education of children. The culture itself educates, and the school is but part of that culture. Teachers have a responsibility to work with other social-minded and competent adults to improve our culture, as well as to assist in the development of boys and girls who will continue that work. Charles Beard sums it up when he writes:

> The solution of specific problems of democracy devolves upon society. Education does not arrogate that function to itself. It does not claim either the competence or the sole power—legal or spiritual. But education does preserve and spread knowledge appropriate to the solution of specific problems, instills the disciplines essential to the acquisition of knowledge, describes the points of view from which problems are discussed, sets forth the assumptions and imperatives on which solutions depend, and in the classroom illustrates the spirit and procedure in which knowledge is applied in coping with the adjustments of society.[24]

Teachers are realizing today that they must heed Vachel Lindsay's exhortation, "Come, let us forget our ivory towers, brothers," and that they must be aware of democracy's problems and should work outside and inside the schoolroom toward their solution. Outside the schoolroom, teachers, the same as other good citizens, should affiliate with organizations whose purpose it is to improve our society. In organization there is strength. Groups can accomplish what individuals cannot do alone. But, as individuals, teachers have a personal responsibility for eternal vigilance, for the growth and use of their critical faculties, for never falling into slothful indifference to the public good or into complete absorption with private and personal interests.

23. Dewey, *op. cit.*, pp. 125–26.
24. Beard, *op. cit.*, pp. 89–90.

What teachers should do within the school room to promote the realization of a better democracy is discussed in later chapters.[25]

SUMMARY

In spite of modern doubts concerning the suitability of democracy for the complex world of today, a study of the history of democracy and of its religious and philosophical foundations demonstrates its superiority. It is based on a conception of the nature of man which seems to be the true one: first, a belief in the worth of every individual and, second, the idea that all normal men are capable of managing their individual and common affairs so as to promote the welfare of all.

In a sense, the history of civilization is the history of democracy: the attempt of mankind to develop social arrangements in which all can live fully and completely. A democratic society is so organized as to provide for men as ends: equal rights for all with attendant obligations; the use of reason rather than of force, except as a last resort; the expectation that the general welfare will be promoted rather than the welfare of the few.

Democracy is best for man—as well as most difficult—because it requires him to *use* his intelligence, his creativeness, his moral sensitivity—the qualities which distinguish him as man. These abilities must be used in order to develop. A democratic society is best because there alone can man achieve self-realization.

Democracy must operate in political, economic, and social life. We have a fairly effective political democracy but less economic and social democracy. This is serious because political arrangements are for the purpose of producing a satisfactory economic and social life. But it would be a mistake to become discouraged with the little democracy we have. Totalitarianism is based on a mistaken conception of the nature of man and his relation to society. It would be better to envision clearly the kind of society we would like to have and then to find the means for its realization. We need to be concerned about the rest of the world as well as about ourselves and should do all in our power to establish everywhere the conditions in which democracy can develop and succeed.

Teachers have a responsibility for the preservation and improvement of democracy which should be done both in co-operation with other citizens and individually, both outside the classroom and inside it.

QUESTIONS TO AID STUDY

1. Have you ever heard anyone question the adequacy or efficiency of democracy? What reasons were given for this doubt? How can we account for modern uncertainty about that which was seldom questioned a generation ago?

25. See chaps. xiii–xvi.

2. On what assumptions is democratic theory based? Is there any reasonable foundation for such assumptions?
3. If a society is organized on democratic principles, for what must it provide? Describe such a society.
4. What is the philosophical basis for faith in democracy? The religious?
5. Can one be certain that democracy is the best form of social organization for man? Explain. Upon what does your argument rest?
6. In what sense is the history of democracy the history of civilization? Show specifically how this is true.
7. Does man have any natural rights? How would you argue for or against such a contention?
8. What is meant by democracy as a "way of life"? How would it operate in different areas of living? In what way is it a difficult way of life?
9. From the suggested readings or elsewhere, look up more about totalitarianism and compare it with democracy as to their teachings concerning the nature of man, the nature of the state, the rights of the individual, the relation of man to his institutions, and the nature of government.
10. Which of the following is merely a means to the others: economic, political, or social democracy? Explain.
11. Why is some measure of economic well-being necessary for political democracy to succeed? Illustrate.
12. Compare the measures, as nearly as you can find out about them, that have been taken in Japan with those used in Germany to reorganize their social structure. Which seem to be more effective? How do you judge?

SUGGESTED REFERENCES

Barzun, Jacques. *Of Human Freedom*. Boston: Little, Brown & Co., 1939.
Becker, Carl Lotus. *Modern Democracy* (New Haven: Yale University Press, 1941), especially chap. i.
Berkson, Isaac Baer. *Preface to a Philosophy of Education* (New York: Columbia University Press, 1940), chap. ix.
Bode, Boyd. *Democracy as a Way of Life*. New York: Macmillan Co., 1937.
Chandler, Albert Richard (ed). *The Clash of Political Ideals*. New York: D. Appleton–Century Co., 1940.
Dewey, John. *Democracy and Education* (rev. ed.; New York: Macmillan Co., 1931), chap. vii.
——. *Freedom and Culture* (New York: G. P. Putnam's Sons, 1939), chaps. i and v.
Edman, Irwin. *Fountainheads of Freedom: The Growth of the Democratic Idea*. New York: Reynal & Hitchcock, 1941 (read according to interest).

EDUCATIONAL POLICIES COMMISSION. *Purposes of Education in American Democracy* (Washington, D.C.: National Education Association and American Association of School Administrators, 1938), chap. ii.
FRIEDRICH, CARL JOACHIM. *The New Belief in the Common Man* (Boston: Little, Brown & Co., 1942), especially chaps. i and ix.
FROMM, ERICH. *Escape from Freedom.* New York: Farrar & Rinehart, 1941.
HORNE, HERMAN HARRELL. *The Democratic Philosophy of Education* (New York: Macmillan Co., 1932), chap. vii.
LEIGHTON, JOSEPH ALEXANDER. *Social Philosophies in Conflict* (New York: D. Appleton–Century Co., 1937), especially chaps. xvi, xxv, and xxxi.
MACIVER, ROBERT M. *Leviathan and the People* (University, La.: Louisiana State University Press, 1939), chap. v, pp. 57–60.
MANN, THOMAS. *The Coming Victory of Democracy.* New York: A. A. Knopf, 1938.
MERRIAM, CHARLES EDWARD. *What Is Democracy?* (Chicago: University of Chicago Press, 1941), especially chap. i.
OVERSTREET, HARRY. *Our Free Minds* (New York: W. W. Norton & Co., 1941), chaps. iii and vi.
PERRY, CHARNER MARQUIS (ed.). *The Philosophy of American Democracy.* Chicago: University of Chicago Press, 1943 (read according to interest).
PERRY, RALPH BARTON. *Shall Not Perish from the Earth* (New York: Vanguard Press, 1940), especially pp. 20–31, 70–96, and 130–35.
ROOSEVELT, ELEANOR. *The Moral Basis of Democracy.* New York: Howell Soskin & Co., 1940.
STACE, WALTER TERENCE. *The Destiny of Western Man* (New York: Revnal & Hitchcock, 1942), especially chaps. vii and ix.

CHAPTER IX
PHILOSOPHY AND THE PROBLEMS
OF DEMOCRACY

Plato's indictment of democracy—Problems of democracy to the study of which philosophy may be applied: (1) Freedom and social justice; (2) Freedom and security; (3) Leadership; (4) Nature of men's equality (a) moral equality and biological inequalities; dangers in disdain for superiority, (b) racial and cultural discriminations; (5) Social change and democracy; (6) Indoctrination and propaganda; (7) War and peace; (8) Education for democracy (a) education for the general welfare, (b) qualities to encourage—Democracy as means; human personality as end

---

IN THE eighth book of Plato's immortal *Republic*, Socrates discusses with the brothers Glaucon and Adeimantus the characteristics of different forms of the state. Socrates makes the point that where there seems avarice in the rulers so that the governed become very poor "the State falls sick and is at war with herself." He continues:

And then democracy comes into being after the poor have conquered their opponents, slaughtering some and banishing some, while the remainder they give an equal share of freedom and power; and this is the form of government in which the magistrates are commonly elected by lot.

Yes, he [Glaucon] said, that is the nature of democracy, whether the revolution has been effected by arms, or whether fear has caused the opposite party to withdraw.

And now what is their manner of life, and what sort of a government have they? For as the government is, such will be the man.

Clearly, he said.

In the first place, are they not free; and is not the city full of freedom and frankness—a man may say and do what he likes?

'Tis said so, he replied.

And where freedom is, the individual is clearly able to order for himself and his own life as he pleases?

Clearly.

158

Then in this kind of State there will be the greatest variety of human natures?

There will.

This, then, seems likely to be the fairest of States, being like an embroidered robe which is spangled with every sort of flower. And just as women and children think a variety of colors to be of all things most charming, so there are many men to whom this State which is spangled with the manners and characters of mankind will appear to be the fairest of States.

Yes.

Yes, my good Sir, and there will be no better in which to look for a government.

Why?

Because of the liberty which reigns there—they have a complete assortment of constitutions; and he who has a mind to establish a State, as we have been doing, must go to a democracy as he would go to a bazaar at which they sell them, and pick out the one that suits him; then when he has made his choice, he may found his State.

He will be sure to have patterns enough.

And there being no necessity, I said, for you to govern in this State, even if you have the capacity, or to be governed, unless you like, or to go to war when the rest go to war, or to be at peace when others are at peace, unless you are so disposed—there being no necessity also, because some law forbids you to hold office or be a dicast, that you should not hold office or be a dicast, if you have a fancy—is not this a way of life which for the moment is supremely delightful?

For the moment, yes.

And is not their humanity to the condemned in some cases quite charming? Have you not observed how, in a democracy, many persons, although they have been sentenced to death or exile, just stay where they are and walk about the world—the gentleman parades like a hero, and nobody sees or cares?

Yes, he replied, many and many a one.

See too, I said, the forgiving spirit of democracy, and the "don't care" about trifles, and the disregard which she shows of all the fine principles which we solemnly laid down at the foundation of the city—as when we said that, except in the case of some rarely gifted nature, there never could be a good man who has not from his childhood been used to play amid things of beauty and make of them a joy and a study—how grandly does she trample all these fine notions of ours under her feet, never giving a thought to the pursuits which make a statesman, and promoting to honor anyone who professes to be the people's friend.

Yes, she is of a noble spirit.

These and other kindred characteristics are proper to democracy, which is a charming form of government full of variety and disorder, and dispensing a sort of equality to equals and unequals alike.[1]

Thus did Plato, through Socrates, turn the full force of his devastating irony upon democracy. Undoubtedly, he saw about him just such abuses of democracy. And if we are honest, we must admit that in our own society such misuse of democratic theory is not unknown. Out of such perversions both Plato and Aristotle agreed that tyranny springs. That has been the sad experience of many peoples of the modern world. As previously pointed out, democracy makes extraordinary demands upon weak human nature, and man's response to these demands is often such as to engender at least temporary pessimism in the most ardent advocate of that way of life.

Under any circumstances, if democracy is not to degenerate into a kind of tyranny—breeding the anarchy which Plato describes—there are many problems which must be met and solved. Some phases of these problems grow out of the difficulties which human nature always has had and probably always will have in managing its own affairs. Other phases grow out of the interdependence forced upon the world by the far-reaching and continuing results of the Industrial Revolution. These latter have brought problems that must be dealt with somehow in every country, whatever its ideology, but they are made particularly difficult here because they must be solved within a misinterpreted and misunderstood ideology. An application of philosophy to the study of some of these problems would assist in their successful solution.

RECONCILING INDIVIDUAL LIBERTY WITH
THE DEMANDS OF SOCIAL JUSTICE

1. Basic to all else is the problem of the reconciliation of individual liberty with the demands of social justice. A modern writer states the dilemma tersely when he writes: "Can our conception of civilization which rests finally on the principle of individual freedom, be reconciled with our knowledge that both war and want can be eliminated only through collective discipline?"[2]

The writer, a French political journalist, by name Raoul de Roussy de Sales, lived in the United States for more than ten years until his

1. Plato *Republic* Book viii (trans. Jowett).
2. Raoul de Roussy de Sales, *The Making of Tomorrow*, p. 231.

recent death. In his last book he discussed the currently accepted "folklore of democracy" in America and pointed out the fact that the idea of individual freedom, the right of each individual to manage his life for himself, has always been a part of American tradition.[3]

It is the same idea that former President Hoover has often expressed in the term, "rugged individualism." He said: "While I can make no claim for having introduced the term 'rugged individualism,' I should be proud to have invented it. It has been used by American leaders for over a half-century in eulogy of those God-fearing men and women of honesty whose stamina and character and fearless assertion of rights led them to make their own way in life."[4]

This idea was in the old political and economic doctrine of laissez faire, a doctrine which has been abandoned with reluctance only within this century and the remnants of which are still clutched, not only by the ruthless and strong, but by many well-meaning and intelligent people. It is a doctrine suited to a simple rural or handicraft economy, but it has been outmoded by the developments in science and industry in the last one hundred and fifty or two hundred years.

In this era man has created the machine. He has harnessed steam, electricity, and now the atom itself, with its tremendous potential energy. As this was accomplished, there grew the dream that the machine could bring to man an economy of abundance such as he had never known.

The natural sciences, industry, and ideas of democracy developed side by side. It is easy to see why. Science and industry promised that, through the machine, basic economic wants of man could be supplied without ceaseless effort on his part. Man might straighten his bent back, lift his head, and be man. It is only under such circumstances that democracy can be secured.

But, as Lewis Browne points out, something went wrong.[5] The benefits of the machine were not equitably distributed. "Capitalism was allowed to grow increasingly monopolistic and nationalism more and more rabid."[6] Man produced enough to banish want forever, but

3. *Ibid.*, p. 224.
4. Herbert Hoover, *The Challenge to Liberty*, chap. v.
5. Lewis Browne, *Something Went Wrong*. This book is a good summary of recent economic history for the layman.
6. *Ibid.*, p. 350.

162   *Philosophy of Education*

the strange phenomenon of want in the midst of plenty ensued. Some nations were wealthy; others poor. Some people within every nation had a great deal; others were starving. Depressions and wars followed.

If man is ever to know freedom from want and freedom from wars, somehow he must solve the economic problem. That means collective action in the interest of all. There is no reason why this cannot be done within the framework of democracy. If the concept of freedom is understood to mean autonomy under the moral law, there is no conflict to be resolved. But men will have to change their concept of freedom from a notion of their right to exercise individual initiative, irrespective of its effect on others, to the idea that each man's freedom depends upon all men's welfare and that his right to freedom is accompanied by the duty to promote the welfare of all. This we must do through our government when individuals do not themselves assume their responsibilities.

Woodrow Wilson saw this clearly. He wrote in his book, *The New Freedom:* "Without the watchful interference, the resolute interference of the government, there can be no fair play between individuals and such powerful institutions as the trusts. Freedom today is something more than being let alone. The program of a government of freedom must in these days be positive, not negative merely."[7]

To formulate and carry through a positive program of a government of freedom is an extremely difficult thing. To strike a happy medium between unbridled individualism and tyrannical bureaucracy is undoubtedly difficult. Theodore Roosevelt saw that distinctly and wrote:

It is no easy matter actually to insure, instead of merely talking about, a measurable equality of opportunity for all men. It is no easy matter to make this Republic genuinely an industrial as well as a political democracy. It is no easy matter to secure justice for those who in the past have not received it, and at the same time to see that no injustice is meted out to others in the process. It is no easy matter to keep the balance level and to make it evident that we have set our faces like flint against seeing this government turned into either government by a plutocracy, or government by a mob.[8]

7. Woodrow Wilson, *The New Freedom*, p. 284.
8. Theodore Roosevelt, in the Introduction to the book by Charles McCarthy, *The Wisconsin Idea.*

To do this has been the purpose of another Roosevelt, Franklin Delano, the thirty-second president of the United States. Through the dark days of depression his championship of the forgotten man was a clarion call which lovers of justice can never forget. De Roussy de Sales says: "Already America is fully engaged on a road which must necessarily lead to a profound revision of the financial and economic structure of democracy. That revision is well advanced in England. It is overdue everywhere and one of the causes of the present world convulsion is to be found in the fact that no attempt at a real readjustment of the traditional concepts of finance and economics was made when the Western democracies made the Versailles Treaty."[9]

In a recent book written by a young economist as he was recovering from injuries received while serving in the army, we read:

This war is not being fought for the past. It is being fought for the future. The determination of the soldiers that the future bring abundance and peace must be recognized and understood. It is the objective of civilians and soldiers alike. This is a war against aggression and dictatorship. Further, it is a war against depression, unemployment, and economic chaos, for out of these unhappy conditions the seeds of war are sown.[10]

I start with the belief that the democratic free enterprise system is the most desirable one, but that it will continue to exist only if it works well.[11]

It cannot be stated too often that the greatest threat to democracy will arise not from economic pressures and military defeat by the fascist states, but rather through a failure of democracy to function effectively on the home front.[12]

The danger of military defeat by Fascist states is over for the present. The danger that democracy will fail to function effectively on the home front is far from over. We can expect that we shall need more and more help from the government to see that our economic system does function for the welfare of all. It is exceedingly unlikely that either businessmen or laborers, even through their organizations, will discipline themselves sufficiently to promote the general good. Political democracy learned long ago that free men had to limit their own freedom through their government. "Freedom within the law" has been understood in that area. Man's freedom has been increased

9. De Roussy de Sales, *op. cit.*, p. 71.
10. Robert Nathan, *Mobilizing for Abundance*, p. ix.
11. *Ibid.*, p. xii.   12. *Ibid.*, p. 221.

by being restricted. If this seems like a paradoxical statement, consider how much freer the average citizen is to attend to his own affairs because the antisocial individual has been restrained by law. How free to drive, or even to walk, would the individual be without traffic regulations? Economic freedom, too, must be "freedom within the law." Unfortunately freedom has become individualism in the eyes of many; and individualism, "the inalienable right to preempt, to exploit, to squander."[13] What does that do to the freedom of others?

People sometimes forget that when their government acts to secure the general welfare, it is acting for them. In a political democracy the government is the people's servant, the people themselves are the state. In commenting on a common misapprehension here, H. H. Schroeder writes: "It is an unfortunate thing that the average citizen does not have a clearer conception as to the meaning of the term 'the State.' It is largely because of such a misconception that his attitude toward state action is so frequently antagonistic. Could he see that the term 'State' simply means 'the people' thus including himself, his attitude would frequently be different."[14]

The writer then quotes from court decisions in which is explained the proper use of the term "state" in a political democracy:

The State itself is an ideal person, intangible, invisible, immutable. The government is an agent, and within the sphere of the agency a perfect representative.[15]

Suppose a state to consist exactly of the number of 100,000 citizens and it were practicable for all of them to assemble at one time and in one place, and that 99,999 did actually assemble: the state would not be, in fact, assembled. Why? Because the state, in fact, is composed of all the citizens, not of a part only, however large that part may be, and one is wanting.[16]

It is in this sense and only in this sense that it is correct to say that the state is more important than the individual. By that is meant that *all* the individuals are more important than *one* individual.

When a man in a political democracy obeys the laws made by his representatives, he is obeying his own will. In exactly the same sense

13. Vernon Louis Parrington, *Main Currents in American Thought*, III, 17.
14. H. H. Schroeder, *Legal Opinion on the Public School as a State Institution*, p. 32.
15. *Ibid.*, p. 33.   16. *Ibid.*

that the student is obeying his own will when he arises at his land-lady's call, knowing that he requested the summons, so is the man living in a political democracy free when he obeys laws made by his representatives.

Suppose that a student takes a package containing his laundry to the post office and asks that it be insured and mailed to his home. The clerk inspects it, finds that it has not been wrapped and addressed in compliance with the law, and points out the deficiency to the customer. In a huff, the student takes the package home, indignantly declaiming: "I'm not going to have that postal clerk telling *me* how to wrap my laundry. I'd rather not mail it at all than obey *him*. I'm a free American citizen."

This is childish, immature, and indicative of a wrong conception of what a free American citizen is. The clerk was put there to obey the instructions of all the people, embodied in law by representatives elected for that purpose. The student should realize that the clerk is part of the government, the people's servant. The clerk was executing the will of the people in enforcing the law.

It is true that laws are sometimes unjust and unwise. If so, it is usually the fault of the electorate. We do have the right to pick our representatives, and men who will keep the ideals of justice and of the common good in mind should be elected. If those elected do not serve their constituents, they should not be returned to office. To be sure, this is not always easy to accomplish, but the people's indifference to their servants is to blame for most of the folly, the inefficiency, and the corruption to be found in our government. Where the people become really aroused and demand good government, they can usually get it.

If in our political democracy we were convinced that goods must be widely distributed as well as bountifully produced, there is nothing in democracy that would have to be sacrificed in order to accomplish it. In fact, that is the only way that our freedom can be retained and democracy improved upon. Individual liberty and social justice are not incompatible. Without social justice, individual liberty becomes merely the tyranny of the strongest. Against that, it is the business of our government to protect the people. Only so can we hope to realize that which, as Aristotle saw, is the highest end of the state: the securing of true justice.

2. The second problem is closely related to the first. Does social justice demand that security be furnished citizens by their government? How much security can one expect in this world? What is the nature of the security we need? Is security compatible with the freedom which we know man needs if he is to achieve his best development?

A generation ago one seldom heard the word "security." Now it is on everyone's tongue. That is easily understood. A generation ago people took their relative security for granted. Then came two devastating wars and between them the worst economic depression the world had seen. No wonder that the people cry for security.

The desire for security is rooted in a human need as fundamental as that for freedom. It comes from the desire to feel adequate for life's struggle, to have some assurance that needs can be met. The point was made in chapter v that it is deeply discouraging to a person to feel that all his attempts to satisfy his wants are going to be frustrated. He needs to feel that his efforts will be crowned with success at least part of the time. Confidence in self and in one's fellow-man is the psychological source of security.

So long as one can see opportunity for utilizing his powers and satisfying his wants, there is little thought given to security. But let society become complex and highly interdependent, let depressions and war stalk the land, let confidence in self and in fellow-man die, let there be more and more danger to self and family preservation, then security is about all of which the average man can think. Then we call upon our governments to make us secure. Then we wish to be rid of the responsibility for our own security and demand that security be furnished us. Then a "strong man" arises who says, "Follow me, and I will make you secure."

But this kind of security imperils man's welfare as much as does extreme insecurity. Complete security, even if it could be obtained through collective action rather than through a "strong man," is probably not good for human beings.

Harry Overstreet points out in *Our Free Minds* that man needs a margin of error for his activities "if the human spirit is to be given its fullest chance." Man needs to fumble, look ridiculous, try, fail, make mistakes, and correct those mistakes. This, says Overstreet, develops people most fully, releases their energies, tightens their wills, gives zest and determination to their purposes.[17]

In other words, we must not let our longing for security remove from our own shoulders the responsibility for meeting and solving our own problems as well as those of the common welfare. Human powers grow through use. It will not develop *our* intelligence to have others solve *our* problems for us.

We do have a right, however, to expect our servant, the government, to provide the conditions in which we can through our own efforts satisfy our needs. The individual cannot prevent depressions and wars. A wise government could. The individual cannot obtain adequate wages, insurance, medical care, sanitation, parks, education, or recreation, but, through collective action to which the individual contributes, perhaps such aspects of life can be made available to all.

The best kind of security is the kind that comes from within a person, the courage with which he faces life, the strength and persistence with which he turns defeat into success, the sturdy independence with which he resolves to play the part of man. The emotional basis for this inner feeling of security needs to be laid in childhood. Children need to be loved, to feel that they are wanted, and that they "belong." They need gradually to assume more and more self-direction. They need to succeed, and they need to fail, the first more often than the second, and they need to learn how to take both success and failure. It goes back to the problem of teaching children to use freedom wisely but always in a home and school where they feel that they are valued and have an important role to play.

LEADERSHIP IN A DEMOCRACY

3. The third problem also is related to the first. In our complex society with its difficult problems, efficiency demands that experts do the work of the government. How can government by experts be combined with democratic methods?

A distinction must first be made between policy formation and policy administration. The people who are to be affected should decide on the policy. Experts who are responsible to the people for carrying out their will should administer the policy. Sometimes the services

17. Harry Overstreet, *Our Free Minds*, p. 52.

of. experts in a consultative capacity are needed also for the wise formulation of policy. If so, they should be called in. Most certainly
democracies need to use experts. It would be very shortsighted not
to do so. "Consent of the governed" means more in a democracy
than saying to a few men: "You attend to public affairs. We shall be
busy looking after our own private business." "Consent of the governed means discussion, debate, seeking information, listening to all
sides, deciding on a policy, and designating experts to carry out the
policy. Then it means holding the persons so elected responsible for
successfully carrying out the policy decided upon. Public opinion
plays an important part in a democracy. It must be an informed public opinion. It is doubtful whether *vox populi* is ever *vox Dei*, but
certainly the only way of approximating such an ideal is through obtaining all the knowledge and wisdom to be obtained from experts.

Suppose that in a town the question of the water supply is raised.
The supply is inadequate and, many believe, inferior in quality.
Should new wells be sunk, or should water be imported from a neighboring city, which has a supply for sale? The counsel of experts
should be sought. Citizens' meetings should be held before which
experts should present facts and figures. Columns in the newspaper
should be opened; radio time should be devoted to the discussion;
clubs should argue pro and con. Then the citizens should decide on
the policy to be followed, and the duly appointed representatives
of the people should carry out the policy. Such representatives should
be held responsible to the people for successfully carrying out the
course of action prescribed.

This is also the method which should be followed in school matters. The people elect a board which ordinarily decides on policy. If
there is to be a radical change, the people themselves should be consulted. But those who decide the policy, be it the people or their
representatives, need the advice of experts, who should be consulted
before deciding upon policy, and the services of experts in carrying
out the policy. For the schools, these experts are trained administrators and teachers.

This is the method to be followed in state affairs and in national
affairs. It is the democratic method. Citizens cannot have the old
town meeting of New England. But they can be informed by newspapers, by magazines, by radio, by speakers. They can discuss in their

homes, clubs, public meetings. They or their representatives can decide, on the basis of all the information they can obtain, what seems best to do. Then they can expect that policy to be carried out by those who know or will find out how best to do it.

While the citizen has a right to demand that the prosecuting attorney, for example, do his best in protecting the citizen against crime, he has no right to dictate to the state's attorney how that is to be done. As an expert in the field of crime, that is his business. The citizen has a right to demand that the board of health, either state or local, protect him against the dangers of the spread of infectious disease, but he has no right to dictate the particular way in which the board of health is to do this. The citizen has the right to demand that the United States Post Office be as efficient as possible, but he has no right to dictate to the Post Office Department the manner in which its members are to render services. The citizen has a right to demand that the schools achieve the purpose for which they were established, but he has no right to dictate to the teachers and administrators, experts in their fields, how this is to be done.

The citizens should always be alert to check on the results of their servants' performance. Human nature has in it a desire for power. Few, if any, men can be trusted with unchecked power. Our government was wisely established as one of checks and balances. Our party system, in which power passes from one party to the other, is a wise one. Citizens quite rightly view with alarm any political machine which builds so strong an organization through patronage or through catering to the demands of particular groups as to defy all rivalry. Aristotle said that the method of the demagogue and the tyrant has ever been to pose as a friend of the people,[18] a friendship which is usually betrayed.

This discussion should point out the answer to the question as how best to prepare leaders in a democracy. We need the best leadership possible. But in a democracy we do not want two permanent classes: leaders and followers. We should not educate a few for leading and the rest for following. Most individuals can learn to be experts in some capacity and to some degree. Everyone must at times follow experts in other fields. But this following should never be a blind, passive, allegiance. Followers as well as leaders must be intelligent.

18. Aristotle *Politics* v. 5.

A teacher in a small-town or country school should be a leader with reference to educational matters in his community. When he calls in a plumber to install a hot-water system in his home, he defers to the judgment of this expert in another field. But he needs to be able to judge whether he is getting value received from this supposed expert.

The abler the person is, the more expert he may become and the more unwise the society which does not avail itself of his services. Not only government by experts but leadership in all our affairs to be exercised by the expert is in harmony with democratic processes, so long as those concerned have a voice in determining policy, and so long as the leaders are responsible to an informed public for doing their work well.

THE NATURE OF THE EQUALITY OF MEN

4. The fourth problem is closely related to the last one, namely, How can democracy deal successfully with the trend toward leveling-down and with the disdain for superiority, too common among us? And, further, how can democracy deal with ideas of racial superiority and inferiority?

These problems seem to be related to misinterpretations of the nature of man's equality. The point has been made that his equality is a moral equality, an equality of rights. Men are equal as *ends*. Inequalities in mankind are very real. Many of these have their basis in our biological nature. We are born with differing capacities, with diverse abilities, with varying potentialities. True, the environment in which we live serves as the directing medium for their development. But heredity itself, as well as the environment, is responsible for inequalities in man.

To resent the fact that Mother Nature has endowed some more favorably than others is foolish and useless. Also, to preen one's self on the fact that he has more ability than others is absurd. The first attitude too often brings pressure for a leveling-down, sure to result in a lowering of standards and in eventual social disintegration and ruin. The second results in an overweening conceit, in the selfish individualism expressed in the saying, "Take all you can get, and bid the devil take the hindmost"—an attitude fatal to democracy.

Plutarch, in his *Lives*, tells a story of Aristides, known in Athens as "the Just" because of his probity in public life. The Athenians had the custom of ostracizing, or banishing, any citizen whom they considered dangerous.

As therefore they were writing the names on the sherds, it is reported that an illiterate clownish fellow, giving Aristides his sherd, supposing him a common citizen, begged him to write *Aristides* upon it; and he being surprised and asking if Aristides had ever done him any injury. "None at all," said the fellow, "neither know I the man; but I am tired of hearing him everywhere called the Just." Aristides, hearing this, is said to have made no reply, but returned the sherd with his own name inscribed.

Many a superior student in school prefers popularity to superior scholarship. Fearing the jealousy of his fellow-students, he refuses to utilize his abilities to the utmost. This is sheer folly. The great majority of human beings, not particularly gifted, should prize and encourage the superior, realizing that the able may contribute to the welfare of all. And, in their turn, those highly endowed by nature should feel under obligation to use their abilities for the welfare of all. There is a sense in which *noblesse oblige* is a fine motto, if unaccompanied by patronizing airs.

A majority can exercise as devastating a tyranny over minorities as can one individual tyrant over all. Boyd Bode says that "democracy easily becomes anonymous tyranny."[19] To secure only the despotism of the many in exchange for the autocracy of one is no advance. Plato conceived this despotism to be an inevitable accompaniment of democracy. We believe that with the opportunity for every man to live a full life, with education available for all, it is not a necessary development.

Not only do majorities become tyrannical in democracies, but well-organized and economically powerful minorities too often seize power. As Theodore Roosevelt said in the quotation cited earlier, political democracy must not permit "either government by a plutocracy or government by a mob."

Nor should any group interpret the fact of biological inequalities among men to mean that there are superior "races" or peoples. In the first place, the term "race" is used in so many different ways that it is a very vague term indeed. Sometimes people mean "one of the major divisions of mankind—black, white, yellow, and

19. *Democracy as a Way of Life*, p. 9.

brown."[20] Sometimes and more often they mean simply an ethnic group, the Jews, for example. Scientists tell us that there is no evidence that any division of mankind, be it biological or ethnic, is superior or inferior to all others. All groups of men have their superior individuals and their inferior individuals. Apparent differences between groups seem caused by differences in the social environment. When members of different races or groups live under the same conditions, with the same educational, economic, and social opportunities, differences between groups tend to disappear.[21]

The belief that I and mine are superior is an old human obsession, says the anthropologist. "My group is uniquely valuable and if it is weakened all valuable things will perish."[22] And so the white man thinks that he is superior to the dark-skinned peoples, the Japanese thinks that he is superior to the white man; the Gentile believes himself to be better than the Jew, and the Jew thinks that he is better than the Gentile.

That this constitutes a serious problem in the world few would deny. In our own country there are many group antagonisms and "racial" discriminations that interfere with treating men as ends, the basic democratic command. But this is something about which the government can do little directly. You cannot legislate racial antagonisms out of existence. Education can do something. Many schools are experimenting with what we are now calling "intercultural" education. But the basic difficulty lies in the lack of justice in our social and economic arrangements. When men have the good things of life in abundance, when there is more economic opportunity for everyone—those of the dominant group as well as of the oppressed group—when all men are less fearful of competition, then we shall be able to teach the facts of "race" and hope to have them accepted. In achieving a more just economic and social system our government can and should help.

An anthropologist writes: "Men have not for all their progress in civilization outgrown the hen yard; a hen who is pecked at by a cock attacks not the cock, but the weaker hen; this weaker hen

20. Julian Huxley and A. C. Haddon, *We Europeans: A Survey of Racial Problems*, pp. 215–16.

21. *Race: What the Scientists Say* (comp. Caroline Singer), p. 13; also Huxley and Haddon, *op. cit.*, p. 223, as well as many other authorities.

22. Ruth Benedict, *Race: Science and Politics*, p. 221.

attacks a still weaker hen and so on down to the last chicken. Man too has his 'pecking order' and those who have been victims, even though they belong to the 'superior race,' will require victims."[23]

SOCIAL CHANGE AND DEMOCRACY

5. The fifth problem might be stated thus: How, in a democracy, can the right attitude toward social change be secured? The point has been made that change is necessary for progress but that not all change is progress; that, to secure changes which will promote progress, we must have our goal in mind; and that we also must know what mankind has already done which has assisted or hindered its attainment.

Both Plato and Aristotle feared change. Reason could tell us, they taught, what the perfect state should be, and any deviation would result only in retrogression. With less of valid reason than these thinkers, many people have the same attitude. Anyone who finds his own life satisfying, quite naturally, does not want any change. Life is as he would have it; he cannot see that the changes proposed hold any promise for improving his condition.

Contributing to this unfortunate situation is the identification of political democracy with all of democracy. The great majority of people in the United States believe that we have a democracy now, not realizing that political democracy without economic and social democracy is empty indeed. Since they firmly believe that we now have democracy, they resent any proposals for change and wish to preserve the status quo. Opprobrious epithets are too often hurled at individuals who criticize our society or propose changes.

Smug complacency with what we have attained will result in disaster. American ideals need to be explored and understood. Then we shall see how far short we are from their realization. Our ideals are the finest man could have; the American dream embodies all that mankind has hoped for in this world. But there is much to be done toward its accomplishment. We must be ready and willing for the changes necessary to bring us nearer the actuality of these ideals. We cannot stand still. To attempt it is to slip backward.

To build this attitude toward change is part of the work of education, both in and out of the school. "Cultural lags" attend our social

23. *Ibid.*, p. 246.

life today because changes in one area have brought dislocations in other areas not yet adjusted to the new conditions. Education is a better tool for social progress than is human suffering. Suffering will certainly result from an unwillingness to study and direct wisely the changes needed for continuing progress.

INDOCTRINATION AND PROPAGANDA IN DEMOCRACY

6. The sixth problem is this: Is the use of indoctrination and propaganda compatible with democratic principles? Should they be used in our society to induce devotion to our way of life?

These questions have a particular interest during these times because the people of nations professing democracy have seen how effectively indoctrination and propaganda were used in totalitarian countries. The young people particularly, in those countries, believed in their doctrines; they have had a devotion to them which induced them to live and, if necessary, die for them. We are told that they were so indoctrinated from childhood that they never even questioned their system. Willard Price in his book, *Children of the Rising Sun,* discusses *Bushido,* the Japanese spirit. It is a spirit of patriotism, of devotion to emperor and state, of willingness to toil or to die for their country. This spirit has been a part of the life of the Japanese people. Bushido was dinned into them from childhood up. We have no counterpart of this in America. We hear little about the American spirit. But not a school day went by in Japan under the old regime without instruction in the Japanese spirit.

Many people believe that our young people would have more devotion to democracy if they had been indoctrinated with its spirit. Should our schools and homes indoctrinate for democracy? That depends upon what one means by the term "indoctrinate." To some it means to produce an uncritical belief in our principles and institutions. William Heard Kilpatrick so interprets the word. So does C. E. Merriam, distinguished student of political science of the University of Chicago. There are other students of the problem who agree with these writers.

On the other hand, Thomas H. Briggs insists that indoctrination is an "earnest attempt on the part of the teacher to make youth intelligent about principles for the common good, inclined to accept them because of an understanding of the justifying reasons, con scious of their bearing on important problems of the day, and stimulated to act in accordance with the program that they indicate."[24]

There is a general conviction among many of our teachers that, where people differ on an important subject, the schools should present both sides impartially and let the individual make up his own mind. That, they say, is the only proper course if one believes in human freedom and respect for human personality. So they would say we must not try to imbue children with anything or attempt to inculcate any beliefs.

There is some truth and much error in this view. Almost any of them would say that it would be a mistake to bring up children to decide for themselves whether or not they will steal. No mother would say to her child:

Now some people let other people's property alone, and some do not. The first group believe that it is wrong to steal; and besides, they argue that people will like you better if you do not take what does not belong to you. Sometimes people who are not skilful in helping themselves to the property of others land in jail. That constitutes a real disadvantage. On the other hand, it is hard work to have to labor for what you get.

There are those who insist that it is more exciting and less trouble to take from others what you want. If you can become skilful at it, it is said not to be very dangerous. And, besides, if you steal large enough amounts, people seem really to admire you. Such "robber barons" seldom land in jail.

I've given you both sides of the question. Now you decide which you want to do.

Instead, nearly every mother tries to teach her child from babyhood on to leave other people's property alone. She intends to induce uncritical belief in the propriety of such behavior while the child is young. She uses praise and blame in such a way as to reach his emotions. When he is older, she explains to him why it is wrong to take the property of others. Children are not born with their moral natures developed. And how wrong it would be to leave them alone to recapitulate all of man's age-long experience and to rediscover for themselves that they should not help themselves to the property of others!

24. Thomas Briggs, "Should Education Indoctrinate?" *Educational Administration and Supervision*, XXII (1936), 575.

So with all of man's ideals. They are the result of the operation of man's finest qualities—his intelligence, imagination, and ability to make moral distinctions—and were developed as a result of his experience, often painful, sometimes grievously so. Why not imbue children with them?

We know that the culture in which we live does inevitably in-doctrinate. The majority of people believe in monogamy, not be-cause they have reasoned out its moral basis, but because they have grown up in a society which accepts it. The same thing is true of their devotion to the church to which they belong, the political party with which they are affiliated, and many of their beliefs and prejudices. As we grow to manhood and womanhood, we should examine the rational bases for these beliefs and prejudices. We are not really mature until we do. But that is no reason that we should have no beliefs until we can examine them with some wisdom and maturity.

We know that the emotions furnish the drive to action. There is no activity from the merely intellectual. Where we want right con-duct we must induce devotion to right ideals. The ideals of democ-racy are the ideals best suited to man's nature. We may be certain that they are right. Then why not induce a strong attachment to them?

With small children this devotion will be uncritical. With adoles-cents, the bases for this devotion should be examined. They need to know why democracy is the best form of social organization for man. They must see it as an ideal toward which mankind has been struggling for thousands of years, an ideal to the further promotion of which they can dedicate their lives. Young people are hungry for ideals which are worth while. We do them a grave injustice when, because of their ignorance and our sloth, they have only the trivial to engage their attention.

Indoctrination does not necessarily imply dogmatism or authori-tarianism. It does give young people access to a living spring of faith which has promoted human progress.

Concerning the means for reaching these ideals, our method should be different. There the scientific method is appropriate. Harold Stassen and Norman Thomas are evidently equally sincere in their devotion to democratic ideals. One believes that these ideals can be realized through capitalism, the other through socialism. High-school boys and girls should know what each of these methods is, what the arguments pro and con are, and should be left to make up their own minds as they get older.

Our attitude toward propaganda will doubtlessly be determined by our attitude toward indoctrination. The word must first be defined; one writer says: "Propaganda is the expression of opinion or action by individuals or groups, deliberately designed to influence opinions and actions of other individuals or groups with reference to predetermined ends."[25]

Propaganda can be good or bad, used properly or improperly. That directed toward the promotion of the general welfare and not promulgated as the whole truth may be good; that directed toward accomplishing selfish ends, particularly those conflicting with the general welfare, and used as if it were truth, not opinion, is probably bad. The wisest plan is to teach people how to analyze propaganda, to see it for what it is, and to decide whether it is or is not disseminated for the public good. Such organizations as the Institute for Propaganda Analysis were doing an excellent work before the war. So long as radio, magazines, and press are open to propaganda from all sides, it should not be dangerous to people so educated. It is partial truth, or uncorrected misrepresentation, which is dangerous to our freedom.

WAR AND PEACE

7. The seventh problem is one of such importance that it dwarfs all that have been discussed. How can democracy exist and improve in a warring world? How can we avoid war and obtain peace? This has always been a problem of man. It is a particularly pointed question for us today. In the first place, it is difficult for democracy to function in a warring world. Men will give up their freedom, as has been pointed out, in order to increase their security. But, since the explosion of the first atomic bomb, the problem is more than that of keeping whatever democracy we may have attained. It has become that of man's survival. Scientists tell us that there is no protection against the atomic bomb. It seems to be a question of keeping the peace or of committing suicide.

25. Will French, "Propaganda," *Frontiers of Democracy*, IV (1938), 152.

The only way to do away with war is to look for the causes of war and then attempt to abolish those causes. It would seem extremely unlikely that the causes of war can ever be abolished without world government, a government based on justice for all and with the necessary power to enforce justice. This would mean the end of sovereign states and nationalism. For this extreme step mankind does not seem to be yet ready.

For many years rulers and thinkers alike have advocated a league or federation of nations. Such a league was not always proposed in order to promote peace and justice. The Great Design of Henry IV of France, who reigned from 1572 to 1610, an account of which is to be found in the *Memoires* of the Duc de Sully, proposed a federation of fifteen European countries, ostensibly to keep the peace of Europe, but perhaps to fight the Russians and the Saracens as well. William Penn was more sincere in his proposals for a European parliament (1693). So was the Abbé de Saint-Pierre with his three-volume work on the *Establishment of Eternal Peace* (1713). These men were a few among those who early saw that nations must learn to co-operate. In 1789, Jeremy Bentham, the English philosopher, published his essay on an *International Tribunal.* And in 1795 appeared Kant's essay on permanent peace, a clearly formulated and wise proposal for a league of nations which would eventuate in world government.

Said the Sage of Königsberg:

> According to reason there can be no other way for nations, in their mutual relationships, to escape from the lawless condition involving the constant menace of war, excepting by surrendering, just as individuals do, their wild freedom, accommodating themselves to public coercive laws and thus forming a society of nations (*civitas gentium*) which would constantly grow in size and finally include all the nations of the earth.[26]

The League of Nations, formed after the first World War, with its forebears the Concert of Europe and the Hague conferences, was a step forward, although it failed for several reasons to keep the peace, perhaps partly because it was not founded on principles of justice and perhaps, too, because the United States was not a member.

The United Nations is man's latest attempt to take steps toward that world organization so necessary for establishing peace. Imper-

26. Immanuel Kant, *Perpetual Peace*, p. 23.

fect as it is and, again, far short of the provisions which would make for justice in the world, it may be hoped that mankind will work toward its improvement.

But a league of nations does not go far enough. It should be but a step on the way to a world state. When Mortimer Adler wrote his book *How To Think about War and Peace,* he thought it would take five hundred years to bring about the kind of world state that would promote a peaceful society. He points out that a man matures slowly and that human society and human institutions mature even more slowly.[27] He thinks that we shall have to go through four stages: "(1) a plurality of independent sovereign states which may enter into alliances with another by treaty; (2) a confederacy or league of independent states which may or may not include all nations and which may or may not be supported by alliances; (3) a world community including all peoples under world government, federal in structure; and (4) a world state which consists of a world community under government that is not federal in structure."[28]

We are still in the second stage, perhaps looking forward in some degree to the third. The United Nations in its present form is still far from including all people in a government federal in structure. But it is probably as far as mankind is ready to go at the present time, and its structure is such that it could be modified more toward the third stage.

Mortimer Adler says that until we stop thinking in international terms and are ready to think in terms of world government we shall not have peace.[29] Emery Reves says the same thing in his book *The Anatomy of Peace:* "What is needed is—universalism. A creed and a movement clearly proclaiming that its purpose is to create peace by a legal order between men beyond and above the existing nation-state structure."[30]

Reves, however, is not willing to let such a movement evolve slowly. Adler sees it as the result of evolutionary steps. Reves wants it now, by conquest if necessary.[31] That, we might remind Mr. Reves, is what Hitler set out to do. We did not like it then.

27. Mortimer Adler, *How To Think about War and Peace,* p. 155.
28. *Ibid.,* pp. 141–42.   29. *Ibid.,* p. 158.
30. Emery Reves, *The Anatomy of Peace,* pp. 187–88.
31. *Ibid.,* p. 269.

Whether the invention of the atomic bomb will hasten the process of unification is impossible to say. People all over the world are frightened. But there are few signs that their fright is forcing their leaders to take steps that will lead away from war. It is easy to be pessimistic today over the possibility of an atomic-weapons race and an atomic war.

If the development of atomic energy should be put under real international control, we might thereby be taking one further step toward world government. There are some signs that this might be done.

One of the most important things that teachers could do would be to help prepare children for *world* citizenship. Anything is worth while that will help boys and girls to understand that men everywhere are more alike than different and that with economic and educational opportunities all are capable of self-government in the interests of all. Young people can learn that we cannot hope to keep either the "secret" of the release of atomic energy or the knowledge of how to make a bomb. They can begin to understand that it actually is "one world or none."

EDUCATION FOR DEMOCRACY

8. The eighth problem is really the subject of this entire book: How educate for democracy? If our efforts in this direction are successful, the child will become a competent, social-minded, human being, able to manage his own affairs with profit to himself and others. He will adopt for himself the task of working with other human beings to improve this world; he will live and help others to live the abundant life; he will regulate his conduct by those rules which make such a life possible; he will become increasingly a free, autonomous human being. This is the only kind of education suitable for any child in any place, because it is based on the needs and potentialities of human nature.

Education is literally our first line of defense. Men can make democracy work only as education makes them free men, that is, helps them to become intelligent, moral, human beings who understand that the general welfare must be our first common concern. The founding fathers of this nation understood this well. But it was forgotten by many in an era in which we were conquering a continent. To them education became an aid, as Charles Beard puts it, in assuring equality of opportunity for economic opportunity. "If America was to be regarded as 'the land of opportunity,' if opportunities were to be 'equal' then education must provide the 'equal start.'"[32] Thus arose the notion that public education was established for the individual, instead of its being a means primarily for promoting the general welfare.

It was taken for granted that our society would be maintained and improved "as the automatic outcomes of individual activities."[33] American ideals became materialistic; success meant economic prosperity. Chancellor Hutchins of the University of Chicago says that love of money, desire for freedom to make it, equality of opportunity to pursue it, are still the current ideals in the United States.[34] In the schools, as a result, we had an overemphasis on the individual, the "child-centered school," in which children, in common with their elders, obtained the grotesque notion that each individual's interest was paramount and more important than those of *all* the individuals, that is, more important than the common good.

For more than a decade now, teachers have been beginning again to see what some few never lost sight of, that democratic ideals need a revival, that our schools must become "society-centered," that democracy does not mean selfish individualism, and that without education aimed at these ideals, democracy will fail. Of this new orientation, Charles Beard says: "As organized education turns to the future, then it discards the theory of automatic democracy. It recognizes that rights to life, liberty, property, work, and the pursuit of happiness are shadows unless those who claim the rights are competent and have the moral power necessary to the creation and maintenance of the social arrangements in which rights may be realized."[35]

There were, of course, some teachers as well as a few educational leaders who never forgot that education was established to pro-

32. Charles Beard, *The Unique Function of Education in American Democracy*, p. 46.
33. *Ibid.*, p. 92.
34. R. M. Hutchins, *The Higher Learning in America*, p. 87.
35. Beard, *op. cit.*, p. 92.

mote the welfare of all, that upon no other basis could universal taxation for education be justly levied, and that education was not made free and universal in our country primarily to benefit merely either the child or his parent.

The judicial branch of our government is one social agency which has perhaps kept this more constantly in mind than has any other. Quoting legal opinion on the purpose of public education, H. H. Schroeder says:

> The public school system was not established merely for the sake of the child who would be the direct beneficiary of its services. Were education merely for the sake of the child or of the parent, the latter would have to foot the bill. Taxes are levied for public purposes. Incidentally, of course, the child derives a benefit, as does the parent. But it was not for that purpose that the public school system was established. It was brought into being in order to promote the general welfare. This is brought out clearly in numerous [court] opinions, as, for instance, in the following:
>
> . . . . The primary purpose of the maintenance of the common school system is the promotion of the general intelligence of the people constituting the body politic and thereby to increase the usefulness and efficiency of the citizens upon which the government of society depends. Free schooling furnished by the state is not so much a right granted to pupils as a duty imposed upon them for the public good. If they do not voluntarily attend the schools provided for them, they may be compelled to do so. While most people regard the public schools as the means of great personal advantage to the pupils, the fact is often overlooked that they are governmental means of protecting the state from the consequences of an ignorant and incompetent citizenship. . . . .
>
> If it is essentially a prerogative of sovereignty to raise troops in time of war, it is equally so to prepare each generation of youth to discharge the duties of citizenship in time of peace and war. Upon preparation of the younger generation for civic duties depends the perpetuity of this government.
>
> Education is one of the functions of government, and the public school system is a department of the government. Education insures domestic tranquillity, provides for the common defense, promotes the general welfare, and it secures the blessings of liberty to ourselves and our posterity.[36]

If education is to do this, it must be directed by socially minded teachers who thoroughly understand the foundations of democracy and the concept of human nature out of which democracy grows. Unfortunately, multitudes of teachers have in the past studied no

36. H. H. Schroeder, *The Public School as a State Institution*, pp. 23–25.

philosophy. Some few have a superficial acquaintance with the philosophy of John Dewey. Whatever the strengths of his philosophy, and there are many, his concept of education as growth with "no aim beyond itself"[37] has been interpreted by many of his followers, particularly those who call themselves Progressives, as encouraging extreme individualism. The Progressives themselves have recently abandoned this view and are now agreeing with many of their critics that education must not be just growth but growth toward that manhood and womanhood necessitated by democratic ideals.[38]

DEMOCRACY AND HUMAN PERSONALITY

Within the last ten to fifteen years much has been written on education for democracy. The conviction is growing that we could do a great deal more than we are doing now to bring up citizens who would preserve and promote democracy. We need to keep in mind in the midst of this discussion, however, that it is not democracy that is important as such, any more than it is the good life that is important in and of itself. Both democracy and the good life are means. Human personality is the end. Democracy is good because it is the only social organization in which human personality can achieve its best development. The good life is the one that is good to live because it results in the nearest possible approximation to human excellence. If we remember that it is superior human beings we are wanting, then it is all right to talk of educating for democracy. It is very important that we do keep this fact in mind, for, as Jacques Barzun says, democracy and good citizenship come "not from a course, but from a teacher; not from a curriculum, but from a human soul."[39]

SUMMARY

The application of philosophy to some of the problems facing us today, which must be solved if democracy is to function more successfully, would seem to point to the following conclusions:

37. John Dewey, *Democracy and Education*, p. 51.
38. See *Progressive Education*, XVIII (June, 1941), 3–9.
39. *The Teacher in America*, p. 9.

Individual liberty can be reconciled with social justice if (1) the individual will remember that he is free only when treating himself and others as ends; (2) the government—the servant of the people in a democracy—acts to promote the welfare of all. Extreme individualism is license, not freedom. Laissez faire results in the rule of the strong, not in freedom for all. Economic, as well as political, freedom must be "freedom within the law." We shall be freer if we restrict our freedom.

Man needs a measure of security. But the best kind of security comes from within a person in the feelings of adequacy, courage, and self-confidence. To demand that outside agencies furnish complete security is probably detrimental to man's best growth. It is, however, perfectly justifiable to plan through collective effort, be it through government or other social agencies, for those conditions which will reward intelligent effort.

In a democracy we need experts. But we do not want a permanent class of leaders and another of followers. All people affected by a policy should have a voice in determining it; experts, who are responsible to the people for carrying out their will, should administer the policy. Most persons can become expert in something. To the extent that he is an expert, a person can lead. We all need to defer to the judgment of those who know more in other fields than do we; to that extent we are all followers. It is also true that in any group of experts there are persons with a higher ability for leadership, whom the rest of the group will follow. This leadership should be utilized. While we wish to foster superiority in every field, any permanent group of leaders and another of followers would be undemocratic.

Men are all equal as ends; we are not equal biologically. We need to encourage and reward, not resent, excellence in every field so that superior human beings may develop their abilities and use them for the general good. Democracy does not mean leveling-down.

While we are not equal biologically, these differences are not "racial." Every division of mankind, racial or cultural, contains individuals of superior ability and those of lesser ability. There is no scientific evidence for the superiority of any race or people over other races or peoples. This wellnigh universal insistence upon the superiority of I and mine goes back to many factors, prominent among them the desire to compensate for feelings of insecurity and inadequacy.

PROBLEM V

Not all change is progress, but to progress, we must have change. Necessary changes are often fought by people who are happy and satisfied with the status quo. Teachers must build the attitude toward change which will judge of its effectiveness in terms of promoting the general welfare rather than of disturbing a vested interest.

PROBLEM VI

Adults should indoctrinate for the ideals of democracy but not for the methods of realizing those ideals, methods in regard to which equally intelligent and sincere people differ. Indoctrination may produce uncritical belief to begin with; it should never be left there. As young people develop, they should study the history and foundation for these ideals. They must learn *why*. We are not afraid of this study of democratic ideals, for we know that they will stand the test. Devotion to these ideals is necessary to obtain right conduct. Propaganda, too, can be used properly or improperly. People need to learn how to analyze propaganda; if all means of communication are free to all sides, little harm will result.

PROBLEM VII

We shall probably have wars until we have a world government based on justice. To work toward such an organization in this atomic age is even more imperative than it has ever been before.

PROBLEM VIII

Education for democracy aims at producing individuals who are imbued with their social responsibilities. The "child-centered" school has too often encouraged a selfish individualism. To educate for democracy our schools must become "society-centered." Schools were not established merely for the sake of the children who attend them but to promote the general welfare.

We need to remember that in educating for democracy, we are attempting to develop human excellence. Society and the individual are interdependent, and one should not be emphasized at the expense of the other. But social arrangements are good in so far as they encourage the development of the best human personalities in all of society's members. It is human personality which is the ultimate. Democracy is the means to that as the end.

QUESTIONS TO AID STUDY

1. What indictments did Plato bring against democracy? What do you think of his view? Have you ever felt the same? Under what circumstances?
2. Can you account for Plato's lack of faith in democracy?

3. Do you believe that individual liberty can be reconciled with the demands for social justice? If so, how? If not, why not?

4. In a democratic society, what is the meaning of the phrase, "the state"?

5. In what sense is a man obeying his own will when he obeys the law?

6. Do you think that we can achieve social justice within a framework of unrestrained capitalism? Why or why not?

7. What does the phrase an "economy of abundance" mean? Compare it with an "economy of scarcity."

8. How important is the desire for security to you?

9. What are the psychological roots of the feeling of security?

10. Why is too much security unfavorable for man's best development? Too little security? How can we obtain the security we need? How can we help children build the sense of security?

11. What is the role of the expert in democracy? Compare Demiashkevich's recommendations for preparing leaders with those of this text. What do you think of each proposal in terms of democratic principles?

12. In what sense are men equal, one to the other? Show how a misunderstanding of the nature of human equality leads to a leveling-down and to social disintegration.

13. What do scientists say about ideas concerning race superiority and inferiority? How account for apparent qualitative differences?

14. How do scientists account, at least in part, for the universal desire to feel superior to someone? What do you think of this explanation? Do you have any other?

15. Under what circumstances do human beings resist change? When do they welcome change? By what standard should the desirability of proposed changes be judged? What should be the teacher's attitude toward social change?

16. Should a democratic society use indoctrination and propaganda? Explain your position.

17. What is meant by saying that a school should be "society-centered"? How would this be done?

18. For what purpose was the public school established? What, then, should teachers aim to accomplish?

19. What qualities does it seem to you should be encouraged through the educative process?

20. Which is the ultimate, educating for democracy or educating for human excellence? Explain the connection between the two.

SUGGESTED REFERENCES

I. LIBERTY AND SOCIAL JUSTICE

BEARD, CHARLES. *The Unique Function of Education in American Democracy.* Washington, D. C.: Educational Policies Commission, National Education Association, 1937.
BROWNE, LEWIS. *Something Went Wrong.* New York: Macmillan Co., 1942.
COREY, LEWIS. *The Unfinished Task of Democracy.* New York: Viking Press, 1942.
COUNTS, GEORGE S. *Social Foundations of Education.* New York: Charles Scribner's Sons, 1934.
GALLOWAY, GEORGE B., and OTHERS. *Planning for America.* New York: Henry Holt & Co., 1941.
HART, ALBERT G. *How the National Income Is Divided.* Chicago: University of Chicago Press, 1937.
NATHAN, ROBERT. *Mobilizing for Abundance.* New York: McGraw-Hill Book Co., 1944.
ROUSSY DE SALES, RAOUL DE. *The Making of Tomorrow.* New York: Reynal & Hitchcock, 1942.

II. FREEDOM AND SECURITY

OVERSTREET, HARRY. *Our Free Minds* (New York: W. W. Norton & Co., 1941), chaps. v and xviii.
UNITED STATES NATIONAL RESOURCES PLANNING BOARD, COMMITTEE ON LONG RANGE WORK AND RELIEF POLICIES. *Security, Work and Relief.* Washington, D.C.: United States Government Printing Office, 1942.

III. LEADERSHIP

BOGARDUS, E. S. *Leaders and Leadership.* New York: D. Appleton–Century Co., 1934.
DEMIASHKEVICH, M. *An Introduction to Philosophy of Education* (New York: American Book Co., 1935), chap. ix.
EDUCATIONAL POLICIES COMMISSION. *Learning the Ways of Democracy* (Washington, D.C.: National Education Association, 1940), chap. i.
JONES, ARTHUR JULIUS. *The Education of Youth for Leadership.* New York: McGraw-Hill Book Co., 1938.

IV. EQUALITY; RACE PROBLEMS

BENEDICT, RUTH. *Race: Science and Politics.* New York: Modern Age Books, 1940.
BOAS, FRANZ. *Race and Democratic Society.* New York: I. J. Augustin, 1945.

188   *Philosophy of Education*

Chatto, C. I., and Hallegan, Alice L. *The Story of the Springfield Plan.* New York: Barnes & Noble, 1945.

Gifford, D. G. "Springfield Plan," *School Executive,* LXIV (January, 1945), 43–45.

Halligan, A. S. "A Community's Total War against Prejudice," *Journal of Educational Sociology,* XVI (February, 1943), 374–80.

Huxley, Julian S. *We Europeans: A Survey of Racial Problems.* New York: Harper & Bros., 1936.

Jennings, H. S., and Others. *Scientific Aspects of the Race Problem.* New York: Longmans, Green & Co., 1941.

Lewin, Kurt; Lippitt, R.; and White, R. K. "Patterns of Aggressive Behavior in Experimentally Created Climates," *Journal of Social Psychology,* X (1939), 271–300.

Overstreet, Harry. *Our Free Minds* (New York: W. W. Norton & Co., 1941), chap. xv.

Singer, Caroline (ed.). *Race: What the Scientists Say.* Camden, N.J.: Haddon Craftsmen, 1939.

Vickery, William E. *Intercultural Education in American Schools.* New York: Harper & Bros., 1943.

V. CHANGE

Boas, George. *Our New Ways of Thinking* (New York: Harper & Bros., 1930), pp. 3–24 and 35–37.

Dewey, John. *Experience and Nature* (Chicago: Open Court Pub. Co., 1925), pp. 47–50, 70–71, and 148-49.

Kilpatrick, William Heard. *Education for a Changing Civilization* (New York: Macmillan Co., 1926), chap. i.

MacIver, Robert M. *Society: Its Structure and Changes* (R. Long & R. R. Smith, 1931), pp. 389–423.

Ogburn, William F. "Change, Social," *Encyclopaedia of the Social Sciences,* II (1937), 330–34.

VI. INDOCTRINATION AND PROPAGANDA

Aries, Leonard P. *Let's Talk It Over.* Chicago: Willett, Clark & Co., 1941.

Briggs, Thomas H. "Should Education Indoctrinate?" *Educational Administration and Supervision,* XXII (1936), 561–94.

French, Will. "Propaganda," *Frontiers of Democracy,* IV (1938), 152.

Institute for Propaganda Analysis. *Group Leader's Guide to Propaganda Analysis.* New York: Institute for Propaganda Analysis, 1938.

Pittenger, Benjamin Floyd. *Indoctrination for American Democracy.* New York: Macmillan Co., 1941.

Ruediger, W. C. "Education, Indoctrination and Realities: A Reply to B. F. Pittenger," *School and Society,* LIV (December 20, 1940), 594–95.

VII. WAR AND PEACE

ADLER, MORTIMER, *How To Think about War and Peace* (New York: Simon & Schuster, 1944), chaps. i–iii, vi, xii, xvi, and xxi.

CARR, EDWARD HALLETT. *Conditions of Peace.* New York: Macmillan Co., 1942.

KANT, IMMANUEL. *Perpetual Peace:* Preface by NICHOLAS MURRAY BUTLER. New York: Columbia University Press, 1939 (any translation).

MASTER, DEXTER, and WAY, KATHARINE. *One World or None.* New York: Whittlesey House, McGraw-Hill Book Co., 1946.

REVES, EMERY. *The Anatomy of Peace* (New York: Harper & Bros., 1945), chaps. i and x–xv.

WILLKIE, WENDELL. *One World.* New York: Simon & Schuster, 1943.

VIII. EDUCATING FOR DEMOCRACY

ASSOCIATION FOR CHILDHOOD EDUCATION. *Toward Democratic Living at School.* Washington, D.C.: Association for Childhood Education, 1943.

BRIGGS, THOMAS H. "Educating for Democracy," *Teachers College Record,* XLIII (October, 1941), 4–5.

BRUBACHER, J. S. "Democratic Education: The Vices of Its Virtues," *Educational Trends,* IX (May, 1941), 10–16.

COUNTS, GEORGE S. *The Schools Can Teach Democracy.* New York: John Day Co., 1939.

DEWEY, JOHN. *Problems of Men* (New York: Philosophical Library, 1946), pp. 23–56.

EDUCATIONAL POLICIES COMMISSION. *Learning the Ways of Democracy.* Washington, D.C.: Educational Policies Commission, National Education Association, 1940 (read according to interest).

EDWARDS, NEWTON (ed.). *Education in a Democracy* ("Charles R. Walgreen Foundation Lectures.") Chicago: University of Chicago Press, 1941.

KILPATRICK, WILLIAM HEARD. *Group Education for Democracy.* New York: Association Press, 1940.

LEWIN, KURT. "Experiments on Autocratic and Democratic Atmospheres," *Social Frontier,* IV (July, 1938), 316–19.

LIPPITT, RONALD, and WHITE, R. K. "An Experimental Study of Authoritarian and Democratic Group Atmospheres," *Journal of Social Psychology,* X (May, 1939), 271–99.

MARITAIN, JACQUES. *Education at the Crossroads* (New Haven: Yale University Press, 1943), especially chap. i.

OVERSTREET, HARRY. *Our Free Minds* (New York: W. W. Norton & Co., 1941), chap. xiii.

REDDEN, JOHN D., and RYAN, FRANCIS. *A Catholic Philosophy of Education* (Milwaukee: Bruce Pub. Co., 1942), chap. xviii.

CHAPTER X
THE UNIVERSE AND MAN: THE SEARCH
FOR ULTIMATE REALITY

The meaning of the terms "ontology" and "metaphysics"—The problem of variety and unity; early ideas concerning the ultimate substance or substances—The problem of permanence and change: (1) Heraclitus; reality of change; (2) Parmenides; reality of permanence; change as illusion; (3) Attempts to reconcile Heracliteanism and Eleaticism (a) mechanism as explanation of change, (b) Logos as the principle back of change—Theories concerning the nature of ultimate reality: (1) Monistic materialism; naturalism; (2) Monistic metaphysical idealism (a) Plato's doctrine of ideas, (b) oriental metaphysical idealism, (c) Hegelian metaphysical idealism; (3) Pluralism; dualism—The nature of mind; its relation to the body: (1) Dualistic view of mind as spirit, body as matter; (2) Mind as epiphenomenon; body as the only reality; behaviorism; (3) Mind as the only reality; body as an incomplete expression of reality; (4) Identity theory of body and mind; Gestalt psychology; (5) Hylomorphism; matter and form; Thomistic interpretation—Metaphysical skepticism; Kant; Dewey—Religion and the problem of ultimate reality

---

SAID Aristotle, "All men by nature desire to know."[1] Because man is a rational creature not content to accept the world of appearances without attempting to understand it, he very early asked the question: Is there some one substance of which everything within the range of man's experience is a variation or transformation, or are there two such substances, or more? We are a part of a universe in which the infinite variety of individual constituents seems to have turned (*vertere*) into one (*unus*), to have combined into a whole. But were the individual components origi-

1. *Metaphysics* A. 980A.

190

nally one, or two, or more? What are they in their essence? What causes the changes into variety? How is man related to the universe? What is he in his essence? The division of philosophy which considers and attempts to solve these problems is known as "ontology," or, more commonly, as "metaphysics."

VARIETY AND UNITY

Thales is credited with having begun this inquiry in the Western world. He thought that water was the basic universal substance, "getting the notion, perhaps," wrote Aristotle, "from seeing that the nutriment of all things is moist."[2] The Greeks had a legend that everything originated from the ocean; we ourselves think that life may have begun there. Then, too, it is easy to see that water takes different forms: It vaporizes; it freezes. Altogether, it is not surprising that Thales came to the conclusion that water was the primary substance.

Thales' pupil, Anaximander, thought nothing so concrete and definite as water could be the ultimate source of all things but taught that everything had come from something he called the Boundless or the Infinite. Another ancient thinker, Anaximenes, believed that air was prior to water and so was "the most primary of the simple bodies."[3] Heraclitus of Ephesus said that fire was the source of all things, and Empedocles said this "of the four elements (adding a fourth—earth—to those which have been named); for these, said he, always remain and do not come to be, except that they come to be more or fewer, being aggregated into one and segregated out of one."[4]

These guesses may seem rather naïve to us, but as a matter of fact they indicate a remarkable step forward in human thought. Another step was taken when thinkers asked: What is this change which is to be seen in all the transformations in this basic stuff? Is change real? Is there anything that is permanent?

PERMANENCE AND CHANGE

The philosopher Heraclitus of Ephesus, spoken of in the foregoing, thought that nothing was permanent, that all things pass,

2. *Ibid.* 983B.   3. *Ibid.* 984A.   4. *Ibid.*

that eternal flux, like fire itself, was the constant state of the universe. "This universe," said he, "which is the same for all, no one, either God or man has made; but it always was, and is, and ever shall be an ever-living fire, fixed measures kindling and fixed measures dying out."[5] He taught that change is real; all is becoming. "One cannot step twice into the same river," said he.[6]

Heraclitus, who lived in that fabulous sixth century of Greece, has come down to us as "the Dark" philosopher. We have but fragments of his teachings through which seems to run a predominantly negative strain. Everybody else is all wrong; he alone has found the truth. His contemporaries seem to have found him conceited and contentious. Says Diogenes Laërtius, the gossipy relator of apocryphal tales of the ancient philosophers: "He [Heraclitus] would retire to the temple of Artemis and play at knuckle-bones with the boys; and when the Ephesians stood around and looked on, he would say, 'Why, you rascals, are you astonished? Is it not better to do this than to take part in your civil life?' "[7]

All of which, if true, probably did not add to his popularity. But in his writings he seems to be criticizing constantly the prevalent beliefs and common opinions of his contemporaries; and probably his contemporaries found his teachings contrary to all that they held to be true and right.

At about this time, there also "flourished," Parmenides, a native of Elea, who, tradition says, was an impressive figure, with many disciples, profound, wise, and some people have thought, unintelligible. It is difficult for us to be sure about his teachings, for but one of his works, a poem, is extant. He seems to have thought that Heraclitus was teaching nonsense, for he developed the idea of Being in opposition to the Heraclitean Becoming. He thought that there was such a thing as permanence and that the way to discover it was not through the senses but through thought. Seen things are temporal; unseen things, eternal and real. "Thus is becoming ex-

5. Charles Bakewell, *Source Book in Ancient Philosophy*, p. 30.

6. *Ibid.*, p. 23.

7. Diogenes Laërtius *The Lives of the Philosophers* ii, p. 409.

tinguished and passing away not to be heard of."[8] A thing to be real must be thinkable. Following is a part of his famous poem:

Listen, and I will instruct thee, and thou when thou hearest shall ponder,
What are the sole two paths of research that are open to thinking:
One path is: that Being doth be, and Non-being is not;
This is the way of Conviction, for Truth follows hard in her footsteps.
The other path is: That Being is not, and Non-being must be;
This one, I tell thee in truth, is an all-incredible pathway
For thou never canst know what is not (for none can conceive it)
Nor cans't thou give it expression for one thing are Thinking and Being.[9]

Therefore, taught Parmenides, thought and some unchangeable, permanent being are identical. The appearance of change is merely an illusion. The differences between Heraclitus and Parmenides have echoed down through the centuries. How often one hears the remark, "This is a changing world!" People who today emphasize the reality of this change and believe that through it emerges the new are called neo-Heracliteans. They, like Heraclitus of old, deny the possibility of absolute truth. On the other hand, those who see permanence in reality are called Eleatics, from Elea, the name of the city where Parmenides and his followers lived. "The more things change, the more they remain the same" is a modern proverb, expressing an ancient view.

The most remarkable guess as to the nature of ultimate reality was made by Leucippus, of whom we know almost nothing, and developed by his pupil, Democritus, one of the best-known and greatest figures in philosophy. Not only did these men try to reconcile the differences between the Heracliteans and the Eleatics, but they formulated the atomic theory and the mechanistic principles of operation concerning the universe. Of this, Fuller says: "Whatever we may think of this theory as a final description of the nature and behavior of Reality, it has been, in the shape in which Democritus advanced it, the basis of all our scientific advance up to the present day. Even now, when science is becoming skeptical of its applicability to the more profound aspects of the physical world, it is still the only theory with which applied science can fruitfully work."[10]

8. John Burnet, *Early Greek Philosophy*, p. 186.
9. Bakewell, *op. cit.*, p. 13.
10. B. A. G. Fuller, *History of Philosophy*, p. 37.

The world stuff, taught Democritus, is nothing but atoms of indeterminate matter, indivisible and infinite in number. It is their nature to move perpetually. The world is matter in motion. Earlier thinkers had necessarily attempted to account for the changes in basic substance whereby variety was produced. As Aristotle said later: "However true it may be that all generation and destruction proceed from some one or (for that matter) from more elements, why does this happen and, what is the cause? For at least the substratum itself does not make itself change; e.g., neither the wood nor the bronze causes the change of either of them, nor does the wood manufacture a bed and the bronze a statue; but something else is the cause of the change."[11]

Aristotle was unimpressed by the mechanistic theory of Democritus. "The question of movement," said he, "these thinkers, like the others, lazily neglected."[12] Aristotle was not quite just to the earlier thinkers. Many of their explanations seem incredibly childish, but there was one, made by Heraclitus himself, the doctrine of the Logos, which competes today with the implications of mechanism. Logos is a term referring to a cosmic reason which gives order and intelligibility to the world. It was this principle, so Heraclitus taught, which caused the constant "becoming" apparent to man's senses. This conception later gave rise to the idea of the "natural law" of the Stoics. With a slightly different meaning, the same term, translated as Word, may be found in the first chapter of St. John's Gospel in the Bible.

Democritus rejected cosmic reason, design, or purpose in the universe. He also rejected chance; according to him the word "chance" merely expresses man's ignorance of the real cause of phenomena. Everything has a cause, and all of nature, including man himself, is explicable in terms of matter in motion.

MONISTIC MATERIALISM

Early Greek cosmology thus gave birth to monistic materialism, one answer to the problems of metaphysics. There seem to be only a few possible answers. All of metaphysics is really concerned with working over and examining the implications of a few recurring theses. Monism designates one of these theses, materialism another.

11. Aristotle *op. cit.* 984A.	12. *Ibid.* 985B.

Sometimes the two are combined. Monism is the theory that there is one fundamental substance. Monistic materialism says that this one substance is matter, something extended in space; that nothing supernatural exists, that there is no purpose in the universe, no world beyond the sensible world, that man himself is of exactly the same stuff that is to be found in sticks and stones, in stars and planets, in animals and plants. Epicurus (341–270 B.C.), the founder of Epicureanism, taught this doctrine; and the famous poem of his follower, the Roman poet, Lucretius (96–53 B.C.), *De rerum natura*, is the most beautiful exposition in literature of this point of view.

That matter in motion is the whole of all that exists is doubtful. But it has been an extremely fertile idea for the development of science. Descartes (1596–1650), known as the "father of modern philosophy," is said to have exclaimed, "Give me matter and give me motion and I will make a universe." Descartes, however, was not a materialist. He believed that man's mind was a thinking substance, not an extended substance, and that God was the first cause of all motion in the physical world. Hobbes (1588–1679), the English philosopher, is known as the "father of modern materialism and of positivism," a doctrine that usually accompanies materialism. He taught that our percepts were merely the result of matter in motion and that the only subject there is for study is bodies and their movements. George Santayana (1863——), the author of *The Last Puritan, Persons and Places,* and the recent *The Middle Span,* as well as numerous philosophical books, is a philosopher of today who calls himself a materialist.

NATURALISM

There have been few philosophers who were thoroughgoing materialists. It seems impossible to understand the totality of the universe and of man in terms of matter alone. Even physics today has abandoned, for theoretical purposes at least, the notion of matter in motion as adequate for all its field. There have, however, been many philosophers who have been naturalistic. Materialism is a kind of naturalism, but not all naturalism is materialism. Naturalism has many varieties; it is a point of view, not a fixed doctrine. According to this point of view, there is in this universe an order and a natural law which, as man discovers it, renders the universe intelligible. This order is identified *with* or *as* nature itself; there is no need to go outside nature to discover its laws and its meaning, according to this conception.

Greek materialism, like all materialism, is one variety of naturalism. Its basic theory was that all nature was matter in motion. The basic theory in naturalism is that whatever is in nature will explain the universe; many naturalistic philosophers have insisted, however, that nature cannot be understood in terms of appearances only. Many scholars interpret Aristotle as naturalistic. All would agree that Spinoza was naturalistic. He taught that God was immanent in nature itself. What nature is, how it is to be understood, is a problem on which thinkers have differed and still disagree. When the great American essayist, Ralph Waldo Emerson, said that there is nothing alien between matter and spirit because they are both from nature, he was thoroughly naturalistic but not materialistic. "Because man is a part of nature, because nature partakes of Deity, there is an unbreakable bond between these elements," wrote the Sage of Concord.

METAPHYSICAL IDEALISM

Greek philosophy was predominantly naturalistic. Many scholars find in Plato, however, the seeds for a philosophy which has sometimes, but not always, been interpreted as naturalistic but which has always been opposed to materialism. It is known in philosophy as "spiritualism" or "metaphysical idealism." As used in philosophy, the word spiritualism is not applied to the belief that spirits may communicate with human beings, a belief that is more properly designated as "spiritism." Spiritualism is the doctrine which holds that the ultimate reality in the universe is spirit, that which is immaterial in its nature. According to this view, the physical universe is an incomplete expression of reality, existing but to subserve the spiritual and requiring a spiritual universe for its foundation and explanation.

In recent years, the term metaphysical idealism has been used by a majority of writers. The word "idealism" has many shades of meaning and is used to denote varying beliefs in all divisions of philosophy. But running through all its uses is the view emphasizing spirit, mind, ideas, or that which is of consequence to the spirit or

mind. Since the term idealism has well established uses and meanings for other divisions in philosophy than metaphysics, it is well to
indicate by an adjective the division in which it is being used. In
metaphysics, the word would be less easily confused with other
meanings of idealism, were it "idea ism." That expresses the meaning much better, but the *l* was inserted by the Romans, we are told,
for euphony.

Spiritualism, or metaphysical idealism (ideaism), stands for another great thesis running through that branch of philosophy known
as "ontology" or "metaphysics." There are many varieties of metaphysical idealism, but they all agree in identifying reality with
mind, spirit, personality, soul, ideas, or something which is not extended in space but is immaterial in nature.

Although not all idealists are Platonic idealists, Plato is regarded
as the "father of idealism" in the Western world. He was said to
have been born on May 21, 427 B.C., of a wealthy and prominent
family. Having been named Aristocles and nicknamed Plato—the
broad—by his physical trainer, but whether because of his shoulders
or his brow we are not told,[13] he has inevitably had many legends
grow about him, as about all the great. He was reputed to have
been the son of Apollo; however, the ancient world often ascribed
divine parentage to its great men. Tradition says that when Plato
was twenty, he met Socrates, who the night before had dreamed that
a swan had appeared to him, rested on his knee, then, singing a
beautiful song, had flown away. It is said that when Plato was introduced to him, Socrates recognized at once the portent of the
dream.[14] Certainly Plato sang so beautifully of Socrates that the
whole world knows and loves them both.

In Plato's philosophy there are many strains and tendencies,
some of them seemingly in opposition. Perhaps something of every
great thesis in philosophy is to be found in his writings. His mind
was undoubtedly one of the greatest in human history and, as such,
extraordinarily fertile. But as the progenitor of idealism his theory
of ideas or forms is the important one. It is very difficult to find this
theory consistently worked out in his own writings. In the dialogues,
he often refers to ideas, but it is in Aristotle's *Metaphysics* that his
supposed views on the forms are presented most systematically.

13. Frederick J. E. Woodbridge, *Son of Apollo*, p. 5.   14. *Ibid.*, p. 10.

Some scholars think that Plato's greatest pupil may have failed to get all the implications of his teacher's thought. Since Aristotle studied with Plato for many years, this seems strange. But if we remember how different the two men were, perhaps we can understand how this could be. And Aristotle is not the first pupil, or the last, to misunderstand his teacher.

The word "idea" comes from the Greek and originally meant shape, form, or image; later it came to mean a prototype as a real entity, creative thought, or notion, a concept. Several of the older Greek philosophers, Heraclitus, for instance, as well as Parmenides, had assumed that there could not be a concept unless there was a corresponding basis in objective reality. That which is common to all members of a class of objects is the "idea," or concept. Aristotle said that Plato believed that, in addition to this, there is a real entity, independent of our intellectual processes, noncorporeal and unconditioned by time or place, yet really existing. These "ideas" are separate from sense objects, they exist in a supersensuous sphere; the objects that we know in this world are nothing but phenomena, imitations, shadow pictures, as it were, of these "ideas" or "forms." The ideas or forms were perfect beings which were eternal—patterns for everything in this changing world of the senses.

In coming to these conclusions, Plato is said to have been influenced by several factors. His first teacher had been Cratylus, a disciple of Heraclitus. The problem of permanence and change was thus one of his concerns, and he undoubtedly saw the force of Heraclitus' arguments. But he also was acquainted with the Eleatic school. In addition, the Pythagoreans and their mathematical speculations evidently appealed strongly to him. The Pythagoreans had some strange doctrines about the relation of numbers to the universe and to its understanding. According to Aristotle:

.... in numbers they [the Pythagoreans] seemed to see many resemblances to the things that exist and come into being—more than in fire and earth and water .... since, again, they saw that the modifications and the ratios of the musical scales were expressible in numbers;—since, then, all other things seemed in their whole nature to be modelled on numbers, and numbers seemed to be the first things in the whole of nature, they supposed the elements of number to be the elements of all things and the whole heaven to be a musical scale and a number.[15]

15. Aristotle *op. cit.* 985B

In mathematics and its axioms Plato found the foundation he needed for permanence in the midst of constant flux. Geometry is based on *ideal* figures; lines, circles, triangles, spheres. Their properties remain the same forever; changes in the material world do not affect them. So he came to believe that there are universal, eternal types for all the fleeting things of sense-perception.

Metaphysical idealism was actually old when Plato lived. In all men there seems to develop early in their thinking the belief that another world than that shown us by our senses must exist. Parmenides reflected that conviction when he insisted that man could not find reality through the senses but only through reason. Some Neo-Platonists have thought that this teaching made Parmenides the father of metaphysical idealism, but other scholars claim that "Parmenides believed in none but a sensible reality, which does not mean with him a reality actually perceived by our senses, but one which might be perceived, if the senses were more perfect than they are."[16] The early Greeks seem to have been incorrigibly naturalistic and, some scholars think, materialistic though not always monistic.

But in India, Brahmanism, already old in Plato's day, taught that reality is an impersonal world soul, pervading and upholding the material universe, to attain union with which is man's chief aim. Lao-tze, in China, found and incorporated in Taoism much the same belief.

From these early days to modern times metaphysical idealism has been, and is, a potent force. The greatest modern philosopher of this school was Hegel (1770–1831), the exponent of objective or absolute idealism. The crux of his philosophy is that the universe is one absolute spirit or idea which expresses itself in the material world through a process of evolution in which apparent opposites become synthesized into unified wholes which approach closer and closer to the ideal or the absolute. Nature is the self-objectification of the absolute, or universal, reason. By the absolute, Hegel meant everything there is: nature, including man. It is a great process striving to know itself. Finding a larger context in which apparent opposites can be understood is the Hegelian method, implying, of course, that everything is somehow related to everything else and

16. Burnet, *op. cit.*, p. 189.

that understanding anything completely will lead one inevitably to understand everything. Tennyson's poem expresses this idea:

> Flower in the crannied wall,
> I pluck you out of the crannies,
> I hold you here, root and all, in my hand,
> Little flower—but if I could understand
> What you are, root and all, and all in all,
> I should know what God and man is.

PLURALISM

It must not be supposed that all philosophical systems are monistic materialism or idealism or some variation thereof. Varieties of pluralism have been recurrent philosophical theses also. Pluralism holds that there is more than one fundamental substance. The earth, air, fire, and water as the ultimates of Empedocles was a pluralistic conception of reality. The commonest form of pluralism is dualism, that is, the belief that there are two ultimate substances from which everything has come. The two substances held as ultimate by most dualists are matter and spirit, or mind. Instead of attempting to explain all spirit in terms of matter, as do the materialists, or all matter in terms of spirit, as do the idealists, dualists insist that matter and spirit are two different substances and that neither can be reduced to the other.

The ancient world had its dualistic conceptions of reality. The Persian teacher, Zoroaster, or Zarathustra, taught that the warfare between the forces of good and evil, light and dark, is the basic principle upon which the universe is built. In China, yang and yin furnished the active male cosmic principle or force and the passive female force, which are objectified in man and woman, sunshine and rain, hardness and softness, large and small, good and evil, and in other such opposites. There are dualistic strains in Plato's conception of the material and immaterial, the sensible and the intelligible, factors of existence.

The most important and thoroughgoing dualism of modern times is that of René Descartes (1596–1650), the French mathematician and philosopher. Living at a time when science was achieving great success in understanding the world through applying the principles underlying a mechanistic conception of the universe, Descartes interpreted philosophy in mechanistic terms. The universe, thought he, is a great mechanism distinct from, but operated by, God. Matter is extended substance; spirit or mind is thinking substance; the two are completely distinct from each other.

THE NATURE OF MIND; ITS RELATION TO THE BODY

Man himself, taught Descartes, is a dualistic creature, composed of a body that is matter and a mind that is spirit, two widely different substances. Such a theory poses the seemingly unanswerable question: How can two substances, completely different, one from the other, affect each other?

And yet it is certain that they do. Man's mind does affect his body, as anyone who has had indigestion because of worry knows. Man's body does affect his mind, as anyone who has taken ether knows. But how? Descartes said by interaction, perhaps through the pineal gland. But the pineal gland has a very definite physiological function of which Descartes was ignorant. Aside from that fact, how could two completely different substances, an extended and an unextended substance, affect one another? To say that they somehow interact does not render such action intelligible. In fact, Descartes's philosophy exaggerated the ubiquitous mind-body problem, a problem still unsolved and one of the chief causes of differences among modern schools of psychology.

Psychology was, until well past the halfway mark of the previous century, a part of philosophy. The nature of man and of his conscious life was investigated by means of philosophical thought. During the 1870's the first laboratories for scientific investigation into these problems were established, and psychology started on its way toward becoming a science. But philosophical problems sat on the laboratory doorsteps. "What is man, as a unity, in the totality of his nature?" eludes a scientific answer. As with most of our fundamental problems, science and philosophy are both needed for an adequate reply. Philosophical dualism did not seem, however, to be of much assistance.

Dualists proposed not only the interaction theory in the attempt to explain the way in which the body and mind affected one another but a theory known as "psychophysical parallelism," which claimed that for every change in bodily or physical processes, there is a

concomitant change in mental or psychic processes but that between these changes there is no causal link. This again was a theory
which posed more questions than it answered.

Some psychologists in the early part of this century settled the
difficulty to their own satisfaction by returning to the old materialistic conception of Democritus. They undertook again to explain the
psychic in terms of the physical. They said that the terms "mind,"
"soul," "consciousness," "purpose," were superfluous and constituted
reifications. All the phenomena of thought could be explained by
the body alone. According to this theory, Cabanis (1757–1808)
would have been right when he said: "Thought is a secretion of the
brain."

This group of psychologists called themselves behaviorists, for
their purpose was to study man's behavior, not some consciousness
or mind impossible to see and check upon. Behaviorism is monistic
materialism in modern dress. In the extreme form taught by its
founder, John Watson, it seems to have been deposed in the psychological world, chiefly because its mechanism made it impossible
to explain the spiritual and cultural values of life, as well as much
of man's intellectual life. With the new interpretation of matter as
an expression of energy, the old mechanism of Democritus and
Hobbes is untenable. However well it may have worked as a tool in
scientific research, mechanism has never been able to provide for
an adequate understanding of man.

There are two other theories concerning the nature of man's mind
which should be mentioned here. They are the identity theory of
Spinoza, a theory seemingly held also by Kant, and the theory of
hylomorphism, which originated, so far as we know, in the fertile
mind of Aristotle and was developed by the great medieval philosopher and Scholastic, Thomas Aquinas, who interpreted Aristo-
telianism in terms of Christian theology.

According to the identity theory, mind and body are two aspects
of some one underlying substance, the exact nature of which, at
least so far as Kant was concerned, we do not and may never know.

Spinoza believed God and nature to be one and that man is part
of this nature. His body is consubstantial with what Spinoza called
the infinite attribute of extension or matter, and his mind is consubstantial with the infinite attribute of thought which is the mind of

nature or God.[17] By "attribute" Spinoza meant that which is indispensable to a substance. He believed that there was but one substance, God or Nature. Spinoza wrote: "You see therefore, how and
why I think that the human body is a part of Nature. As regards the
human mind, I believe that it also is a part of Nature."[18]

Spinoza's metaphysics is a classic example of a naturalistic,
monistic, philosophy which was emphatically not materialistic.

In discussing the relation of body and mind, Kant wrote: "What
in one relation is entitled corporeal would in another relation be at
the same time a thinking being, ... that is, the very same being
which, as outer appearance, is extended, is (in itself) internally a
subject and is not composite, but is simple and thinks."[19]

And, again: "Neither the transcendental object which underlies
outer appearances nor that which underlies inner intuition is in
itself either matter or a thinking thing, but a ground (to us unknown) of the appearances which supply to us the empirical concept of the former as well as of the latter mode of existence."[20]

Some students of the problem think that in the new physics may
be found a clue to such a relation between matter and spirit. Writes
James Gurnhill:

Matter is no longer to be thought of as very minute particles of solid
substance, but as a form of physical energy.[21]
There is no radical antagonism between matter and spirit. Both are
forms of energy proceeding from the same source, the one physical, the
other spiritual. Both are necessary as contributory and cooperating factors
in carrying on the work of Creative Evolution though each has its function
and sphere of operation.[22]
The materialist must give up his idea that matter will suffice to account
for all the forms of energy, all the phenomena and noumena of which we
are conscious in our varied and complicated environment both physical

17. Joseph Ratner, Introduction to The Philosophy of Spinoza, p. xliv.

18. Baruch de Spinoza, Nature and Origin of the Human Mind (ed. Joseph
Ratner), p. 164.

19. Immanuel Kant, Critique of Pure Reason (trans. Norman Kemp Smith),
p. 340.

20. Ibid., p. 352.

21. James Gurnhill, Christian Philosophy, pp. 46–47.

22. Ibid., pp. 43–44.

and metaphysical. And the spiritualist must cease to regard matter as a principle in nature obstructive and repressive to the upward tendency and aspiration of spiritual life.[23]

Modern hylomorphism rests on Aristotle's teachings concerning the nature of ultimate reality. Aristotle was equally dissatisfied with Democritus and the other early materialists and with Plato's theory of ideas as the ultimate reality. He believed that everything in our universe is a union of two ultimate principles: matter, the substance of which it is made, and form, that which determines the kind of being which it is. The form is not something external to the matter; matter always possesses form as an integral part. According to Plato, ideas or forms were entities or realities outside of or separate from matter itself. Aristotle believed that forms are in matter—the formal, efficient, and final cause for matter becoming whatever it does become. Matter, pure potentiality, becomes actualized through the form which is its essence. The acorn becomes the oak because there is a determining factor within the acorn which causes the actualization of a potentiality.

So with man. He, too, is matter and form, body and soul:

We must describe it [the soul] as the first grade of actuality of a natural organized body. That is why we can wholly dismiss as unnecessary the question whether the soul and the body are one: it is as meaningless to ask whether the wax and the shape given to it by the stamp are one, or generally the matter of a thing and that of which it is the matter.....
Suppose that the eye were an animal—Sight would have been its soul, for sight is the substance or essence of the eye which corresponds to the formula (i.e. which states what it is to be an eye), the eye being merely the matter of seeing: when seeing is removed the eye is no longer an eye, except in name—it is no more a real eye than the eye of a statue or of a painted figure.[24]

This sounds naturalistic and is so interpreted by many philosophers and psychologists. It seems in harmony with modern biology and psychology, which is no longer mechanistic but organismic, not materialistic but naturalistic. It could be reconciled with the identity theory of mind and body. It is definitely not dualistic in the Cartesian sense.

23. *Ibid.*, p. 44.
24. Aristotle *De anima* ii. 412B.

Thomas Aquinas interpreted Aristotle's philosophy in terms of Christian doctrine, an interpretation accepted by the Catholic church today. According to this view:

Man is not merely a spirit or intelligence; nor simply an organism, but one substance composed of two principles. He is body and mind united in one complete substance.[25]

Man is a composite substance, neither body nor soul separately, but one substance resulting from intimate union of both. . . . . This view is monistic in admitting a unity of substance; dualistic in admitting two principles necessary to constitute this substance.[26]

Soul is the substantial form of the organism.[27]

The most widely and generally accepted psychology at the present time is known as Gestalt psychology. It takes its departure from the belief, arrived at after much experimentation with human perception, that conscious life is patterned into wholes from which parts derive their distinctive character. Configuration seems to be the best translation for the word *Gestalt*—a word which has come to mean that an awareness of form or pattern seems to be imposed on sense-experience by man's nature. This much of Gestalt psychology is certainly Kantian.[28]

Gestalt psychologists reject materialism because it makes matter more important than mind and because it seems impossible to explain such phenomena of the intellectual life as organization, abstraction, meaning, and significance in terms of the merely material. Gestaltism is more than a psychology; it is a concept used in physics and in physiology as well as in studying mental phenomena. It may become an entire philosophy. Beyond insisting that the older psychologies, including dualistic as well as materialistic, were inadequate for a complete understanding of man and that Gestalt psychology is thoroughly naturalistic, Gestalt psychologists seem to have little disposition to discuss the nature of mind. They would probably agree with a recent writer who says: "That which is termed 'mental' is really a derivative or special manifestation of the physical and not a distinct order of existence."[29]

25. George Albert Dubray, *Introductory Philosophy*, p. 489.

26. *Ibid.*, p. 483.

27. *Ibid.*, p. 501.   28. See chap. xi.

29. G. W. Hartmann, *Educational Psychology*, p. 45.

This is not particularly helpful, unless one understands just what the physical is. The newer physics has broken down the old distinction between matter and energy as two phases of the physical. Authorities in this field write: "According to the theory of relativity, there is no essential distinction between mass and energy."[30]

But to say that mind, like body, is an energy system and that energy is, in the last analysis, positive and negative particles of electricity may be useful in breaking down the traditional dualism between mind and body, but it does not explain what either life or mind is. To give a phenomenon a name is not to explain it.

There have been philosophers who have insisted that man can never know what ultimate reality is, no matter how far he probes. Such a position is often called "metaphysical skepticism." The writings of Immanuel Kant illustrate that view. Because our knowledge cannot transcend our experience and because that is exactly what metaphysics attempts to do, there are many questions which we cannot hope to answer with the certainty with which we can demonstrate a theorem in geometry. In writing of metaphysics, Kant says:

> For we are brought to the conclusion that we can never transcend the limits of possible experience, though that is precisely what this science is concerned above all else, to achieve. This situation yields, however, just the very experiment by which, indirectly, we are enabled to prove the truth of this first estimate of our *a priori* knowledge of reason, namely that such knowledge has to do only with appearances, and must leave the thing-in-itself as indeed real *per se*, but as not known by us.[31]

Perhaps it is only through religion and a reliance on faith that we can achieve any certainty as to the nature of ultimate reality. Kant himself said: "For although we have to surrender the language of knowledge, we still have sufficient ground to employ, in the presence of most exacting reason, the quite legitimate language of a firm faith."[32]

It seems certain that man will not drop the attempt to speculate

30. Albert Einstein and Leopold Infeld, *The Evolution of Physics*, p. 208.

31. Kant, *op. cit.*, p. 24. See chap. xi for the meaning of the "thing-in-itself" as contrasted with "appearances."

32. *Ibid.*, p. 597.

about metaphysical problems. Though he may be convinced that he can never, through the use of his reason, discover the nature of ulti-mate reality; though he may be certain that he will never be able to solve the mystery of his own being, of life itself, of mind and all its activities, still he comes back again and again to try once more.

Thales pointed out the fact that the most difficult thing for man to do was to know himself. So far as discovering his ultimate na-ture, to know himself seems impossible. Kant expressed the futility of such a quest when he pointed out that, to take cognizance of the inner self or mind, one has to use this inner self or mind.[33] How can the same thing be both the subject and the object of thought? It is like trying to lift one's self by one's bootstraps.

The fact that we are not able to prove through reason all that we would like to prove does not mean that the only things which exist are those which we can apprehend through sense-experience. The further that science investigates into this universe of ours, the more certain we become that there are "more things in heaven and earth than have been dreamt of" in any positivistic philosophy.

It would seem that Kant was right when he wrote:

Whenever I hear that a writer of real ability has demonstrated away the freedom of the human will, the hope of a future life, and the existence of God, I am eager to read the book, for I expect him by his talents to in-crease my insight into these matters. Already, before having opened it I am perfectly certain that he has not justified any one of his specific claims; not because I believe that I am in possession of conclusive proofs of these important propositions, but because the transcendental critique, which has disclosed to me all the resources of our pure reason, has completely convinced me that, as reason is incompetent to arrive at affirmative asser-tions in this field, it is equally unable, indeed even less able to establish any negative conclusion in regard to these questions.[34]

Even though ultimate reality may forever escape man's attempts to penetrate its mysteries, there are plenty of problems which he may hope to solve. It is easy to agree with Kant's statement: "Thus even after reason has failed in all its ambitious attempts to pass be-yond the limits of all experience, there is still enough left to satisfy us, so far as our practical standpoint is concerned."[35] To turn our

33. *Ibid.*, p. 167.
34. *Ibid.*, p. 602.   35. *Ibid.*, p. 650.

reason to "fruitful, practical employment"[36] is good advice, whether we always follow it or not.

This is the counsel which John Dewey also gives. He has paid less attention to the field of metaphysics than to epistemology—the branch of philosophy dealing with problems of knowledge—and to social problems. Dewey is naturalistic; he finds no division between nature and life and mind. He says that if there is any wonder or mystery, it lies in the fact that there is a nature and with it, existential events. But it is not wonderful that man should be a thinking, knowing, creature. "The world is subject matter for knowledge," says he, "because mind has developed *in* that world; a body-mind whose structures have developed according to the structures of the world in which it exists will naturally find some of its structures to be concordant and congenial with nature, and some phases of nature with itself."[37]

In discussing the mind and its relation to the body, Dewey insists that the mind is not an entity; he prefers to use adjectives and adverbs rather than a noun in speaking of mental life: The mind is what it does, an instrument for man's adjustment to and in his environment. Mind emerges in social interaction; it is not something with which man is born. In his preoccupation with change, Dewey is neo-Heraclitean, but for Dewey there is no Logos back of the change, bringing law and order, a cosmic harmony. He notes that Aristotle comes nearer our conception of change than most of the philosophers who followed him, for Aristotle recognized contingency in the world. "But," says Dewey, "he never surrendered his bias in favor of the fixed, certain, and finished. His whole theory of forms and ends is a theory of the superiority in Being of rounded out fixities."[38] For Dewey, change is welcome because it is the necessary condition for making this world a better place. He, like Kant, would have man turn his attention to improving his social life.

Like Kant, Dewey insists that we cannot know reality; all we can know are the constant relationships with which science is concerned. Science, says he, is never certain of essences or qualities but

36. *Ibid.*, p. 377.

37. John Dewey, *Experience and Nature*, p. 276.

38. *Ibid.*, p. 48.

only of relationships.[39] This is, of course, the central teaching of the relativity theory.[40]

That man seems unable to solve the problem of ultimate reality but that he seems driven to continue the search and that each one of us inevitably adopts some theory concerning it is an impressive fact. We might not all agree with the conclusions of Dostoevski, but we can all understand the mood which prompted him to write: "Much on earth is hidden from us, but to make up for that, we have been given a precious mystic sense of our living bond with the other world, with the higher heavenly world, and the roots of our thoughts and feelings are not here but in other worlds. That is why, the philosophers say, that we cannot apprehend the reality of things on earth."[41]

SUMMARY

In all probability man will be unable to solve the problem of the nature of ultimate reality by means of either science or philosophy. There have been thinkers who thought it most likely that matter, whatever that may be, is the only reality and that all which we call "spiritual" can be explained in material terms. Other thinkers have believed that spirit is the ultimate reality, that matter is an incomplete expression of reality, needing spirit for its explanation and support. Still other students of the problem have held that there is more than one ultimate substance; the commonest variety of this view holds that there are two ultimate substances, matter and spirit; that neither is reducible to the other but that each is irreducible and independent in its existence.

It is likewise difficult to understand the changes which we see about us. Is there some underlying reality which merely takes different forms? If so, what is the underlying reality, and what causes the changes in form? Can change be explained in mechanistic terms, or must we postulate some directing cosmic reason back of these changes? Or is there some creative force at work in the universe? How real are the changes? Does change merely mean the old in new garb, or does it mean actual novelty? Each of these theories is held by careful students, and no one can say with certainty who is right.

Likewise, when we apply the theories concerning ultimate reality to man in an attempt to understand his ultimate nature, particularly the relation of his mind to his body, we find disagreement among thinkers.

39. Dewey, *Quest for Certainty*, p. 290.

40. Sir Arthur Eddington, *The Philosophy of Physical Science*, p. 31.

41. Dostoevski, *The Brothers Karamazov*, Part II, Book VI, chap. iii.

Some would say that he is really just a body; others would say that his mind is the reality; still others believe him to be both body and mind, each an ultimate substance. Two attempts to synthesize the disagreements between monists and dualists have resulted in the identity theory and hylomorphism. The identity theory holds that body and mind are two different aspects of one underlying reality; perhaps the reality is energy, perhaps something we do not and cannot know. Hylomorphism says that man, like all reality, is matter and form, body and mind, two principles united during life into one substantial reality.

If man insists upon certainty concerning his ultimate nature and that of the world about him, he will have to go to religion and accept on faith what is taught him there. At any rate, it is well not to spend too much time attempting to solve the metaphysical problem. We had far better attempt to solve our social problems in the light of what we *can* learn from science and philosophy of man's nature and needs.

QUESTIONS TO AID STUDY

1. With what questions does ontology or metaphysics deal?
2. What were some of the early guesses concerning the basic substance? Can you account for these views?
3. Summarize the ideas of Heraclitus and Parmenides concerning permanence and change.
4. Does this dispute concerning the relative importance and nature of change have any significance in the modern educational world? Explain.
5. Does it seem to you that there is any permanence in this world of change? Explain.
6. Contrast the mechanistic and organismic points of view. Are either or both of these views necessarily teleological or nonteleological?
7. How many principal theories concerning the nature of ultimate reality are there? Name them.
8. Compare materialism and spiritualism as to basic metaphysical tenets.
9. What is naturalism? What is the relation of naturalism to materialism? To spiritualism?
10. Identify Plato, Aristotle, Democritus, Epicurus, Thomas Aquinas, Descartes, Hegel, Spinoza, Kant, and Dewey with a metaphysical position.
11. What is meant by the mind-body problem? In what way is it a problem? Summarize the attempts to solve it.
12. Compare behaviorism and Gestalt psychology on their solutions to this problem.
13. Can we be certain of attaining truth in attempting to solve metaphysical problems? Explain.

14. Do you think that your metaphysical views make any difference in your philosophy of life and of education? Read H. H. Horne, *Democratic Philosophy of Education*, pp. 2–4 and 7–9, to see what he thinks about the importance of metaphysics. Do you agree or disagree? Why?
15. What do both Kant and John Dewey advise us to do about the metaphysical problem? What do you think of the advice? Toward what end would they have you use your intellectual ability? Why?

SUGGESTED REFERENCES

BRENNAN, ROBERT EDWARD. *Thomistic Psychology* (New York: Macmillan Co., 1941), Introd. and chaps. iii and xiii.

BRIGHTMAN, EDGAR. *Introduction to Philosophy* (New York: Henry Holt & Co., 1925), pp. 212–29, 201–11.

BROWN, PEARL F. *Highlights of Philosophy*. Dallas: Story Book Press, 1944.

BURTT, EDWIN ARTHUR. *Types of Religious Philosophy*. New York: Harper & Bros., 1939 (read according to interest).

DEMIASHKEVICH, MICHAEL. *Introduction to Philosophy of Education* (New York: American Book Co., 1935), pp. 44–63 and 67–107.

DOUGHTON, ISAAC. *Modern Public Education* (New York: D. Appleton-Century Co., 1935), pp. 3–37.

DURANT, WILL. *The Story of Philosophy*. New York: Simon & Schuster, 1926 (read according to interest).

EDMAN, IRWIN. *Four Ways of Philosophy*. New York: Henry Holt & Co., 1937.

EDMAN, IRWIN, and SCHNEIDER, H. W. *Landmarks for Beginners in Philosophy*. New York: Reynal & Hitchcock, 1941 (read according to interest).

ELLIOT, HUGH. "Materialism," *Readings in Philosophy*, edited by J. H. RANDALL, JUSTUS BUCHLER, and EVELYN SHIRK (New York: Barnes & Noble, 1946), pp. 206–24.

FOSDICK, HARRY EMERSON. *On Being a Real Person* (New York: Harper & Bros., 1943), chap. ix.

HOCKING, WILLIAM E. *Types of Philosophy* (New York: Charles Scribner's Sons, 1929), chaps. iii, xvi, and xix.

———. "What Man Can Make of Man," *Fortune*, XXV (February, 1942), 91.

HUXLEY, JULIAN. "The Biologist Looks at Man," *Fortune*, XXVI (December, 1942), 139.

KRIKORIAN, YEWANT HOVHANNES (ed.). *Naturalism and the Human Spirit*. New York: Columbia University Press, 1944.

McWILLIAMS, J. A. *Philosophy for the Millions*. New York: Macmillan Co., 1942.

MARITAIN, JACQUES. "Christian Humanism," *Fortune,* XXV (April, 1942), 106.

MONTAGUE, W. P. "Philosophy in a World at War," *Fortune,* XXV (March, 1942), 103.

——. *The Ways of Things* (New York: Prentice-Hall, Inc., 1940), chaps. iv–v.

MORRIS, CHARLES W. *Six Theories of Mind.* Chicago: University of Chicago Press, 1932.

ORCHARD, W. E. *Humanity: What? Whence? Whither?* (Milwaukee: Bruce Pub. Co., 1944), chap. vii.

SMITH, T. V. *The Philosophic Way of Life in America.* New York: F. S. Crofts & Co., 1943.

SMITH, T. V., and GRENE, MARJORIE. *From Descartes to Kant.* Chicago: University of Chicago Press, 1940 (read according to interest).

SPERRY, W. S. "Our Moral Chaos," *Fortune,* XXV (May, 1942), 102.

TOWNSEND, H. G. *Philosophical Ideas in the United States* (New York: American Book Co., 1934), pp. 233–52.

TURNER, WILLIAM. *History of Philosophy* (Boston: Ginn & Co., 1903), use Index.

WAHLQUIST, J. T. *The Philosophy of American Education* (New York: Ronald Press Co., 1942), chap. iii.

WEBER, ALFRED. *History of Philosophy* (New York: Charles Scribner's Sons, 1906), pp. 573–603.

CHAPTER XI
THE NATURE OF KNOWLEDGE
AND TRUTH

Meaning of the term "epistemology"; relation to metaphysics and psychology—Sources of human knowledge: (1) Sense-experience: empiricism; (2) Reason: rationalism; (3) Aristotle's unification; (4) Kant's synthesis—Validity of human knowledge; relation of knowledge to reality: (1) Naïve or natural realism; (2) Idealism (a) validity of knowledge for epistemological idealist who is also a metaphysical idealist, (b) Skepticism for epistemological idealist not a metaphysical idealist; (3) Realism: scholastic, neo-, and critical—The nature of truth: (1) The realist's and the idealist's conception of truth; (2) The pragmatist's conception of truth (a) importance of pragmatism in education, (b) original meaning; common-sense use, (c) as a philosophy; contributions of Peirce and James, (d) John Dewey's pragmatism, (e) failure to distinguish between knowledge and truth, (f) dangers in pragmatism, (g) value of pragmatism—The value and importance of the search for truth

AFTER Kant (1724–1804) in his monumental work, *Critique of Pure Reason,* had examined the sources of man's knowledge, he wrote of the territory covered:

This domain is an island, enclosed by nature itself within unalterable limits. It is the land of truth—enchanting name!—surrounded by a wide and stormy ocean, the native home of illusion; where many a fog bank and many a swiftly melting iceberg give the deceptive appearance of farther shores, deluding the adventurous seafarer ever anew with empty hopes, and engaging him in enterprises which he can never abandon and yet is unable to carry to completion.[1]

The size of this land of truth, how man gets to it, the boundaries between it and the ocean of illusion, even its actual existence, have

1. Immanuel Kant, *Critique of Pure Reason* (trans. Norman Kemp Smith), p. 257.

long been the subject of man's speculation and inquiry. As Aristotle observed, it is man's nature to want to know, and to know the truth, the way things are. The nature of ultimate reality eludes him. What can he know? How can he know? What are the sources, the extent, the limitations of human knowledge?

The branch of philosophy which deals with problems of knowledge is known as "epistemology." The answers to its problems both condition and are conditioned by metaphysical theories. These answers underlie psychology. They undergird and aid scientific investigation. Eddington says that "it is actually an aid in the search for knowledge to understand the nature of the knowledge which we seek."[2]

One of the important problems of epistemology is to investigate the sources of our knowledge. How do we learn what we think we know? It is evident that our senses have something to do with getting knowledge of the world we live in. A child is born equipped with certain reflexes, possibilities for emotional expression, and potentialities for interacting with his environment, but he *knows* nothing. Conditions, things, and people begin to make impressions upon him through his sight, hearing, smell, touch, and other senses. He reacts to these impressions. We say that he is learning.

If a human being were so unfortunate as to be born with no sense organs, it is doubtful whether he could ever learn anything, for all knowledge begins with sense-experience. The story of Helen Keller illustrates the necessity for such experience if understanding and intelligence are to develop.

Any epistemology which emphasizes the role of sense-experience in obtaining knowledge is called "empiricism." There are many varieties of this school of thought, its supporters ranging all the way from those that insist that experience is the *sole* source of knowledge to those who merely say that no knowledge is possible without experience.

The most thoroughgoing empiricists of the ancient world were that group of philosopher-teachers known as the Sophists. They were men who thought the efforts of the early cosmologists to pierce

2. Sir Arthur Eddington, *The Philosophy of Physical Science,* p. 5.

to the heart of reality were foolish. Why not be practical? Study man and his life; then teach other young men how to get along in this world, how to make friends, and to influence people. For this teaching, Sophists took money, something that philosophers had not done before and a practice which was frowned upon.

The Sophists were impressed by the teachings of Heraclitus concerning constant change and by the views of Democritus concerning the material nature of man. They believed that man knows nothing but his own sensations and that what he feels, perceives, and experiences is the only way to knowledge. Since what he felt, perceived, and experienced was constantly changing, there was no truth beyond the individual notions. "Man is the measure of all things," said Protagoras of Abdera (480–410 B.C.), one of the best known of the Sophists.

Plato's famous dialogues record the attempt which Socrates made to combat what seemed to him the unfortunate influence and false teachings of the Sophists. Socrates seemed to be concerned chiefly with the moral aspects of their teachings. While it is difficult to separate the interests of Socrates from those of Plato, it would appear that Plato was concerned also with epistemology. He emphatically was not an empiricist but a rationalist, for he stressed the role of reason in obtaining knowledge.

In the preceding chapter, it was pointed out that Parmenides taught that one could not rely upon sense-experience for obtaining knowledge of reality but must reason. Plato agreed with Parmenides in this respect. The secret society known as Pythagoreans also, little as we know of them, seems to have taught that only through thought, and particularly mathematical thought, could one obtain knowledge.

The rationalists argue that our senses give us but the raw material from which knowledge comes. Knowledge, say they, is not to be found in sense-perception of particulars but in concepts, in principles, which our senses cannot possibly furnish us; the mind itself is active, an organizer and systematizer of our sensory experience. For the rationalist, mathematics furnishes the correct pattern for thought. The ideal circles, triangles, spheres, and the other figures with which it deals are only in the mind. It was through the use of mathematics, and particularly the method of geometry, which is the method of deductive logic, that man made many of his intellectual advances. Science never could have developed without the use of mathematics.

In addition to emphasizing the activity of the mind itself, rationalists point out the fact that our senses often deceive us. There are often discrepancies in their reports. Illusions, hallucinations, fantasies, grow either directly or indirectly out of sense-experience. Plato believed that the world perceived by our senses is not the true world but a mere shadow of the real world of thought. He wrote:

> Behold! human beings living in an underground den, which has a mouth open toward the light and reaching all along the den; here they have been from their childhood, and have their legs and necks chained so that they cannot move and can only see before them, being prevented by the chains from turning round their heads. Above and behind them a fire is blazing at a distance, and between the fire and the prisoners there is a raised way; and you will see if you look, a low wall built along the way, like the screen which marionette players have in front of them, over which they show the puppets.[3]

This den, said Plato, is the world of sense-experience; the fire is the sun; what we see here is a mere shadow of reality. To find the real world, man will have to be loosed from his chains, turn around, and travel upward. Then he will find knowledge and reality in the world of ideas and ideals, in the world of thought. It is the work of education to free man from the bondage of the sense life and to aid him in this search for knowledge.

This famous allegory of the cave represents not only Plato's own belief but that of the Eleatics and the Pythagoreans of the ancient world. Descartes, Spinoza, and Leibnitz were modern rationalists who agreed with Plato that knowledge is reached through reason and that mathematical thought is the proper pattern for its attainment. Spinoza wrote his ethics in the form of a geometry, with definitions, postulates, and axioms. Descartes and Leibnitz are remembered for their mathematical contributions as well as for philosophical thought.

Aristotle adopted a middle position between the extreme empiricism of the Sophists and the extreme rationalism of Plato.

3. Plato *Republic* Book vii.

Knowledge, he believed, needed both sense-experience and reason; the sum of sense data constitutes merely a potentiality which reason actualizes; thus, concepts, principles, knowledge, are realized.

Unfortunately, most medieval thinkers followed Plato rather than Aristotle. They thought that they could rely exclusively upon reason to discover the facts about the world. It was not until man learned that observation as well as reason is required and that sense-experience as well as thought is needed for discovering the truth that scientific advances began. Thomas Aquinas, following Aristotle, was one medievalist to insist that all knowledge comes from reflection upon sense-experience.

Because of the untenable claims of many of the thinkers of the Middle Ages and the resultant stultification of science, there came in the seventeenth century a violent reaction against rationalism and a revival of empiricism. John Locke (1632–1704), the English thinker, epitomized this position when he wrote: "Let us suppose the mind to be like white paper, void of all characters, without any ideas; how comes it to be furnished? Whence comes it by that vast store which the busy and boundless fancy of man has painted on it with an almost endless variety? Whence has it all the materials of reason and knowledge? To this I answer in one word, from *experience;* in that all our knowledge is founded and from that it ultimately derives itself."[4]

Locke taught, "Nihil in intellectu quod non prius in sensu," and would have none of Leibnitz' addition, "sive intellectus ipse." Hume (1711–76), another of this school, taught that what we call the mind is nothing but the sum total of our sensations.

It remained for Kant to take these two streams of thought from the past and to integrate them into an epistemology which has been more influential than any other and which modern scientists concede to have "anticipated to a remarkable extent the ideas to which we are now being impelled by the modern developments of physics."[5] It was Kant's self-imposed task in the *Critique of Pure Reason* to investigate not only the sources of knowledge but whether man is justified in thinking that knowledge is at all possible.

So far as the sources of knowledge are concerned, he found them

4. John Locke, *Essay on Human Understanding,* Book II, chap. i.
5. Eddington, *op. cit.,* p. 189.

in both sense-experience and in the activity of man's mind. He said very definitely that all our knowledge begins with experience. "But," he continues, "though all our knowledge begins with experience, it does not follow that it all arises out of experience."[6]

Through our senses, "objects are given to us"; then by thought, or understanding, as Kant calls it, an organization of this sensory material takes place. "Thoughts without content are empty, percepts without concepts are blind."[7] Reason is the highest mental power and is that ability which enables man to grasp and understand the ideal, that which ought to be. Ideals do not come from experience any more than does the idea of a perfect sphere. They come from man's mental life. "All our knowledge starts with the senses, proceeds from thence to understanding, and ends with reason, beyond which there is no higher faculty to be found in us for elaborating the matter of intuition [sense-experience] and bringing it under the highest unity of thought."[8]

In effecting the synthesis of sensory materials, man thinks in terms of time, of space, and of cause and effect. He cannot help but do this. Hume had shown that none of these principles is deducible from sense-experience. Kant argued that if they cannot be deduced from sense-experience, they must be a priori to sense-experience. Here he is talking of logical priority, not temporal. Man's sense organs and mind seem to be of such a nature as to impose *forms* upon all our sense-experience.

Since Kant's synthesis of empiricism and rationalism, no one who knows philosophy could be an ultra-empiricist or an ultra-rationalist. Some writers do emphasize the greater importance of one or the other. Not all thinkers have agreed with Kant. Many students of philosophy have not understood him. But the great majority would agree that the source of knowledge is in both sense-experience and thought. Just *how* any student would explain the role of each depends upon the theory he holds concerning the nature of man and particularly of his mind.

VALIDITY OF HUMAN KNOWLEDGE

Epistemology's second important problem is this: What is the relation of knowledge to reality? Is our knowledge valid? Do we actu-

6. Kant, *op. cit.*, p. 25.   7. *Ibid.*, p. 93.   8. *Ibid.*, p. 300.

ally know the object directly, or do we know only our own ideas? There is even less agreement on this problem than there is on the problem of the sources of knowledge, for this question involves not only the nature of man but the nature of all reality. Here is a wider unknown than that concerned in the first problem.

If a group of average college Freshmen were asked whether the campus is just the way they perceive it, they would consider their interrogator as peculiar, to say the least. The majority of people take it for granted that the world is exactly as they see, hear, smell, taste, and feel it. But give each member of this group a collection of many colored pieces of yarn and ask each to pick out a color to match that of the foliage of the tree of heaven, of white pine, of the elm, or a color to match that of the red geraniums, of the purple petunias—all before them on the campus—and see the varieties of shades picked! Who is right? Who knows? Even if most of the group agree on a certain shade of yarn for each, that does not prove that each tree and each flower is in reality that color. Physicists tell us that our sensation of color is the result of a nerve impulse started through an interaction between the rods and cones in the retina of our eyes and the light rays of different length reflected from an object. In other words, color is probably not "out there" but in our minds.

Students hear sounds which seem to emanate from the campus. Are those sounds "out there"? Something is out there, something which starts vibrations in the air which reach sensory equipment of the ear. But there are vibrations so rapid that the human ear does not respond to them. Man does not "hear" them. But they are as much a part of reality as those vibrations he does "hear."

Suppose that man were equipped with a sense organ enabling him to pick up radio waves. Reality would seem very different to him. Suppose that he were a thousand times stronger than he is; would the wood of a tree seem hard? Suppose that he were the size of an amoeba. Would the table top now in the student's study seem smooth?

Is a rose "really" the lovely, fragrant, red, silky, soft flower which we perceive, or is it "really" an agglomeration of molecules, fundamentally of an electrical nature, causing certain vibrations, which cause effects in us? Or is it something else?

The assumption that reality is as man perceives it, is known as natural or naïve realism. As soon as a thoughtful person becomes aware of the fact that things are not as they seem, such an assumption will not satisfy him. He then inevitably asks: In what sense is this world we live in "real"? What is the relation of our assumed knowledge to what we call "reality"?

This is one of the most difficult and fundamental problems in philosophy. It would be impossible to discuss it adequately in the few pages which can here be devoted to it. The two principal points of view on this problem have been called "idealism" and "realism." There are many varieties of each school of thought; not all idealists have agreed in the past, nor do they agree with each other today; realists also differ in some respects, one from the other. But all idealists hold to one fundamental principle, one which is opposed by all realists. And all realists agree on one essential doctrine, however they may disagree in other respects.

If a person plucks a rose, looks at it, touches it, smells it, and then tries to describe the lovely flower to another, he thinks that he is describing something outside himself. But its appearance was an appearance *to him;* its odor, a smell which *he* experienced; the silky feel was the way it impressed *his* sense of touch. He finds that he is describing his own ideas. Epistemological idealists all agree that all we know are our own ideas; the mental life alone is knowable. All anyone can know of the rose is his idea of it.

If the epistemological idealist is also a metaphysical idealist, he believes that man can obtain knowledge of reality. If reality is spiritual in nature and man's mind is part of this spiritual substance and if all that we call material depends upon the spiritual or mental, then there can be nothing apart from or independent of a knowing mind. *Esse est percipi,* observed Berkeley, one of the most famous of idealists. Since the universe is in itself mental, it is possible for man through his mind to know it as it is. Man may not be able to know the whole of reality, for his mind cannot comprehend the mind of God, but he can obtain knowledge; he knows things as they are.

If the epistemological idealist is not a metaphysical idealist, he lands in skepticism as to the possibility of knowledge. If the world about us is material in nature and if all we know are our own ideas

—immaterial in nature—the problem becomes that of how man can know anything about the universe. In fact, perhaps he himself, as an immaterial substance, does not exist. As Hume asked: Should not the theory that "we have no idea of external substance distinct from the idea of particular qualities"[9] make us ask if a like theory does not apply to man's mind? "When I turn my reflection on myself," Hume said, "I never can perceive this self without some one or more perceptions; nor can I ever perceive anything but the perceptions." . . . . "Tis the composition of these, therefore, which forms the self."[10]

Against these views realism protests. Such subjectivity concerning the universe they cannot abide. All realists would agree that the objects of knowledge in this universe about us, are independent of any knowledge process and that matter exists apart from any percipient mind. As to whether we can know it as it is, realists do not agree. But they all agree that it is "out there" and would be there whether it were perceived or not. "To be" is not necessarily "to be perceived."

In the United States today there are three chief groups of realists. The scholastic realists hold that "reason is capable of reaching with complete certainty the most sublime truths of the natural order, but with difficulty, and only when duly trained. . . . . There are also truths of the supernatural order which the mind can never know unaided. For this revelation is needed."[11] The neo-realists also hold that man's knowledge corresponds to reality; he knows things as they are. This is the point of view from which Frederick Breed, the author of *Education and the New Realism*, writes. The third group call themselves critical realists; they come nearer the Kantian epistemology than do either of the other groups of realists.

In the *Critique of Pure Reason*, Kant made his position clear. There undoubtedly is a reality, he said, independent of thought. For example, he wrote: "All outer perception, therefore, yields immediate proof of something real in space, or rather is the real itself.

<hr/>

9. David Hume, *A Treatise of Human Nature*, p. 105.

10. *Ibid.*, pp. 104 and 84.

11. William McGucken, "The Philosophy of Catholic Education," in *Forty-first Yearbook of the Society for the Study of Education, Part I: Philosophies of Education*, p. 285. Also see R. E. Brennan, *Thomistic Psychology*, pp. 176–86.

In this sense empirical realism is beyond question: that is, there corresponds to our outer intuitions something real in space."[12]

But what those objects are in their essence, man cannot know. Our sense organs and our minds, being what they are, interpret the world of sense-experience according to certain forms implicit in our own nature, the schemata of which we are not at all conscious. Said Kant: "This schematism of our understanding, in its application to appearances and their mere form, is an art concealed in the depths of the human soul, whose real modes of activity nature is hardly likely ever to allow us to discover, and to have open to our gaze.[13]

Sir William Cecil Dampier, writing of the Kantian epistemology, says: "Nineteenth century empiricists often failed to see the strength or bearings of the view, that experience does not lead us directly to things as they are, but is only a process by which the appearance of things arises in our minds and that therefore the picture of nature we construct is partly determined *a priori* by the structure of our minds, as also is the fact that we have experiences at all."[14]

Kant's argument is not easy to follow, and it is not strange that he was, and is still, misunderstood. Many readers thought that he was teaching idealism, but of this accusation he wrote:

> Idealism consists in the assertion, that there are none but thinking beings, all other things, which we think are perceived in intuition, being nothing but representations in the thinking beings to which no object external to them corresponds in fact. Whereas I say, that things as objects of our senses existing outside us are given, but we know nothing of what they may be in themselves, knowing only their appearances, i.e., the representations which they cause in us by affecting our senses.[15]

In other words, there is undoubtedly a real world independent of human knowledge. The objects in that world man probably can never know in any ultimate sense; the essence, the thing-in-itself, escapes him. But scientific knowledge is possible for man because, being more alike than different, in spite of individual differences, human beings all interpret the world in terms of the same intellectual rules. The more scientists discover about the world in which we

12. Kant, *op. cit.*, p. 349.

13. *Ibid.*, p. 183.

14. Sir William Cecil Dampier, *A History of Science*, pp. 315–16.

15. Kant, *Prolegomena to Any Future Metaphysics*, p. 43.

live, the more certain it seems to many who know philosophy that Kant was right in his fundamental position.[16] Of course there is much about reality which we can know. The human mind is competent enough for all practical purposes. We can know that there is oil in some sections of southern Illinois. We can know that man is able to fly. We can know that the atom may be split to release its energy. We can know enough about man's nature and destiny here to predicate the components of a life good for him to live. But what oil is, what atoms are, what vitamins are, in and of themselves, no one knows. What man himself is we do not know. That is no reason why we should not continue the search for truth. As Kant put it: "We cannot indeed, beyond all possible experience, form a definite notion of what things in themselves may be. Yet we are not at liberty to abstain entirely from inquiring into them; for experience never satisfies reason fully, but in answering questions, refers us further and further back, and leaves us dissatisfied with regard to their complete solution."[17]

A scholar and philosopher of today who has studied Kant and written exhaustively of his *Critique of Pure Reason* has the following to say:

Knowledge is developing so rapidly that the physical world as it appeared to science the day before yesterday is very different from the physical world as it appears to science today. Who knows how it will appear tomorrow? There are few thinkers who would claim that modern science gives us adequate knowledge of the world as it really is; and even the fundamental concepts of physics are being subjected to criticism and revision. The scientists themselves are finding paradoxes and inconsistencies thrust upon them—as in the case of the quantum theory and the theory of Relativity. It is even asserted that time is merely a human way of looking at things and is not to be found in the physical world; and that we are aware only of our own measurements but have no idea of what it is that we are measuring. Such assertions, made quite independently of Kant's influence, look very like a revival of the Kantian doctrine, and give an added interest to the argument of the *Kritik*.[18]

I believe that the attitude of Kant is much nearer to the modern attitude than was that of his immediate successors; and I believe that a real, as

16. See W. H. Werkmeister, *A Philosophy of Science*, chap. iv, for a modern interpretation of Kant's epistemology.

17. Kant, *Prolegomena to Any Future Metaphysics*, p. 121.

18. Herbert James Paton, *Kant's Metaphysic of Experience*, I, 68–69.

opposed to a superficial, knowledge of the *Kritik,* may help to save modern philosophy from unnecessary errors and to keep it in the path of progress.[19]

Sir Arthur Eddington says that the modern scientist would choose Kant as the leader among philosophers because Kant anticipated to a remarkable degree what today science is being impelled to believe.[20]

THE NATURE OF TRUTH

The reader should now be in a position to understand better the quotation from Kant with which the chapter began. Kant never doubted but that there is a "land of truth" and that it is possible for man to apprehend much of the truth. He may not know all truth, but within the bounds of a wide and stormy ocean he can know. Kant would never have assented to the modern doctrine known as pragmatism, which holds as its fundamental doctrine a theory as to the nature of truth. Philosophers, be they idealists or realists, have taught that the locus of truth is in reality. If an idea corresponds with reality, it is true. If it does not correspond with things as they are, it is not true. Idealists and realists alike would say that if a thing is *true,* it will work in experience. That is one way of finding out whether it is true—put it into practice and see whether it will work.

Pragmatists turn this around and say that if a thing works in experience, that makes it true—that its working makes it true. The truth of a proposition is measured by its efficiency, by whether it works, by what it can do to guide human action toward achieving human purposes. Truth is man-made, say the pragmatists. There is no absolute truth. Truth changes and is purely a matter of consequences; that is true which works in any particular set of circumstances. Circumstances change, so truth changes; what is true today may not be true tomorrow.

Pragmatism is so important in the modern educational world that it needs careful scrutiny and understanding by every teacher. It is the philosophy which underlies Progressive education today, although some Progressives show signs of abandoning some of its tenets. As a philosophy it has not been entirely understood by many teachers who tried to follow its educational applications.

19. *Ibid.,* II, 464.　　　　　20. *Op. cit.,* p. 189.

The word "pragmatism" comes from the Greek word *pragma*, which means "a thing done, business, effective action." Aristotle used the term in distinguishing the practical, empirical, life from the life of thought. Polybius, a Greek historian who died about 123 B.C., used the term in explaining that his historical study was for the purpose of investigating the facts of the past in order to draw from those facts practical lessons for guiding posterity in its action. The word has come to mean "practicality." Anything with that connotation appeals to the practical American people, and, with the exception of most university teachers of philosophy and some of their students, pragmatism has been and perhaps still is the most popular philosophy in the United States. It has never had much standing in Europe, although F. C. S. Schiller's "Humanism" and Hans Vaihinger's "Alsobism" have been developments along the same line. Friedrich Nietzsche's theory of knowledge is indistinguishable from pragmatism, and his philosophy is the inevitable and logical result of this theory of truth.

There is a sense in which all men are sometimes pragmatists, and quite properly so. If a person who drank coffee in the evening always stayed awake whenever he indulged; if he were certain that drinking coffee was the only variable, and it happened repeatedly, he would be foolish to continue drinking coffee unless he wanted to stay awake. But the fact that he stayed awake after drinking coffee did not make the proposition "coffee keeps me awake" true. The thing that makes that proposition true is the actual effect of the caffeine upon the nervous system, resulting in the drinker's wakefulness. Truth lies in the agreement of a proposition with reality. Man did not make that truth. The truth is to be found in the constituents of the nervous system and of the caffeine and in the effect of the latter on the former.

As a philosophy, pragmatism, like all philosophies, has ancient roots. The Sophists taught that "man is the measure of all things" and that man himself makes all the truth there is. Modern pragmatists would not say, as did the ancient Sophists, that truth is anything which works for any individual. It must work for a large number of people over a long period of time. As a modern philosophy, pragmatism began in this country with Charles Peirce (1839–1914). William James (1842–1910) further developed the ideas of Peirce,

226 *Philosophy of Education*

applying them in a way not altogether approved of by their progenitor. John Dewey (1859——) has continued the tradition but
prefers that his philosophy be called instrumentalism or experimentalism.

Charles Peirce intended pragmatism merely as a theory of logical
analysis. In a paper entitled "How To Make Our Ideas Clear" he
wrote: "Consider what effects that might conceivably have practical
bearings we conceive the object of our conception to have. Then
our conceptions of these effects is the whole of our conception of
the object."[21] He continues: "Let us illustrate this rule by some
examples; and, to begin with the simplest one possible, let us ask
what we mean by calling a thing *hard.* Evidently that it will not be
scratched by many other substances. The whole conception of this
quality, as of every other, lies in its conceived effects. There is absolutely no difference between a hard thing and a soft thing as long
as they are not brought to the test."[22]

It is said that Peirce arrived at his theories after studying Kant's
Critique of Pure Reason. Many people argue that the roots of pragmatism are in the Kantian epistemology. Kant did use the term
"pragmatic" several times. For instance, in *The Metaphysic of
Morals,* when discussing different kinds of imperatives, he calls that
hypothetical imperative pragmatic "which refers to the choice of
means to a definite end."[23] That is, if one wishes to be happy, one
must do so and so. The command to do "so and so," *if* one desires
happiness, is a pragmatic and hypothetical imperative. In a footnote
Kant says: "It seems to me that the proper signification of the word
pragmatic may be most accurately defined in this way. . . . . A history is composed pragmatically when it teaches prudence, i.e. in-
structs the world how it can provide for its interests better, or at
least as well as the men of former time."[24] This reminds one of
Polybius' use of the word.

In Kant's writing, "pragmatic" always referred to a method of determining means, never to the determination of ends. If pragmatists
had used the term only in this sense, there could have been no criti-

21. *The Philosophy of Peirce* (ed. Justus Buchler), p. 31.
22. *Ibid.,* p. 31.
23. Kant, *Fundamental Principles of the Metaphysic of Morals,* p. 33.
24. *Ibid.,* p. 34.

cism—and, of course, no philosophy of pragmatism, but pragmatists make no distinction between means and ends.[25]

In addition to a logical method, William James made pragmatism a theory of truth; formulating the teaching which is its fundamental position and differentiating characteristic. He said:

Truth for us [pragmatists] is simply a collective name for verification-processes, just as health, wealth, strength, etc. are names for other processes connected with life, and also pursued because it pays to pursue them. Truth is made, just as health, wealth, and strength are made, in the course of experience.[26]

The true is the name of whatever proves itself to be good in the way of belief, and good, too, for definite, assignable reasons.[27]

Some persons have argued for this theory of truth, saying: Why not admit that man makes truth? If we cannot know reality, why put the locus of truth there? To say that we cannot know reality is to say that we can never know truth, which means that we can have no knowledge. Why not admit, since man knows only phenomena, that truth is man-made, that there is no valid distinction between truth and knowledge, and that truth is merely that which works for man?

John Dewey is today the foremost exponent of the pragmatic theory of truth. He prefers to be called an instrumentalist, from his theory of mind, which he looks upon as a biological instrument for aiding man in his adjustment to his environment, or to be called an experimentalist, because of his devotion to the scientific method. Realists, particularly, object to his pre-empting the name "experimentalism" for his philosophy, for, say they, the scientific method is not the private property of those who are pragmatic in their theory of truth. In fact, many realists believe that pragmatism destroys science in that it denies the possibility of obtaining knowledge about the objective world. The pragmatist holds that truth is not in the world for man to discover; man makes truth through the scientific method. John Dewey writes:

In physical matters men have slowly grown accustomed in all specific beliefs to identifying the true with the verified. But they still hesitate to recognize the implication of this identification and to derive the definition

25. John Dewey, *Democracy and Education,* p. 124.

26. William James, *Pragmatism,* p. 218.   27. *Ibid.,* p. 76.

of truth from it. For while it is nominally agreed upon as a commonplace that definitions ought to spring from concrete and specific cases rather than be invented in the empty air and imposed upon particulars, there is a strange unwillingness to act upon the maxim of defining truth. To generalize the recognition that the true means the verified and means nothing else places upon men the responsibility for surrendering political and moral dogmas and subjecting to the test of consequences their most cherished prejudices.[28]

According to other philosophies than pragmatism, Dewey should have said that in physical matters men have slowly grown accustomed in specific beliefs to identifying *knowledge* with the verified. Even that statement would have to be qualified. Pragmatists, however, do not distinguish between truth and knowledge. Idealists and realists say that truth is in the way things are, whether we *know* it or not; knowledge is apprehended truth, what we have learned of truth. The phrase "true knowledge" is a tautology. If it is knowledge, it must be true. The phrase "false knowledge" is a contradiction.[29] Knowledge, apprehended truth, could not be false. To be sure, men have often thought that they had knowledge only to discover that they did not. But what man had was not false knowledge; it was simply not knowledge. Where man possesses knowledge, he has discovered truth, that is, that much of reality. As Bertrand Russell writes: "I conclude that 'truth' is the fundamental concept and that 'knowledge' must be defined in terms of 'truth,' not vice versa. This entails the consequence that a proposition may be true although we can see no way of obtaining evidence for or against it."[30] "He [Dewey] judges a belief by its effects, whereas I judge it by its causes."[31]

Though there can be no knowledge without truth, there can be truth without knowledge as Russell points out. Which of these

28. John Dewey, *Reconstruction in Philosophy*, pp. 159–60.

29. In reading the manuscript Dean Emeritus Schroeder commented on this point as follows: "In view of the possibility that some well-informed student might call attention to the statement 'knowledge is false' in such a thinker as Kant, on page 97 of Smith's translation of the *Critique of Pure Reason*, it is pertinent to say that this is a mistranslation; that the correct translation would be 'cognition is false' as the original reads '*Erkenntnis ist falsch,*' not '*Wissen ist falsch.*'"

30. Bertrand Russell, *An Inquiry into Meaning and Truth*, p. 23.

31. *Ibid.*, *A History of Western Philosophy*, p. 826.

statements is true: There once lived a woman named Helen of Troy; there never lived a woman named Helen of Troy. Who knows? But Helen of Troy either lived, or she did not live. Man's inability to say with certainty does not change the fact. Some day, some record may turn up by which we shall discover whether her life was fact or fiction. But our knowledge or lack of it does not affect the truth.

One sees today on a drive through parts of southern Illinois a very different landscape from that of fifteen years ago. Oil has been discovered. That oil was there fifteen years ago, twenty years ago, probably thousands of years ago. Man did not know it. The statement: There is oil in parts of the region we call southern Illinois would have been a true statement one hundred years ago or a thousand years ago. Only it would not at that time have been verified; man did not know it. But the truth was there, some day to be discovered.

Leonardo da Vinci more than four hundred years ago predicted that man would fly. To have said then or at any time "man will be able sometime to fly" would have been a true statement. Man did not have the knowledge which made it possible for him to fly until fairly recent times, but such a statement would always have been true whether man knew it or not.

But, the reader inquires, does this imply the old concept of a closed universe, with fixed species or forms, eternally complete, in which nothing new comes into being? Does that not contradict the newer concept of emergent evolution, of unpredictability? Not at all. Of course this is a changing world. But the potentiality for those changes was here all the time, else they could not have occurred. That they could not have been predicted by anyone does not change that. There is a continuity; something does not come from nothing in the natural universe. We do not know what reality is; but suppose that this is a universe infinite in time and space; suppose that there is a creative force at work in it all the time and that new things are constantly coming into being; even so there are things which do not change. The earth rotates on its axis, there is the constant pull of gravitation, living organisms need food, and fundamental human nature remains the same.

If a man says "It is warm" or "The sun is shining" or "It is raining," he is not giving expression to his whole thought. He is understood by inference on the part of the person to whom he is speaking. What he means is: "At this moment the weather is warm here"; "The sun is shining here and now"; "It is raining at this particular time and place." If this be true, it will always be true that at that place and moment the weather was warm or that the sun was shining at that particular time and place or that it was raining at that time and place. If Lincoln was born on February 12, 1809, it will always be true that Lincoln was born on February 12, 1809. So with all facts. A fact is an individual datum of knowledge. Of course, there are changes going on all the time at any time. But any assertion or judgment about any one of them, if true at the time, will always be true in the sense that that particular thing happened at that particular time and place. The truth in regard to facts does not change.

Does it not seem a little presumptuous as well as slightly ridiculous to say with the pragmatists that man is "making truth" as he acts? Does he "make truth" as he plants a garden, teaches school, takes a journey, writes a book, eats a meal, goes to war, or builds a home? One may make assertions and judgments about his activity which are true or false. But to say that he is making truth seems to indicate muddled thinking. If man acts always to satisfy his wants— if that statement is true, and it seems to be—then what man does comes from his nature; he is acting in accord with his nature. He acts within an environment in which there are permanences to which he must adjust and changes, some of which he may direct, but always within a framework and toward ends which he did not invent and cannot change.

In discussing Dewey's concept of truth, Bertrand Russell writes in his recent book, *A History of Western Philosophy:*

> In all this I feel a grave danger, the danger of what might be called cosmic impiety. The concept of "truth" as something dependent upon facts largely outside human control has been one of the ways in which philosophy hitherto has inculcated the necessary element of humility. When this check upon pride is removed a further step is taken on the road toward a certain kind of madness—the intoxication of power which invaded philosophy with Fichte and to which modern men whether philosophers or not, are prone. I am persuaded that this intoxication, which however

unintentionally contributed to, is increasing the danger of vast social disaster.[32]

When Dewey says in the quotation previously noted: "That the true means the verified, and means nothing else places upon man the responsibility for surrendering political and moral dogmas and subjecting to the test of consequences their most cherished prejudices,"[33] he is saying something that might be dangerous.

We might agree that all human beliefs, whether they be cherished prejudices or not, should be subjected to critical review in the light of human reason. But it is quite another thing to say that one should believe nothing save that which has been subjected to the test of consequences. Under the impact of pragmatism many persons have surrendered not merely political and moral dogmas but all political and moral principles, not prejudices alone but faith in anything not verified by consequences. The notion has grown that there are no absolutes, no generalizations on which one can depend as *truths*. This is most unfortunate for our society, for there are generalizations which are true just as there are statements of facts that are true.

Many accepted generalizations are not true even though accepted as true. It was not true that all metals sink in water, although this was generally accepted by scientists before Davy discovered sodium and potassium. It was not true that the earth was the center of the universe before the days of Copernicus, Kepler, Bruno, and Galileo. In spite of the belief of Aristarchus of Samos, who lived in the third century, B.C., and of some few other scientists, practically all people from the time of Aristotle thought that the earth was the center of the universe because Aristotle had so taught. But that did not make it so.

But if a generalization expresses that which agrees with reality, it is true. Though man cannot know all of reality or know it in any ultimate sense, it does not follow that he can know nothing of the way things are.

Many things that man has discovered have been verified. There are other truths to which his reason assents which cannot be verified by experiment. It is only through reason that the infinite value of the individual can be proved. But that he has infinite value is true, and that he should be treated always as an end and never merely as a means is an absolute; that is, it is a principle which is always true.

That a democratic society, a society in which all human beings are treated as ends, is the best form of society for man was always true and will always be true. This truth has not been proved by any actual experimental means but by the use of reason. It can be proved in experience as well and verified through practicing democracy.

Of course, our beliefs and our principles need to be scrutinized, examined in the light of new knowledge, put into practice constantly, and reviewed in the light of human reason. Verification through experimentation is one way of determining whether we do have the truth or not.

Realists and idealists would say that a statement is true if it corresponds to reality. They recognize that one way of discovering whether a proposition is true or not is to put it to a scientific test. Scientists are doing that all the time. But few of them would say that they are thereby making truth; rather, they would say that they are discovering it. Idealists also emphasize coherence as the test for the truth of a statement or judgment. It must express an idea which is a necessary part of a coherent and systematic whole.

These criticisms of pragmatism do not mean that pragmatism has no value. Mankind insists on going to extremes. A rationalism which never refers to sense-experience will not arrive at truth. There is a need both for first principles and for looking at consequences in deciding upon and judging of man's conduct.

In the earlier chapters the source of those principles which we know to be true was indicated. It is apparent that we do not know all the truth as yet. We must be ready and willing to accept truth as it is discovered, to discard a principle as false when it is so proved, even though it may have been held to be true. But to believe that there is no truth in the sense of any principles that are always true, to believe that truth changes or that man makes it, seems false, and a serious handicap to man's progress.

Kant pointed out the proper and suitable area for pragmatism to operate: for the determination of means. It is never suitable for determining ends. The ends of life, our values and purposes, grow out of human nature. Man does not make that or contrive it. He *discovers* what these criteria are through the use of reason operating within and upon experience. He should and does contrive ways and means of achieving these ends, his proper goals, the components of the good life, and the kind of social organization we should have. Then he looks at the consequences to see whether his conduct has brought him nearer his goal.

How else can one judge "consequences"? To say that the truth of a principle of conduct depends on consequences, on operations, on how a thing works, is no help unless one has a standard by which to judge the success of consequences. To study whether a line of conduct will work for man's welfare is of no avail unless we know what man's welfare demands. Man needs a standard, a clear concept of his ultimate goal, to guide him in deciding whether the consequences of his conduct are good or bad. Pragmatism holds that there are no ultimate goals, no absolutes, no unchanging truths. That seems to be a mistake. But after man has discovered his goals, then the pragmatic theory has value as a guide toward discovering means. Then man should look at consequences to see whether his conduct is furthering his aim. This is particularly necessary when the knowledge for the best method of reaching aims is not available. Of this, Kant says:

> The physician must do something for a patient in danger, but does not know the nature of his illness. He observes the symptoms and if he can find no more likely alternative, judges it to be a case of phthisis. Now even in his own estimation his belief is contingent only, another observer might perhaps come to a sounder conclusion. Such contingent belief, which yet forms the ground for the actual employment of means to certain actions, I entitle pragmatic belief.[34]

Throughout all history man has sought the truth; he has tried to learn how things are in this universe. In attaining knowledge, not only has he assuaged his thirst to know but he has used the knowledge gained as an instrument for his welfare. Knowledge *is* power, and truth *does* set man free; not completely free because he does not yet know all truth—and probably never will—and certainly does not yet use all the truth that he knows.

34. Kant, *Critique of Pure Reason*, p. 648.

Any man who has once beheld "the bright countenance of truth" would be less than a man if he did not hold fast to proved truth and do all in his power further to explore the "island of truth." He will be content with nothing less than truth, preferring the agony of doubt to the acceptance of an inadequate theory of knowledge.

Men of thought have always been of importance in guiding human conduct. The poet Heine wrote: "Mark this you proud men of action. You are nothing but unconscious hod carriers for the men of thought, who often in humble silence have prescribed for you your every act, even to the uttermost detail."

If this be true, men of thought have considerable responsibility for guiding human conduct aright. They should diligently seek and hold fast to the truth.

SUMMARY

Men have long debated the question of the source of knowledge. Some, who are called "empiricists," emphasize the role of sense-experience in obtaining knowledge; others, known as "rationalists," say that human reason is the source of knowledge. Of attempts to synthesize these two positions, Aristotle's and Kant's are the most famous. Aristotle said that the senses furnish us mere potential knowledge; reason actualizes it. Kant said that all knowledge begins with sense-experience, but our minds impose *forms* upon the sense-experience. For Kant, forms are ways of knowing.

Men also have not agreed upon the relation of reality to knowledge. The epistemological idealist insists that all we can know is our ideas. If the epistemological idealist is also a metaphysical idealist, thus believing that reality itself is mental, he would believe that knowledge could be valid; if the epistemological idealist were not a metaphysical idealist, he would be skeptical about obtaining any knowledge of reality. The realists, scholastic, neo-, or critical, all agree that in some sense knowledge is of a real world, a world independent of a percipient mind. The scholastic realists and neo-realists believe that knowledge of reality is possible; the critical realists in some manner and to some degree follow Kant, who believed that knowledge was a joint product of an external world and of man's sense organs and mind. This knowledge comes out of experience; experience furnishes the content and mind the form of knowledge.

This raises the question of the nature of truth. If we cannot know reality, how can truth be conceived of as correspondence with reality or even as a necessary part of a coherent and systematic whole? Pragmatists identify truth with that which works in human experience. They make no distinction between truth and knowledge but say that truth is man-made, that it changes, that truth means simply the verified.

Other philosophies identify knowledge, or apprehended truth, with the verified and insist that because truth has its locus in the way things are, whether we know about them or not, there may be truth which has not and perhaps never can be verified. Truth is discovered, not made. It is our knowledge which changes. While we probably shall never know all the truth, we can discover much through both sense-experience and reason.

QUESTIONS TO AID STUDY

1. With what questions does epistemology deal?
2. Who were the Sophists? What were their principle tenets?
3. Contrast empiricism and rationalism, giving the arguments for each as an explanation for the chief source of knowledge. Name famous philosophers identified with each point of view.
4. What did Aristotle teach about the source of knowledge?
5. How did Kant reconcile empiricism and rationalism?
6. Did it ever occur to you that your sense organs do not report things as they are? How does the physicist explain the phenomenon of color? Does this mean that the world is *really* one without color?
7. Compare the central positions of idealism and of realism on the problems of the nature and validity of knowledge.
8. How does pragmatism differ from idealism and realism on the nature of truth and on the relation of truth and knowledge?
9. Does truth change? What is the difference between saying that man makes truth and that he discovers truth?
10. What is dangerous about pragmatism as a philosophy?
11. In what area of life does pragmatism properly operate? For what does it seem a mistake to attempt to use it?

SUGGESTED REFERENCES

BERKELEY, GEORGE. "Are Things Different from Ideas?" *Readings in Philosophy,* edited by J. H. RANDALL, JUSTUS BUCHLER, and EVELYN SHIRK (New York: Barnes & Noble, 1946), pp. 77–100.

BLANCHARD, BRAND. *Nature of Thought.* London: G. Allen & Unwin, 1939.

BRADLEY, FRANCIS HERBERT. *Appearance and Reality.* New York: Macmillan Co., 1906.

BRENNAN, ROBERT EDWARD. *Thomistic Psychology* (New York: Macmillan Co., 1941), pp. 176–86.

BRIGHTMAN, EDGAR. *Introduction to Philosophy* (New York: Henry Holt & Co., 1925), pp. 34–66.

BUCHLER, JUSTUS (ed.). *The Philosophy of Peirce.* New York: Harcourt, Brace & Co., 1940.

DEWEY, JOHN. *Reconstruction in Philosophy.* New York: Henry Holt & Co., 1920.

HOCKING, WILLIAM E. *Types of Philosophy* (New York: Charles Scribner's Sons, 1929), chaps. ix and x.

HOLMES, ROGER. "Your Nature and Mine," *Atlantic Monthly,* CLXI (April–May, 1938), 547 and 692.

HORNE, HERMAN HARRELL. *Democratic Philosophy of Education.* New York: Macmillan Co., 1932.

JAMES, WILLIAM. *Pragmatism* (New York: Longmans, Green & Co., 1907), especially Lecture II.

KANT, IMMANUEL. *Prolegomena to Any Future Metaphysics,* edited in English by DR. PAUL CARUS. Chicago: Open Court Pub. Co., 1902. Also in SMITH, T. V., and GRENE, MARJORIE. *From Descartes to Kant.* Chicago: University of Chicago Press, 1940.

MONTAGUE, WILLIAM P. *Ways of Knowing.* New York: Macmillan Co., 1925.

———. *Ways of Things* (New York: Prentice-Hall, Inc., 1940), chaps. ii–iii.

PATRICK, G. T. W. *Introduction to Philosophy* (rev. ed.; Boston: Houghton Mifflin Co., 1935), use Index.

RUSSELL, BERTRAND. *A History of Western Philosophy* (New York: Simon & Schuster, 1945), chap. xxx.

———. *An Inquiry into Meaning and Truth.* New York: W. W. Norton & Co., 1940.

WERKMEISTER, WILLIAM HENRY. *A Philosophy of Science* (New York: Harper & Bros., 1940), chap. iv.

CHAPTER XII

EDUCATIONAL PHILOSOPHIES AND
EDUCATIONAL AIMS

Questions to be answered by philosophy of education: what, why, and how of education—Source of educational objectives—Ultimate law of the school—Differing philosophies and their relation to philosophy of education: (1) Materialism and education; (2) Idealism and education; (3) Realism and education (a) scholastic realism, (b) neo-realism, (c) critical realism; (4) Experimentalism and education—Agreement among philosophies of education: (1) Need for study of educational problems, beginning with areas of agreement; (2) Work of the Educational Policies Commission—Progressivism, traditionalism, and essentialism: (1) Philosophy or philosophies on which each is based; (2) Principal proposals of each concerning education; (3) Choosing among competing philosophies of education—Educational aims in democracy: (1) Work of the home; (2) Work of the school: (a) inculcating respect for human personality, (b) helping pupils master tools of learning and the social heritage, (c) assisting pupils to learn self-discipline and concern for the common welfare, (d) developing independence in thinking in relation to the authority of truth, (e) developing an understanding of and devotion to social goals

---

ANY adequate philosophy of education must answer three questions: What is education? What ought it to accomplish? How can these aims be realized? In other words, philosophy of education is concerned with the what, the why, and the how of education. The nature of the educative process was discussed in the second and third chapters. To lead the reader to formulate an answer to the second question, what education ought to accomplish, has been the purpose implicit in all the intervening chapters.

237

The ends and purposes of education, like the ends and purposes of life itself, grow out of human needs and cannot be understood apart from an understanding of man's nature, of the meaning of life, of the chief end of man, and of the kind of life that is good for man to live in this world. Whatever man's ultimate destiny, it seems apparent that his task in this world is to build a social organization in which all men can realize their best potentialities. It is only in and through such a mutual enterprise that men can be truly men, that they can develop human personality.

If this be true, it should be clear that the purpose of education is to promote our common welfare through helping boys and girls to grow in capacity for intelligent and social-minded participation in group life. To do all in their power to help each child develop into the finest human being he is capable of becoming, able to live life to its fullest and to do his part in making that possible for every other human being—this is the task of all who guide the development of youth. There is no work in the world of greater importance.

Because education is more inclusive than schooling, this task is that of practically all adults. Primarily, education is a function of the state, meaning by that term, *all* the people organized for political purposes. Parents must take the first responsibility; the church must play its part; libraries, radio, the press, and other agencies have a share. But the school, organized and established by the people for the express purpose of promoting the general welfare through guiding the development of children, has particularly heavy responsibilities.

It is essential that every teacher know why we have schools and what education should aim to accomplish, because the purpose for which schools were established and the aims of the educative process must determine the policy and practice within the school. It is only in the light of what education should accomplish—in other words, by reference to the ultimate goal of education—that a teacher can decide on immediate and specific aims and on the course that ought to be followed in the daily life of the school. This principle might be called the philosophical or ultimate law of the school.

Every day the teacher has many problems to solve. Three boys, separately and collectively, pommeled Billy, during recess. What to do? Mary's listlessness pointed to the possibility of her having come to school without breakfast again. John worked none of his arithmetic problems at the time he was supposed to be doing them. The children seem bored with the present unit in history. The teachers have been asked to discuss and decide the question of dismissing school on Lincoln's Birthday. Is there any principle to guide a teacher in making such decisions?

Teachers certainly need to know as much about boys and girls as possible—their interests, their growth and development, their homes, and their surroundings. But it is not enough to know and like children.

Teachers need to know a great deal about the world we live in, to have assimilated as much of the social heritage as possible, and to be avid for more knowledge. But knowledge of subject matter is not enough, any more than knowledge of children is all the professional information a teacher needs.

Teachers need to know how children learn; the best methods to use in assisting them and in guiding the learning. They need to know how to select suitable subject matter and illustrative material, how to test for evidence of growth, how to use remedial measures.

But these are all tools, techniques, means. The ways in which they should be used, the ends toward which the educative process should be directed, are to be found in the purposes and aims of education. The ultimate purpose of the school furnishes the directing principle for deciding what shall be done in any particular situation.

For this reason, a teacher's philosophy of education is extremely important. Consciously or unconsciously, what any teacher considers important in life, and therefore in school, will affect the decisions made during every minute of the day. It is too true that education has not done for our society what it could and should do. One cause of this is the unfortunate lack among teachers of a philosophy of education based on an understanding of human nature and human needs.

Differing philosophies of education grow out of different philosophies. Materialism, realism, idealism, pragmatism—all philosophical schools have varying proposals for education. Many of these proposals can be reconciled. Some are so diametrically opposed one to the other that they cannot be harmonized. They should all be studied thoughtfully by every teacher in the light of the philosophy from which they sprang. It is only as such study is intelligently pursued that teachers will be in a position to make decisions about their own work and to appraise proposals for education made by others.

MATERIALISM AND EDUCATION

Materialism has never, for any length of time, been important as a source of educational theory. As pointed out previously, the psychology known as "behaviorism" was rooted in monistic materialism. It was popular for a time. Some of its vocabulary is still to be found in educational discussions. It contributed some valuable ideas to education. That psychology should be as objectively scientific as it is possible to make it is a valuable concept; a purely introspective psychology has difficulty in meeting such a standard. The idea of learning as "conditioning" is a useful notion, so long as the entire process of learning is not interpreted in such terms. But as a philosophy or a psychology, materialism has proved inadequate. It has seemed impossible to explain how matter in motion can give rise to moral ideals, to spiritual values, to creative activity, to reason itself. Perhaps the newer concepts of matter which seem to make it possible to bridge the ancient gap between materialism and idealism will give rise to a more adequate explanation of man's nature.

IDEALISM AND EDUCATION

Idealism, on the other hand, has been extremely influential. The ideas and ideals of a few leaders in the educational world have entered deeply into the thinking of many teachers who have themselves never studied philosophy but who have been influenced by the teachings and example of those leaders who have.

Hegelian idealism was particularly important in the United States during the latter part of the nineteenth century. W. T. Harris (1835–1908), superintendent of schools in St. Louis from 1867 to 1880 and national commissioner of education from 1889 to 1906, was a Hegelian who applied this philosophy to the study of educational problems. John Dewey started his philosophical career as a Hegelian.

One of the most characteristic things about Dewey's present philosophy is his attempt to achieve unity out of apparent contradictions, an indication of the influence of Hegelianism on his thinking.

It was Karl Rosenkranz (1805–79), a Hegelian, who wrote the first textbook on *Philosophy of Education*. This book, edited by W. T. Harris, was used widely in this country during the 1890's and the early 1900's.

In our country the late Herman Harrell Horne, of New York University, has been the most prominent present-day spokesman for the philosophical idealist in education. He has written numerous books and articles from this point of view and was the author of "An Idealistic Philosophy of Education" in a symposium of philosophies of education.[1]

This symposium is a valuable collection for the student of educational philosophy. In it representatives of differing schools of thought state tersely and succinctly the philosophy on which they base their educational theories and explain briefly their convictions on the nature of education and on educational aims and procedures. Because of the book's convenience and suitability for students, it is used as the source for most of the quotations in this chapter. In the article written by him, Horne said:

In the light of the total philosophy of idealism, we conclude that the objective of living and learning is to develop the natural man into the ideal man.[2]

The school should really be centered in certain ideal conceptions of what man and his society should be in view of the kind of world in which he really lives.[3]

The objective of all method in teaching is the cultivation of the personality of the pupil.[4]

A modern ethical theorist . . . . under Hegelian inspiration finds the highest good in "self-realization," a concept requiring a social as well as a personal application, and involving the maximum fulfillment of man's capacities in all desirable directions.[5]

Idealism emphasizes the spiritual side of man. Because, to the idealist, spiritual values are the most important aspect of man and

1. National Society for the Study of Education, *Forty-first Yearbook of the Society for the Study of Education,* Part I: *Philosophies of Education,* p. 139.
2. *Ibid.,* p. 194.   4. *Ibid.,* p. 172.
3. *Ibid.,* p. 160.   5. *Ibid.,* p. 181.

of life, the philosophy of education growing out of metaphysical idealism would emphasize spiritual growth. Horne held that education is growth, but growth toward a goal. Of the goal one may be certain: It is ideal human personality. A teacher who was a metaphysical idealist would believe that the search for ultimate reality may best be furthered by inference from the nature of man, that man's finite mind springs from the Infinite Mind, that both the individual and the world are expressions of intelligence, that the material world is to be explained by the mental, and that the enduring substance of the world is of the nature of mind. This teacher would be very certain of the goal of education and would accept these goals as determining the ultimate law of the school.

REALISM AND EDUCATION

Realism is represented in this symposium by three writers; two of them, Adler and McGucken, wrote from what is practically the same point of view. The third, Breed, wrote from one slightly different. Mortimer J. Adler contributed "In Defense of the Philosophy of Education," and the late William McGucken of St. Louis University wrote "The Philosophy of Catholic Education." The two men are both Aristotelians; Adler's interpretation is secular and naturalistic and rooted in epistemology, while McGucken's interpretation is Thomistic and rooted in metaphysics as well as in epistemology; it is religious as well as secular and concerned with the supernatural as well as with the natural.

Adler is primarily a logician. He is intent on proving that "the ultimate ends of education are the same for all men at all times and everywhere. They are absolute and universal principles."[6] He says that "the ends of education are always properly determined by the nature of man,"[7] that "he who serves the common welfare ultimately works for his own welfare,"[8] and that "education is the process by which those powers (abilities, capacities) of men that are susceptible to habituation, are perfected by *good* habits, through means artistically contrived, and employed by any man to help another or himself achieve the end in view (i.e., good habits)."[9]

Adler firmly believes that man may know truth; there are, he says,

6. *Ibid.*, p. 221   8. *Ibid.*, p. 231.
7. *Ibid.*, p. 230.   9. *Ibid.*, p. 246.

self-evident truths from which to proceed, by reasoning, to build a superstructure of truth. "I say: *either* there are self-evident truths at the foundation of philosophical demonstration, *or* there is no such thing as philosophical knowledge."[10]

There is, according to Adler, but one philosophy of education. He is certain of this because he is sure of the principles here stated. He does not say that either he or anyone else knows what this philosophy of education is with all its ramifications, but he is certain that, to discover it, one must proceed from the aforementioned principles.

Adler and Chancellor Hutchins of the University of Chicago have had a great deal to say in recent years about education and the philosophical background necessary for determining its policies and content. Their proposals will be referred to later.[11]

The key to the Catholic philosophy of education, says McGucken, is the supernatural.[12] "Without God, the Catholic maintains there is no ultimate purpose in life, no ultimate purpose in education. For God made man, according to the words of the penny catechism, 'to know, love, and serve Him in this life and be happy with Him forever in the next.' "[13]

Quoting from the *Encyclical on Christian Education* of Pius XI, McGucken says that "education consists essentially in preparing man for what he must do here below in order to attain the sublime end for which he was created."[14] For the Catholic, "the thing of ultimate importance is not here but hereafter."[15] However, Catholicism insists on a social organization in this world which recognizes the essential dignity of man, his natural and inalienable rights, and in which ideals of social justice may be increasingly realized.[16]

The second realistic philosophy, that of neo-realism, is represented by Frederick Breed, who contributed "Education and the Realistic Outlook."[17] Breed's book *Education and the New Realism* was a cogent and intelligent criticism of pragmatism and Progressive education. He has written many articles from the realistic point of view,

10. *Ibid.*, p. 237. 11. See chap. xiii.
12. National Society for the Study of Education, *op. cit.*, p. 264.
13. *Ibid.*, p. 252.
14. *Ibid.*, p. 263. 16. *Ibid.*, p. 284.
15. *Ibid.*, p. 287. 17. *Ibid.*, p. 87.

in which he emphasizes that any philosophy of education in this country must be in harmony with democratic principles. He points out in this symposium that the first principle of democracy is respect for individuality, that education as growth must be understood to receive its direction from social as well as from individual demands,[18] and that the term "democracy" needs to be redefined in terms of social welfare and control.[19] "Democracy," says he, "has been taken for granted by our population to such an extent that knowledge of its foundation has been wanting."[20] And, again, he continues: "Could youth but see that concessions to the freedoms that wrought the Lindbergh tragedy [the "democracy" from which they fled] are violations rather than applications of the principles of democracy, they could unite in a sweeping crusade for the clarification of democratic principles and their proper application."[21]

Because Breed firmly believes in the apostolic injunction, "Hold fast that which is good," he would have the school transmit the social heritage in such a way as to impress youth with the fact that "truth . . . . constitutes an important element of the general social tradition."[22] He emphasizes repeatedly the necessity for helping youth adjust to inexorable fact, to the independent nature of the reality which is back of our experience.[23]

A third group of realists, the critical realists, are not represented in the symposium *Philosophies of Education*. In so far as the critical realists are Kantian, this textbook may be said to be written from their viewpoint. Kant was a great synthesizer. It is probable that each of the great schools of philosophy has something of truth and value in it. Else it could not have been held and convincingly argued by the great intellects espousing it. One of the strengths of Kant's philosophy was that he saw the unification possible between empiricism and rationalism, between skepticism and certainty, between eudaemonism and puritanism. This was not a shallow eclecticism but a genuine synthesis, in which the errors of each position were avoided and a consistent philosophy erected. Time seems only to confirm and strengthen the fundamental positions of this philosophy.

18. *Ibid.*, p. 131.   20. *Ibid.*, p. 134.   22. *Ibid.*, p. 133.

19. *Ibid.*, p. 133.   21. *Ibid.*, p. 135.   23. *Ibid.*, pp. 108–9.

The point of view expressed in this book has much in common with all the educational philosophies quoted. All these educational philosophies agree that the educative process centers in the task of developing superior manhood and womanhood; that our task in this world is to promote justice and the common welfare, and that we should look to the ultimate purpose of education for direction in solving educational problems. Breed does not specifically discuss any ultimate purpose, but his emphasis on the role of democratic principles carries that implication.

EXPERIMENTALISM AND EDUCATION

There remains one other educational philosophy to discuss—"Philosophy of Education from the Experimentalist Outlook," written by William Heard Kilpatrick, the foremost exponent of Dewey's philosophy in the United States. This is the philosophy which underlies the Progressive movement in this country. Any educator worthy of being a teacher is a progressive; those who build their educational theory on pragmatism call themselves Progressives. Teachers who do not accept the philosophy of pragmatism resent the pre-emption of the term "progressive" by those who do accept that philosophy, just as realists and idealists resent the imputation implied and expressed that it is only experimentalism that is the philosophy of democracy and of the proper use of science and the scientific method. Breed says that "the teaching profession has already been rescued from the delusion that Dewey's instrumentalism is *the* philosophy of education, or *the progressive* philosophy of education, or even *the democratic* philosophy of education."[24]

There is much that is excellent in Progressive theory; much of it that has been in educational teaching since the days of Plato. But there are other practices which have so aroused groups who hold other philosophies that they have organized rather loosely into a unit calling themselves Essentialists. One point of dispute between the groups is, of course, the theory of knowledge held by the pragmatists, their belief that truth is changing and man-made and the resulting implications for morality and for education. Kilpatrick says: "We know no absolute principles, that is, none which now stand properly above criticism or which may not conceivably be

24. *Ibid.*, p. 89.

modified, perhaps in intent, perhaps in application, as new conditions arise."[25]

He insists that there are no principles that admit of no exceptions. With that understanding, he says that the following are moral principles issuing from man's experience: "Each person is to be treated always as an *end* and never merely as *means*. In this ethical respect all men are to stand equal. Conversely, each person is under moral obligation so to act as, negatively, not to hurt the good life of others and positively, to foster the good life for all."[26]

It is difficult to understand how the same principle can admit of exceptions and still be acted upon *always*; how can one treat a person *always* as an end unless this principle is a true one, an *absolute*? And if exceptions are to be allowed, who is to decide on them? Individuals? Majority opinion? The good life for man, his chief end, morality itself, democracy as a society in which each man is treated as an end, are impossible unless this principle is held inviolate, a truth which permits no exceptions. Dewey himself has always held that because there are no concepts of universal validity, there are no ultimate and general aims for education. He wrote:

> Education, as such, has no aims; "education" is an abstract idea. Only persons have aims. And the aims of persons are indefinitely varied, differing with different children, changing as children and their teachers grow. Stated aims, such as we are about to make, will do more harm than good unless they are taken only as suggestions as to how to look ahead for consequences, to observe conditions, and to choose means in the liberating and directing of children's energies. As a recent writer has correctly said "To lead this boy to read Scott's novels instead of old Sleuth's stories; to teach this girl to sew; to root out the habit of bullying from John's makeup; to prepare this class to study medicine,—these are samples of the millions of aims we have actually before us in the concrete work of education."
>
> Bearing these qualifications in mind, there are three characteristics found in all good educational aims, viz., (1) they are founded on the activities and needs of the pupils; (2) they enlist the cooperation of the pupils; and (3) they are specific and immediate, not general and ultimate.[27]

Dewey quotes with approval a writer who gives examples of a few of the "millions of aims" teachers have before them. Exactly.

25. *Ibid.*, p. 54.   26. *Ibid.*

27. John Dewey, *Democracy and Education*, p. 121.

How can one decide which aims to promote? Why lead any boy to read Scott rather than old Sleuth? Why root bullying out of John's makeup? One is in the same dilemma as was pointed out in the previous chapter. Pragmatism says, "Look at consequences." Consequences for whom? In the light of what? In the same way, what is the criterion by which one decides on specific and immediate aims? Certainly one must have aims that are specific and immediate. They are the steps by which one travels toward the ultimate goal. But one also needs a general and ultimate goal in order to have a criterion for deciding on which of the million immediate and specific goals one should concentrate.

The nearest to a general and ultimate goal which experimentalism allows is that of growth. "Education," says Dewey, "is all one with growing, even as growing is all one with living."[28] This concept of education as growth with no goal beyond further growth has been severely criticized. Growth can be in the wrong direction as well as in the right. The direction must be defined, not merely a dynamic direction indicated.

Of this, Boyd Bode, also philosophically an experimentalist, wrote:

The chief defect in American education today is the lack of a program, or sense of direction. It has no adequate mission or social gospel.[29]

We have made no serious effort to provide young people with a gospel to live by.[30]

Progressive education has a unique opportunity to become an avowed exponent of a democratic philosophy of life, which is the last remaining hope that the common man will eventually come into his own.[31]

There are few thinkers who have written more than John Dewey about democracy. But to follow the philosophy of experimentalism would be to make it well-nigh impossible to achieve democracy. To deny the necessity for an ultimate goal, an ideal of a society in which every man is treated as an end, to insist that respect for human personality is not an absolute, i.e., a principle that is always true, to deny the possibility of objective knowledge of truth, to subordinate reason to purpose, ideas to acts, duty to interest, and to

28. *Ibid.*, p. 51.
29. Boyd Bode, *Progressive Education at the Crossroads*, p. 100.
30. *Ibid.*, p. 58.   31. *Ibid.*, p. 122.

identify the good with that "which works" would seem to make it
impossible to achieve true democracy.[32]

Fortunately, the majority of teachers use experimentalism as it
should be used: as an aid to the means which will assist in realizing
those ends, denied as ultimate goals by the philosophy of experimentalism but toward the formulation and realization of which human nature itself impels us.

It would seem that Dewey's third characteristic of good educational aims should read: "They are specific and immediate *as well
as* general and ultimate." The other characteristics which he states
also seem to need some revision. The first one states that educational
aims are founded on the activities and needs of pupils. If this is understood to mean children's activities and needs with reference to
becoming competent and social-minded human beings, able and willing to promote the general welfare, the statement might be acceptable. But without a general and ultimate purpose in mind by which
to decide on the actual needs of pupils, the application of such a
principle will result in the extreme individualism which has been
the curse of Progressivism, for teachers are very likely to interpret
wants as needs. The second characteristic of educational aims,
Dewey says, is: "They must enlist the cooperation of the pupils."
Eventually, they should. If children are wisely managed, in time
they will. But human nature being what it is, there will often
be resistance on the part of children to any means used for stimulating the growth which they must make if they are to become the
kind of human beings they should become. Coercion is often necessary in bringing up children. But it should be used so as eventually
to result in willing co-operation, if at all possible.

There is some indication that the criticism directed at any educational philosophy based on pragmatism is having some effect. Some
of the Progressives themselves have definitely adopted the concept
of democracy as an ultimate goal. Teachers over the entire country
are examining the meaning of the word "democracy" and seeking to
discover how education can develop the kind of men and women
able and willing to further the ideals of the democratic way of life.

Brubacher says that, as a matter of fact, experimentalism has its

32. The student should recall what was learned in studying chaps. vi, viii,
and xi as a background for this statement.

absolutes just as does every philosophy; that democracy and respect for human personality are actually absolutes for them.[33] If they would frankly admit that this is true and make the necessary changes in their theories of knowledge and of ethics, experimentalism would be much like realism.

At present, Kilpatrick sees learning as closely interrelated with the process of living[34] and says that our schoolrooms must "become living democracies,"[35] that "in a democracy it is self-directing personalities that we try to build, the kind that can carry forward life ever more successfully in a developing world,"[36] and that the progressive development of a better life for all men is the basis out of which morality and moral conduct arise.[37] These proposals for education must of course be understood within the frame of reference furnished by the pragmatic theory of knowledge and truth.

AGREEMENTS AMONG ALL PHILOSOPHIES

All these philosophies agree that respect for human personality is the crux of their educational theory. They are all interested in building a society which recognizes the dignity of mankind and provides for man's best development. When one begins with these points of agreement, is it not true, as Kilpatrick says, that if all teachers "study their common problems honestly and carefully, the greater is the likelihood that they will reach common results."[38]

The Educational Policies Commission of the National Education Association has been encouraging and aiding this study of our common problems through a series of publications on education within the framework of democracy. In one of the commission's books, *The Purposes of Education in American Democracy,* there is a detailed analysis of what it means to educate boys and girls for a democratic society. Four aspects of education are identified and described as follows:

These aspects center around the person himself, his relationship to others in home and community, the creation and use of material wealth

33. J. S. Brubacher, "The Absolutism of Progressive and Democratic Education," *School and Society*, LIII (January 4, 1941), 1–9.

34. National Society for the Study of Education, *op. cit.,* p. 66.

35. *Ibid.,* p. 78.   37. *Ibid.,* pp. 48–49.

36. *Ibid.,* pp. 85–86.   38. *Ibid.* p. 54.

and socio-civic activities. The first area calls for a description of the educated *person;* the second for a description of the educated *member of the family and community group;* the third of the educated *producer or consumer;* the fourth of the educated *citizen.* The four great groups of objectives thus defined are:

1. The Objectives of Self-Realization
2. The Objectives of Human Relationship
3. The Objectives of Economic Efficiency
4. The Objectives of Civic Responsibility.[39]

Each of these areas is subdivided into from eight to thirteen more specific objectives, with each of these discussed in relation to the daily work of the teacher.

Other publications of this commission, such as *The Unique Function of Education in American Democracy, Education and Economic Well-being in American Democracy, Learning the Ways of Democracy,* and *The Education of Free Men in American Democracy,* are all practical and helpful. The point of view is Essentialist rather than extreme Progressive, but the writers have wisely concentrated on points of agreement rather than on differences. The later *Education for All American Youth* is perhaps more controversial in nature. Many of the proposals of the authors of this book for the secondary schools are those advocated by Progressives.

PROGRESSIVISM, TRADITIONALISM, AND ESSENTIALISM

It has been pointed out that the principal philosophical support for the movement known as Progressive education came from Rousseau's conception of child nature and from Dewey's pragmatic empiricism. The Progressive Education Association was organized in 1918 and for twenty years or more was a potent force in American education. It is doubtful whether many teachers really understood its philosophical foundations. Certainly, few had studied Dewey's philosophy against any background of other philosophy. Many ill-advised and extreme practices were advocated in the name of Progressive education, practices which John Dewey himself vigorously condemned.

To some extent the movement was popular because it constituted

39. Educational Policies Commission, *The Purposes of Education in American Democracy,* p. 47.

a revolt against the boring formalism of the traditional school, a formalism of which no educational leader approved. Further, the organization had a name which appealed to teachers. We all desire progress, and hope for progress ran high immediately after the first World War. Some teachers joined because Progressive education was the current band wagon; it is human to want to be in the parade.

It was the outbreak of the second World War which spelled doom for the organization. Rightly or wrongly, Progressive education was blamed for certain weaknesses in our educational system which became apparent in our war experience. Membership fell off. Early in 1944 the organization voted to change its name to the American Education Fellowship, to include laymen as well as teachers in its membership, and to extend its interest beyond the school into the community.

This does not mean that the movement is dead. But it is not so popular as it was. There is some danger that the reaction from its teachings may carry educational practice too far from progressive tenets. F. Alden Shaw, headmaster of the Detroit Country Day School and one of the advocates of essentialism, has written an article in which he exhorts teachers "not to throw out the baby with the bath."[40]

Progressives have not always agreed among themselves on school procedures, but the following seem to be essential tenets:

1. Pupil freedom, initiative, and independence in thinking.
2. An "activity" curriculum based on children's experiences, not on subject matter organized to be learned. Teacher and children plan the curriculum together on the basis of problems arising within their experience. Subject matter is to be used in order to understand experience and thereby enable the individual to direct and redirect it better.
3. Individual interests are used as the basis of motivation; schools are to be child-centered; learning must be purposeful: to solve problems which seem important to the pupil.
4. No general or ultimate aim for education; education is growth to produce further growth.[41]

40. "Let's Not Throw out the Baby with the Bath," *School and Society*, LVIII (August 21, 1943), 123.
41. See articles by W. H. Kilpatrick on progressive education.

It is easily seen how such proposals for the school have grown out of empiricism and pragmatism. During the twenties the Progressive theory was highly individualistic, but this was corrected to some extent in the succeeding decade. Progressives advocate democracy because it allows the individual the highest degree of freedom. But their interpretation of democracy has often been too individualistic and with far more emphasis on rights than on duties.

The criticisms of Progressive education most often heard, and those probably responsible for the loss of prestige, were two: (1) pupils have not learned thoroughly our social heritage; they do not know what an educated person needs to know; (2) they are too selfish and self-centered; they are not self-disciplined or willing to sacrifice for the common good.

Whether these criticisms are to be laid at the door of Progressive education alone might be questioned. They are without doubt the possible results of Progressive theory which many persons have been pointing out for years. Chief among these critics has been the late William Chandler Bagley. He said repeatedly that out of the experience of the race have come lessons so important to social welfare and to social progress that it is folly to let the child decide on the basis of his interests whether he will learn them or not. He also said that there is no rigor in Progressive education; children do not learn to tackle the unpleasant or difficult things of life.[42]

Bagley called himself an Essentialist. Essentialists have no elaborate organization nor do they constitute a movement. A group of educational leaders, among whom were Bagley, Michael Demiashkevich, and F. Alden Shaw, pledged themselves in February, 1938, to protest against the "widespread skepticism and cynicism of Progressives toward values imbedded in the cultural heritage, which mankind has laboriously and painfully evolved for thousands of years and within which are rooted ideas and ideals that have endured the test of time."[43]

Many persons not in this original group consider themselves Essentialists. The name indicates their belief: that certain essentials

42. W. C. Bagley, "Crux of the Conflict between Progressives and Essentialists," *Educational Administration and Supervision*, XXVI (October, 1940), 508–11.

43. Alfred Hall-Quest, "Three Educational Theories: Traditionalism, Progressivism, Essentialism," *School and Society*, LVI (November 14, 1942), 457.

from the experience of the race cannot safely be overlooked in education; they are values by which we must be guided. The philosophy of essentialism is either that of realism or that of idealism, although scholastic realists and many idealists are Traditionalists rather than Essentialists.

One deciding factor between essentialism and traditionalism seems to be the belief concerning the source of knowledge. Neo-realists and critical realists are neither extreme empiricists, as are the pragmatists, nor rationalists, as are the idealists and scholastic realists. Neo-realists follow Aristotle, and critical realists follow Kant in a synthesis of empiricism and rationalism. The Thomistic Aristotelians are likely to be more inclined toward rationalism than the modern Aristotelian who does not accept the Thomistic interpretation.

Although realists and idealists differ in their philosophies, they would agree (1) that man's nature is such that he must learn to use freedom and that he needs adult discipline before he can be self-disciplined and (2) that man is in possession of much truth about himself and the world in which he lives which young people need to learn for their own best development and for social welfare. Therefore, those who are Essentialists advocate:

1. Discipline from adults, directed always at developing young people who can use freedom wisely.
2. An organized, planned, curriculum. The "activity" experience approach in lower grades; informal learning gradually giving way to a curriculum in which symbols play a larger part. Any planning done by pupils is to be within a framework of subject matter selected by adults.
3. Social interests and needs paramount; society-centered school; individual interests may be used, but it should be remembered that such interests are often selfish and need redirecting; interest follows effort as well as effort following interest.
4. Promotion of the general welfare conceived as the general and ultimate aim; general welfare thought of in terms of real democracy.[44]

Essentialists are in sympathy with many of the Progressive emphases and practices. They want a functional approach to the problems of learning and think it wise to use the individual experience of the learner as the starting-place in learning lessons from the ex-

44. See any article by W. C. Bagley or F. S. Breed on essentialism.

perience of the race. Essentialists condemn parrot-like *memoriter* methods and do not want a return to the traditional school which used them. Sound educational principles, say they, are old, and good teachers have practiced them for generations.

Scholastic realists and many idealists incline toward traditionalism. Back of this educational theory there is a philosophy of the changeless and the eternal and often a belief in a supernatural order as well as in a natural world. The world is controlled by universal reason; man should develop his reason and live in accord with its dictates. The Traditionalist is likely to think of education as a process of rigid intellectual training through the logical use of symbols.[45] This, it is thought, will develop his mental powers and increase his ability to use his reason, the source of knowledge, in practical affairs. Thus, the Traditionalist advocates:

1. Strict and authoritative discipline; free men can become free only through the discipline, physical and mental, which subordinates man's lower nature to his higher nature and develops his reason.
2. An organized, planned, curriculum, with emphasis upon the liberal arts. Logical use of symbols important. "Activity" should be mental. Even small children should not get the idea that learning is all play. Much memorization needed.
3. If the teaching is good, students will be interested in much of their work, particularly after they learn the joy that comes from exercising reason. But young people must learn to exert effort whether they are particularly interested or not. Otherwise their mental powers do not develop.
4. The purpose of education is to make man intelligent and good and so to prepare him for his eternal destiny. But to do that, man needs a society here in which the ideals of social justice are increasingly realized, so he should concern himself with improving this world as well as himself.[46]

The beginning student of educational philosophy will have to decide for himself which of these groups has the best program for educating young people in and for a democratic society. Herman Harrell Horne, in discussing the problem of the teacher's educational philosophy, suggests that the young teacher try to reach his most fundamental idea and then build his philosophy upon that

45. Hall-Quest, *op. cit.*, p. 452.

46. See *ibid.* and also writings of Catholic educators. The writings of Chancellor Hutchins advocate a secular type of neo-traditionalism.

idea, taking care that what he builds is consistent.[47] The study of this text and readings from the Suggested References should by this time have given the beginner enough help so that he can understand what the fundamental ideas of differing philosophies are and, with that assistance, begin to decide upon his own philosophy.

EDUCATIONAL AIMS IN A DEMOCRACY

If education is a process of growth and development, taking place as a result of the interaction of an individual with his environment, both physical and social, a process beginning at birth and lasting as long as life itself, during which the finest potentialities for manhood and womanhood are to be developed, it seems evident that to realize the objective of education—promoting the welfare of all mankind —children must live in a society which will induce the proper growth.[48]

Children need, first of all, a healthful and happy home life where they are managed with affectionate firmness. Nothing can take the place of a good home. Good health, both physical and mental, unselfishness, respect for the other fellow's rights and points of view, good will to others, self-control, ability to do hard things and to sacrifice one's own desires for those of others, a willingness to take responsibility, are all best and most successsfully developed in home life. If the school is to be successful in its share of the educative enterprise, it must be able to build upon a foundation begun in the home and to continue building with the help of the home. It is a mutual enterprise, in which home and school must work together.

Love of native land and of a specific way of life begins with a love of home and the kind of living that goes on in a genuine home. As Kilpatrick emphasizes, if we want children to learn to live democratically, we must see that our homes as well as our schools are laboratories for that kind of living.

Schools, too, must be organized in such a way as to promote democratic living. What this involves should be clearly understood. Too many teachers have acted as if democracy meant anarchy and

47. H. H. Horne, "Three Competing Philosophies of Education," *Educational Forum*, IX (January, 1945), 133–38.

48. What is said in this section should be connected with all that has gone before, particularly with the discussions of democracy in chap. viii.

have been responsible for classrooms where bedlam reigned. Teachers should remember that, while freedom is a natural right of man, its proper use must be learned and that the freedom of any one individual is always limited by the freedom of others.

If the school is to be successful in its task of educating for a truly democratic society, the following policies and practices seem to be among the most important:

1. The principle of respect for human personality should be acted upon. It ought to be remembered that this means treating each child as an end, promoting his best development.[49] It does not mean letting him follow all his own whims and caprices. It does mean treating him so that the best in his nature may develop. The best in human nature is that which promotes the welfare of all men.

The primary responsibility for securing an atmosphere of mutual respect lies with the teacher. The son of the poor man should be treated with as much consideration as the son of the rich man. The child of the school-board president should have no special favors. Children of different races should meet no discrimination; instead, the teacher should work to build up mutual respect and understanding.

No child should ever be treated with sarcasm or contempt. Every child should be helped to do things at which he can succeed; in this way a feeling of competence is built up out of which comes self-confidence and self-respect. But he must not get the idea that success in everything is easy of attainment. Children need to learn that only effort brings success.

Children should themselves be helped to develop respect for others. This is a long, slow process. Sometimes the influence of the home is such that a teacher works under an insuperable handicap. But the teacher should do all in his power to counteract selfishness, snobbishness, and cruelty on the part of some children, directed toward other children.

The teacher's own example is of great importance. There is something in human nature which delights in the use of power. Teachers need to learn to use power wisely and not to abuse it. It is unfortunately true that teachers are themselves sometimes selfish, snobbish, and even cruel. It is impossible to teach others what is not

49. See chap. vi.

practiced in one's own life. As Emerson put it: "Do not say things. What you are stands over you the while, and thunders so that I cannot hear what you say to the contrary."[50]

2. Children should master the tools of learning and as much of the social heritage as each has time and ability for. They certainly should leave school realizing that education is a continuing process and knowing how and where to learn more. But they should *know* something when they leave school. The alleged mathematical illiteracy of our Army population seems inexcusable. Some teachers have interpreted Progressive education to mean that children should learn only what they were interested in, that to know specific facts was not important, that drill was useless and coercion immoral. Dewey and Kilpatrick have always been more sensible than many of their followers.

It is the teacher's business to interest children, if possible, in what they need to know. The old dry-as-dust, recite-what-was-written-in-a-textbook, word-for-word, formalism was contrary to all educational theory and practiced only by teachers who knew little themselves and nothing of how children learn. Since at least the days of Comenius, real teachers have known better.

But it is not possible to interest all children all the time in everything they need to know. The better the teacher, the nearer he comes to doing this, but even the best teacher finds it necessary to use extrinsic motivation and sometimes coercion. Both while they are learning to use the tools of education and after they have become proficient in their use, young people should learn what specialists in each field consider it most fundamental to know about (1) our natural environment, (2) man himself, (3) his history and group life, and (4) the products of his culture: language and literature, practical and fine arts, religious and philosophical thought.

As they study, they learn the story of man's upward struggle, the background out of which came the idea of democracy, the story of the American dream and of American democracy. They study the development of science and learn of the rise of industry which accompanied applied science. As they grow older, they study the problems of today and learn how far short we are of having realized

50. Ralph Waldo Emerson, *Letters and Social Aims* (Vol. VIII of *Complete Works*, 1883 ed.), p. 95.

the ideals of a society in which each man can live as man should live. But they also learn of the progress which has been made, and it is hoped that they will study other social programs, their strengths and their failures.

Science can and has aided in discovering the level of maturity at which children are ready for specific learnings, but whatever they study, they should learn thoroughly.

3. Children must learn self-control, self-discipline, intelligent self-direction, in the interests of all. This is never learned without discipline from without, but it must be a discipline aimed at making itself unnecessary.

Little children learn to take turns, to play fairly, to share their playthings. Children in the lower grades can begin discussing and deciding questions which involve their group welfare, whenever the problem is one which they can understand and for which they have sufficient judgment; for example, the problem of where roller skates may be used and where their use is dangerous or the problem of snowballing. The discussion, however, must always be led by the teacher, and decisions must be made in the interests of all and therefore with the teacher's help. Teachers are supposed to have more wisdom than their pupils. They should never abdicate their position of leadership. But they can and should obtain the co-operation of their pupils. We all prefer to obey rules which we have helped to make.

Schools should make more use of co-operation than many of them do. Competition has its place. It is a powerful motive in human nature, and, as such, young people should learn to use it in the right way. Fair play and sportsmanship have to be developed. But schools have probably overdone the use of competition and have not emphasized co-operation as they should.

To learn to take responsibility is one of the lessons a child emphatically needs. This responsibility is, first, a responsibility for right conduct, for studying his lessons, for learning, for taking care of himself as a member of the group. Then comes the assumption of responsibility in group enterprises. For much of this, the extra-class activities are valuable. But it is a mistake to believe that these activities are of more importance in teaching young people to assume responsibility than are those of the classroom. Student committees, school councils, clubs, assemblies, all have their values; but the pupil's first responsibility to himself and to the society which is paying for his education is to assimilate as much of the social heritage as he can, in such a way as to develop his finest powers and abilities. Every classroom furnishes opportunity for co-operative as well as individualized work. Both are valuable. Gradually, a devotion to the common good should be developed.

4. Young people need to become as independent as possible in their thinking, to learn how to arrive at truth, to use the scientific method, to withhold judgment until all the facts are in, to think things through for themselves. In a school where personality is respected, there is freedom to discuss controversial issues, there is practice in the development of reliable opinion, and there is respect for opinions other than one's own. This does not mean that everyone has a right to form any opinion he pleases about matters for which facts are known and the truth has been established. Young people need to learn a respect for truth and a desire to know it. Their opinions have nothing to do with truth. The square root of 36 is 6; the chemical formula for hydrochloric acid is HCl; the first group of so-called Pilgrims landed in the New World in December of 1620; Delaware was the first state to ratify the Constitution of the United States; the physical basis for all life is a substance which we call protoplasm.

Even where truth has not been established, children must learn that they should not form an opinion until they have studied the question and learned all that they can discover about it. Prejudice and ignorance are never worthy of respect. But after they have studied and then have come to differing conclusions on controversial matters, their opinions should be respected.

The word "respect" has here a better connotation than does the term "tolerance." It is sometimes said that a society of free men is tolerant. It is a moot question how far a society can tolerate that which might undermine the public welfare. It has sometimes been said that people should be free to express any ideas in which they believe but that overt acts against the common good must not be condoned. It is ideas, however, which provoke acts, and why the thinker should be immune while the actor is not is difficult to say. We need to remember that rights carry attendant obligations, and the right to express thought should be used for the public good. Where differences of opinion do not threaten the public good, we should *respect* these differences. To bring up children to be as concerned with their duties as with their rights and to teach them to respect the rights of others is an important obligation of education.

Children can learn to respect, particularly, the opinion of the expert, of anyone who has really studied a problem. If democracy is to use experts as leaders, children must be brought up to demand that leadership be based on knowledge and on study. A respect for talent, for ability in any line, needs to be engendered in school. A child feels, intuitively, a respect for persons who embody those things he believes to be of value; he needs to be taught to value true worth, wherever found.

In these days of propaganda, schools must help children to learn how to detect and to analyze it. Young people need assistance in reading newspapers and in listening to the radio with intelligence and in recognizing when a one-sided presentation of any question is being given; otherwise they will not be able to obtain the information on the basis of which they can think a problem through and arrive at valid conclusions.

Another lesson that the school should help the child to learn is that in a democracy a minority must always be heard, its point of view examined, and its claims investigated. Its rights must always be guarded. But after this has been done and the majority has decided on a policy concerning a controversial matter, the minority must fall in line and act in accordance with the decision. This is the method of democracy and should always be followed unless the matter involved is an ethical question. In that field there is a higher authority than majority decision.

5. Young people need a great and ennobling goal for which to work. It is the business of the school to help boys and girls see the attainment of true democracy in this light. If they can understand that such a society has its roots in the needs of human nature; if they are convinced that man is more than an animal and should therefore always be treated as an end; if they see that a society in which man can live as man should live can be built only through mutual endeavor, then perhaps social progress can be speeded up and man will attain it without so much suffering.

Education for democracy means education for social progress. If every human being could have a healthy body, a good character, and as much intelligence and creative imagination developed as his physical limitations allow, the aims of education would be realized. To promote the general welfare means to promote the welfare of *each* and *every* individual; this means that each individual must be helped to become as fine a human being as *he* can become; he must be as intelligent and as good as we can help him become. On this all schools of educational philosophy would agree. On *how* this is to be accomplished there might be considerable difference of opinion. That difference is not so important. If we can agree on our aims and then set out to find out how to accomplish them through intelligent study, we shall, in time, come nearer to their realization.

SUMMARY

A philosophy of education must answer the questions of the what, why, and how of education. To determine the why of education, it is necessary to study human nature and its needs, for educational aims, like life's aims, grow out of human needs. In the light of the interdependence of the individual and society, it would seem that the purpose of education is to promote our common welfare through helping boys and girls develop into intelligent and social-minded members of a democratic society. To do this is the particular and joint responsibility of the home and school.

It is by reference to the why of education that the teacher can solve his daily problems, for it is the ultimate purpose of the school which should determine the policies and practices within the school. For this reason it is very important to study different philosophies and thoughtfully to appraise what each proposes as the aim of education and as the program for attaining that aim.

Materialism has never been of any lasting importance as a source of educational theory. Idealism, on the other hand, has been extremely influential. Idealists emphasize the spiritual and take for their goal the development of ideal human personality. There are three different schools of realism in educational philosophy. Scholastic realism centers its philosophy in the supernatural and conceives the purpose of education to be that of preparing man for what he must do here in order to attain eternal happiness in the next life. Neo-realism emphasizes the inexorable necessity for man's adjustment to the natural world in which he lives and the social responsibilities that grow out of man's nature and needs. Critical realism stresses not only adjustments but improvement of this world; respect for human personality is the central thesis in its educational philosophy; the study of man's nature and needs is its method for determining the provisions necessary for living life fully and completely and thereby discovering what education should accomplish. Experimentalism has no ultimate aim other than that of encouraging growth. Its aims are specific and grow out of the individual needs and interests of the pupils.

All philosophies agree that human personality has value and that society should be such that man can live with dignity, exercising his powers and abilities. But beyond this general statement there are wide divergencies concerning educational objectives and their attainment.

The popular names for differing schools of educational philosophy are Progressivism, Essentialism, and Traditionalism. Progressives are pragmatic and empiricist and propose a program for the schools in line with those epistemologies. Essentialists include neo-realists, critical realists, and some idealists. Idealists are rationalists, while neo-realists and critical realists are neither extreme empiricists nor rationalists but combine the two in either an Aristotelian or Kantian fashion. Because idealists are rationalists, they and the scholastic realists, who lean toward rationalism, are likely to be Traditionalists and so to emphasize the development of reason through the logical use of symbols.

Since all philosophies of education accept in some way the goal of educating for a democratic society, it would seem that we should all work together to (1) inculcate in young people a respect for human personality; (2) help our pupils attain, first, a mastery of the tools of learning and, second, a mastery of as much of the social heritage as each has time and ability for; (3) assist pupils in learning the difficult art of self-discipline and concern for the general welfare; (4) develop in each person the ability to think for himself but always within the framework of established truth; and (5) help young people understand democracy and to take the promotion of an improved society as their aim in living.

QUESTIONS TO AID STUDY

1. What questions must an adequate philosophy of education answer? Where must we go to find these answers? State the philosophical or ultimate law of the school. Why is it needed?

2. What is the aim of education in the light of the argument presented in this text?

3. In about two hundred to two hundred and fifty words write the gist of this argument so as to answer the question: "What should education accomplish?" Be sure you write a gist; do not attempt a summary.

4. What has materialism contributed to modern educational theory?

5. Name some persons prominently connected with an idealistic philosophy of education. What would they consider the aim of education to be?

6. Summarize the viewpoint of Thomistic philosophy of education on educational aims.

7. How would other realists state the aim of education?

8. What is the pragmatic view of educational aims? What seems to be the difficulty in using only immediate and specific aims without a general or ultimate aim?

9. Can teachers reach relative agreement on educational aims? How? Where does the point of agreement seem to be?

10. How does the Educational Policies Commission analyze educational aims?

11. What are the principal emphases in Progressive education? Show how each one is related to pragmatic empiricism.

12. In what do the Essentialists agree with the Progressives? In what do they differ?

13. In what philosophies is essentialism rooted? Show the connection between these philosophies and what essentialism advocates for the school.

14. From what philosophies does traditionalism come? How does traditionalism differ from essentialism? Show how the educational proposals of traditionalism come from their philosophies.

15. What seem to be the two most essential ideas in the philosophy of the Progressives? From what branch of philosophy do they come?

16. What seems to be the most essential idea in the philosophy of idealism? From what branch of philosophy does it come?

17. What seems to be the most essential idea in the philosophy from which this text is written? From what branch of philosophy does it come?

18. What seems to be the most essential idea in scholastic realism? In neo-realism?

19. With which essential idea do you propose to begin in building your philosophy of education? Why?

20. Can you see any evidence in the school you are attending that the policies and practices are determined by the purpose for which your school was established? Illustrate and explain.

21. If we accept the attainment of true democracy as our ultimate goal, what policies and practices must be followed in the school?

22. Write a paper illustrating *specifically* the way in which educational aims determine educational procedure. Using some unit of work, show how you will use subject matter and method toward the realization of an educational goal or goals.

264   *Philosophy of Education*

SUGGESTED REFERENCES

BODE, BOYD. *Progressive Education at the Crossroads.* New York: Newson & Co., 1938.

BREED, FREDERICK S. *Education and the New Realism.* New York: Macmillan Co., 1939.

BRUBACHER, JOHN S. *Modern Philosophies of Education* (New York: McGraw-Hill Book Co., 1939), chap. xiv.

DEWEY, JOHN. *Democracy and Education* (New York: Macmillan Co., 1926), chap. viii.

EDUCATIONAL POLICIES COMMISSION. *The Purposes of Education in American Democracy* (Washington, D.C.: Educational Policies Commission, National Education Association, 1938), chaps. iii–viii.

HARDIE, CHARLES D. *Truth and Fallacy in Educational Theory.* Cambridge: University Press, 1942.

HORNE, HERMAN HARRELL. *The Democratic Philosophy of Education* (New York: Macmillan Co., 1932), chap. viii.

———. "Three Competing Philosophies of Education," *Educational Forum,* IX (January, 1945), 133–38.

HUTCHINS, ROBERT MAYNARD. *The Higher Learning in America.* New Haven: Yale University Press, 1936.

JAARSMA, C. R. "Comparative Philosophies of Education," *Education,* LVIII (June, 1938), 630–35.

JUSTMAN, JOSEPH. *Theories of Secondary Education in the United States.* New York: Teachers College, Columbia University, 1940.

KANDEL, I. S. *Conflicting Theories of Education.* New York: Macmillan Co., 1938.

LODGE, RUPERT C. *Philosophy of Education* (New York: Harper & Bros., 1937), especially chaps. i–iv.

NATIONAL SOCIETY FOR THE STUDY OF EDUCATION. *Forty-first Yearbook of the Society for the Study of Education,* Part I: *Philosophies of Education.* Bloomington, Ill.: Public School Pub. Co., 1942.

REDDEN, JOHN D., and RYAN, FRANCIS A. *A Catholic Philosophy of Education* (Milwaukee: Bruce Pub. Co., 1942), chaps. iii and xvii.

ROCHE, PATRICK JOSEPH. *Democracy in the Light of Four Current Educational Philosophies.* Washington, D.C.: Catholic University of America Press, 1942.

REFERENCES ON TRADITIONALISM, PROGRESSIVISM
AND ESSENTIALISM

BAGLEY, WILLIAM CHANDLER. "The Case for Essentialism in Education," *N.E.A. Journal,* XXX (October, 1941), 201.

———. "Crux of the Conflict between Progressives and Essentialists," *Educational Administration and Supervision,* XXVI (October, 1940), 508–11.

———. "An Essentialist Platform for the Advancement of American Education," *ibid.*, XXIV (April, 1938), 241.

———. "Progressive Education Is Too Soft," *Education*, LX (October, 1939), 75–81.

BRAMELD, T. B. H. "Progressive Education on the Defensive," *Current History*, VII (August, 1944), 95–100.

BREED, F. S. "Has the 'Progressive' a Monopoly on Democratic Education?" *Education*, LX (October, 1939), 87–90.

BRUBACHER, J. S. "The Absolutism of Progressive and Democratic Education," *School and Society*, LIII, 1–9.

———. "A Proposal for Judging What Is and What Is Not Progressive Education," *ibid.*, XLVIII (October 22, 1938), 509.

HALL-QUEST, ALFRED. "Three Educational Theories: Traditionalism, Progressivism, Essentialism," *School and Society*, LVI (November 14, 1942), 452.

HOOK, SIDNEY. "The Case for Progressive Education," *Saturday Evening Post*, CCXVII (June 30, 1945), 28–29.

HOROWITZ, ARNOLD. "Experimentalism and Education," *Educational Forum*, I (May, 1937), 403–25.

KILPATRICK, WILLIAM HEARD. "Progressive Education," *N.E.A. Journal*, XXX (November, 1941), 231.

———. "Reconstructed Theory of the Educative Process," *Teachers College Record*, XXXII (March, 1931), 530–58.

KILPATRICK, W. H., and OTHERS. "What Is Progressive Education Today?" *Progressive Education*, XVII (May, 1940), 321.

OWEN, WILLIAM. "My Case against Progressive Education," *Saturday Evening Post*, CCXVII (June 23, 1945), 14–15.

PRESTON, R. C. "Stereotypes in Education," *School and Society*, LV (January 3, 1942), 1–5.

SHAW, F. ALDEN. "Let's Not Throw out the Baby with the Bath," *School and Society*, LVIII (August 21, 1943), 123.

CHAPTER XIII
THE DEVELOPMENT OF INTELLIGENCE

The nature of intelligence: (1) Its definitions; (2) Its components; (3) Its physical basis—The source of intelligence: (1) Contribution of heredity; (2) Contribution of environment; (3) Constancy of the I.Q.; relation of nature and nurture—The recognition of intelligence: (1) Use of intelligence tests; (2) Levels on which intelligence operates (a) obtaining facts, (b) organizing facts, (c) applying facts to life's problems; (3) Teachers' lack of appreciation for independence of thought—Development of intelligence; (1) Responsibility of the home, of the school; (2) Basic philosophical problem involved (a) empiricism: intelligence develops as human beings attempt to solve the problems which arise in their individual experience, (b) rationalism: intelligence develops as human beings exercise their reason through following the reasoning of great reasoners, (c) empiricism and rationalism as two aspects of a whole; synthesis of these two formulas; (3) Relation of activity to the development of intelligence (a) physical activity; mental activity, (b) history of the activity movement; (4) Relation of the wisdom of the past to the solution of modern problems

---

O N REGISTRATION day in a teachers college, two attractive young women were interviewed by the director of elementary education. To the friendly questioning of the director one replied:

Oh, I came because my girl friend was coming, and this school is close to home. I want to go home every weekend. I've always been told that I had a nice way with children, so I thought I might as well teach awhile. No-o-o, I have no brothers or sisters. I've never tried teaching Sunday school. But I've sometimes stayed with a neighbor's children. The little girl was sweet; I loved fixing her curls. But the boy was pretty hard to manage; he didn't mind very well. No-o-o, I didn't like school work so well; that was one reason I thought I'd like to teach little children; their work is easier. I don't like to read very much. But I do like children, especially when they are little and sweet. I'd like to take the kindergarten course, I think.

266

In her turn, the other one replied to the same inquiries:

I've always wanted to teach. One of my teachers, Miss Walters, told me about this school. She was tops. I selected elementary education because I like to work with children of that age. I have two young brothers and a sister, and I've helped my mother with them. I taught Sunday school for three years. Yes, I particularly like boys and girls, from eight to eleven or twelve—especially boys. You can *do* things with them. I've helped my two brothers and some boys in the neighborhood make airplanes this summer. Oh, yes, they behave themselves. If they're busy doing something they want to do, they don't get into mischief. Yes, I liked school work all right. I like to read, too. I just finished reading Marjorie Rawlings' *The Yearling.* Miss Walters told me she thought I'd like it. She said it might help me understand more about boys. Yes, I'd like to enroll in a curriculum that would prepare me to teach in the intermediate grades.

One would not need to be a director of elementary education to decide that the second girl was more intelligent than the first in her attempts to solve the problems that had evidently confronted each: What shall I, a high-school graduate, do next? Shall I go to college? Why? For what?

THE NATURE OF INTELLIGENCE

In what way was the second girl more intelligent than the first? What causes such differences? Just what is intelligence? That is a question with which psychologists have concerned themselves for at least fifty years. Intelligence is the name given to the ability to see and successfully solve one's problems. It is a more inclusive term than either intellect or reason; memory undoubtedly plays a part; so does imagination. Intelligence is sometimes defined as the ability to learn or to adapt behavior to varying circumstances. Some psychologists identify intelligence with the ability to see relationships; they point out that the intelligent person sees resemblances where the less intelligent sees no kinship and sees differences where others see only the superficial likeness. This ability the Gestaltist calls "insight." By some, speed of thought is considered the most important factor in intelligence. A good memory has been thought by others to be the most significant factor. Still others have emphasized the ability to do abstract thinking.

Philosophy of Education

George D. Stoddard, a psychologist of note and president of the University of Illinois, defines intelligence as "the ability to undertake activities that are characterized by (1) difficulty, (2) complexity, (3) abstractness, (4) economy, (5) adaptiveness to a goal, (6) social value, (7) emergence of originals, and to maintain such activities under conditions that demand a concentration of energy and a resistance to emotional forces."[1]

Ebbinghaus seems to have been the first of the modern psychologists to attempt to determine the essential nature of this thing called intelligence. He raised the question: "Of what does that higher intellectual activity of the mind consist: the performance of reason or understanding (judgment) in the higher sense? How is it to be characterized more specifically?" He continues:

What is an efficient physician? One who knows a great deal? True, he must know a great deal, but if he has nothing more than the knowledge he will probably be good as an author of a text-book, but not an efficient physician. For that, there is necessary in addition, the ability of a peculiar utilization of this knowledge; he must, by its means, be able to make a correct diagnosis and to help his patients. That is to say, he must be able, in the presence of certain symptoms, in themselves rather capable of a variety of interpretations, and described by the patient in a quite distorted way, to judge correctly: "That is such and such a disease," its present stage of development, the medicaments recommended for its cure, but also with reference to the individuality of the patient, his social position, ancestry, etc., to prescribe the treatment that will prove to be correct.[2]

The possession of knowledge is an important factor in the operation of intelligence; one cannot solve problems without information. A highly intelligent person usually has a good *memory*, well stored with information. If he has had the opportunity for schooling, he has usually assimilated more of the cultural heritage than has a less intelligent person. Questions of motivation, however, so often enter into the situation and some few highly intelligent children are so bored with what they get at school that unfortunately they do not always assimilate as much as they could. But a good memory is one factor in intelligence, and those children who show a high degree of

1. George D. Stoddard, *The Meaning of Intelligence,* p. 4.
2. A. L. Lee, "An Experimental Study of Retention and Its Relation to Intelligence," *Psychological Monographs,* Vol. XXXIV. No. 4.

ability to meet problems successfully do so partly "because of a richness and variety of basic mental organization which is exactly what we mean by good memory."[3]

Insight, the ability to see relationships, enters into what we call intelligence. The physician sees or hears of symptoms. He must find their cause, see connections, similarities to other cases, differences from previous situations. To return to the two candidates for admission to a teachers college: The first girl was not intelligent, so far as one could judge from her replies, for she thought she saw a relation between teaching school and her fondness for playing with a pretty, docile, child as if she were a doll. The only relation she saw between teaching and her dislike of school work and inability to manage an obstreperous boy was that she would do better with younger children because their "work" was easier. Even she might have been disabused of such an idea by a day's observation in the kindergarten.

Imagination is a factor in intelligence. The abilities to foresee the probable consequences of any contemplated behavior, to construct hypotheses, and to initiate and to create are important factors in what we call intelligence.

The *capacity for conceptual thought* is an essential phase of intelligence. Man's sense-experience is with particulars, with individual items. In some way, seeing the relationships among these particulars, he is enabled to organize and classify them into groups. Thus concepts—ideas of classes of things—arise.

The *ability to reason* is an intrinsic factor in intelligence. This is the highest mental power that man has. It enables him to infer from propositions which he knows or assumes to be true other propositions which necessarily follow but which are distinct from what is already known.

These factors, memory, insight, imagination, capacity for conceptual thought, and ability to reason, are not separate faculties but are simply different phases of the way man's mind works. What man's mind is, no one knows.[4] It has a physical basis in the brain and nervous system. Certainly, man's intelligence seems to be con-

3. J. L. Mursell, *The Psychology of Secondary School Teaching,* p. 234.
4. See chap. x.

270 Philosophy of Education

nected in some way with the organization and structure of the cortex of the cerebral hemispheres.

Whether the difference between human intelligence and animal intelligence is merely one of degree, accounted for wholly by differences in bodily structure, is a moot question. The majority of modern psychologists seem to be inclined to believe that man's superiority is dependent only upon a superior nervous system and some few other anatomical differences and that differences in intelligence rest upon corporeal differences of some kind. Their agreement does not, of course, prove that such a belief is true. That man's consciousness of self; his development of language, of art, of science and industry; his moral sense; his religion; are the result merely of a superior brain, an opposable thumb, a particular kind of larynx, etc., is an assumption which many thoughtful persons find difficult to accept.

THE SOURCE OF INTELLIGENCE

The source of man's intelligence is likewise a controversial question, although it seems to be less difficult of solution than does the problem of the exact nature of intelligence. Whether man's ability to solve his problems successfully depends upon hereditary factors or upon environmental factors or upon each to some degree is a question still arousing acrimonious dispute. There are psychologists of note, Terman, Goodenough, and the late Leta S. Hollingworth, for instance, who emphasize the role of heredity. Other psychologists, Stoddard and Wellman particularly, emphasize environmental influences.

It has been assumed by most psychologists not only that the ratio between chronological age and mental age, the so-called "intelligence quotient," is the most reliable indication of an individual's intelligence but also that this ratio is a constant one. The dispute at the present time seems to rage about the question of this constancy. Is the intelligence quotient always practically the same, or does it change radically with fundamental changes in the environment and the person's reactions to it? Is the development of intelligence merely an unfolding of a fixed and determined-at-birth ability? Hartmann quotes Karl Pearson, the distinguished English biometrician, as saying "that intelligence as distinct from knowledge is a congenital character and that it is not a *mutable* quality capable of being molded in any way by the doctor, the teacher, the parent, or any other human and natural agent."[5]

Stoddard calls attention to the fact that Binet, the father of the famous intelligence test, did not hold such a view. Stoddard writes, beginning with a quotation from Binet:

"Some recent philosophers appear to have given their moral support to the deplorable verdict that the intelligence of an individual is a fixed quantity, a quantity which cannot be augmented. We must protest and act against this brutal pessimism. We shall endeavor to show that it has no foundation whatsoever."

Binet then cites various observations and experiences in the teaching of subnormal children, summing up his final verdict in the year of his death as:

"A child's mind is like a field for which an expert farmer has advised a change in the method of cultivating, with the result that in place of a desert land, we now have a harvest. It is in this particular sense, the only one which is significant, that we say that the intelligence of children may be increased. One increases that which constitutes the intelligence of a school child; namely the capacity to learn, to improve with instruction."[6]

The Thirty-ninth Yearbook of the National Society for the Study of Education, issued in 1940, was devoted to a description of original studies and experiments dealing with the effect of changing environments on the intelligence quotient and to a discussion of the implied problem. At the present time, the environmentalists seem to have the better of the dispute. That is, experimental evidence seems to indicate that intelligence is a mere potentiality at birth, depending upon interaction with the environment for its development. No one claims that this potential is the same for all men or that there are not differences, the causes of which lie in hereditary factors. But the environmentalists affirm that human beings are dependent for the nature and degree of their development upon an environment with which they are inextricably united. "To deny this is to affirm that the organism and its properties are independent of the world in which they are found and that it leads a wholly self-determined life of its own. Such a view flies in the face of all contemporary science."[7] There seems to be an increasing amount of experi-

5. G. W. Hartmann, *Educational Psychology,* p. 153.

6. G. D. Stoddard, "The I.Q.: Its Ups and Downs," *Educational Record,* XX (January, 1939), 54–55.

7. Hartmann, *op. cit.,* p. 159.

mental evidence to show that with a radical change of environment, either toward improvement or deterioration, there is a corresponding change for better or worse in the intelligence quotient. Particularly is this true in early childhood.

Undoubtedly, part of the difficulty here lies in the nature of intelligence tests—the means by which we attempt to measure intelligence and to obtain the mental age. It is impossible to measure innate capacity itself. The only way by which we can approximate the measurement of intelligence is by measuring what intelligence can do. And what intelligence can do depends in part upon the environment in which and with which the person possessing the potential intelligence has interacted since birth.

Intelligence tests are made up of items about matters presumably common to the experience of all children, wherever they live. It is extremely difficult, if not impossible, to find items common to the experience of all children, even to those who live in the United States. Cultures differ within the country. City children and rural children, children of the plains and children of the mountains, children of high socioeconomic levels and children of the slums, children of the white race and children of other races, come in contact with widely different environmental conditions, know different things, and have differing opportunities. Not only would *what* they can do and *what* they know differ—and no intelligence test can measure intelligence in terms other than those of achievement—but their *ability* to learn and to solve problems, the sharpness of their wits, would differ, first, because they started with differing potentialities and, also, because their environments had been favorable or unfavorable for developing the potential power with which they started. Identical twins, supposedly with identical potential intelligence, in widely differing environments, show widely differing abilities to solve problems.[8] Children whose environment changes radically for the better or for the worse usually show corresponding changes in intelligence.[9]

Psychologists often assume that the more difficult the problems

8. National Society for the Study of Education, *Thirty-ninth Yearbook*, Part I: *Intelligence: Its Nature and Nurture*, p. 240.

9. *Ibid.*, pp. 230, 205–7, and 314–97.

successfully solved, the greater the number and variety of correctly solved problems, and the greater the speed with which problems are solved, the higher the intelligence; but it is a mistake to use mere rapidity of reaction as the sole criterion. Unfortunately, that is done by too many teachers. The child who reacts quickly, who talks glibly, who responds accurately and rapidly in school, is often favored above the more thoughtful and less articulate pupil. Intelligence tests themselves often contain items which favor the superficial thinker as compared with the more intelligent person. Tests too often encourage a person to jump to conclusions rather than to deliberate and to analyze, to see relations, to synthesize, and to hold one's attention to a difficult problem for a long period of time.

Not only is too much importance attached to speed as a supposed measure of intelligence, to the neglect of more important factors, but achievement tests in general too seldom demand the use of the higher intellectual powers. Intellectual activity may be thought of as operating on three different levels. The first and lowest of these is that of *acquiring information* or facts. To do this successfully requires sense-perception and memory. It is this particular form of intellectual activity that is measured by true-false tests and most of the short answer, so-called "objective," tests for which there has been such a craze during the last twenty or thirty years. Many teachers use only such tests for measuring the achievements of their pupils. That the ability to deliver facts is esteemed and too often confused with intellectual power is indicated by the popularity of and admiration for radio "quiz programs" of various kinds.

Information is important; one cannot think successfully without knowing facts. But the knowledge of isolated data is merely the lowest grade on which intelligence operates. The next plane is that of the *organization of these data* into a connected whole in which relationships are apparent. This demands the use of insight, and it takes time if the individual is to think for himself rather than merely to accept the dictum of author, teacher, or some other authority.

But the highest level on which intelligence operates is that of *application:* the use of knowledge in actual life-situations. Intelligence is the ability to solve life's problems successfully. Can the physician use what he has memorized and organized to heal his patients? Can the teacher use what he has learned to guide success-

fully the education of his pupils? This calls not only for memory
and insight but for imagination and the ability to reason.

Too many teachers have neither prized nor sought to develop
these higher intellectual powers. Docility, quickness, and ability to
memorize have been rewarded and independence of thought often
frowned upon. This may account for the fact that many 'great men
were poor students in school and many pupils who have made good
records in the classroom have never been heard of outside the
school. The University of Königsberg had this to say of the scholarship of Immanuel Kant as a student there: "The departments of
language and mathematics report that young Kant is doing well,
but the department of philosophy reports that it is impossible to get
any philosophy into his head." Young Kant probably thought for
himself. There is an old proverb that says: "One cannot tell from
the appearance of the tadpole how far the frog will jump." Our
merely "bright" pupils are often not so intelligent as some pupils
who appear less bright but who have more actual independence
and power for dealing with difficult problems.

Young Kant was not the only potentially great man who was un-
appreciated in school. Thomas Aquinas was named by his fellow-
students the "Dumb Ox." He happened to have a teacher who
appreciated his pupil and who foretold his future renown: "Nos
vocamus istum bovem mutum, sed ipse adhuc talem dabit in doc-
trina mugitum quod in toto mundo sonobit."[10]

Many great men have not been so fortunate during their school
days as to have such discerning teachers. There have been literally
hundreds of boys and girls considered dull in school who later have
become leaders in the intellectual world.

The father of Linnaeus was told by the director of the school
attended by the boy that he was unfit for a learned profession and
had better become a cobbler. Charles Darwin was considered at
school a very ordinary boy, below the common standard in intellect.
Harriet Martineau was considered to have' a dull, unobservant, and
unwieldy mind. Sir Isaac Newton, at twelve, stood low at school and
was taken out of school at fifteen. Later, he did very badly in the

10. May be freely translated as: "We call that ox speechless, yet he will bellow
forth a teaching that will resound through the whole earth" (quoted by William
Turner, *History of Philosophy*, p. 344).

university examination in Euclid because he would not be restricted by "approved" methods of demonstration. Robert Fulton was considered a dullard. Heinrich Heine made a poor showing at school because he was impatient of the imitative class work. George Eliot learned to read with difficulty. Oliver Goldsmith's teacher thought him one of the dullest boys she had ever tried to teach.[11]

The enumeration could continue for many pages. The truth of the matter is that teachers have too often failed to recognize real intelligence. To estimate justly and to assist in developing the potential ability of every child is a difficult problem. Psychologists are only beginning to understand some of the requisite factors, and there is much yet to learn.

THE DEVELOPMENT OF INTELLIGENCE

To raise the general level of intelligence in the population would be an important factor in promoting human progress. There are two ways by which this might be done: one through eugenics, by securing a better congenital endowment of potential intelligence; the other through education, by developing the potential intelligence already in the possession of the race. Teachers must work with the human beings already here. Indirectly, teachers may contribute to eugenics by inculcating in children a respect for parenthood and a recognition of the responsibility each person is under to insure that his children be well born. As citizens, teachers should study problems of eugenics. But the immediate contribution which teachers can make to this problem of improving the intelligence of the population is to do all in their power to develop the intellectual powers and abilities that children already possess in potentiality.

One real difficulty for the school lies in the fact, well established by experimental studies, that the early years of childhood seem to be the most important for the development of intelligence. Changes in intelligence quotient are most pronounced with radical changes in the environment during the preschool years. This indicates a need for nursery schools but, even more, the necessity for parent education. Parents are now, and always have been, the most important factor in a child's education.

11. Edgar J. Swift, *Mind in the Making*, chap. i.

Experimental evidence seems to indicate that a home favorable for developing the best in a child is one not of wealth but of economic security; one in which there is at least one adult, and, better, a mother and father, warmly interested in the child, furnishing affection and engendering a feeling of security and treating him as a personality.

If the development of small children is to proceed as it should, they must have opportunities to explore their environment and a chance to learn more and more about it. Children have inquiring minds. Their curiosity should be encouraged and properly directed. Their legitimate questions should be answered. To be sure, children ask questions in order to be noticed and to keep an adult's attention as well as to find out something they really need to know. It is not difficult to distinguish between questions prompted by the two motives. The first kind of question can be good-naturedly turned back to a child: "Suppose that *you* tell me." The second kind should be patiently and intelligently answered. Small children can ask questions that will tax the ability of the best-informed adult to answer. When the grown person does not know the answer, he should not try to hush the child or to bluff. If there is an answer, the proper reply is, "Let's find out," with recourse to the encyclopedia or dictionary. If no answer is possible, an honest explanation on the child's level of understanding should be made.

Children have minds far better and more alert than many adults give them credit for. It is a mistake to talk "down" to them, continually to "hush" them up, or to treat them with a discourtesy one would not dream of using with an adult. That does not mean that children do not need to learn consideration, manners, or appropriate conduct. It does mean that they should be treated with the same consideration that we hope to teach them to use.

To teach children self-reliance is to encourage the development of intelligence. They need practice in solving their own problems if they are to grow in ability to exercise this power. They should be encouraged to manipulate and to handle tools and to learn to use them, but the precaution should always be taken to see that they do not attempt what is clearly beyond their ability or that which is dangerous for them. Self-reliance grows with self-confidence, and that comes with success. On the other hand, children must not be too much shielded from the consequences of their behavior. It is from those consequences that they learn best. So they must not be allowed to take responsibility for conduct, the consequences of which would be dangerous or too painful. To help children think through the possible consequences of a line of action, to relate, to compare, to assume responsibility, and to take the consequences is to help them develop their ability to solve problems.

Parents should also acquaint children with language, literature, art, and drama. Mother Goose, children's classics, poetry, pictures, plays, if properly selected, appeal to all children and have an important place in their development.

To summarize, little children in the home need a gradually widening environment with which to interact; they need practice in solving those problems of their own for which they have the needed maturity; they must develop self-reliance, learn to assume responsibility, become acquainted with art, literature, drama, on their level of appreciation; they should be treated as intelligent human beings; they should have mental stimulation and experiences which challenge their interest and their powers.

The same recipe could be written for the development of intelligence in the school. The point is that, unless the process has been begun at home, almost irreparable damage is done the child. It is the first five years that are most important. Nursery schools and kindergartens with teachers who understand child growth and development ought to be established in every town and city. Parent education, of some kind, is even more imperative. If the proper development of intelligence has begun in the home, the school, working with the home, can continue the process.

The ability to solve life's problems successfully takes not only a capacity for insight and for reasoning but also knowledge. It is only as one obtains knowledge, organizes it, and applies it that his potential intelligence develops. It is one of the functions of the school to help children obtain knowledge in such a way as to develop their ability to apply it.

BASIC PHILOSOPHICAL PROBLEM INVOLVED

Before teachers can be sure that they know how to help children obtain the knowledge needed for complete and successful living, the basic epistemological question concerning the source of knowledge must be answered. Because leaders in the educational field differ on this question, we have differences of opinion on both curriculum and method. These differences were spoken of in the previous chapters.[12] Empiricists and rationalists do not agree on how to develop intelligence. This disagreement accounts for much acrimonious dispute in the educational world, as well as for lack of uniformity in practice. In the previous century the dispute centered about the opposition of the idealist, W. T. Harris, to the empiricism of the followers of the English philosopher, Herbert Spencer (1820–1903). In this generation the controversy rages between John Dewey and the Progressives, on one hand, and Chancellor Hutchins and the neo-traditionalists, on the other.

The question might be stated thus: Is intelligence best developed through meeting and solving your own problems, obtaining from the experience of the race what is needed for this solution, or through rigid intellectual training by the use of symbols, using books written by great thinkers and following their thought so as to develop one's own ability to think? Perhaps a further examination of the proposals of Dewey and of Hutchins might clarify the issue.

Basic to all of Dewey's educational philosophy is his concept of experience. "On the active hand, experience is *trying* . . . . on the passive, it is *undergoing*. When we experience something we act upon it, we do something with it; then we suffer or undergo the consequences.[13] . . . . Experience is primarily an active-passive affair; it is not primarily cognitive. But the measure of the value of an experience lies in the perception of the relationships or continuities to which it leads up."[14]

For an experience to have educational value, it must further growth, not arrest or distort the growth. Everything, says Dewey, depends upon the quality of experience. The criteria by which one may judge the worth-whileness of experience for education are the categories of continuity and interaction. If an experience leads on to other experiences, and those to still others, and those on and on

12. See chaps. xi and xii.
13. John Dewey, *Democracy and Education*, p. 163.
14. *Ibid.*, p. 164.

in such a way "as to arouse curiosity, strengthen initiative and set up desires and purposes that are sufficiently intense to carry a person over dead places in the future,"[15] then it has value for education. An experience must also furnish the opportunity for both phases of experience, the outer and the inner, the passive and the active, to operate.[16] Neither should be emphasized at the expense of the other; nor are the two principles of continuity and interaction separate from one another.

Within experience, human beings are continually meeting problems. When one meets a problem the solution of which seems important to the person meeting it, then, and only then, does one think. For this reason, Dewey would develop intelligence through having the curriculum grow out of those problems which children meet in their experiences and which meet the criteria of continuity and of interaction. Thinking and action are parts of the same process, says Dewey. Thinking guides action, and action tests thinking. "Thinking . . . . is the intentional endeavor to discover specific connections between something we do and the consequences which result, so that the two become continuous."[17]

Dewey's famous analysis of how we think contains the following steps:

1. Perplexity, confusion, doubt. (A felt need.)
2. A conjectural anticipation, a scrutiny of the given elements. (Analysis of the problem and conjecture concerning possible hypotheses.)
3. Marshaling all the data which will define and clarify the problem.
4. Selection and elaboration of tentative hypothesis.
5. Trial, testing, verification.

This is, as has often been pointed out, an analysis of the scientific method. Whether we *do* think this way or whether it is the way in which we *ought* to think, there are probably few people who would take issue with Dewey on the validity of this analysis.

One of the severest critics of modern education within the past few years has been Chancellor Hutchins of the University of Chicago. Dewey's influence has been felt in elementary education more than in secondary. It is for the higher levels of education that Hutch-

15. John Dewey, *Experience and Education*, p. 31.
16. *Ibid.*, p. 39.
17. Dewey, *Democracy and Education*, p. 170.

ins has made specific proposals, but his indictment of our entire educational system has been most severe. He calls attention to the fact that man is a rational animal and that the aims of education are the same as the aims of life: the attainment of wisdom and goodness. Therefore, in schools we must concern ourselves with developing man's ability to reason. Any study which does not bring man closer to wisdom and goodness does not belong in the curriculum. Our university graduates, says Hutchins, have far more information and far less understanding than did the college graduates in the Colonial period.

Hutchins finds the cause of this condition in (1) the neglect of philosophy in universities, (2) the abandonment of the prescribed classic curriculum for the elective system, and (3) the importance attached to vocational education. He would banish from higher education that vocationalism and unqualified empiricism which he blames for the disorder in education today.[18]

Dewey emphasizes the role of sense-experience, advocates learning by doing and the development of intelligence through meeting and solving problems of importance to the pupils. Hutchins advocates mental discipline, emphasizing that young people should take studies in which the operation of reason is manifest and should follow the thoughts of great thinkers by studying the classics. Hutchins has suggested curriculums very different from those of today, for both the secondary school and the university. He says that schools will soon be called upon to provide for all adolescents up to the age of twenty. Two-thirds of this adolescent population can profit from studying books; one-third should probably have some other type of educational experience. For the two-thirds he would prescribe a curriculum centering about the study of books written by the giant intellects of the world. These books should include not only drama, history, poetry, literature, and philosophy but mathematics, science, politics, and economics as well. All the greatest books of man's creation should have been read by the time a person has finished this secondary school. Euclid's *Elements,* Galen's *On the Natural Faculties,* Dante's *Divine Comedy,* Bacon's *Novum organum,* Newton's *Opticks,* Hume's *An Enquiry Concerning Human Understanding,* Kant's *Prolegomena,* Adam Smith's *The Wealth of*

18. Robert Maynard Hutchins, *The Higher Learning in America,* p. 117.

Nations, and Karl Marx's *Das Kapital* are a few suggestions on his list.

Hutchins says that this study of the classics would do two things: Students would learn what has happened in the past and what the greatest men have thought, and they would also learn to think for themselves; for he would have this study carried on always with reference to the problems of today. He believes these problems can be solved only in the light of principles and wisdom already in the possession of the human race and through using minds which have been disciplined to think.

The only provision he would make for individual differences in these secondary schools is in the length of time it would take students to finish the curriculum. Man's nature, he says, is everywhere much the same; therefore his general education should be much the same. For some it may take a longer, for others a shorter, time. At the completion of this curriculum he would award a Bachelor's degree. The majority of students would then go to technical schools or enter industry. But they would *know* something, and their minds would be trained for thinking. They would have had their potential intelligence developed. The few who have superior intellectual abilities and interests should enter the university for further study, where they might qualify for a Master's or perhaps a Doctor's degree. Hutchins believes that under these circumstances the emphasis on athletics and social life, which infects colleges and universities to their detriment, would be lessened.[19] Hutchins' proposals are not completely in force at the University of Chicago. But they are being experimented with at St. John's College in Annapolis, Maryland, where two young men, Stringfellow Barr and Scott Buchanan, impressed with Hutchins' indictments, have been conducting an interesting experiment in college curriculum and teaching.[20]

As is usually true where intelligent men hold differing opinions, there probably is some value in each position. The Aristotelian mean, or, better yet, a Kantian synthesis, seems to be needed. This,

19. *Ibid.,* p. 11.

20. See Stringfellow Barr, "John Doe Goes to St. John's," *Progressive Education,* XVI (January, 1939), 18–23, or a series of articles entitled "St. John's College: A Critical Appraisal," in the *Journal of Educational Sociology,* XVIII (November, 1944), 129–72.

of course, would not connote a superficial eclecticism. It has been pointed out previously that empiricism and rationalism seem each to be a partial answer to the problem of obtaining knowledge and that man needs both sense-experience and reason. It is quite likely, then, that educational proposals, each stemming from a partial view of the problem of knowledge, would themselves be incomplete, one without the other.

All knowledge is rooted in experience, that is, in personal acquaintance with reality. Experience may be either first hand or vicarious. A person has firsthand experience when his contact with reality is through his own senses. His experience is vicarious when it is a communicated experience. This communication is usually through symbols. In chapter iv the point was made that this ability to use symbols is man's distinguishing feature. Because he has this ability, he is able to reason, to use his imagination, and to make moral distinctions—to be human rather than animal. The use of symbols makes it possible for man to profit from vicarious experience. It is because man, unlike animals, can profit by vicarious experience that he has been able to profit from the experiences of previous generations and to build upon their accomplishments. A given generation does not have to repeat through firsthand experience what preceding generations have learned. It is fortunate indeed that human beings can learn through vicarious experience but very unfortunate that they do not always profit even from their own experiences, to say nothing of learning from others.

It is undoubtedly true that firsthand experience is more likely to make a deep impression upon an individual than does a communicated experience. It will usually be better remembered. On the other hand, to learn everything through firsthand experience would be very slow, tedious, and often dangerous. Vicarious experience can be vivid and impressive. The ability to communicate experience in a way which will make it remembered is part of the art of teaching. It is this ability which makes a great actor; he can make the stage seem life itself, and the play, a story come true. Dramatic ability is just as necessary in a teacher. The greatest teachers would have made superior actors and actresses, for they have the ability to teach the experiences of the race so that young people never forget them. If a child is so fortunate as to have a parent or a teacher who knows how to teach effectively, he will learn many of life's lessons vicariously.

The circumstances under which teachers should use firsthand experiences for teaching purposes and those under which vicarious experience is appropriate will vary with the teacher, the subject, the age of the pupils, both chronological and mental, and the pupils' former experiences. The Progressives advocate much firsthand experience. This proposal was originally a reaction against a meaningless symbolism and verbalism too prevalent in schools which overstressed memorization. The fact that pupils can repeat words is no indication that they have obtained any information, understanding, or insight which will help them solve life's problems. But it is just as great a mistake to overemphasize the use of firsthand experience in teaching. Human beings seem to insist on going to extremes.

In general, firsthand experience is needed (1) when children are young and unacquainted with their environment; (2) when a skill is being learned; one cannot learn to swim by reading about it in a book, although that may help; (3) when beginning any completely new topic for which there has been no adequate background already laid through firsthand experience; (4) whenever one wishes to teach that certain causes inevitably produce certain effects; science teaching needs the laboratory to teach the scientific method rather than to teach the facts of science; (5) where children are dull; the brighter the child, the better able he is to learn through the experience of others.

ACTIVITY AND THE DEVELOPMENT OF INTELLIGENCE

Not only do the Progressives advocate much firsthand experience, but they claim that intelligence is best developed in the "activity school" of modern education. Many teachers interpret the activity movement as meaning primarily trips to the dairy or post office or the hammering of orange crates. They believe the movement to have originated in this country and that John Dewey was its progenitor—something he himself never claimed.

To be sure, the activity school is the implacable foe of mere verbalism. But activity means more than physical activity. And pragmatism was neither its original nor ever its principal philosophy. The modern activity movement began in Europe; Comenius and

Rousseau were its fathers;[21] its primary tenet is the belief that children develop best through their own activity. The majority of its advocates have held that activity is mental as well as physical and that, while initiative, self-expression, and self-activity are a necessary part of the program of any good school, there is need for a prescribed curriculum, discipline, and memorization, as well.

In ancient Athens and Sparta the major emphasis in education was on the pupil's activity, an emphasis which was largely lost in medieval days. In modern times, John Amos Comenius (1592–1670), a Bohemian and a member of the Moravian Brethren, is given credit for planting the seed of the activity movement. He advocated instruction for the eye, for the tongue, and for the hand and proposed pupil activity as a principle of instruction.[22] He it was who said that we must either take our pupils into the world or bring the world into the classroom.

But it was Jean Jacques Rousseau (1712–78) who was the father of the modern movement for pupil activity. He taught that the activities which spring from actual life-situations should form the curriculum of the school.[23] He wrote of the education of Émile:

> In proportion as a sensitive being becomes active, he acquires a discernment proportional to his powers; and it is only with the power which is in excess of what is needed for self-conservation that there comes to be developed in him the speculative faculty suited for employing that excess of power for other uses. If then, you would cultivate the intelligence of your pupil, cultivate the power which it is to govern. Give his body continual exercise; make him robust and sound in order to make him wise and reasonable; let him work and move about, run, and shout, and be continually in motion; let him be a man in vigor, and soon he will be such by force of reason.[24]

Much of the work of Johann Bernhard Basedow (1724–90) and the Philanthropinists in Germany was the outgrowth of Rousseau's

21. Perhaps Wolfgang Ratke (1571–1635) should be given some credit for basic teachings which developed into the activity movement. Two ideas permeating his pedagogy were (1) first the thing itself and then the explanation of the thing and (2) all things through experience and experiment.

22. G. G. Schoenchen, *The Activity School*, p. 6.

23. F. Eby and C. F. Arrowood, *The Development of Modern Education*, p. 492.

24. J. J. Rousseau, *Émile*, Book III.

influence. Rousseau would have Émile learn through his own activities. Basedow followed this principle closely. His pupils went on excursions to studios, to farms, to mines, to shops, to markets, and to military camps.[25] He taught languages by the conversational method and through games. Henry Barnard has a most interesting description of the method used in Basedow's school, the Philanthropinum.[26] This name was given to the school to express the idea that it grew out of and was to serve humanitarian purposes—from a love of mankind. Associated with Basedow were many men of note in educational history, who, when the school was discontinued in 1793, scattered to various parts of Germany, where they put the ideas they had learned into practice.

Paul Monroe, the historian, says:

> The fundamental idea of the reform was "education according to nature," which was interpreted to mean that children should be treated as children, not as adults; that language should be taught by conversational methods, not through grammatical studies; that physical exercises and games should find a place in the child's education; that early education should be connected with "motion and noise," since children naturally love these; that each child should be taught a handicraft for reasons partly educational, partly social; that the vernacular rather than the classical languages should constitute the chief subject-matter of education; that instruction should be connected with realities rather than with words.[27]

Here, indeed, we have the first of the Progressive schools. Operating upon the theories of Rousseau, they were, however, guilty of the same fault too often found in modern schools: the neglect and disparagement of hard work and of emphasis on the assimilation of the social heritage: "They insisted that all learning should be made not only pleasant but easy. It must involve no hardship and require no effort. All learning must be sport or play. In a word, they advocated what in the present day has been called 'soft pedagogy.'"[28]

The modern activity school owes more to Pestalozzi (1746–1827) than to any other educator.[29] "The central idea of Pestalozzi's peda-

25. Eby and Arrowood, *op. cit.*, p. 523.
26. Henry Barnard, *German Teachers and Educators.*
27. Paul Monroe, *History of Education*, p. 581
28. Eby and Arrowood, *op. cit.*, p. 763.
29. Schoenchen, *op. cit.*, p. 12.

gogy is his concept of the nature of man as having two aspects, the individual and the social,"[30] an idea which Dewey has elaborated and which is, perhaps, his most important educational emphasis. Pestalozzi interpreted activity to mean not mere bodily activity but mental activity as well. He also called attention to the fact that the value of doing a thing by hand, experimentally, is that one can *see* whether it is right or wrong, a theory which Dewey elaborated in his teaching that experimentation applies the pragmatic test to ideas.[31]

Froebel (1782–1852), the father of the kindergarten, should be mentioned among the important contributors to this movement. From his point of view, "self-activity, or doing, leads to feeling and knowing, and is therefore the dynamic factor in education."[32]

It would be impossible to mention the names of all the men who have contributed to this important movement in the modern educational world. One of the most important figures of recent days is W. A. Lay (1862–1926), whose Tatschule (activity school) in Germany had for its aim "self-development: growth through self-activity, through expression," a place where "creative work and constructive and expressive activity follow all impressional observational activity."[33]

The Austrian, Eduard Burger (1872–1938), of pre-Hitler Vienna, was the foremost present-day European promoter of activity pedagogy. His work in establishing activity schools in a metropolitan school system and his book *Die Arbeitsschule* ("The Work-School") are not so well known in this country as they are in Europe.[34] Burger understood the activity movement to mean for each child that (1) through self-activity he would become independent, (2) in a very real sense all education was self-education, and (3) mental activity is as important in an activity school as is physical activity.

John Dewey (1859—) is regarded as the chief promoter of activity schools in this country, although there is little agreement among

30. *Ibid.*
31. *Ibid.*, p. 15.
32. *Ibid.*, p. 16.
33. W. A. Lay, *Experimental Pedagogy*, Introd. by P. R. Radosavljevich, p. 25.
34. Schoenchen, *op. cit.*, p. 303.

educators as to what an activity type of education is.[35] It is usually thought of as synonymous with Progressive education and Progressive education as synonymous with one founded upon John Dewey's philosophy. It is interesting to note in this connection that no other founder or contributor to the activity movement has been a pragmatist. Some of the recent advocates of this emphasis in education have been followers of the voluntarism of Fichte (1762–1814), but the others have based their educational principles on various philosophical positions. Usually they have been naturalistic and humanistic in the sense that they look to human nature to find the foundation for aims and procedures in education. Sometimes their understanding of human nature has been narrow and incomplete, but their purpose has been, in the light of their understanding, to find the method best adapted for securing the optimum development of human personality. All of these important advocates of activity as a means of acquiring knowledge would disagree with Dewey's conception of the nature of knowledge and truth.

The chief points of difference between the followers of Dewey and other advocates of the activity school are: (1) Dewey's disciples would abandon prescribed curriculums, letting the curriculum grow out of the activities of children in solving their problems; (2) they minimize teacher guidance and direction to the extent that many of them talk of their pupils spontaneously "choosing their own activities"; (3) they would subordinate discipline to interest, insisting that discipline from without is unnecessary if school work is intrinsically interesting, as it can be if the teaching is good and the curriculum grows out of children's problems; in fact, any artificial means of obtaining interest through rewards, prizes, or marks cannot be too severely condemned; and (4) they beg the question of an ultimate aim for educational endeavor. Many advocates of the activity school say that the principal fault to be found with the activity movement in this country is the fact that many of its features grow out of a faulty theory of knowledge and truth.

If experience is understood to be vicarious as well as first hand and if activity is thought of as mental as well as physical, we can see perhaps how Hutchins' proposals could fit into the total picture.

35. J. W. Wrightstone, *Appraisal of Newer Elementary School Practices*, p. 38; also, L. C. Mossman, *The Activity Concept*, pp. 61–67.

Man is a symbol-using creature. The ability to use symbols in abstract thinking is the essence of his intelligence. We should do all we can to develop this ability in the boys and girls whose schooling we direct.

In the elementary school, children need much firsthand experience. There are times all through the school and throughout life outside the school when firsthand experience is necessary for learning. But man can learn through the use of symbols; and if that ability is *the* distinctive human ability, it would seem to be a great mistake not to help boys and girls gradually to learn through the use of symbols. If they have normal human abilities, they should not be left on the level of learning through firsthand experience alone.

Great thinkers have important lessons to teach to those who can learn them. It would seem to be true that following the thoughts of great thinkers stretches one's own mind. Those thoughts must be applicable to today's problems to appeal to the student. But that is what makes a great thinker. He is able to see and extract the universal and the true from the welter of particulars with which life surrounds man and to express it so that other men can understand and profit by his insight. Few men could have invented the differential calculus, but the majority of men could learn to use it. Lesser minds can profit by the discoveries and inventions of great minds. So effective intelligence can be developed in the population.

It would be a mistake to read great books merely for the mental exercise or simply for exegesis alone. But to study the masters of thought in order to obtain wisdom to apply to the solution of today's problems seems eminently worth while.

It is doubtful whether two-thirds of the adolescent population would profit from the type of study recommended by Hutchins. There is some doubt whether the curriculum, as he proposes it, would be entirely suitable for the needs of today. But it is a fact that we have neglected the wisdom to be gleaned from the past. It is a misfortune for modern man that he is, as Bertrand Russell puts it, so provincial in time that he "feels for the past a contempt it does not deserve and for the present a respect it deserves still less." In the great books of the past we find the accumulated intellectual riches of mankind. Many of the problems of yesterday are still the problems of today. Greece knew wars, tyranny, depressions. Her thinkers were concerned with problems of morality, of the ends of living, of the life good for man to live. Great books have only to be read to be respected. Let the school provide firsthand experience with first-class minds, to the profit of youth.

SUMMARY

Intelligence is best defined in terms of what it can do, which is, see and solve human problems successfully. It has its basis in hereditary factors but is merely a potentiality at birth, depending upon environmental factors for its development. This puts upon the home and the school the responsibility for recognizing and developing the factors which compose it.

Human intelligence is what it is because of the ability to do abstract thinking. Man can think abstractly and, as a result, reason, because of his ability to invest symbols with meaning and to use them in his mental processes.[36] It would seem, then, that to develop intelligence we must help young people go from learning through firsthand experience—in which all learning is rooted—to learning through symbolic experience; from learning through use of the concrete to learning by means of the abstract; from learning accompanied by physical activity to learning through mental activity without overt action.

It would seem that the following principles might point the way toward the maximum development of children's potential intelligence:

1. A good home is imperative: this means not wealth but a measure of economic security and parents interested in and willing to learn all that they can about child development.

2. Since mind and body are one during life, a healthy body is a necessary foundation for an intelligent mind.

3. Since intelligence is the ability to solve life's problems successfully, children must have practice, on their own level of maturity, in solving problems.

4. These problems should arise out of or be related to children's experience; children can and do learn through vicarious, as well as through firsthand, experience.

5. Children learn through their own activity; this activity is mental as well as physical. Physical activity is particularly important for young children; as children get older, mental activity without overt action becomes more possible and more necessary. To assist children to independence, both physical and mental, is our purpose.

6. To solve problems successfully takes knowledge. Children not only should learn *how* to think but also should acquire knowledge of what

36. See chap. iv for the background for this statement.

the great have done and thought. Out of the experience of the race have come tools, techniques, knowledge, and wisdom so important for individual and social welfare that it is dangerous to leave their mastery to incidental learning. There should be a planned curriculum, subject to revision when need or new insight makes this necessary. It should be suited to children's maturity and related to their interests.

7. The law of interest usually is interpreted as: "Lead the child in the direction of what he likes to do." We should interpret it to mean: "Lead the child to do what mature wisdom dictates it would be well for him to do." There is no excuse ever for dull, dry, teaching. Learning never takes place without some kind of motivation. The better the teacher, the greater the amount of intrinsic motivation. But extrinsic motivation has to be used part of the time, with the majority of children. It should be pointed toward the development of intrinsic interest, but teachers should not be discouraged when they find it impossible to interest every child in every phase of what he needs to learn.

8. Intelligence will not develop unless children expend effort. They must learn to work hard; children naturally prefer play. So do we all, even when we have learned to tackle uninteresting jobs which need to be done. Education should produce disciplined, unselfish, young people willing to work at the unpleasant, difficult, things in life, as well as at those which are fun. It is impossible and unwise to make play out of all school work.

9. Memorization has an important place as a basis for the development of intelligence. For too long a time teachers have assumed that it is a mistake to require children to memorize poetry or fine bits of prose. The stupid, parrot-like, *memoriter* methods of some of the older schools were bad. But it is cheating children of their birthright to swing to the opposite extreme and to require no exact memorization. To have beautiful words, wise sayings, noble passages, as part of one's mental equipment is to have some available basis from which to start in meeting life's problems.

10. Drill is necessary in fixing much that needs to be memorized. Drill can and should be interesting. Children should understand what they are doing and why. Drill should be varied, suited to differing needs of different pupils. Mere verbalism should not be tolerated. But neither can words that express noble and wise ideas have as much meaning for children as they will come to have with more experience. Words should, however, have some meaning for the learner, else they will be nothing more than nonsense syllables and will be memorized only to be soon forgotten.

11. There should be no hypocrisy about "letting children choose their own activities." If teachers know children and their interests, as they should, they can lead children in the direction in which they know they

should go. Children may be unaware of the teacher's leadership. The greater the artist in the teacher, the less aware the children are of his guidance. It is the teacher's business to manage pupils with skill and tact. But the teacher should never abdicate. He has the maturity and the preparation, supposedly, to direct young people's growth toward aims which children cannot be aware of but which he must keep constantly in mind. Let him never play the hypocrite.

12. In developing intelligence, the brightest children are often the most neglected. School work is too often planned for the average child, and other children are treated as if they were in the bed of Procrustes. The problem of providing for individual differences is an extremely difficult one, paticularly for the harried teacher of large groups. It needs much more study. Particularly do we need to study how to challenge and utilize to the fullest degree the best abilities of the most intelligent. There are several centers experimenting now with various attempts to solve this problem, but every teacher should work at it to the limit of his time and ability. In the proper development of these potentially most intelligent human beings lie our highest hopes for advancing modern civilization.

13. If education does its work both inside and outside the school, we may hope to raise the level of effective intelligence in the population. While human nature remains about the same in its inherent capacities, we have not done all that we could do to develop and utilize what is potentially there. In addition, ordinary human beings can assimilate and use what extraordinary human beings have discovered. If we cherish and promote the best minds and help the rest of the population to climb toward the shoulders of the giants of the past and present, the ability of the general population to solve life's problems successfully, that is, their intelligence, will certainly improve.

QUESTIONS TO AID STUDY

1. Point out specifically the ways in which the second girl in the opening anecdote was more intelligent than was the first girl.
2. Define intelligence. What factors enter into the nature of what we call intelligence?
3. What does experimental evidence seem to show concerning the problem of the constancy of the I.Q.? What light does this throw on the question as to the source of intelligence?
4. In what terms is intelligence always measured? What does this mean for the notion that innate ability can be measured?
5. On what three levels does intelligence operate? What conclusions can you draw concerning the kind of examinations teachers should use for testing achievement?
6. Discuss the home's responsibility for the development of intelligence.
7. What basic philosophical problem is involved in the differing opin-

ions of educational leaders concerning how best to develop intelligence?

8. What does Dewey believe to be the best method for developing intelligence? Why does he hold this view?
9. What is Hutchins' advice on how to develop intelligence? Why does he hold this view?
10. What is meant by saying that the two views are merely two aspects of a larger whole? In what epistemological position is such a statement rooted? Explain.
11. Under what circumstances should the school use firsthand experience? What limitations are there on the use of firsthand experience? Why is vicarious experience important? How can it be used successfully?
12. What do you understand the most important principle of the activity school to be?
13. Summarize briefly the history of the activity movement. Was it an outgrowth of pragmatism? Explain.
14. On what points would the followers of Dewey and other advocates of the activity school differ? Can you explain why Dewey's followers hold these beliefs?
15. Summarize the means by which intelligence may be developed.
16. Write a paper in which you show *specifically* how you think you can work as a teacher to develop the intelligence of your pupils. State the epistemology to which you are inclined, and show how this is connected with what you propose to do.

SUGGESTED REFERENCES

BAGLEY, WILLIAM C. "Danger of Sweeping Generalizations in the Science of Education," *School and Society,* LXII (December 29, 1945), 419.
DEMIASHKEVICH, M. *Introduction to the Philosophy of Education* (New York: American Book Co., 1935), pp. 165–81.
DEWEY, JOHN. *Experience and Education.* New York: Macmillan Co., 1938.
GLASER, EDWARD. *Experiment in the Development of Critical Thinking.* New York: Teachers College, Columbia University, 1941.
HARTMANN, GEORGE W. *Educational Psychology* (New York: American Book Co., 1941), chap. vi.
HORNE, HERMAN HARRELL. *The Democratic Philosophy of Education* (New York: Macmillan Co., 1932), chaps. xi–xii.
HOROWITZ, ARNOLD. "Experimentalism in Education," *Educational Forum,* I (May, 1937), 403–25.
HUTCHINS, ROBERT MAYNARD. *The Higher Learning in America* (New Haven: Yale University Press, 1936), chaps. i and iii.

KILPATRICK, WILLIAM HEARD. *Group Education for a Democracy* (New York: Association Press, 1940), chaps. xvi–xvii.

MOSSMAN, LOIS C. *The Activity Concept* (New York: Macmillan Co., 1938), especially chaps. iii–v.

NATIONAL SOCIETY FOR THE STUDY OF EDUCATION. *The Thirty-ninth Yearbook of the Society for the Study of Education. Part II: Intelligence: Its Nature and Nurture.* Bloomington, Ill.: Public School Pub. Co., 1940.

NEAL, NATHAN A. "The Philosophy of Science Teaching," *Education,* LXII (January, 1942), 267–74.

REDDEN, JOHN, and RYAN, FRANCIS A. *A Catholic Philosophy of Education* (Milwaukee: Bruce Pub. Co., 1942), chap. vii.

SCHOENCHEN, GUSTAVE G. *The Activity School* (New York: Longmans, Green & Co., 1940), chap. xii.

STODDARD, GEORGE D. "The I.Q.: Its Ups and Downs," *Educational Record,* XX (January, 1939), 44.

———. *The Meaning of Intelligence* (New York: Macmillan Co., 1944), chaps. i, xiii, and xv–xvi.

THURSTONE, L. L. "Theories of Intelligence," *Scientific Monthly,* LXII (February, 1946), 101–12.

WAHLQUIST, JOHN T. "Is the I.Q. Controversy Philosophical?" *School and Society,* LII (November 30, 1940), 539–47.

———. *The Philosophy of American Education* (New York: Ronald Press Co., 1942), chap. xi.

WELLMAN, B. L. "I.Q. Changes of Pre-school and Non-pre-school Groups during the Pre-school Years: Summary of the Literature," *Journal of Psychology,* XX (October, 1945), 347–68.

WITTY, PAUL. "Reconstruction of the Concept of Intelligence," *Educational Method,* XIX (November, 1939), 64–72.

CHAPTER XIV
DEVELOPING CREATIVE IMAGINATION

The significance of the creative imagination—The universality of creative ability—The nature of creative thought: (1) Its possible identity with the creative forces of the universe; (2) Descriptions of the way the mind works in creative ability; (3) Characteristics of creative thought—Creative imagination and the arts: (1) Importance of the arts in developing creative imagination; (2) Relation of the arts to the study of beauty; aesthetics; (3) The problem of the nature of beauty (a) aesthetic objectivism, (b) aesthetic subjectivism, (c) Kantian synthesis; (4) The universal in human nature as the source for aesthetic standards—Discovery and creation; education as creative—Educational philosophies and creative education: (1) Emphasis of progressive education; (2) Emphasis of other philosophies; (3) Strengths and weaknesses of progressive education in this field—The development of creative imagination

---

THE British poet and naturalist, Arthur William Edgar O'Shaughnessy, sang in the previous century:

> We are the music makers
> And we are the dreamers of dreams,
> Wandering by lone sea-breakers
> And sitting by desolate streams;
> World-losers and world-forsakers,
> On whom the pale moon gleams:
> Yet we are the movers and shakers
> Of the world forever, it seems.

HUMAN NATURE AND CREATIVE IMAGINATION

Since the days of Aristotle, it has been a commonplace to say that man differs from the other animals in that he is capable of reasoning. There have been thinkers, however, who have stressed other aspects of man's nature: Sometimes it is his ability to make moral

294

distinctions; again it has been his creative abilities, his power to dream dreams and to embody those dreams in beauty.

Coleridge, for instance, insisted that the creative imagination is the supreme power in man. He himself exhibited that ability to a high degree; he also tried to understand it, thinking and writing about this gift of the gods to human beings. One of the most interesting studies of the way in which creative imagination works in a highly gifted man is to be found in John Livingston Lowe's study of the way in which Coleridge worked. In *The Road to Xanadu*, based chiefly on a study of Coleridge's journal, Mr. Lowe says: "Coleridge's most precious contribution to our understanding of the imagination lies, not in his metaphysical lucubrations on it after it was lost, but in the implications of his practice while he yet possessed the power."[1]

Teachers might well follow the implied advice. If we wish to understand man's creative imagination, we perhaps will learn more from studying its fruit than from either philosophy or psychology. Very little is known about imagination which would help us to understand either its source or the way in which it works. But because in educational circles today the word "creative" is used very loosely and because the schools have an important task to perform in developing, so far as possible, this potential ability of man, it behooves teachers to learn all that they can from every source.

A recent writer in the field of philosophy, Joseph A. Leighton, in saying that man is not only an animal but a spiritual being, agrees with Coleridge in saying that the greatest difference between the two is man's power of creative imagining. Leighton writes: "He does not merely reproduce his past experience. He can break up the images which arise from the traces of past experiences, and form them into new combinations. Like the musician, man as an inventor and genius in the useful and fine arts and in the art of living itself can form out of three sounds, not a fourth sound, but a star."[2]

This emphasis does not belittle reason nor deny its importance. The two, imagination and reason, are complementary. Properly, they work together, as pointed out in the previous chapter, on the highest level on which intelligence operates. Goethe said that imagi-

1. J. L. Lowes, *The Road to Xanadu*, p. x.
2. J. A. Leighton, *Social Philosophies in Conflict*, p. 233.

nation was the "forerunner of reason." On this point a modern
writer and teacher of philosophy, says: "The first stage in solving a
problem or getting out of a predicament is concocting a plan or
hypothesis. It is not *reason* but *imagination*, which, working on the
data of the situation and on the memories of similar situations in the
past, concocts, or creates, or discovers by intuition, a hypothesis, a
plan, a possible way out. Then and only then does reasoning in the
proper sense of the word really begin."[3]

UNIVERSALITY OF CREATIVE ABILITY

Creative ability probably exists to some degree in every normal
human being. Men exhibit it to the extent that they show resource-
fulness, initiative, and independence in the successful solution of
their problems. It is an important factor in leadership in any field:
in business, in engineering, in technology, in politics, in education,
in farming, in war. Creative imagination has produced most of our
art, has been responsible for those inventions not merely stumbled
upon, and is paramount in the thought life of those whom we call
"geniuses." They possess creative ability to a higher degree than do
the majority of people. Children seem to exhibit the fruits of imagination more freely than do adults. Daydreaming, playing with
imaginary playmates, constructing, dramatizing, are common occu-
pations; whether adults are less imaginative because they have become acquainted with a world of fact which checks the world of
fancy or whether their imaginations have been repressed through
inhibitions and self-distrust is a controversial question.

It seems certain, however, that the power to create varies in degree as does every aspect of intelligence and, indeed, every human
trait. Hughes Mearns says that "all God's chillun got wings," although many are not permitted to use them.[4] This is probably true,
but some of these wings would never grow very strong or large, no
matter how much use was given them, while others enable their
fortunate possessors to soar among the stars. But every human being
should have the opportunity to use and strengthen whatever wing-
power he may possess. He must also learn when he may use his

3. W. P. Montague, *The Ways of Things*, p. 33.
4. G. Hartmann and A. Shumaker (eds.), *Creative Expression*, p. 13.

wings and when he should walk circumspectly in the sober world of fact.

To assist in the development of creative imagination is much more difficult than to help children acquire knowledge. As a modern psychologist points out, men have been interested in the laws of mental acquisition since the days of Aristotle and have been studying them experimentally since the time of Ebbinghaus. But of the nature of creative thinking little is known.[5]

NATURE OF CREATIVE THOUGHT

Because ideas in creative thinking seem to come to one without the conscious effort entailed in other thinking, men have been inclined to ascribe them to some supernatural agency, operating through a few chosen men. The Greeks had their Muses and later man his doctrine of inspiration: the belief that creativity transcends personal capacity and is the result of a divine "breathing in." Emerson wrote of the Oversoul. More recently Freud and his followers have written of the subconscious mind, and some students of the problem would relegate the source of creative thought to some such sphere. Spearman, the great British psychologist, thinks it unlikely that there is any such fountainhead of genius as either a subconscious mind or an Oversoul. Psychology is not limited, he says, to one or the other explanation.[6]

Other modern thinkers believe that creative imagination in man is identical with the creative force in nature which causes evolutionary changes. While creativeness in man and in nature are diverse in mediums, they are identical in activity.[7] All of which is just another way of saying that we do not understand man's nature any more than we understand the nature of the universe but that what we believe to be divine operates in both.

Certainly we do not understand what causes the creative imagination to work as it does. Alfred Russell Wallace, the English naturalist, said: "I have long since come to see that no one deserves either praise or blame for the ideas that come to him. . . . . Ideas and beliefs are certainly not voluntary acts. They come to us—we

5. J. M. Fletcher, *Psychology in Education, with Emphasis on Creative Thinking*, chap. xi.

6. C. Spearman, *Creative Mind*, p. 81. 7. Montague, *op. cit.*, p. 453.

scarcely know *how* or whence, and once they get possession of us we cannot reject or change them at will."[8]

Helmholtz, the great physicist, at a banquet in honor of his seventieth birthday, described the way his mind worked in creative activity. He said there seemed to be three stages: (1) preparation, in which the problem is investigated in all directions; (2) incubation, in which the mind is not consciously active on the problem but is evidently engaged in a process of assimilation; and (3) illumination, in which occurs the sudden insight, fertile suggestions, and happy ideas.[9]

The French psychologist, Ribot, said that creative imagination, whether in art or science, works differently in different men. Some individuals seem more spontaneous and intuitive than others. He gives the names of Wallace, Mozart, and Poe as identifying men of this type. The instant of imaginative synthesis, of original thought, comes very early in the attack upon a problem. With other men, there is a long incubation before the flash of inspiration. Darwin gathered specimens of natural life for many years, then read Malthus —and arrived at his theory. Newton is said to have studied his problems for seventeen years before formulating his theory. Hamilton says that after fifteen years of study the famous discovery of quaternions burst upon him as he stood upon a bridge.

Ribot makes the point that this seeming difference in the way in which creative minds work is a superficial rather than an essential difference. While temperament and disposition undoubtedly do operate with some individuals to induce an inclination toward one method rather than toward the other, with the majority of persons there seems to be a mixed procedure rather than a clear-cut difference between one process and another.[10]

The characteristics of creative thought, according to those who have studied available material,[11] seem to be:

1. It is effortless; it "comes to one" and seems not volitionally directed.

8. Quoted by Fletcher, *op. cit.*, p. 368.

9. Graham Wallas, *Art of Thought*, p. 80.

10. T. A. Ribot, *Essay on the Creative Imagination*, pp. 157–62.

11. See, e.g., Fletcher, *op. cit.*, pp. 371–77.

2. It is more like play than work; Edison is said to have remarked that he had never done a day's work in his life.

3. It involves not just cognitive elements but deep-seated feelings, complexes, and life-urges.

4. Usually one cannot bid it begin when a clock strikes or a bell rings, although some creative workers say that they do best under the impulsion of a necessity to meet a dead line.

5. Breaking away from routine seems essential; a spirit of freedom, of nonconforming, of breaking loose, is characteristic.

6. It seems impossible to observe introspectively.

7. It can be easily destroyed in the nascent stage if neglected or mishandled.

A psychologist reminds us that "all so-called inspirations occur strictly within the limit of the individual's training and previous cogitations. It was to Hamilton, the mathematician, not to Byron, the poet, that the famous discovery of the quaternions came."[12]

Ribot calls our attention, also, to the dependence of the creative intellect upon what has been accomplished in previous generations.

Let us suppose that in the Samoan Islands there had been born a child having the unique and extraordinary genius of Mozart. What would he be able to do? At most, extend the gamut of three or four to seven, and create melodies a little more complicated; but he would be as incapable of composing symphonies as Archimedes would have been to invent an electro dynamo. How many creators have been thwarted because the conditions necessary to their inventions were lacking! Roger Bacon foresaw many of our great discoveries; Cardan, the infinitesimal calculus; Von Helmont, chemistry; and it has been possible to write a book on the forerunners of Darwin. All of this is well known, but it deserves to be recalled to mind. We talk so much of the free flight of the imagination, of the absolute power of the creator, that we forget the sociological conditions (not to mention others) on which this power at every instant depends. In this respect, no invention is personal in the strict sense; there always remains in it a little of that anonymous collaboration.[13]

If this creative ability, so widely distributed, is to promote progress, it must then be founded upon a wide knowledge of what man has already accomplished. It can readily be seen that one of the

12. June Downey, *Creative Imagination*, p. 158.
13. Ribot, *op. cit.*, pp. 154–55.

problems of the teacher who earnestly desires to develop creative ability in pupils would be to determine how to leave children's imaginations free and yet see to it that they acquire the facts, the information, the knowledge, on which and through which they can build.

CREATIVE IMAGINATION AND THE ARTS

While undoubtedly true that creative imagination is not the possession of poets, artists, and novelists alone but to some degree a possession of every human being, operating in every phase of human life where intelligence is being used, its development can perhaps be more readily furthered through working in the arts, both practical and fine, than through any other medium. Man seems most truly to create in this field. There is more opportunity here for the exercise of imagination unhampered by the necessity for an exact and uncompromising correspondence with reality.

Does this mean that in art there are *no* objective standards by which to judge the work of man's imagination? Is his imagination completely unhampered? May he create, in the name of art, anything he likes and call it good? Is it true that *de gustibus non disputandum est?* This question raises several problems. What is art? How is it related to beauty, the pursuit of which has been part of the famous triumvirate of man's highest endeavors. What is the nature of beauty? What makes an object beautiful? Art is not, of course, concerned only with beauty. Sometimes man has sought to give expression through an art to anger, horror, pain, indignation, sorrow, disgust, fear, or some other unpleasant emotion. Sometimes the artist has sought to objectify the sublime or the comic. Sometimes it has been art for art's sake; sometimes it has been art for the sake of the useful. The purpose of art, says DeWitt H. Parker, "is a sympathetic vision of some part of human experience."[14]

But to produce and objectify beauty has been the artist's chief concern. Aesthetics is the name given to that branch of philosophy which is concerned with the systematic study of the nature of beauty. Whether beauty is a part of the world in which we live, to be identified with a structure or pattern possessed by an object independent of its relation to a percipient, or whether the pleasure

14. DeWitt H. Parker, *The Principles of Aesthetics*, p. 119.

produced in the percipient is the sole determinant of beauty has been a moot question with students of aesthetics.[15]

The classic writers on aesthetics taught that beauty is intrinsic in beautiful objects. They are called objectivists because they insisted that there are objective standards to which anything must conform if it is to be beautiful. Beauty, say they, is independent of man's liking, and aesthetic value lies in the nature of the object itself. A thing is not beautiful, either in nature or in art, because man likes it but because of what it is, in and of itself. Beauty is intrinsic in the poem, picture, music, building, or statue. It is *in* the very nature of the landscape, the sunset, the rolling waves. Objectivists emphasize the rational elements in art. They point, for example, to the mathematical relations at the basis of music. They speak of "form" in art—an arrangement of line and color which combines order and variety.[16]

Plato, Aristotle, Thomas Aquinas, and Hegel were aesthetic objectivists. A modern objectivist, Lessing, writing in the *Hamburgische Dramaturgie,* said that "the laws laid down by Aristotle in the *Poetics* were as certain in their application to the drama as Euclid's Elements in geometry."[17]

Thomas Aquinas, interpreting Aristotle in terms of Christianity, defined beauty as that which gives pleasure on sight. Maritain, the foremost Thomistic philosopher of the modern world, says that Aquinas believed that "to say that beauty is the splendour of form shining on the proportional parts of matter is to say that it is a lightening of mind on a matter intelligently arranged."[18] Aquinas argued that, while God is one, the world is multiple. This multiple world in emulating the oneness of God achieves unity in variety, or what we call "harmony." The reason, then, that harmony and order in physical objects are beautiful is that harmony is the highest degree of God-like oneness that the secular world can achieve.[19]

Hegel likewise believed beauty to be a part of the world of ob-

15. Montague, *op. cit.,* p. 129.

16. Earl of Listowell (William Francis Hare), *A Critical History of Modern Esthetics,* p. 148.

17. Parker, *op. cit.,* p. 104.

18. Jacques Maritain, *Art and Scholasticism,* p. 25.

19. *Ibid.,* pp. 23–25.

jects because of the relation of the world to God. He defined beauty as the shining of the Absolute through the veil of sense-experience.

It was in modern times that aesthetic subjectivism, the belief that man puts beauty into objects, became important. It flourished in England in the eighteenth and nineteenth centuries and found expression in the writings of Lord Kames, Shaftesbury, and Edmund Burke. These men and others who followed them insist that a thing is beautiful if it is pleasant to the producer and consumer. Santayana, a modern philosopher, defines beauty as objectified or externalized pleasure.[20] If any object gives man pleasure, that is evidence of its beauty, according to this view. The aesthetic subjectivist would insist that there are no standards to which appeal can be made for determining excellence, save those of man's emotions. The idea that beauty is that which pleases the senses and satisfies the emotions, and that alone, is called a hedonistic aesthetic.

One person may like Brahms's *First Symphony*. Another may prefer Gershwin's *Rhapsody in Blue*. The subjectivist would say that neither man's taste is better than the other one's, providing that they both had wide and inclusive experience. Subjectivists do admit that liking based on wide experience is superior to that which comes from narrow experience. But it is man's liking of, his emotional reaction to, an object which determines its excellence. Santayana says: "Preference is ultimately irrational; it is good only because we desire it."[21]

Perhaps each of these groups has grasped a partial truth. In any aesthetic experience there is probably both a rational and an emotional aspect. We do not distinguish between them at the time of the experience, but they are both there. In all probability, there are some aesthetic experiences in which the feeling aspect predominates. In others, the rational is more important. But they must both be there for beauty to be present.

As in ethics and in epistemology, it took the genius of Kant to bring these two streams of thought together and to show in what way the recognition of beauty is both rational and emotional and how both the objectivists and subjectivists had something of truth

20. George Santayana, *The Sense of Beauty*, p. 49. The exact quotation is: "Beauty is pleasure regarded as the quality of a thing."

21. *Ibid.*, p. 18.

in their positions.[22] William Pepperell Montague, in his recent book, *The Ways of Things*, says: "Kant, in his theory of aesthetics, set forth in the *Critique of Judgement*, dealt more justly and penetratingly with the two aspects of beauty than any other philosopher."[23]

Kant says that an object which appeals only to the senses is merely agreeable, not beautiful.[24] Animals find some things agreeable; *beauty* has "significance only for human beings, i.e., for beings at once animal and rational.[25] It is true that "beauty is for itself, apart from any reference to the feeling of the subject, nothing."[26] But this does not mean that feeling is the only aspect of man involved in judging whether an object has beauty. There is a cognitive element involved also. If a thing is beautiful, it appeals to both the intellect and the senses in such a way as to put them spontaneously and naturally in harmony with each other.[27]

This harmony we feel is caused by the reaction of our own natures to a physical object in the relation it produces between our senses and our intellect. But we have a tendency to believe that the harmony is in the object we observe. We want the pieces of our experience to fit together. We require a principle of design—our nature demands it. This, of course, was what Aquinas was saying, as well as other students of aesthetics.

Modern students of aesthetics define beauty as that which produces harmony between the subject and the object. Kant would go further than this to say that an object is beautiful if it appeals to both the rational and sensuous in us in such a way as to put them in harmony with each other.

This seems to be what the modern Samuel Alexander has in mind in his recent book *Beauty and Other Forms of Value*. He comes to the conclusion that beauty arises out of a relation between the sub-

22. Benedetto Croce, whom many students consider the foremost writer in the field of aesthetics today, says in the article on "Aesthetics" found in the 1946 edition of the *Encyclopaedia Britannica*: "The principles he [Kant] laid down were laid down once for all. After the *Critique of Judgment* a return to hedonistic and utilitarian explanations of art and beauty could (and did) take place only through ignorance of Kant's demonstration" (I, 271).

23. P. 132.

24. Immanuel Kant, *The Critique of Aesthetic Judgement* (trans. J. C. Meredith), p. 46.

25. *Ibid.*, p. 49.   26. *Ibid.*, p. 59.   27. *Ibid.*, pp. 57–60.

ject and object, created by mind in co-operation with material reality. Nature, he believes, does not contain beauty. He who calls a landscape beautiful makes it so by the operation of his own mind. He, like the artist who paints a landscape, imputes his mind to nature.[28]

Kant characterizes beauty as that which not only produces harmony between our rational and sensuous natures but produces pleasure which is disinterested, i.e., untainted by concern for self. We value beauty for itself alone, not because it is good for something, as is a utensil or a tool. Neither is the pleasure one feels in the presence of beauty caused by a desire to own that beauty. Aristotle, too, had made the point that pleasure in beauty is a disinterested pleasure. The wealthy man who collects jade and feels a pleasure in his possession is not expressing thereby an aesthetic interest. He may, of course, have such an interest, but pride in possession is not part of it. The aesthetic attitude might be compared with the pleasure we have in a friend. We value a friend for what he is, for himself alone, not for what he can do for us. So we value beauty for itself alone. It is its own excuse for being.

Again, Kant characterized beauty as "purposiveness without purpose." We value beauty for itself alone, and yet we feel that some aim or purpose has been satisfied. These things that please us asthetically look as if they had been designed for us with our needs in mind. Certainly beauty meets human need. But we cannot reasonably suppose, thought Kant, that any designer really had us and our needs in mind in producing the object. We feel content, as we do when we have accomplished something we set out to do, when we have reached a goal we ourselves set. We feel *as if* purpose must be there, and yet we cannot assume that there was any conscious purpose to meet our needs.

It is the combination of all this which produces the deep harmony between the rational and the sensuous parts of our natures. Man's nature and needs, as well as external objects, are responsible for what we call beauty. Does this mean that there are no standards by which we can judge of the excellence of the art which attempts to embody beauty? Is the man who prefers Maxfield Parrish to

28. Samuel Alexander, *Beauty and Other Forms of Value*, esp. chap. i; see also Earl of Listowell, *op. cit.*, on Alexander's views.

Leonardo da Vinci justified in the belief that one picture is better than another only if someone prefers one to the other? Kant thought not. He argued that human nature is the same everywhere; men are more alike than different; standards for beauty grow out of our *common* nature and *common* needs.

On this point DeWitt Parker writes: "Art has been identified now with one interest and now with another; what people want of art differs from one age to another, and each must define that for itself; yet throughout there has been a core of identity in the purposes it has served."[29]

This is why great art lives. It meets the universal needs of men, needs that persist from age to age. So imagination has something to conform to even here. In search for truth, man's imagination is constrained by facts, by the way things are in this world. In the search for beauty, his imagination is constrained by the nature of beauty. The nature of beauty is determined, however, by the nature of man. Beauty speaks with a universal language but only to man. The forms of beauty grow out of man's cognitive and sensuous nature. We all seem to possess, according to Kant, a common sensitiveness to whose authority we can appeal in judging that this or that object is one of beauty.

This sensitiveness to beauty must be developed. To develop it is the purpose of aesthetic education. Aesthetic education is necessarily a part of the education designed to develop creative imagination. One should know and recognize beauty as one learns to create it. As previously said, in the creation and appreciation of beauty is to be found one of the best mediums for the operation of creative imagination. It is because man has embodied not only that which gives us pleasure but that which excites other emotions as well and has done it so successfully as to arouse the same emotion in those who contemplate the objectification, be it picture, music, novel, or poem, that artists "are the movers and shakers of the world forever, it seems." Their imaginations have seen visions, and they attempt, by objectifying that dream, to inspire others to the action necessary for realizing the vision. Because the appeal of art is primarily to the emotions and because the emotions are the springs of conduct, the artist in any field has great power.

29. Parker, *op. cit.*, p. 113.

Plato saw this clearly. In the *Republic*, Socrates says: "When the modes of music change, the fundamental laws of the State always change with them." So, having set up a perfect state, poets, musicians, and all such disturbers of the status quo must not be allowed within its borders. They might induce change. This seems such strange advice from Plato, the great artist, that at least one scholar has believed that by such a proposal Plato was trying to impress his readers with the undesirability of trying to attain absolute perfection in a state, for to do so would mean the suppression of so much that was pleasant to man.[30]

However that may be, it seems certain that creative imagination needs guidance not only by other elements of intelligence itself but by being harnessed to the ideals which will promote social progress. To develop creative imagination in such a way that life is enriched both for the possessor and for all other human beings is the task of the teacher. The use to which the imagination is put is not a private matter. As Kant said:

> The empirical interest in the beautiful exists only *in society*. And if we admit that the impulse to society is natural to mankind, and that the suitability for and the propensity towards it, i.e., sociability, is a property essential to the requirements of man as a creature intended for society, and one therefore, that belongs to humanity, it is inevitable that we should also look upon taste in the light of a faculty for estimating whatever enables us to communicate even our *feeling* to every one else, and hence as a means of promoting that upon which the natural inclination of every one is set.[31]

Science and art Kant saw as the great humanizing influences:

> Fine art and the sciences, if they do not make man morally better, yet by conveying a pleasure that admits a universal communication, and by introducing polish and refinement into society, make him civilized.[32]

DISCOVERY AND CREATION

Much of the work of the imagination is more properly thought of as discovery than as creation. Imagination operates wherever intelligence is at work; if this is an attempt to discover truth, imagination is checked upon by reason and sense-experience as, through their operation, man discovers the way things are. The scientist starts

30. F. E. Woodbridge, *Son of Apollo*, pp. 82–85.
31. Kant, *op. cit.*, p. 155. 32. *Ibid.*, p. 97.

with a hypothesis which may be the result of imaginative thought; but if this hypothesis does not explain or fit reality, it is abandoned. A man concocts in his imagination a plan for action; he sets forth upon it; if by the plan he cannot achieve his purposes or if the plan does not fit the situation as it develops, it is abandoned. Imagination takes the initial steps, but sense-experience and reason follow to check upon the efficiency of its activity. Man does not create truth; he discovers it. We live in a world, the facts and truths of which are as they are, wings or no wings.

Using the facts and truths which he discovers, man invents, i.e., he forms new combinations of things already here, using his imagination intentionally toward an end. Newton *discovered* the law of gravity; Watt *invented* a steam engine. We have doubtless called many discoveries "inventions." There are many accounts of "inventions" which were stumbled upon, in much the same way as the princes, in the old tale "Three Princes of Serendip," were always finding in their travels valuable or agreeable things not sought for. Perhaps we should use the word coined by Walpole, "serendipities," for such "inventions."

It seems correct to speak of creating when man forms a new combination out of pre-existing materials. He never creates something out of nothing. But inventions, applied science, and the arts, both practical and fine, are the results of the working of his creative imagination in a somewhat different sense from the role it plays in discovering knowledge. To remember that any work of the imagination is merely a new combination of old and pre-existing material is not to belittle it. A modern writer in the field of aesthetics points out that it is "the combination, not the material that matters. A Shakespearean sonnet and a jumble of letters; a Gothic cathedral and a heap of stones; does the identity of material in each case detract from the significance of the difference in the way it is combined?"[33]

The loose and incorrect use of the term "creative" in today's educational parlance has grown out of the pragmatic theory of truth and knowledge. Progressives are likely to speak of all education as creative, implying that children create knowledge, as they learn.[34]

33. Montague, *op. cit.*, pp. 88–89.

34. John Dewey, *The Quest for Certainty*, p. 44; also W. H. Kilpatrick, *Remaking the Curriculum*, pp. 26–27.

Facts they do not create. *Truths* they do not create. The imagination undoubtedly plays a part in the discovery of truth, but the results of imaginative thought must be constantly referred to reality itself in order to determine whether imagination has conceived a truth or an error.

The most common criticism of Dewey's analysis of thought is that this analysis is not of creative thought but only of rational thought. As a matter of fact, the two cannot be separated. The second step, in which various hypotheses are formulated, is usually the place where creative thought enters the process. But, while Dewey's analysis has a place for the work of imagination, it would be strange, indeed, if he made any distinction between creative thought and rational thought. For him, not only imaginative ideas, but all ideas, are creative. The difference is a mere matter of emphasis. His analysis seems to be as follows: Life goes on in an environment, but not alone in it, rather because of it, through interaction with it. No creature lives merely under its skin. All living things are bound up in the most intimate way with the interchanges between them and their environment. Every need is the indication of a temporary absence of adjustment. Life consists of phases in which the organism falls out of step with the march of surrounding things and then recovers unison with them but is always changed thereby. This process reaches to the roots of the aesthetic. Here, in germ, are balance and harmony attained through rhythm. Equilibrium comes about not mechanically and inertly but out of and because of tension. "Order cannot but be admirable in a world constantly threatened with disorder." The rhythm of loss of integration with the environment and the recovery of union with the environment becomes conscious in man. "The difference between the aesthetic and the intellectual is thus one of the place where emphasis falls in the constant rhythm that marks the interaction of the live creature with his surroundings. The ultimate matter of both emphases in experience is the same, as is also their general form. The thinker has his aesthetic moment when his ideas cease to be mere ideas and become the corporate meaning of objects. The artist has his problems and thinks as he works. But his thought is more immediately embodied in the object." In a world of mere flux or in a world where there was no suspense and crisis there would be no aesthetic experience. Art is prefigured in the very processes of living. "Because experience is the fulfillment of an organism in its struggles and achievements in a world of things it is art in germ. Even in its rudimentary forms, it contains the promise of that delightful perception which is esthetic experience."[35]

No Oversoul as the explanation of man's imaginative and creative activities in the philosophy of John Dewey! He finds the roots of aesthetic activity in the biological processes of life itself. Other philosophers who find the basis of the creative and the aesthetic in the nature of man might not be so certain that this aspect of man can be explained in biological terms alone. But, taken in conjunction with Dewey's theory of truth, his theory of art helps us understand why for many Progressives all education is creative. To teach this is unfortunate, not only because it seems untrue, but because it obscures the issue and may block the effort to develop that aspect of the educative process which is properly called creative.[36] In the past too many teachers concerned themselves only with guiding pupils in the acquisition of facts. That is important and must not be neglected. Teachers in some modern schools have gone to the opposite extreme; and, as a result, children have a very hazy grasp when they leave school of the knowledge which man has accumulated. These young people have little real mastery of facts and truths. In the reaction which seems imminent, and needed, from "soft pedagogy," it would be unfortunate again to stress mere acquisition of information and to neglect entirely the development of the power of creative thought.

EDUCATIONAL PHILOSOPHIES AND THE DEVELOPMENT

OF CREATIVE IMAGINATION

The foregoing discussion of all education as creative constitutes perhaps the most vocal controversy among the differing educational philosophies concerning the use of man's creative powers. It will be noticed that this disagreement concerns fundamentally a theory of knowledge rather than of aesthetics. It asks that the relation between discovering and creating be clarified.

It is probably true that all educational philosophies are heartily

---

35. Quoted and paraphrased from John Dewey, *Art as Experience*, pp. 13–19.
36. See pp. 312–17 for further discussion.

in favor of the development of man's creative imagination. That there is so little discussion among them or even mention of its importance may be a reflection of the fact that education has been concerned chiefly with helping children acquire a knowledge of the social heritage. Until recently there has not been much attempt to help children develop creative ability even through the arts. And in the recent past educational philosophers have been so busy disagreeing on the nature of the true and of the good that they have not gotten around as yet to much discussion of basic differences concerning the beautiful. There are differences among them, differences in emphases and methods which go back to differing conceptions of the nature of beauty and of art.

Whatever the faults of Progressive education have been, we have that movement to thank for an emphasis on artistic expression in education and for a method of teaching the arts much more suited to child nature and child need than was the older method. It is Kilpatrick who says in the symposium of educational philosophies referred to in earlier chapters: "The activity type of school will show more of creative drawing, painting, music, dancing, writing."[37] Breed says nothing in this symposium about the education of the creative abilities, although he protests vigorously against the belief of the experimentalist that "the qualities of objects are instituted by the creative activity of man's intellectual operations."[38] Horne advocates a curriculum of science, fine arts, and practical arts, saying that the pupil "will need also to appreciate one of the arts like literature or music, and even try his hand at the production of something artistic and beautiful."[39] McGucken writes that education must teach the child to appreciate "the true, the beautiful, the good."[40] But concerning the importance of creative expression, he has nothing to say.

It is probably significant that both Horne and McGucken emphasize appreciation. Idealism and scholasticism have a classical basis. Such philosophies, it will be remembered, teach that beauty is inherent in objects and has definite qualities which make the objects beautiful. If there are relatively fixed standards for beauty, they

37. National Society for the Study of Education, *Forty-first Yearbook: Part I: Philosophies of Education,* p. 75.

38. *Ibid.,* p. 99.   39. *Ibid.,* p. 162.   40. *Ibid.,* p. 286.

should be learned. Children would need much experience with forms of beauty already created before they can do anything worth while themselves. So a boy or girl should be exposed to the beautiful and learn to appreciate it; then perhaps, as Horne says, he can "try his hand at the production of something artistic and beautiful."

The following quotations from Redden and Ryan make clear the scholastic position on the nature of beauty and on the function of aesthetic education: "The science of aesthetics treats the problem of the nature and objective conditions of beauty. By the term objective conditions of beauty is meant in general, unity, truth and goodness; and in particular, completeness, proportion and clarity."[41] "Full and complete appreciation of beauty is . . . . essentially rational."[42] "The function of aesthetic education is to acquaint the individual with the correct notion of beauty, so that he may contemplate, appreciate, and enjoy it."[43]

Progressive education, on the other hand, has little to say about standards for artistic endeavor. Progressives stress art as self-expression. Children are stimulated to express their emotions freely through all kinds of art mediums. It makes no difference whether the result seems good to adults; if it seems good to the child, that is all that matters.

Sometimes Progressives seem to forget that art is not only a means of self-expression but also a valuable means for communication. The expression that fails to communicate is an incomplete expression. Self-expression without any emphasis on communication is probably a necessary emphasis with small children, but young people need to learn how to express themselves so as to communicate. Again let it be emphasized that the ability to communicate through the use of symbols is man's unique power.[44] Early man first used pictures for recorded communication, later, more abstract symbols. Modern man uses both. If he is learning to use words, he will need to learn that to communicate he must observe conventions of spelling, punctuation, and sentence structure. If he is learning to use other art mediums, there are standards of excellence there which he must learn as he experiments and expresses himself.

41. John D. Redden and Francis A. Ryan, *A Catholic Philosophy of Education*, p. 294.

42. *Ibid.*, p. 296.   43. *Ibid.*, p. 300.   44. See chap. iv.

Psychologically, the order in which the child practices self-expression and then learns gradually the better form for his expression is probably sounder in Progressive practices than in the older traditional school.

Even in the use of problem-solving, the Progressives seem to be in advance of the older schools of thought. The Progressives advocate problem-solving as the only method suitable for teaching children how to think. There can be no quarrel with this thesis if children at the same time are obtaining knowledge of the experience of the race so that they will have available the essentials of human experience for solving their problems. We need to remember that, as June Downey puts it, "all so-called inspirations occur strictly within the limits of the individual's training and previous cogitations."[45] We all need to learn *how* to think, to solve problems, to use the imagination and the reason. But the imagination and the reason need materials with which to work.

If a human being is to live successfully and solve his problems, he needs to know what others have discovered. The wisdom of the past should be his, so far as he is able to acquire it. He needs to know *what* to think, where truth has been established, as well as *how* to think in solving new problems.

THE DEVELOPMENT OF CREATIVE IMAGINATION

The teachers of the arts, both practical and fine, and the teachers of English seem to be in the vanguard of those who have made a start toward working intelligently to develop in every child whatever potential creative ability he may have. Some few psychologists are beginning to investigate problems connected with this phase of the educative process and are asking, as does June Downey, why it is that "some persons' cogitations (conscious and unconscious) issue in original patterns and others in stereotyped or conventional ones"?[46]

She continues: "Undoubtedly poets are made as well as born, and in part this 'making' involves the throwing off of fetters that for most individuals keep them from being as original as they might be."[47]

In New York City at an exhibit of the remarkable work done by children in Professor Cizek's classes at the School of Arts and Crafts in the pre-Hitler Vienna, astonished beholders told how they finally

45. See p. 299.   46. *Op. cit.*, p. 160.   47. *Ibid.*, p. 167.

came to the teacher: " 'How do you do it?' we asked at last, when we had looked at some hundreds of the productions of Professor Cizek's pupils, each more delightful and original than the last. 'But I don't do it,' he protested with a kind of weary pity for our lack of understanding. 'I take the lid off, and other art masters clap the lid on— that is the only difference.' "[48]

This process is not so simple as Professor Cizek made it sound. *How* to take the lid off is in itself a difficult psychological problem. And most authorities hold that just to take it off is not enough. But getting the right atmosphere, one of noninterference and sympathy, is undoubtedly an important part of the problem. Any kind of stiff or elaborate methodology is bad. Even the methods suitable for acquisitive learning are not suitable for the operation of creative power. Genius has always been recalcitrant toward system and order in education. One writer charges that our society acts on the assumption that a person of creative mind thrives best when he is scorned and cuffed about.[49] This recalcitrance toward rigidity may help to account for the long list of persons of superior ability who have done so poorly in school. Geniuses have at least occasionally survived the treatment received in school; but we do not know that genius always develops in spite of the stupid treatment its possessor too often receives. We do feel quite certain that whatever creative ability the majority of human beings have is damaged and often killed outright in the early school years.

The teacher seems to be the most important factor. That is not surprising, for the teacher is always the most important agent in the success of any aspect of the educative process. The teacher must, of course, recognize excellence in creative activity; he must know *how* it is attained as nearly as this is possible. It is even better if he himself is capable of creative work, so that he can *do* as well as know *how* to do. But, most important of all, he must be able to act as a kind of catalytic agent that is, to accelerate the development and activity of creative power without actively entering into the process of creation himself. Such teachers seem to be able to start the emotional quickening which accompanies creative work. They are sympathetic but never maudlin. They know that one "laugh may seal forever one outlet of the spirit."[50] They know how to give instruc-

48. Hughes Mearns, *Creative Youth*, p. 7.
49. Rollo Brown, *Creative Spirit*.   50. Mearns, *op. cit.*, p. 5.

tion which assists and guides growth but never kills or shackles. On this point, Hughes Mearns says:

> One group of "progressives," for instance, believes so much in the "growth theory" that it will hardly permit any instruction at all. It banks all upon Nature. With these "naturalists" some of us have delightful disputes. Nature is wonderful, as all the poets tell us, but we, some of us, don't trust her altogether. . . . . Because of having written a book on the poetry of youth I am in constant receipt of sheaves of bad poetry from all parts of the country. "See what my children have done without any instruction whatever!" is the tenor of the accompanying letters. My pity goes out to the children; so obviously have they needed someone to be by to point out the way. . . . . If growth under pleasantly free surroundings were all of the new education, then my occupation is gone; for I conceive of my professional skill as something imperatively needed to keep that growth nourished.[51]

Evidently, it is more than simply taking the lid off that has to be done. There must be a teacher who knows how to instruct. On this same point another student of the problem writes:

> From observation of children in the nursery school, the author leans toward the view that more adult-directed imaginative activities and more closely supervised creative activities at earlier levels might better foster the development of imagination than undirected freedom of expression. This assumption is based on the belief that the most socially acceptable and possibly the most satisfying expressisons of imagination are based on adequate knowledge. Adult guidance of the child's learning activities and imaginative play contributes to the building of a background of concepts and generalizations, whereas the undirected activity of the child is often likely to be fanciful and imaginative merely because it is incorrect and irrational.[52]

Mearns insists that a coldly intellectual stage must always follow creative fire, in which work must be appraised in the light of the best standards. It is most unfortunate that some teachers have the notion that spelling, punctuation, grammar, paragraphing, are unimportant. Good teaching, it will be remembered, is a matter of combining instruction, training in habit formation, and inspiration. They are all needed for the proper development of the creative imagination.

Thomas H. Briggs, himself a most skilful teacher, has written of a study which he conducted with a high-school class, concerning

51. Hughes Mearns in Hartman and Shumaker, *op. cit.*, p. 19.
52. Francis V. Markey, *Imaginative Behavior of Pre-school Children*, p. 138.

the formal aspects of poetry, in which such interest was awakened as to bring an outburst of creative effort, resulting in a privately printed book of verse.[53]

Teachers could learn much from the answers to a questionnaire sent to chemists by two investigators, in regard to the conditions under which the best creative work seems to be done. Many of them replied that mild exercise seems to be helpful; that their best "hunches" have come when doing such things as driving a car, shaving, gardening, fishing, golfing, playing solitaire, dressing. They all agreed that fatigue, worry, noise, anger, and interruptions militate against effective thought.[54]

Undoubtedly the modern activity school with its emphasis on self-activity, initiative, thinking things through for one's self, etc., furnishes a much better atmosphere for the development of creative imagination than did the traditional school with its insistence on *memoriter* learning, its formality, and, too often, its poorly prepared teacher. Various types of unit assignments used in the modern school, most of which furnish some opportunity for self-initiated projects of various sorts, if wisely used, can contribute to originality and creative effort.

Children need to learn to do things as well as to learn what is in books. The home, in previous generations, attended to much of this phase of education. It can still have an important part in it. But much of what young people need to learn to do cannot be taught in homes. This is an increasingly technical and mechanical age. Technical expertness is in demand. This requires not only an ability to understand and use tools and machines but an ability to use the imagination as well. Contriving, building, visualizing, planning, constructing, all need a highly developed imaginative ability. The skilled trades, engineering, practical arts, designing, homemaking, aeronautics, radio development, and business activity of all kinds are a few examples of fields in which imagination is increasingly needed.

There are many children in our schools who are interested in the contents of books and who are also interested in the manipulation of

53. "The Teaching of Prosody: A Means and an End," *Bulletin, Illinois Association of Teachers of English*, Vol. X, No. 2.

54. Quoted by Fletcher, *op. cit.*, p. 367, from the *Journal of Chemical Education*, October, 1931.

materials. There are other children who care little for the contents
of books but who have excellent minds for dealing with concrete
materials. The abilities of these youngsters are needed by our civilization as badly as are those of the first group or those of young
people who are interested primarily in ideas.

We seem to have inherited from the past a notion that persons
whose work is primarily mental are somehow superior to those
whose work is physical in nature. In a technical and industrial age
such a view seems to be indefensible because of the fact that much
of the work of the world today takes both mental and physical
effort. Wherever a person can do the best, in whatever field his interests and abilities lie, that is the place where he should have the
opportunity to work. The school must not neglect any individual.

Imagination has been an important factor in the development and
continual improvement of the machine into the shining, streamlined,
beautiful, complex mechanism of today. Imagination is needed in its
improvement and in planning to bring its benefits to all mankind.
There will be more and more call on the school to assist in laying
the proper foundation for life in this world of machines.

In a technological society the school's attention to the development of the creative powers of man is important for still another
reason. Many men who work at machines all day perform highly
repetitive and very simple operations. There is nothing creative
about their work. The craftsman of yesterday used his creative abilities constantly; the worker on an assembly line or in any type of
mass production scarcely ever does.

Newton Edwards says that the machine fractionalizes experience
and dulls the individual's creative abilities.[55] This gives the "worthy
use of leisure" a new meaning. Fortunately, the machine makes
more leisure possible. The school, beginning in the lower grades and
through the upper grades and high school, needs to emphasize
creative activities for leisure time. These pursuits may be in intellectual fields, in physical activities, in practical or fine arts, but they
should have within them the possibilities for the unifying effect and
emotional satisfaction that modern industry denies so many.

Many experienced teachers know what miracles of changed behavior the harnessing of excess energy into creative lines can effect.

55. In a lecture at the University of Chicago, summer of 1946.

When all a pupil's attention is centered on producing something which he feels is peculiarly his, he has no time for mischief or desire for troublemaking. Teachers would do well to attempt to discover latent interests and abilities in their pupils and to put them to work along creative lines. It may be chemistry for this child; it may be music for that one. It may be the making of a poster for the school or perhaps the writing of a story or the reporting of a sports event for the school paper. It may be the making of a simple piece of furniture for the school or home; it may be the concoction of some apparatus for a school project. It may be drawing, modeling, painting, or playing a musical instrument.

Teachers of industrial arts, of shop courses, of home economics, of business, have as much responsibility and opportunity for the development of creative thinking as have the teachers of the fine arts. Many of these teachers, particularly in home economics and in industrial arts, are living up to their opportunities.[56]

Physical education teachers have opportunities here, too. Competitive games offer the chance for original thinking within the rules of the game. A successful player is one not only with physical skill but with the ability to lay plans, to imagine possibilities, and to display originality in thought.

Honors courses for the superior student in both the secondary school[57] and the college promise favorable opportunity for pursuing individual research and encouraging originality. Every teacher, from the elementary school through the graduate school, must be constantly on the alert to encourage special interests, to develop individual gifts, to stimulate original thought, and to discourage mere verbalism. On the other hand, teachers need to remember Goethe's warning: "The most foolish of all errors for clever young men to believe is that they forfeit their originality in recognizing a truth which has already been recognized by others."

SUMMARY

Some thinkers have insisted that the creative imagination is the supreme power in man, a power which links man to the creative forces in the universe. Like the intelligence of which it is a part, creative imagi-

56. See, e.g., F. Theodore Struck, *Creative Teaching.*

57. See, e.g., L. H. Burnside, "An Experimental Program in Education of the Intellectually Gifted Adolescent," *School Review,* L (April, 1942), 274–85.

nation is found to some degree in all normal human beings. Psychologists do not understand very well either the nature of creative thought or the way in which it works. Mental activity, which is creative, seems to have characteristics which distinguish it from other types of mental activity. But it always operates within and upon previously acquired knowledge.

The arts are particularly effective mediums through which to develop the creative imagination. The artist has been especially concerned with the embodiment of beauty. Aesthetics is the branch of philosophy which studies the nature of beauty. Aesthetic objectivists have believed that beauty is a quality inherent in objects themselves and have emphasized rational elements which man could discover through the use of his mental powers. They have also taught that there are objective standards to which art should conform. The aesthetic subjectivist believes that a thing is beautiful because it appeals to the senses of man; because men differ in what appeals to their senses, there can be no objective standards. The Kantian synthesis sees beauty as appealing to both the rational and the sensuous in man so as to put them in immediate harmony. There are standards for beauty and for excellence in artistic production which grow out of the universal aspects of human nature. The aesthetic sense in man must be developed through the educative process.

Progressives have probably done more than other educational philosophies in recent years to encourage the development of creative ability. They stress creative activity more often as self-expression than as communication. The traditional philosophies, stemming from aesthetic objectivism, emphasize appreciation. Progressive education has encouraged the use of problem-solving; traditionalists have in the past been more likely to emphasize the acquisition of knowledge.

We need a synthesis of all these emphases for an adequate philosophy of education. This is what we seem to know concerning the development of the creative imagination:

1. Creative imagination needs to be encouraged from early childhood on; the reality of the early development of the creative urge has been demonstrated in work with grade-school children.[58]

2. There seems to be a close connection not only between creativeness and intelligence but between the creative urge and the emotional urge. It does seem to be true that some of the world's greatest art was born out of unhappiness and maladjustment. Failing to find happiness in the world of men, the artist creates his own world. Dante's *Divine Comedy* and Beethoven's *Ninth Symphony* come to mind as illustrations. This may be true of some geniuses, but it does not seem true of the average individual, especially not of children. The relation needs further study, but it seems that conditions favoring a healthy, happy, emotional adjust-

58. See Hartman and Shumaker, *op. cit.*

ment favor the development of creative ability in the majority of persons. Emotional drive is connected somehow with effective creativeness. Life that is too easy is not likely to stir the emotions.

3. The most difficult problem for the teacher seems to be to learn how to encourage originality and creativeness within the necessary bounds set by reality and by what man has already discovered and invented, to help children acquire knowledge already in man's possession and go on from there to original activity. It is usually wasteful for children to have to rediscover what is already known.

4. The teacher's attitude toward the children and the atmosphere of the classroom growing out of this attitude are essential factors. Rapport is essential; thinking and acting toward each child as an end, as important in himself, is the background out of which the most favorable atmosphere grows.

5. The teacher himself needs to be interested in, and capable of, creative production. Teacher-education programs should contain features designed to develop this appreciation and ability in prospective teachers. To have great artists and creative thinkers on our college faculties is a privilege most advantageous to youth.

6. Home economics, industrial arts, music, drawing, modeling, puppetry, painting, dancing, and writing plays, short stories, verse, or radio skits all give opportunity for creative activity; but it should not be thought that these fields exhaust the opportunity for the development of man's creative imagination. Teachers in *every* field should remember that acquisition of facts is merely the beginning of knowledge and should encourage their pupils to continue on to those higher levels of thought pointed out in the previous chapter.

7. Each child, as Arthur T. Jersild of the Child Development Institute points out, should be observed in several situations with differing materials and companions. Only so can his potential creative abilities and interests be discovered.

8. Very seldom does creative ability produce its best at first trial. Children must be encouraged to work over the results of thir first efforts in order to get a better product. But how to do this without discouraging children is not easy to determine. Too great perfectionism on the part of a teacher may dishearten a child. The greater the ability a child has, the higher the standards to which he should be held. Creative fire burns easily for its possessor; perfecting the result is hard work.

9. Genius is rare; encouraging creative activity in all children will probably not produce any appreciable increase in the contributions from extraordinary human beings. But such encouragement should help all human beings to live on a higher plane, to appreciate genius where it does arise, to utilize a growing leisure profitably, in short, to live so as to raise the level of civilization. If imaginative creation is, as it seems, an exten-

sion of a creative process in nature into the realm of the mind, man is most truly man when he is exercising this ability, to whatever degree he is able to employ it.

10. Although it is still a controversial question whether everyone can learn to appreciate the fine arts, especially when his creative abilities run along other lines, there seems to be enough evidence to justify the conclusion that there is no better way to develop the common sensitiveness to beauty which seems to be a general, if potential, possession of man than through the wise guidance of an enthusiastic teacher. It takes imagination to enjoy as well as to produce art. Art appreciation courses need further development and improvement.

11. Psychologists should assist teachers by investigating further the way in which the creative imagination works and the best conditions for developing it. Teachers need to learn how to keep inhibitions and distrusts from forming, how to remove them if they have already developed, and how to provide the kind of environment favorable for the work of creative minds.

12. Teachers should remember that it is their responsibility not only to develop creative imagination but to inspire their pupils to use their abilities, particularly if they be great, for man's welfare. Few teachers will ever have a genius to instruct, one of those who really are "movers and shakers of the world." But we all dream dreams, and we can all work to exchange dreams for reality.

QUESTIONS TO AID STUDY

1. In what sense does man create? How are imagination and reason complementary?
2. How widely does creative ability seem to be distributed among human beings? In what life-activities is its presence shown? At what age does it seem particularly active? How might this be accounted for?
3. What theories are there concerning the source of man's creative imagination?
4. Compare creative thought with assimilative thought. How is creative thought dependent upon acquired knowledge?
5. What seem to be the characteristics of creative thought? In what sense is creative thought effortless?
6. How do you understand the relation of the arts to beauty?
7. How would you define aesthetics? Examine a book in that field to see the kinds of problems with which it deals. Are you interested? Why or why not?
8. Summarize the two points of view concerning standards by which the excellence of man's artistic efforts may be judged.

9. What was Kant's view of the nature of beauty? What two viewpoints did he attempt to synthesize?
10. Compare Santayana's conception of beauty with that of Kant. How are they alike? How different?
11. Discuss the distinction between discovery and creation? Why is it important to make this distinction? What philosophic school of thought fails to make such a distinction? Why?
12. What have been the strengths and what the weaknesses of progressive education in the field of education for creativeness?
13. What differing emphases concerning the development of man's creative powers are found in differing philosophical schools? Why?
14. Explain the significance of the saying: "Let me make a people's music and I care not who makes their laws." What responsibility do artists have?
15. Summarize the factors which seem important for success in developing creative imagination in the school. What connection do you see between success in this endeavor and the elimination of disciplinary problems?
16. Write a short paper showing through a specific illustration how you, in your particular field or fields, with children of the age you are preparing to teach, could work for the development of creative imagination.
17. What seems to be the most difficult problem of the teacher who desires to encourage originality and creativity in children?

SUGGESTED REFERENCES

ARISTOTLE. *Poetics* (any translation).

BREED, FREDERICK S. *Education and the New Realism* (New York: Macmillan Co., 1939), chap. vi.

BRUBACHER, JOHN S. (ed.). *Public Schools and Spiritual Values*. Seventh Yearbook, John Dewey Society (New York: Harper & Bros., 1944), chap. ix.

CROCE, BENEDETTO. *Essence of Aesthetics*. Translated by DOUGLAS AINSLIE. London: William Heinemann, 1921.

CROW, CHARLES SUMNER. *Creative Education*. New York: Prentice-Hall, Inc., 1937.

D'AMICO, VICTOR. *Creative Teaching in Art*. Scranton, Pa.: International Textbook Co., 1942.

DEWEY, JOHN. *Art as Experience* (New York: Minton Balch & Co., 1934), especially chap. i.

———. *Creative Intelligence*. New York: Henry Holt & Co., 1917.

DICKINSON, G. LOWES. *The Greek View of Life* (New York: Doubleday, Page & Co., 1911), chap. iv.

Downey, June. *Creative Imagination.* New York: Harcourt, Brace & Co., 1929.

Eaker, J. G. "Aesthetics and Education," *Educational Forum,* III (November, 1938), 63–68.

Fox, Lillian Mohr, and Hopkins, Thomas. *Creative School Music.* New York: Silver Burdett Co., 1936.

Gilbert, Katherine Everett, and Kuhn, Helmut. *History of Aesthetics* (New York: Macmillan Co., 1939), especially pp. 321–43.

Hartman, Gertrude, and Shumaker, Ann (eds.). *Creative Expression.* Milwaukee: E. M. Hale & Co., 1939.

Hartmann, George W. *Educational Psychology* (New York: American Book Co., 1941), chap. xi.

Langfeld, Herbert S. *Aesthetic Attitude* (New York: Harcourt, Brace & Howe, 1920), especially chaps. i and iii.

Leighton, Joseph A. *Social Philosophies in Conflict* (New York: D. Appleton–Century Co., 1937), chap. xvi.

McCall, Lucie Ann. "Child's Experience and His Art," *Educational Method,* XVII (May, 1938), 395–403.

Maritain, Jacques. *Art and Scholasticism.* Translated by J. F. Scanlon. New York: Charles Scribner's Sons, 1937.

Mearns, Hughes. *Creative Power.* Garden City, N.Y.: Doubleday, Doran & Co., 1930.

———. *Creative Youth.* Garden City, N.Y.: Doubleday, Doran & Co., 1925.

Montague, William Pepperell. *The Ways of Things* (New York: Prentice-Hall, Inc., 1940), chap. vii.

Overstreet, Harry. *The Enduring Quest* (New York: W. W. Norton & Co., 1931), chap. xi.

Parker, DeWitt H. *The Principles of Aesthetics* (New York: F. S. Crofts Co., 1946), chap. vii.

Redden, John D., and Ryan, Francis A. *A Catholic Philosophy of Education* (Milwaukee: Bruce Pub. Co., 1942), chap. ix.

Ribot, Theodule A. *Essay on the Creative Imagination.* Translated from the French by Albert H. V. Baron. Chicago: Open Court Pub. Co., 1906.

Santayana, George. *The Sense of Beauty.* New York: Charles Scribner's Sons, 1910.

Stace, Walter Terence. *The Meaning of Beauty.* London: G. Richards & H. Toulman, 1929.

Struck, Ferdinand Theodore. *Creative Teaching; Industrial Arts and Vocational Education.* New York: J. Wiley & Sons, 1938.

Whitford, William G. "Changing Philosophy of Art Education," *Education,* LX (November, 1939), 169–71.

CHAPTER XV
THE DEVELOPMENT OF CHARACTER

Relation of education to character development—Nature of character; etymology of the term; relation of character to conduct—Obstacles to the development of moral character: (1) Misunderstanding of the nature of morality; (2) Diminishing influence of religion; (3) Lack of agreement on the constituents of desirable character; (4) Social conditions and arrangements; (5) Teachers who do not exemplify human excellence; (6) Factors in human nature itself—Methods of character education: (1) Direct; (2) Indirect—Three phases in character development: (1) Knowledge of what is right and what is wrong; (2) Love of right; hatred of wrong; (3) Habits of right conduct—Developing altruism and social attitudes: (1) Relation of values to wants; (2) Identification of self with others; gradually widening sphere of identification; (3) Principles for accomplishing identification; (4) Illustration of the use of these principles—Organizing school life to provide a favorable environment for development of character—Educational philosophies and character education: (1) Differences of opinion on nature of morality; (2) Differences of opinion on emphasis to be placed on knowledge and on experience; (3) Differences of opinion on relation of religion to character development (a) religion and spiritual values, (b) the teaching of religion in the public schools

IN PLATO'S dialogue known as the *Meno*, a young man by that name who has been a pupil of the Sophist Gorgias inquired of Socrates whether virtue is acquired either by teaching or by practice or whether it is perhaps a natural possession of man. Socrates, with an innocent air, replied that in Athens no one knew just what virtue was, so how could anyone know how it could be acquired: "When I do not know the 'quid' of anything, how can I know the 'quale'? How if I knew nothing at all of Meno, could I tell if he was fair, or the opposite of fair; rich and noble, or the reverse of rich and noble. . . . . I confess with shame that I know literally nothing about virtue."[1]

Gorgias had taught Meno, as Socrates well knew, that there was no common moral law binding on all men but that excellence consists in something different for every age and every condition of life. Meno fell into the trap which Socrates had set for him, and there followed a conversation, amusing to everyone but Meno, in which this human gadfly, Socrates, developed the idea that virtue is knowledge. He is, however, a little doubtful as to whether it can be taught, as can geometry. There is so little agreement on the nature of excellence; and, besides, where are the teachers?

From the days of Plato to the present time, the problem of the development of excellence and fine character has concerned the philosophers, the theologians, and the teachers. It is agreed that Socrates could easily be misunderstood in identifying virtue with knowledge. As we use the word "knowledge," more than that is needed to induce moral conduct. But Socrates was right in the lesson he seemed to want to teach young Meno—that before we can teach virtue we must agree upon its meaning and that the Sophist conception of virtue made it impossible to teach excellence to human beings.

This dialogue might help the modern teacher to understand some of the causes operating against the successful development of character in schools. Too many people again believe that there is no one moral law binding on all men alike. Too many identify morality with the mores. There is still little agreement as to what constitutes excellence. The influence of religion is at a low ebb. These points have all been made and discussed in a previous chapter.[2] In addition, there is not even agreement on the part of men who write on character development as to what character itself is.

NATURE OF CHARACTER

Books on character education contain long lists of varying definitions of the term "character," among which one often searches in vain for any harmony of opinion. This much seems apparent: that all explanation of its meaning may be classified as either psychologi-

1. Plato *Meno* (trans. Jowett).   2. See chap. vi.

cal or ethical in nature.[3] In the psychological sense one's character is his distinctive nature, that which makes him himself rather than another. In this sense everyone has character. In the ethical sense the term means that quality of human nature which makes for dependability. Character in this sense means an inner consistency or unity of personality. It means constancy, steadfastness, dependability. It implies stability. A man of character is no weather vane. He acts as he does because of principles or ideals within rather than from expediency or because of pressure from without. In this sense there are many people who have little or no character. It is in the ethical sense that the word is used in philosophy.

The etymology of the term should help in understanding this latter meaning. The word "character" comes from the Greek and seems to have meant first "a sharp-pointed instrument or engraving tool." Later it was applied to the mark made or to the thing engraved. It meant something stable and constant because it was cut into the material. The term was applied to man in this sense by Theophrastus (378–288 B.C.). Augustine (354–430) used the word character to mean a holy sign or symbol imposed upon the soul by the sacraments. La Bruyère (1645–96), the French author and moralist, seems to have been one of the earliest moderns to use the word in the ethical sense, although the idea for which the word stands is very ancient. Breasted, the eminent investigator of ancient Egyptian culture, found in the writing of King Ptahhotep, who lived twenty-seven centuries before Christ, a word which seemed to mean what we mean by the term character: "Precious to a man is the virtue of his son, and good character is a thing to be remembered."[4]

The original meaning of the term is in agreement with common usage. It is often said of a man, "He has no character," meaning that he is an unknown and unknowable quantity, acting not upon principle but upon policy. It is about as futile to depend upon such an individual as it is to try to pick up a blob of mercury in one's fingers. A person with no character is a menace. But so may be a man with character, unless that character be headed in the right

3. See H. C. McKown, *Character Education*, pp. 1–6; H. Hartshorne, *Character in Human Relations*, pp. 125–86; and D. C. Troth (ed.), *Readings in Character Education*, pp. 4–34.

4. J. H. Breasted, *The Dawn of Conscience*, p. 396.

direction. A man of character is a man of principle. But principles may be immoral or moral in nature, and a moral character is more than just a character. Kant says, "In a bad man, character is very pernicious."[5] To have character is not enough—although that is probably preferable to having no character; others at least know what to expect. Character must be moral. By this is meant that men must learn to act upon those principles which will promote the development of the finest personalities in human beings, those which will further the life good for man to live. Man not only must be intelligent but must use his intelligence to promote the welfare of all, instead of merely his own selfish interests.[6]

Conduct is the outer expression of character; what a man does tells us what he is. Conduct and character are the outer and the inner phases of the same thing. It is because character determines conduct that its development in boys and girls is so important.

OBSTACLES TO THE DEVELOPMENT OF MORAL CHARACTER

To say that children should be brought up in such a way as to get them to act upon the principles necessary for promoting the general welfare is easy; to state what those principles are is not difficult. particularly in the light of the aid given man for this formulation by religion and philosophy; but actually to develop in children the willingness and ability so to conduct themselves is the most difficult task of education. Developing intelligence or even creative imagination is easy compared to developing moral character. But its development is so crucial that, without at least a modicum of success, it may be actually dangerous to raise the level of intelligence in the general population. Some educators, Herbart (1776–1841) among them, have insisted that the development of moral character is *the* aim of education. It is certainly an important educational aim. However, intelligence, creativeness, and goodness are all needed for man's welfare. The omission of any one of these from educational endeavor would be a serious handicap to the realization of social progress. "Be good, sweet maid, and let who will be clever," is inadequate advice. Every maid should be both good and clever, as far as it is possible. So should every man.

5. Immanuel Kant, *Pädagogik* (trans. J. H. Kirchmann), VIII, 264.
6. The student should call to mind the discussion in chaps. iv, v, and vi.

A misunderstanding of the nature of morality, the diminishing influence of religion, the lack of agreement on what constitutes desirable character, or even character itself, are not the only factors operating to render the development of fine character difficult. Too often the school furnishes children the only contact with ideals that they have. When young people see all that the school teaches constantly trampled under foot in the community and sometimes even in the home, teachers can accomplish little. As long as we have a society which, by its very organization, brings out the worst in man, it will be impossible for the school to develop the best. With other responsible adults, teachers must work to improve social arrangements while they work with boys and girls to improve their individual development.

In addition, society needs to look at its teachers and to take steps to attract superior men and women of the finest personality into the profession. Too many teachers have led lives apart from reality. Primness and priggishness are not goodness. The celibacy imposed upon women teachers has too often resulted in a type of instructor unable to understand or appreciate adolescence and young adulthood and therefore unsympathetic with them. If men and women are to understand and influence young people, they must be persons not only of superior character themselves but intelligent, gifted, capable, creative. They should have personality in its best and truest sense—that is, they should approximate the best in human development. Too few such men and women are teachers, although their numbers in this profession have been growing during this and the previous decade. Such persons can teach excellence in the best way—through the example of what they themselves are.

The greatest obstacle to the development of fine character lies in the selfishness and self-seeking of human nature itself. It is often extremely difficult to act from the motive of sympathy for others and still more difficult to act from a sense of duty. It is very easy to act for the interests of the self. Man has not yet seen and does not understand that the interests of all are his interests, that a hungry man on the other side of the world is a menace to him, that ignorance hundreds of miles away may have repercussions that engulf him, and that suffering or evil anywhere in the world concerns him. To convince human beings of this truth, to instruct them in the principles upon which man should act, and to engender in them the desire to act upon these principles are the problems of character education.

METHODS OF CHARACTER EDUCATION

A few years ago educators were debating whether the direct or the indirect method of character education was the better. Using the direct method, a teacher attempts to develop moral character by giving instruction in morality at a definite time and place in the daily program, much as one might allocate a definite time to arithmetic or reading. At the designated period the children would discuss various virtues, read material designated to rouse interest in ideals, talk over moral problems. During the remainder of the day, there might be references to the lesson in morality growing out of the other activities of the school which were always utilized and connected. Slogans and mottoes were often used. The teaching was conscious and direct.

It will be readily seen that such a plan may have at least two serious faults. It concentrates attention on the intellectual aspects of moral behavior, but it does little to affect motivation. Unless children's emotions are reached so that they earnestly desire to do right, character education has not been effective. In addition, it too often encourages hypocrisy and priggishness. Both children and adults who talk a great deal about their goodness often do little but talk. "Man talks most of those virtues which he least possesses." With older children and with young adults, all authorities would agree that there is a place for formal ethical discussions. But the indirect method seems to be better for younger children and for many phases of character education with older boys and girls.

In the indirect method character education is considered a part of all education. Advocates of this method believe that the life of the school should be organized in such a way as to develop character through all that is done. If an occasion arises that seems to demand some discussion of a moral problem, that discussion should take place. But the principal emphasis is put on helping children live so that they develop as they should. Morality, say the advocates of this method, is not a separate department of our lives but enters into all our living and can be taught successfully only in connection with life's experiences.

Today the majority of teachers believe that the indirect method is the better. The only serious fault with it is that teachers are too likely to forget to use it—and that is really a fault with the teacher, not with the method. This does not mean, of course, that the direct method should never be used.

THREE PHASES IN CHARACTER DEVELOPMENT

No thinker has been wiser than Aristotle in analyzing the factors necessary for helping children develop moral character. They must know what is right and wrong, of course. But Aristotle did not think that that was enough. Children must also love what is noble and hate what is base.[7] Even that is not enough; good habits are also necessary.

The virtues we acquire by first exercising them, as also happens in the case of the arts, as well. For the things we have to learn before we can do them, we learn by doing them, e.g., men become builders by building and lyre-players by playing the lyre; so too we become just by doing just acts, temperate by doing temperate acts, brave by doing brave acts. . . . . It makes no small difference then, whether we form habits of one kind or of another from our very youth; it makes a very great difference, or rather, *all* the difference.[8]

Knowledge of the right, love of right and hatred of wrong, habits of right conduct—these three phases of character education must be taken care of if the work is to be successful.

The point has been made that the educative process has three interrelated aspects: instruction, training, and inspiration. Character education illustrates well each of the three. Instruction will take care of the knowledge of what is right and what is wrong; training is concerned with forming habits of right conduct; and inspiration is needed in order to induce love of right and hatred of wrong. Giving young people information as to what is right is the least difficult of the three, but it can be done so as to aid or so as to hinder progress in the more difficult aspects.

Young people certainly must learn somewhere what is right and what is wrong and why; they must learn the distinction between morality and the mores; but they should also learn that the mores of

7. Aristotle *Nicomachean Ethics* Book x. 1179B.
8. *Ibid.* Book ii. 1103B.

a group are the result of generations of experience of mankind, that they embody those principles of conduct which the group believes to be right, and that there are good reasons for following such conventions.

Coming from so many kinds of homes, with such different cultural patterns represented, it is no wonder that adolescents and young adults become confused about ethical standards. The advocates of direct moral instruction are probably right when they stress the fact that young people do not always know the what and the why of moral behavior and when they recommend that the school should offer opportunity for adolescents to discuss problems of moral conduct.

One of the most valuable of these suggestions is the group case-conference plan formulated by R. D. Allen of Providence, Rhode Island. It is particularly suitable for use in the junior and senior high school. The teacher presents to the group, in club, homeroom, or classroom, a hypothetical, concrete case involving a controversial problem in ethics. It must deal with questions which boys and girls themselves meet, the answer to which is of importance to them, and in which the line of action is not clear upon first examination. The teacher acts merely as a chairman, never in any way indicating his stand. This is very difficult for the teacher, but it is imperative for the success of the plan. The teacher may ask a question if he thinks some phase of the problem is being neglected; he may summarize what has been said and indicate issues, but he must not, ex cathedra, state solutions. Young people enjoy these discussions and find them helpful, not only in bringing to light their own prejudices, but in discovering the standards of other young people. Conflicting ideas are an effective gadfly to thought, as Socrates well knew. Whether a decision is reached or not is irrelevant, just so all aspects of the situation are brought up and freely discussed. To see that this is done is the role of the teacher.[9] The necessary emotional sensitivity to moral conduct is much more likely to result from such procedure than from any amount of adult preaching.

This, of course, should not be the only source from which young people can obtain knowledge of what is right. From literature, from social studies, from assembly programs, from the lives of their teach-

9. R. D. Allen, *Case-Conference Problems in Group Guidance*, esp. pp. 1–22.

ers, as well as from home and church, such lessons should be learned. It is a mistake to make such teaching too obvious. Young people respond with enthusiasm to ideals wherever they find them sincerely and genuinely lived; they do not respond to moralizing.

Wherever there is discussion with adolescents about moral conduct, that discussion should be specific, objective, and as scientific or philosophical as possible. Young people want to know what to do or say when cocktails are passed, when petting is proposed, when a problem of cheating arises. Vague, general talk about sin and wrongdoing leaves them uncomfortable or even resentful.

It is not so difficult to teach children what is right and what is wrong; it is not so hard to get them to practice right conduct, at least when the desire for social approval is operating. The most difficult factor in character education lies in inculcating the proper loves and hates, in getting young people to love what is noble and to hate what is base. It is also the most important factor. Without it, mankind will not follow the prompting of duty. With it, virtue is its own reward. *How* to develop this love of right is the crucial element in the process.

DEVELOPING THE LOVE OF RIGHT

Human beings, it will be remembered, act to satisfy their wants. Anything which satisfies a human want has value.[10] It is, then, our sense of values which motivates our behavior—our attitude toward those things, material and immaterial, which appeal to us because they satisfy our wants.

The baby "values" his mother because she brings him food, because she ministers to his comfort. The small child "values" and will fight for *his* food, *his* playthings, *his* family. He has identified himself with those things which satisfy *his* wants. The valuing of the object as a means to the satisfaction of wants comes in time to be a value attached to the object as an end in itself. The child comes to *love* his mother, his father, other members of the family, if he can first identify himself with them. Love of friends, of the community, of the nation, of all mankind, comes about in the same way. As it is with the child, so it is with the adult. It is the emotions, man's likes

10. See previous discussions in chaps. iv and v.

and dislikes, which furnish the motivating force for his conduct. The problem, then, is to get a child to identify himself with other selves, so that each will act, not from a narrow self, but from a wider self, a self which has identified itself with a constantly widening group of human beings. The truly civilized man has identified himself with all mankind and acts from a regard for all human beings.[11] The more nearly man can do this, the closer he comes to achieving his chief end: co-operative self-realization.[12]

As in all education, the early years are the most important for this process. If the home does not build the proper foundation, the task of the school becomes even more difficult. When a child starts school, he should have, already developed, an attitude of love and considerateness to his family and to a circle of relatives and friends. Children who have not gotten this start may never attain a proper attitude toward mankind; many of them become the maladjusted and antisocial members of society. If such children are to be helped, they must be able to identify themselves with the teacher and with fellow-pupils. They particularly need friendly interest and sympathetic understanding.

When the proper foundation has been laid in face-to-face groups, the skilful teacher will, from the kindergarten through the university, endeavor to "widen this sphere of fellow feeling until it includes a greater and greater number, not only of his own social set, his own class, his own community,"[13] or his own nation, but rich and poor, ignorant and learned, black, brown, red, and white, those of all races and all lands. Teachers will widen the sphere of brotherly love by helping children "to see our common interests, our common humanity, our common fears and aspirations, our common cares and tribulations, our common destinies."[14] When teachers themselves obtain this vision and this insight, the problem of character education will be on its way to solution.

But concrete measures for putting such a program into effect must be worked out. The chief contribution of the school to character education will be made through the life that is lived in that school and the influence of the teacher and the schoolmates. Is the

11. See H. H. Schroeder, *Psychology of Conduct*, p. 31, and John Dewey, *Democracy and Education*, p. 408.

12. See chap. iv.   13. Schroeder, *op. cit.*, p. 33.   14. *Ibid.*

teacher the kind of person whom the child can admire? Does the teacher exemplify in his life ideals which the child will want to build into his own personality? Are the child's schoolmates boys and girls who are healthy and normal in their common life? Is the life of the school one that is in harmony with the nature of the child, one that gives each child an opportunity to grow and develop toward a happier, more satisfying individual group life? Are his needs and legitimate wants being met? Is he having the opportunity to develop his particular abilities and talents in such a way that the welfare of the group is being promoted? Is he being helped to live a life which is satisfying to him because it is promoting the development of *his* best potentialities?

To organize the school so that this is being done for every child to the best of the teacher's ability takes ingenuity and all the knowledge of human nature and its needs that teachers can obtain from biology, history, sociology, psychology, and philosophy. Human nature is exceedingly complex, and any understanding of the springs of human conduct is the result of years of study. There is a constantly growing body of knowledge gained by research and through insight into the problem with which all teachers should be familiar. It is a difficult matter to reduce all this to principles, but the following seem to cover the crux of the necessary procedure in character education:

1. See that each child has a legitimate way of satisfying his needs and reasonable wants.

2. See that he does not obtain satisfaction from unacceptable ways of gratifying needs or from any attempt to satisfy any unreasonable want.

3. See that through group life and personal experience he becomes aware of the needs of his entire nature; this is only possible, as has been pointed out, when his basic needs have been cared for.

The following two cases illustrate how these principles are used in actual experience: (*a*) David was a seventh grader in a city junior high school, the oldest son in a large family of a highly respectable but very poor workman. His mother had died a few years before, and an older sister was trying to take her place. David was shabby, not too clean, somewhat overaggressive, indifferent to school work and below average in achievement.

At the close of the homeroom period in mid-morning it was customary for those children for whom the school nurse or parents
made the request to go to the lunchroom to drink a glass of milk or
orange juice. The money for this was collected by the homeroom
teacher at the beginning of the week, because the parent-teachers
association furnished the money for a few children who needed the
nourishment but whose parents could not pay for it. These children
would feel less conspicuous if no child carried his nickel and if the
entire bill was paid weekly by the homeroom teacher. David's homeroom teacher, Miss Ellis, kept the money locked in a drawer in her
desk but one Monday forgot to lock the drawer and, to her con-
sternation, found it gone on Tuesday morning. She consulted the
principal, Mr. Haley, at once. They agreed to say nothing about the
disappearance but to watch the children carefully.

It took no detective work to see that David had money. He
had a pocketful of candy and chewing gum which he passed out
with an air. He was highly popular with the other children for
awhile. David had never "treated" before, so far as Miss Ellis knew.
In fact he never had any money, although he never was allowed to
be the recipient of charity. Mr. Haley called David to his office; and
as the result of a friendly approach, the boy readily confessed that he
had taken the money, about three dollars in all. He had already spent
something over a dollar but returned the remainder to the principal.
Mr. Haley learned, in his conversation with David that, though the
boy delivered papers, he was not allowed to keep any of his money.
David was very much afraid of his father and begged that he not
be informed. David was, in fact, a very unhappy boy at home; he
missed his mother greatly and felt that he had no friends and no
standing anywhere, at home or at school.

Mr. Haley could see no possibility for improvement unless the co-
operation of the father could be enlisted, so, in spite of David's
pleading, the father was sent for. His reaction was what could have
been expected: He would thrash David within an inch of his life; he
had disgraced a respectable family! Finally, he was persuaded that
such treatment would not solve the difficulty and that the *cause*
must be found and removed. He agreed that David was to keep
part of the money he made, that he should pay Miss Ellis each week
until all he had spent was replaced, and that he should have a little
spending money each week. His father reluctantly agreed that Da-

vid should have a gradually increasing amount of responsibility for purchasing his own and family necessities.

But this was not all that was done. David needed some way to obtain status in the group. Miss Ellis made him treasurer of the milk fund. He was responsible for its safekeeping and its transfer to the lunchroom. He had to keep an account of all the money that came in. Not a penny was lost or unaccounted for during the rest of the year. His teacher could not have done this if the children had known of his misdemeanor. It would have looked to them as if he were being rewarded for doing wrong. They would not have understood. But it was a fine thing for David. He was passionately grateful to both Miss Ellis and Mr. Haley. He grew to take more pride in his appearance, was cleaner, more assured, less aggressive; he was important in the group; and, while he made some mistakes, as was natural, on the whole, he gradually earned the respect of the other children. His school work improved. He was a different and a better boy—though far from a perfect one—when he left the junior high school two years later for the senior high school.

David *needed* status, friendship, and recognition in the group; he tried to buy it. Children often do this. They do not have the judgment to understand that one cannot purchase permanent liking and respect from others but must earn it. He was not allowed any enduring satisfaction from the wrong method of satisfying his need; he had to *earn* money to replace that which he took; he realized his conduct had the disapproval of the principal, his teacher, and his father. But he was helped to obtain legitimately what he needed: self-respect through having a little of his hard-earned money in his pocket, a place of growing importance at home and at school, a feeling that he was trusted with responsibility.

Henry Carleton was a young lawyer who had hung out his shingle in his large, midwestern, home town and sat down to wait for clients, who were slow to appear. Judge White of the juvenile court and a lifelong friend of Henry's father called him one day to have lunch with him.

"Henry," said he, "I have a job for you. You'll get no fee for it; you'll probably get a lot of worry, work, and even heartache. But I want you to take it."

Henry looked his inquiry.

"I had a fifteen-year-old boy in court yesterday. He needs a big brother. You're elected. Wait a minute, now—let me tell you about him.

"His name is John S——. He lives in an upper flat on the fringe of the business district, with no place to play but the street. He's got a gang of boys in his neighborhood, and he's their idol. He holds that position because he can lick any two of them and because he has brains enough to figure them out of trouble—at least, until recently. The boy's worth saving, and if you won't help him, I've got to send him to reform school, and that is not likely to save him!

"The kid thrives on fights; there's another gang with which they are continually in trouble. But recently his gang has been raiding small shops and businessmen. He and his gang broke a window in a grocery night before last and made off with a bunch of bananas and some other food. The man who owns the grocery was hopping mad and you can't blame him. The kid's been in court before. His father drinks, and his mother scrubs offices most of the night. There are two younger children. I've got to do something with John—but great Scott, Henry, I've robbed more than one watermelon patch and been chased by irate farmers out of more than one orchard. This boy robs grocery stores, instead. Of course, it's got to be stopped. And you're the fellow to do it."

Henry Carleton reluctantly consented and met the boy in the judge's chambers. A lunch followed, but the lad was ill at ease, secretive, and on the defensive. Wild West shows, meals, and invitations to Henry's home followed, but Henry felt that he had made no headway in winning the youngster's friendship. Then the Golden Gloves tournament began at the Y.M.C.A.

"How would you like to go, John?"

"Gosh, Mr. Carleton, could I . . . .?"

So they went to the Golden Gloves tournament, and John was an eager, excited, natural lad that night.

"How would you like boxing lessons, John?"

"How'd I like them? Gosh, Mr. Carleton . . . ."

So John took boxing lessons. Henry boxed with him as soon as he had a little skill. Henry's mother—a forbearing and understanding woman—helped Henry fix up a recreation room in the basement of the Carleton home. There, a few at a time, came other members of John's gang to learn boxing and to spend an evening. An electric corn popper and a barrel of apples helped morale considerably.

It was uphill work. The youngsters got into trouble occasionally. However, the gang organized as a club in Henry's basement and meted out its own justice to offending members. The worst punishment was temporary exclusion and loss thereby of the privilege of meeting with the group in the clubroom.

Henry's hobby was photography. He had a darkroom in the basement, in which he often worked. John became interested in watching him develop his pictures. The boy's keen mind was stimulated, and Henry discovered that the lad had latent technical ability. He was allowed to help, but John wanted a camera of his own. He got a job out of school hours, earned money for his own equipment, and joined Henry in a common interest.

In the meantime his school work had improved, particularly studies in science. Judge White saw him in court no longer but did meet him in the clubroom occasionally when he called on Henry's father. John had been worth saving.

He had *needed* a place to play and an opportunity to exert leadership and to develop his abilities. He was attempting to satisfy these real needs in the wrong ways; very wisely, Henry began with an interest which he had—the interest in physical prowess—and helped him satisfy it in a legitimate way. As this was done, new interests on a higher plane developed.

An entire book could be written about John, for this is a true story[15]—as was the previous one.[16] Not all accounts of attempts to redirect the growth of children have such happy endings. Many times family life and other social forces which lie outside the control of the school are not only antagonistic to educational aims but are stronger than all the forces of the school. Teachers cannot always redirect the development of the children in their classes. But their best guide for accomplishing what can be done is the principles which have been here illustrated.

THE LIFE OF THE SCHOOL AND CHARACTER DEVELOPMENT

With many children—fortunately a majority—the problem is not one of redirection so much as of continuing the direction in which their development is already started so as to assist them to the best possible growth.

15. Told by a student in one of the author's classes.
16. This first example came from the experience of a friend.

Fortunately the kind of school best suited for the development of intelligence and creative imagination is likely to be the kind best suited for proper development of moral character. As pointed out, the principal problem in character education is that of the education of the emotions, the springs of conduct. When a child is engaged in activity which develops his abilities and utilizes his powers, he is most amenable to character education. It is the continually frustrated child, the constantly unhappy child, who becomes withdrawn, unfriendly, and antisocial. It is this child who fails to identify himself with others, to develop an ever widening self, and who thus does not learn to treat others as ends.

This is not meant to imply that the extroverted child is necessarily superior in character to the introverted. Many an extrovert is extremely selfish; many an introvert has made a great contribution to the welfare of mankind. Great scientists, thinkers, and artists are often introverts. A true introvert is happy in his absorption with his own ideas. Teachers need to learn to distinguish between genuine introverts and unhappy, withdrawn children. The majority of children are by nature neither complete extroverts nor complete introverts; usually they have some qualities of each but sometimes tend more toward one type than toward the other.

The growing interest in mental hygiene and in the techniques of case study testifies to our increased concern with the development in our pupils of a healthy, integrated personality. Children who do not respond to the ordinary life of the school, who are unhappy and withdrawn, need to be studied carefully by the teachers and perhaps referred to experts for study. Every teacher should have a course in mental hygiene as a part of his preparation; he should also be acquainted with case-study technique. Sometimes, of course, a little knowledge is a dangerous thing here, as elsewhere; and one important lesson every teacher needs to learn is when to call on an expert in mental hygiene, if one is available for assistance. Too often in the average small town such an expert is not available, and teachers, working with the home, will have to do whatever is done for the child.

A classroom in which democracy is practiced provides the kind of situation in which the best character development can take place. All that has been said in previous chapters about education for a

democratic society applies to education for moral character, just
as it applies to education for the best development of potential intelligence and of creative ability.[17] It is only where children are
treated as ends and where they learn to treat others as ends that
there may be the best development of intelligence, of creative
imagination, and of excellence in character.[18]

Out of the class with which a teacher starts in the fall he must
develop a group, to which every child will feel that he belongs, in
which he has status, for which he has a definite responsibility, and
to which he can make a contribution. As children contribute, they
identify themselves with the other members of the class. There is
nothing like common service for building common interests and concern with common welfare. These contributions and services should
be extended to the entire school. Such is the only lasting source of
school spirit.

Gradually, contributions and services can be extended into the
community itself. Many schools are making valuable contributions
to the communities supporting the schools. We have not yet learned
to utilize the idealism of youth or its eagerness to contribute to
group life. The best of the programs so far worked out seem to be
those which involve actual work and responsible activity in the
community under adult leadership.

Some schools, in their eagerness to have children participate in
social enterprises, have set them to doing tasks which aroused antagonism. Certain kinds of community surveys might be of this type.
To ask children to go to every home, inquiring there about sanitary
provisions, for instance, is not wise. This prying is resented by
people, quite understandably, as unjustifiable curiosity. Citizens
feel that such tasks encourage children in presumptuous and patronizing instruction of their elders. While the elders may need instruction, children's manners are not helped by being led to feel that
this instruction is their prerogative.

On the other hand, children and young people can profitably aid
in landscaping school grounds, planning and providing for play-
grounds, reclaiming waste and junk, working on erosion projects,
gardening, harvesting crops, aiding community drives, obtaining
recreational facilities for teen-agers, etc.—all jobs in which there is

17. See pp. 315–17.   18. See chap. vi.

ample opportunity for youth to take responsibility, to sacrifice ease and comfort, and to do hard things in order to advance the common welfare.

School life itself furnishes many opportunities to obtain such lessons. Children should learn that their first responsibility lies in doing their school work well. Their present development and their future value to society depend upon their assimilating as much of the cultural heritage as they possibly can. Unless young people learn this lesson in school, they are likely to grow up thinking that the really valuable part of school life is the extra-curricular instead of the curricular. To be sure, clubs, homeroom, and school council, as well as the classroom, offer opportunities to serve the common good. But children's responsibility to society is only discharged as they do their work in the classroom, assimilating knowledge and skills which will enable them to further the welfare of society. Thus, gradually they learn that life means responsibility and duty as well as wants and inclinations.

EDUCATIONAL PHILOSOPHIES AND CHARACTER EDUCATION

Little that has been said so far on the problem of the development of moral character could be a matter for dispute among teachers, whatever their philosophies of education. All schools of thought unite in emphasizing the importance of character education, and the majority would probably agree on the procedure outlined so far. There are, however, some basic differences among the schools of thought.

As previously pointed out, there is disagreement among philosophies as to the nature of morality. For the philosophy of experimentalism, morality is nothing but the mores and there are no moral principles of universal and timeless validity. Idealists and scholastic realists distinguish between morality and the mores; they both believe that there are absolutes in morality——principles of universal validity for rational creatures. With this latter view the Kantian realist concurs. These schools might have different grounds for their belief, but the attitude toward morality is the same.[19]

There might be some difference in opinion concerning the relative emphasis to put on knowledge and on experience in character edu-

19. See chap. vi.

cation. Traditionalists are likely to emphasize knowledge. For example, Chancellor Hutchins has said repeatedly that the aims of education are intelligence and goodness. But he has nothing but scornful words for the college which has character-building for its aim rather than the training of the intellect. He writes: "Since character is the result of choice it is difficult to see how you can develop it unless you train the mind to make intelligent choices."[20] He points out that from the curriculum "we have excluded body-building and character building. We have excluded the social graces and the tricks of the trade. We have suggested that the curriculum be composed principally of the permanent studies."[21]

These permanent studies are those that will cultivate the intellect. If the intellect is cultivated, man will choose intelligently and will be good as well as intelligent.

Progressives emphasize experience rather than knowledge of first principles derived from study. Character, say they, is formed through one's experiences in living. With this the essentialists would be inclined to agree. But they would believe that vicarious experience could be effective in developing moral character. Effective character education on the higher levels might well include a study of the great books from which men have drawn inspiration through the ages. But it should also include the kind of experiences through which young people learn to identify themselves with more and more of their fellow-men and to work with them for the common good.

There would be some difference of opinion on how much emphasis to place upon the concept of duty. Dewey seems to say that there is no real conflict between duty and interest and that the solution for any apparent conflict lies in being interested in what one is doing. If Dewey means that we all need to learn to interest ourselves in doing our duty, that is one thing. But if he means, as he is usually interpreted to mean, that concentrating on interest alone without reference to duty will be sufficient, then other schools of thought will differ with him.[22] It is precisely here that Progressive education has been criticized. It is said to encourage young people in following

20. Robert M. Hutchins, *The Higher Learning in America*, p. 29.

21. *Ibid.*, p. 77.

22. See John Dewey, *Democracy and Education*, chap. xxvi, or H. H. Horne, *The Democratic Philosophy of Education*, chap. xxvi.

self-interest rather than interest in self-discipline or in working for the common good. Teachers and parents need to work together to develop in their pupils an interest in assuming responsibilities, in doing right because it is right, in acting on the principle of the practical imperative.

Probably the most serious differences concerning character education between philosophies of education are to be found in their beliefs on the relation of religion to moral education. Those who believe that morality is nothing but the mores, that "moral" and "social" are synonymous, that there are no absolutes in morality and no ultimate goals or ideals, and that the only sanction for morality lies in consequences would either omit religion entirely or define religion in secularized terms. This is the position of those Progressives who follow Dewey.[23]

Those persons, however, who believe either that morality has been revealed to man by God or that man has discovered morality to be immanent in him—an expression of the divine nature within him and a manifestation of a power in the universe, not himself, which makes for righteousness—would hold that religion is both a powerful sanction for and an inspiration toward moral conduct. To man's mind, it looks reasonable that there must be in this universe a first cause. It also seems reasonable that man's personality, his selfhood, is more than his physical body. It looks, to man's reason, as if *his* idealism and *his* intellect are evidences of a goodness and an intelligence in the universe out of which he has come and that his creative imagination may be identical with the creative force of the universe. But this cannot be proved as one can prove a geometric theorem. Religious faith is needed to establish belief in God and in the divine nature of man. The intuitions of faith seem to many intelligent persons a more reliable basis for truth than any other means available to man.

Although the teaching of religion has been excluded from the curriculum of the public school, religion operating through the lives of teachers and pupils could not and should not be excluded from its life. Any religion worthy of the name should make better human beings of its adherents. Horne points out that because religion gives man convictions about the nature and origin of life, it helps him see

23. See John Dewey, *Human Nature and Conduct,* esp. Part IV, sec. IV.

that children are not just behaving organisms and children of time but are also images of their Great Original and children of eternity. This, he says, makes teaching an extraordinarily important task: "Our sense of the dignity of teaching as a profession and life career . . . . depends considerably on our conception of the origin and nature of life."[24] A teacher's influence for good, his example, his own personality, are enhanced by a living, functioning religion. It is unfortunate for our civilization that the influence of the church has decreased markedly within this century.

Scholasticism holds that religion should be a part of the curriculum of the school. Writes Father McGucken: "Since man has a supernatural destiny any educational system that fails to impart religious instruction is not acceptable to the Catholic. For the Catholic believes that religion is an essential part of education since it is indispensable for right living here and for eternal life hereafter."[25] And again, in Redden and Ryan: "There can be no true moral or character education that is not founded primarily on religious education."[26]

Until we all can agree upon our religious beliefs, it would be impossible for religious instruction to be given in the public schools to all the children gathered into one class. There is not enough common content in the teachings of all churches—Jewish, Catholic, Protestant—to draw from for a course of study. And yet it seems far from ideal to have religious education only on Sunday. How can it affect the quality of our everyday living if children get the idea that it is something for Sunday only?

Many persons are so disturbed over the situation and so convinced of the necessity for religious instruction both to satisfy man's spiritual cravings and to serve as a sanction for moral conduct that they are advocating religious education on the "released-time" plan as a part of public education. They suggest that a certain period in the school program be set aside weekly, that parents be asked to designate the religion in which their children are to be instructed— or to say that thy are to have no such instruction—and that ministers

24. Horne, *op. cit.*, p. 9.

25. National Society for the Study of Education, *Forty-first Yearbook: Part I: Philosophies of Education*, p. 285.

26. J. D. Redden and F. A. Ryan, *A Catholic Philosophy of Education*, p. 245.

of churches indicated be asked to do the teaching. Some towns are experimenting with such a program.

There are problems connected with such a proposal that need to be thought through very carefully. This country was established on the basis of complete religious freedom. This necessitates the separation of church and state. Public schools are under the control of the state. This must be in order to promote the general welfare. Because our religious views differ and we are free to belong to any church or to no church, the state rather than the church must control public schools in order to see that all children are educated for the general welfare. It is unfortunately true that religion divides us rather than unites us. But the state unites us in a common devotion to the ideals of democracy.

Many persons fear the influences of sectarianism in the public schools. In the first place, it violates the principle of separation of church and state and may thus interfere with religious freedom. In the second place, it introduces a divisive influence into the school which now is the one uniting influence in the life of the nation. In the third place, people who do not wish their children to have religious training—and religious freedom implies the right to have no religion as well as to choose among religions—dread the social pressure which would be brought to bear upon their children by the other boys and girls. Children find it hard to be different in any respect from their fellows. Conformity is important to them.

There are persons who believe that spiritual values are not dependent upon religion for their acceptance. The life of the school can be organized so that children learn through living to respect their fellow-man and to treat him as a creature of value. A science teacher can teach science so as to impart a sense of awe before the mysteries of the natural universe. A teacher of literature has an opportunity to bring children in contact with persons of nobility, both fictional and actual, thus helping the young person in his search for values. A teacher of social sciences can teach so as to make the child aware of social interdependence and mutual responsibilities. And so on, through the entire curriculum.

It might be possible to have courses *about* religions in both the high school and the college. There are many teachers who could treat the subject objectively and fairly. For the sake of widening information this might be advisable. We need to know about all the great religions of the world as well as about the different interpretations of Christianity. But this would not by itself be very effective in changing conduct. Religious teaching is effective only if it reaches the emotions, the springs of human conduct. Knowledge *about* religion does not necessarily do that, although it should increase the understanding.

The problem of daily religious instruction probably goes back to the responsibility of the home and the church. The public school should not be asked to take on this task.

Many adults feel that if churches were doing their work in the Sunday school and as a center for recreational activities for their young people and that if church schools utilized sound principles of education, they could do more through their own efforts than in connection with public schools. Parents would, of course, have to be convinced of the necessity for religious education. Unfortunately many of them are not. Perhaps some of the fault for this lack of conviction lies at the door of the churches themselves. It is undeniably true that man has a spiritual nature and that he needs food for that nature as he does for his material body. Is it not possible that when man has asked for bread he has too often been given a stone?

Can virtue be taught? Where are the teachers? Among those who know the psychology of human conduct and who have an understanding of the true nature of morality and of man.

SUMMARY

Character, in the ethical sense, is an inner consistency and unity which gives steadfastness and dependability to man's conduct. A person of moral character acts upon moral principles. To develop the disposition in our pupils so to act is one of the most difficult tasks a teacher has. Such factors as the common misunderstanding of the nature of morality, the diminishing influence of religion, the lack of agreement upon what constitutes a desirable character, the kind of competitive "dog-eat-dog" society in which we live, the selfishness and self-centeredness of human nature itself, to say nothing of the lack of teachers who exemplify human excellence, all militate against success in developing moral character in the rising generation.

The following seem to be the important conclusions concerning the development of moral character:

1. It is better to depend upon indirect rather than direct methods of

character development. The life of the school should be organized so as to develop desirable character through all that is done rather than through depending upon discussions of morality as a part of the day's or week's study. This does not mean that there is no place for discussions of ethical principles and practices. In the lower grades these discussions should grow out of children's experiences. On the higher levels more formal discussions may be arranged for.

2. If moral character is to be developed, three factors must be provided for: Children must learn what is right and what is wrong; they must learn to love the right and to hate the wrong; they must form habits of right conduct. The first is the easiest of the three; the second is most difficult. How to accomplish it is the crux of character education.

3. We come to love, or value, the good as it satisfies our wants. The foundation for our values is laid in the home. Children must live there and at school so that they gradually learn that their happiness and welfare depends upon the happiness and welfare of others. They gradually learn to identify themselves first with family and friends, then with a gradually widening group of persons. The truly civilized human being identifies himself with all mankind. But it is experience in living, particularly in the early years of life, which enables a person ultimately to do this. It is the business of the school to see to it that every child, as nearly as possible, (1) has a legitimate way to satisfy his needs and reasonable wants, (2) fails to obtain satisfaction from unacceptable ways of gratifying needs or from any attempt to satisfy an unreasonable want, and (3) becomes aware of the needs of his higher nature. If these principles are not followed, a child is not likely to learn to love the right and to hate the wrong.

4. The life of the school should be so organized as to provide a favorable environment for character development. This is the same type of school as the one most suited to the development of intelligence and creative ability: one in which democracy is practiced; one in which each child feels himself an integral part of the group; one in which children are living, learning, growing, together as they contribute to their common welfare and, gradually, to the welfare of the society in which they live.

5. The most serious disagreement among educational philosophies is in regard to the relation of religion to character development. The extreme positions seem to be taken by the Progressives, on one hand, who insist that spiritual values are not dependent on religion for their sanction and the scholastic philosophy, on the other, which holds that religion and character development cannot be separated. The idealists and other philosophical realists take their positions between these two—idealism closer to scholastic realism and neo-realism, at least, closer to the Progressives.

It would seem that man needs religion whether or not it be considered essential for the proper development of moral character. But religious education should be given by the home and church rather than on school time. It would be unwise to introduce divisive influences into our schools or to jeopardize religious freedom through anything tending to nullify our traditional separation of church and state.

QUESTIONS TO AID STUDY

1. What is meant by the term *"character"*? Could a man have no character? When is character moral? What is the etymology of the term?
2. How are conduct and character related?
3. What factors operate to render the development of fine character difficult?
4. What connection is there between one's convictions concerning the nature of morality and effective character education?
5. What is meant by the direct method of character education? By the indirect? Which seems better? Why?
6. What are the three phases of character education? Which is most difficult?
7. Illustrate specifically how you could provide, through the life of the school, for each phase.
8. What is the relation between these two statements: "Man acts to satisfy his wants" and "Man acts from his sense of values"? Explain.
9. How does the process of identification of the self with others proceed?
10. What are some of the signs in children that this process is not proceeding normally?
11. What does mental hygiene have to do with the development of character?
12. Summarize the principles which must be followed if children are to learn to love the right and to hate the wrong.
13. Write a short paper in which you show specifically how this was done in an actual instance or in which you plan how it might be done. Be sure that you show how these principles were or could be applied.
14. Describe the school and the life lived there which will best further the development of fine character in its teachers and pupils.
15. In what do the differing schools of educational philosophy agree and in what do they disagree concerning the development of moral character?
16. Do you think religious teaching is necessary in order to obtain moral character? Explain why you think as you do.
17. What arguments are there for and against religious education in the public schools?
18. How can the school utilize religious influences without the teaching of religious views?

SUGGESTED REFERENCES

ALLEN, RICHARD DAY. *Case-Conference Problems in Group Guidance.* New York: Inor Pub. Co., 1933.

ALLERS, RUDOLF. *Character Education in Adolescence.* New York: J. F. Wagoner, 1940.

BRUBACHER, JOHN. *Modern Philosophies of Education* (New York: Mc-Graw-Hill Book Co., 1939), chap. xiii.

——— (ed.). *The Public Schools and Spiritual Values* (New York: Harper & Bros., 1944), especially chaps. vi, vii, and viii.

CHAVE, ERNEST J. *A Functional Approach to Religious Education* (Chicago: University of Chicago Press, 1947), chap. viii.

DEMIASHKEVICH, MICHAEL. *Introduction to the Philosophy of Education* (New York: American Book Co., 1935), chap. vi.

DEWEY, JOHN. *Human Nature and Conduct* (New York: Henry Holt & Co., 1922), pp. 38–57.

GARNETT, MAXWELL. *Knowledge and Character* (Cambridge: University Press, 1939), pp. 1–7, chaps. xiv–xv.

HARTSHORNE, HUGH. *Character in Human Relations.* New York: Charles Scribner's Sons, 1932.

HEATON, KENNETH LOUIS. *The Character Emphasis in Education.* Chicago: University of Chicago Press, 1933.

KUNKEL, FRITZ. *Character, Growth and Education.* New York: J. B. Lippincott Co., 1938.

McKOWN, HARRY C. *Character Education.* New York: McGraw-Hill Book Co., 1935.

MUMFORD, LEWIS. *Faith for Living* (New York: Harcourt, Brace & Co., 1940), pp. 280–302.

REDDEN, JOHN D., and RYAN, FRANCIS A. *A Catholic Philosophy of Education* (Milwaukee: Bruce Pub. Co., 1942), chap. viii.

ROUCEK, JOSEPH S., and ASSOCIATES. *Sociological Foundations of Education.* New York: Thomas Y. Crowell, 1942.

SCHROEDER, H. H. *Psychology of Conduct* (Chicago: Row, Peterson & Co., 1911), chap. ii.

THAYER, VIVIAN T. "Religion and the Public Schools," *Harper's,* CLXXXVIII (April, 1944), 458.

CHAPTER XVI

THE GOOD SCHOOL

THE point has been made repeatedly that Progressive education and what usually has been referred to as "traditionalism" are not, at their best, so much opposing theories between which one must choose as each a partial view of the educative process. It has been the purpose of the writer to synthesize the two on the basis of critical realism. This synthesis would seem to point to the following conclusions.

A good school is one which contributes in the highest possible de-

349

gree toward the realization of the aims of education, as formulated through the study of philosophy of education. Every philosopher worthy of the name has been interested in an attempt not only to understand the universe and man's place in it but also, on the basis of that study, to formulate a conception of the kind of life that would meet man's needs; that is, philosophers are concerned not only with what is but also with what ought to be. In addition, philosophers have universally recognized education as the most potent means for achieving what ought to be. Although the school is by no means the only educational agency, it is, next to the home, the most important. If all our schools were *good* schools, social progress would be more certain and more swift.

THE TEACHER OF THE GOOD SCHOOL

The crucial factor in accomplishing the purpose of a good school is the good teacher. We need men and women of superior personality and adequate professional preparation who see education as a means for promoting man's welfare and who are enthusiastically devoted to the work of teaching. Yale's late William Lyon Phelps wrote:

> I do not know that I could make entirely clear to an outsider the pleasure I have in teaching. I had rather earn my living by teaching than in any other way. In my mind, teaching is not merely a life-work, a profession, an occupation, a struggle: it is a passion. I love to teach as a painter loves to paint, as a musician loves to play, as a singer loves to sing, as a strong man rejoices to run a race. Teaching is an art—an art so great and so difficult to master that a man or a woman can spend a long life at it, without realizing much more than his limitations and mistakes, and his distance from the ideal.[1]

If all teachers felt so about teaching, the first step toward universally excellent schools would have been taken. Of course it takes more than enthusiasm for teaching to make a good teacher. It is imperative that we have superior young people to educate professionally. Society is the loser in that too few of the ablest young people turn to teaching for their lifework. It takes superior individuals to make superior teachers.

Superior persons are those of fine personality, in the best sense of

1. William Lyon Phelps, *Teaching in Schools and Colleges*, p. 1.

that much abused term. It will be remembered that "person" is the term used in philosophy to denote man as distinct from other animals. "Personality" is the word used to mean that composite of human characteristics which entitles man to respect: his rational, creative, and moral qualities. A man possesses fine personality to the degree that these qualities are developed in him so that he approaches ideal manhood. To develop personality is the task of a lifetime; one cannot expect that young adults will have more than a start toward its growth; but that start, prospective teachers should have.

The development of personality is dependent to a high degree upon a strong, healthy body and a sound nervous system. It is impossible during life to separate mind and body. Physical health and mental health are conjoined. Teachers should be concerned about their health, not only for their own sake but because its presence or absence is a prerequisite for their real effectiveness in the school. Teaching is strenuous and demanding work. Teachers must have good humor, serenity, balance, and stability. If health is lacking, such qualities are usually absent. It should be remembered also that if poor health is traceable to an infection, a teacher so afflicted may be an actual physical menace to children with whom he is thrown in contact.

Anyone who does not like children or adolescents should not teach. *Liking* children or young people does not mean feeling a maudlin sentimentality for them, nor does it mean using them as playthings or as means to gratify one's own desire for adulation and affection. It means genuine concern for their welfare and best growth, respect for their developing personalities, kindness and real interest. It means a willingness to study their needs and a constant endeavor to find the best way to guide them.

To do this, teachers need to know a great deal. They must be scholarly enough so that they will not need continually to think of the subject matter which they wish to teach but can focus their attention on the children. Many a teacher has found it impossible or extremely difficult to control a group of children because he did not know enough about the field in which he was teaching to arouse and hold the interest of the boys and girls. To help children become desirous of learning those things we believe that they should learn, teachers must themselves be interesting, resourceful, and informed. The more they know of our social heritage, other things being equal, the better. They must also know all they can learn about human growth and development, children's interests, and adolescent enthusiasms.

It is not enough for teachers to know a great deal about what is in books. They should also be able to *do* things. Proficiency in an art, a craft, in sports, in constructing, designing, gardening, cooking, in any aesthetic or practical accomplishment, is of value to the teacher as it is to most people. Teachers need hobbies, both for widening their own interests and for stimulating the growth of new interests in boys and girls. One of the marks of a highly intelligent and cultivated person is the variety and breadth of his interests and accomplishments. An intellectual curiosity which leads one to seek new and valuable experience, travel, and further study is an outstanding characteristic of superior human beings.

No man is superior without moral character. It takes more than fine character to make a superior man, but without it all else is but "sounding brass and a tinkling cymbal." Because of the influence over pupils exerted by any successful teacher, high character is especially important in those who guide children's growth.

Attracting superior men and women to the teaching profession depends upon rewarding them not only with adequate salaries but also with the respect and recognition that such important work deserves from society. Extremely high salaries can never be obtained for teachers. It is doubtful whether the prospect of comparative wealth, if such a thing were possible, would attract the kind of young person needed in the teaching profession. Service to society rather than personal gain should be the actuating ideal for teachers if they are to perform in accordance with educational aims. But, on the other hand, salaries must be high enough to attract and hold young people who do have the desire to serve society but who also have enough self-respect to demand a decent livelihood, somewhat proportionate to the service they render. The low standards at the present time attract too many individuals who could not make more in any other work. When such persons become teachers, they do not command the respect of laymen; and their salaries remain low.

Only as competent men and women now in the teaching profession work for adequate salary schedules, security of tenure, and provisions for retirement and at the same time endeavor gradually to raise the requirements for entering the teaching profession will the highest type of young persons in any adequate number be attracted to this most important work. The two processes seem to go hand in hand. When teaching draws to it men and women who are worthy of society's respect, then the teaching profession will be more likely to receive its due; and when teachers can live in some comfort and security, then and only then will any appreciable number of superior persons be willing to enter and remain in the profession. Raising the professional requirements and obtaining suitable rewards for superior service seem to be concomitants.

Although the situation has been slowly improving, there are still too few men in the profession. Men are needed as teachers from the elementary school through the college. Every home needs both masculine and feminine influence. So does every school. A school which is exclusively or predominantly feminine in its atmosphere, as are too many of our elementary schools and some of the secondary schools, does not provide the best environment for either boys or girls, but it is perhaps worse for boys. Preadolescent and adolescent boys, especially, need the influence of strong and manly men whom they will admire and wish to imitate. Such men will be attracted to teaching only when salaries are paid which will enable them to support families in decency and comfort and when a man who chooses to teach in the elementary school is considered no more eccentric than is the pediatrician. Men, as well as women, like and can learn to understand and teach young children. Both are needed in a good school.

Salaries should always be based upon preparation, efficiency, and years of service, rather than upon the particular age level at which the teaching is done. Why should primary teachers receive lower pay or, for that matter, need less preparation, than high-school teachers? Nowhere in the entire school system is more important work done than with young children. The best-prepared and the most able teachers are needed during these important years. If children were guided and taught more wisely, at home and at school, during the first eight or nine years of their lives, there would be fewer personality and learning problems during preadolescent and adolescent years.

If we have men and women, intelligent, scholarly, capable, and interested in children and also in promoting the common good, we have the most important factor for obtaining good schools. Such teachers will think seriously and intelligently about educational problems and will be in a position to contribute to their solution. The point was made in the first chapter that every problem in education must be referred to the answers given to such fundamental questions as: What am I trying to accomplish? For what were the schools established? This child being what he is and the demands of society being what they are, how can I best guide his growth so as to realize the purposes of education? Young people who wish to become teachers need to acquire a philosophy of life and of education which will furnish the directive principles for school practice. Only on such a firm foundation are teachers in any position to decide questions concerning the curriculum, methods to be employed, and the management to be used.

Unless philosophy of education does function in this way, it is of no use. If a student has not changed during his study so that he sees and manages his life and his responsibilities in the school differently from the way he would have seen and managed them before he started this study, he might better have been doing something else. Unless the teacher, confronted with a constant succession of problems, uses philosophy in solving these problems, he has not achieved a philosophy of education. Discrepancies between professed theory and actual practices indicate an inadequate, faulty theory; a lack of acceptance or of understanding; or laziness and unwillingness to make the effort to put sound theory into practice. It is quite human to prefer to stay in the comfortable groove of habitual performance and to object to making a change, even for the better. But a philosophy which one has actually understood and assimilated cannot fail to affect one's practice.

THE CURRICULUM OF THE GOOD SCHOOL

The thoughtful student of philosophy of education should now have, for example, some basis on which to answer the question:

What shall we teach in our schools? Out of the vast amount of knowledge which man has obtained—and which, after all, is a mere start toward all that is yet to be discovered—what shall we choose for the curriculum?

The philosophical law of the school states that what we wish to accomplish determines what we shall do. We know that we want to promote the general welfare by helping each boy and girl to develop whatever excellence he is capable of so that he will be able to live a truly human life. We shall want to select from the social heritage those things which will promote these ends.

The word "curriculum" originally meant "racecourse." Robert Ulich of Harvard University says in his recent book that that is still just what a curriculum is.[2] Young people go round and round but seldom go to the heart of life and its problems. The curriculum too seldom meets human needs.

In planning any curriculum, teachers need to keep in mind this principle: Boys and girls must learn those things which will help them grow in ability to live the good life in so far as we understand it. Schools must see that (1) children get the basic learnings necessary for obtaining the physical necessities of life; (2) they have increasingly satisfying human associations; (3) they learn to work when they work and to play when they play and they gain the deep satisfaction that comes from learning to do a difficult task well; (4) each child has an opportunity to develop his talents, his gifts, his abilities; (5) he has opportunities for success and he learns how to meet failure; (6) he begins to develop and enjoy intellectual and aesthetic interests; (7) he learns gradually how to use freedom wisely; and (8) he lays the foundation for a philosophy of life which will be a rock under his feet in a world of chaos and uncertainty.[3]

Because of our common human nature, there are many things all boys and girls need to learn. Because of individual differences, there will be varying emphases and diversified specialization. All children must have the tools of reading, arithmetic, spelling, writing, and grammar. These tools, both while they are being acquired and after their acquisition, should be used in learning (1) of the world about us, both nonliving and living; (2) of man's slow and arduous

2. *Conditions of Civilized Living,* p. 146.
3. Connect this with the analysis of the components of the good life in chap. v.

climb from primitive life to the very moderate amount of civilization which he has so far attained; (3) of man himself, of his own nature, and of his relation to the rest of the world and to his fellow-man; and (4) of man's creations: his culture, with its languages, industry, art, music, literature. This is general education.

In addition, each individual will have special needs. He must learn how to earn a living. He must have an opportunity to develop his particular abilities and to specialize along the line of his own interests. As children go from elementary levels to secondary, general education might be provided through a core curriculum. There ought to be an early opportunity for one elective; and as the boy or girl proceeds through the secondary school, opportunity for more choice may be given if it seems advisable.

In the past we probably went too far with the elective system. High-school pupils and even college students seldom have the maturity or the judgment to make wise choices. Chancellor Hutchins says that when President Eliot of Harvard instituted the elective system, he robbed youth of their cultural heritage. Few young people have the wisdom or the self-discipline to choose difficult but rewarding subjects. Instead they often pile up credits in "snap" courses. The growth of the elective system has also resulted in a bewildering number of subjects among which it is hard to choose.

George Stoddard, president of the University of Illinois, says that the two basic problems in education today are the search for a core of general or liberal education and for the place of science in a liberal education. "The real struggle in education today," says President Stoddard, "is an attempt to achieve unity and direction on some basis, be it ancient, medieval, or modern, or a merging of all three."[4]

Chancellor Hutchins would achieve this unity through the study of the great books of our heritage; John Dewey, through science and the application of the scientific method to our modern problems.

During 1945 a book was published by the Harvard University Press which dealt in a particularly wise and balanced way with the problem of general education. Sponsored by a group of Harvard University professors and entitled *General Education in a Free Society*, the book presents a philosophy of education for a democratic society, examines the relation between general and special educa-

4. *Frontiers in Education*, pp. 1–2.

tion, and advocates a definite program for the secondary school as well as for Harvard University.

The group believes that unity can be achieved through an examination of the vital aspects of our cultural heritage. This does not mean that the schools should appeal only to the authority of the past but that the past should be used to clarify the present.

Jewish, Greek, and Christian thought in this heritage have all contributed to the formulation of the most basic concept of all: the dignity of man. "To the belief in man's dignity must be added the recognition of his duty to his fellow man," according to the Harvard report.[5] "This concept is essentially that of the Western tradition: the view of man as free and not slave, an end in himself and not a means."[6]

Our society rests on this common belief. But it also relies on science "to implement the humanism which classicism and Christianity have proclaimed."[7]

To continue these strains in a modern setting is the task of general education. Without an understanding of these concepts and all that has come from them we cannot understand our society, communicate effectively with each other, or work together to improve what we have. The study of the humanities, of natural science and mathematics, and of the social studies seems to be indicated by this analysis.

The committee recommends, therefore, that every high-school student complete at least half the sixteen units usually required for graduation in the three fields of the humanities, natural science and mathematics, and the social studies. Some additional work in these fields is recommended for each student according to his interests and needs. General education on both the secondary and higher levels is to be spread over all four years rather than concentrated in two. On the college level the committee recommends that two courses, "Great Texts in Literature" and "Western Thought and Institutions" should be required of all students and that the rest of their general education should be worked out according to individual needs by a committee set up for that purpose.

5. Committee on the Objectives of a General Education, *General Education in a Free Society*, p. 46.

6. *Ibid.*   7. *Ibid.*, p. 50.

The report has been criticized by friends and foes alike. Some friends, even those who speak of it as the most important educational document of our time, regret that foreign languages are given a place of so little importance. Some persons think that vocational education has not received enough emphasis. But the blasts of opposition have come from the pragmatists and the Progressives. They quite consistently deplore the emphasis on tradition and upon the study of books.[8] The recent publication of the Educational Policies Commission called *Education for All American Youth* is more to their liking. This book recommends that the core of secondary-school education be found in the social studies, concentrating on problems of today as young people find them through their experiences in living. This latter report also goes much farther than the Harvard report in advocating a breaking-down of barriers between subject-matter fields.

For many years the curriculum was highly compartmentalized. Children in the elementary school might spend twenty minutes in reading, thirty minutes in studying arithmetic, ten minutes in writing spelling words, and then ten minutes in handwriting. There was usually no relationship among any of these activities; no one idea seemed to draw them together in any way. High schools were quite as bad and much more dilatory in effecting any reform. A large number of subjects were taught, each independently of the other. The average high school in a large city had as many as two hundred and fifty different subjects with which to bewilder boys and girls. The mathematics teacher taught algebra but was not aware of the mathematics which the physics teacher thought it necessary for his pupils to know. The geometry teacher taught with no reference to social science or to any other subject. Pupils too seldom saw relationships between fields and so gained little real understanding of the world and of society.

To rectify this situation the movement for "integration" has gained impetus. Properly, this word should be used only for the physiological and psychological processes by which parts are woven into organized wholes. The knowledge that this in some way does take place in man is not new. There are references to it in Plato's *Theae-*

8. See, e.g., Boyd Bode, "Harvard Report," *Journal of Higher Education*, XVII (January, 1946), 1–8.

tetus. In modern times, Herbert Spencer called attention to the fact that we hear rapid taps not as separate sounds but as a tone, which rises in pitch and changes in timber as the taps and blows become more rapid.[9] William James also discussed the process of integration in a famous passage. He said: "It is as if a long file of men were to start one after the other to reach a distant point. The road at first is good and they keep their original distance apart. Presently it is intersected by bogs each worse than the last, so that the front men get so retarded that the hinder ones catch up with them before the journey is done, and all arrive together at the goal."[10]

Gestalt psychologists believe today that the older psychologists were mistaken in their attempts to explain wholes in terms of the combination of sensory elements. No perception, say they, is the sum of sensations. No whole is merely the sum of its parts. It is an organization from which the constituent parts take their characteristics. It is to the whole that we first react, not to parts which we combine into a whole. These parts exist, they teach, not as the primitive stuff that makes up experience but as the products of our analysis.[11]

The infant, according to gestaltism, begins life as a crudely organized whole, reacting with and toward whole situations. He reacts to a human face long before he would recognize a nose, an eye, or any of the constituent parts of a face. As he reacts to wholes, he becomes aware of parts in relation to the whole. But in order to see these relations, he must first experience the whole. These unified wholes are separate and distinct from what the gestaltists call "the field" or a background. This field or background helps determine the pattern or organization which we perceive as a whole. That is, the entire situation seems to determine our perception of the properties of any object or event.[12]

Integration, in other words, is a psychological process, imperfectly understood, but a process which educational procedure seems to have sometimes hindered rather than helped. However, teachers learned long before Gestalt psychology was heard of that children

9. Herbert Spencer, *Principles of Psychology*, chap. xiv.
10. William James, *Principles of Psychology*, I, 156.
11. Edna Heidbreder, *Seven Psychologies*, p. 339.
12. George Hartmann, *Educational Psychology*, pp. 133–34.

learn to read much more quickly and with more comprehension by becoming familiar with sentences and words before they learn letters and their sounds. Also, the organization of subject matter into units in high schools antedated any widespread acceptance of Gestalt psychology. But in spite of this recognition that parts are more easily understood and relations between them better seen if they are studied in relation to a whole, the majority of schools have failed to put into practice, until recently, any considerable reform. Now it looks as if some schools are about to go to unwise extremes in giving pupils experiences with "wholes."

A curriculum in which barriers between subjects are broken down is often called an "integrated curriculum." Such a curriculum provides experiences which are supposed to facilitate the psychological process of integration and in connection with which children will learn the subject matter suitable for understanding or "reconstructing" their experience. Such an experience curriculum abolishes the old compartmentalization and the categories of "subjects" as such, introducing subjects only as they pertain to the "centers" of child interest.

With small children a skilful teacher can probably use such a curriculum to advantage. Whether it is wise completely to abolish subjects as such, even on the lower elementary levels, is doubtful. On this point, Carleton Washburne, for many years superintendent of schools in Winnetka, Illinois, wrote:

It is manifestly absurd to suppose it contrary to sound education to be systematic and orderly, to suppose that thoroughness is the antithesis of good learning. Yet the time has come when a person almost has to apologize for a kind of education that develops a subject in an orderly, systematic manner.

Yet the answer does not lie in a reversion to the old compartmentalization of the curriculum, but neither does it lie in an attempt at a complete correlation and the kind of "integration" which assumes that all subjects must be "integrated" with each other and with some center of interest or grow out of some one activity.

The solution lies in having a basic course required of each child as he reaches the right stage of development, and including in that course only those items which really function or can be made to function in the experience and training of the child. Each of these things—call them subjects if you wish—should be taught in relation to the child's life and interests. They should be taught when the child is ready to use them through having his interest aroused and when he has reached that mental age found by research to be most suitable to the learning of a given topic. And in doing this, the school may well use a number of the old categories —arithmetic is after all quite different from social science, and spelling is not related to creativeness and initiative.[13]

It would seem to be an even greater mistake to abolish or to "integrate" subjects on the high-school level. Fewer secondary schools have attempted any such radical transformation of their curriculums. It is entirely in harmony with any present-day psychology to recognize that, as man interacts with his environment, learning more and more about it, the "wholes" to which he reacts are less crude and more complex and that he desires to analyze, abstract, specialize. That is the way the human mind works. If we keep in mind the kind of creature man is and the way in which he grows and develops, we will recognize that a type of curriculum suitable for the primary grades is not suitable for high school and certainly not for college.

That does not mean that the high-school curriculum does not need an overhauling and revision. Change has been long overdue. Such investigations as the Pennsylvania Study, the Regents' Inquiry of New York, and the Eight Year Study of the Progressive Education Association emphasize this need. An organization into broad fields and a core curriculum required of all, with some electives for specialized interest, seem to be the type of reorganization holding the most promise.[14] But just what that core shall be seems to be the storm center in American education today.

Within any modern curriculum, teachers need to plan carefully and in advance the large units best suited to the age and needs of their pupils and to the realization of educational objectives, so that there may be sequence, continuity, orderliness, and cumulative learning. These broad outlines need to be agreed upon by all the teachers, so that there will be no overlapping and useless duplication and that the whole educational process will be a cumulative one. Within the broad outlines there may be flexibility and opportunity for changing emphases and for differentiation. But to brand a

13. Carleton Washburne, "The Case for Subjects in the Curriculum," *Journal of the National Education Association,* XXVI (January, 1937), 5.

14. See Harold Spears, *The Emerging High School Curriculum,* chap. iii; also John Dewey Society, Eighth Yearbook, *The American High School,* chaps. vii–ix.

curriculum planned in advance of its teaching as anathema and a violation of children's rights, as do some extremists, is to lose sight of valid educational objectives. It is probably more a violation of the rights of the immature to deprive them of adult guidance and contact with the experience of the race than it is to decide what they are to study without consulting them.

As children grow toward adulthood, there should be opportunity for all who can profit thereby to study that part of the social heritage to be found in the great books of all time. Outside the direct and immediate personal experience, contact with great minds is the most important educative experience which we can have. The high school and the college which do not furnish such an opportunity for young people are not doing for their students what should be done for them.

The social heritage should be thought of as a precious tool by which man is enabled to develop his best powers and to further his progress. The curriculum should be composed of both firsthand experience and vicarious experience drawn from the social heritage; it is, in fact, all those experiences, firsthand and vicarious, for which the school assumes responsibility and from which learning is expected to result. The selection and the proper allocation of all these experiences are exceedingly important; in these tasks teachers should and do have an increasingly important part. Through the use of a wisely planned curriculum, children should grow in intelligence, creative ability, and moral character.

They should learn to be increasingly respectful of and eager to obtain truth, the ultimate source of which lies outside man, his desires, and his purposes. The universe, in fact, seems quite indifferent to our desires and our purposes. If we wish to achieve any success, we must learn to work with things as they are in the world. Thomas Carlyle is said to have exclaimed when told that Margaret Fuller had said, grandiloquently, that she accepted the universe, "Egad, she'd better!" The sooner we accept the universe and attempt to learn all that we can about it, the more effectively we shall be enabled to control and to harness it to our purposes and the faster we shall progress.

Education should make man not only desirous of truth but very humble in regard to his ability to know the truth. There is so much to learn and life is all too short to learn it. Although we cannot hope to know the universe in any ultimate sense, we can learn enough for practical purposes and enough to enable man to live as man should live. Compared with all there is to know, that is a mere drop in the proverbial bucket. The average high-school pupil may not understand, but any scholar knows what Sir Isaac Newton meant when he said, near the end of his life: "I do not know what I may appear to the world, but to myself, I seem to have been only a boy playing on the seashore and diverting myself in now and then finding a smoother pebble or a prettier shell than ordinary, whilst the great ocean of truth lay all undiscovered before me."[15]

War makes special demands upon all areas of life. The school curriculum was certain to be affected. Greater interest in health and in sports for all rather than for a few athletes; more emphasis on mathematics, science, and history; an interest in cultures other than the Anglo-Saxon or even the European; an increasing attention to technical education, particularly to that relating to preflight training; and a return to thoroughness and a stricter regime—these seemed to be the trends most in evidence during and immediately after the war. Whether they will continue in evidence remains to be seen.

THE METHOD USED IN THE GOOD SCHOOL

For accomplishing results, education is quite as dependent upon the method used by teachers as upon a suitable curriculum. How can teachers help children learn? What method is best suited to this purpose? Again, the question should be asked: What do we want to accomplish? If we want to develop intelligent, creative men and women, capable of living in and promoting a democratic society, the implications are clear. We must use a method which will teach our pupils how to think, i.e., the problem-solving method; we must use a method which will encourage creative performance; we must use a method which will develop attitudes of good will, habits of moral conduct, and skill in democratic procedures. The development of intelligence, of creative imagination, and of moral character, with the method suited to each, has been discussed in earlier chapters. Teachers will recognize that educational psychology is especially

15. Sir David Brewster, *Life of Sir Isaac Newton*, p. 303.

helpful in assisting them to understand and guide the learning process.

There are, however, many problems in method which must be referred to philosophy of education. For example, the question is often raised as to whether children should be taught *what* to think or *how* to think. As pointed out in a previous chapter, they need to learn both. It would be a great pity if every child had to discover for himself everything the race has learned. On the other hand, children should have the opportunity from early childhood to solve their own problems on the basis of the information which they have already assimilated.

Another problem in the realm of method is that of whether methods should be used to make school work like play—activity which is an end in itself; or like work—activity which is a means to an end. The answer again is: Both. Each, by itself, is only a partial view of the method by which children learn. Play can be truly educative. The more children can learn that way, the better. Skilful teachers in primary grades do much of their teaching through play. Creative activities, all through life, partake of the play spirit. Anything in which one is absorbedly interested is likely to be an end in itself and therefore like play.

But not all that children need to learn can be learned through play. That, after all, is just as well; for if children did not learn gradually to work at difficult and uninteresting tasks that need to be done, they might never develop the self-discipline which young people and adults must have in order to tackle the unpleasant things in life. Life demands that we work as well as play. Man's nature needs the discipline of work to develop its best. Children should learn to work.

This does not mean that school work should not be interesting, nor is it meant as an excuse for dull formalism in the schoolroom. Work is always directed toward some end. Effort results only from interest in something. The work itself may not be intrinsically interesting. But it is the business of the teacher to help children learn to work toward remote goals which they are interested in reaching. Where children cannot see the value of these more remote goals, teachers resort to extrinsic motivation. The more skilful the teacher, the less extrinsic motivation will be needed. But it is far better for a fun-loving, mischievous, normal boy to learn thoroughly the multiplication tables in order to have the fun of "spelling down" his opponents or to earn a blue ribbon or a gold star than for him never to know them because his teacher had been taught that extrinsic motivation is immoral. Teachers sometimes use incentives that have bad effects. But extrinsic motivation can be used effectively and properly. If an incentive concentrates attention on the task to be done rather than on the reward itself and if, in time, it can be dropped out and the activity continues without its impetus, the type and use of the incentive was probably justified.

Marks, correctly used, are perfectly proper forms of extrinsic motivation. They are often misused, however, so that they become the end sought rather than an indication of success or failure in attaining an end. True, the numerical or letter mark does not tell parents or school authorities all that needs to be told about children's growth. Such marks need to be supplemented by reports using adjectives or adverbs. But as an indication of success in scholastic achievement, they have value. Some of this value lies in letting the boy or girl know whether he is meeting the teacher's requirements and expectations. For little children, this may not be necessary or advisable, but with upper-grade and high-school pupils, marks can be of real psychological value. Of course they can do great harm, also. Teachers should learn to use marks so that they may be helpful, not harmful.

Many a person, induced to study through some extrinsic motivation, has become vitally interested in a field once detested or held in indifference. As we have said before, effort engenders interest perhaps as often as interest begets effort. There is no field of knowledge which is uninteresting *if* one knows enough about it. It is for inducing the first necessary steps toward obtaining the beginning knowledge that incentives are often necessary. It should be pointed out, of course, that in those fields where a child lacks the ability to assimilate the knowledge, he should not be asked to labor, with or without incentives. It is the business of the school to discover pupils' abilities and to see that children work at tasks where they can, with some effort, succeed.

Educational method today is influenced particularly by two psychological points of view: developmentalism and the Gestalt theory.

Developmentalism sees education as resulting from a utilization of the child's development from within rather than as an imposition of adult standards from without. There is nothing new about such an idea. Rousseau's reaction against the doctrine that the child was depraved by nature and must be fashioned by nurture into a different sort of creature was one of the early phases of the movement. Pestalozzi, Froebel, Herbart, G. Stanley Hall, and William James all contributed to this view of education. As a principal emphasis it was interrupted and almost eclipsed by the scientific movement in psychology—using measurement, analysis, experiment—during the early years of this century. With the growing acceptance of Gestalt psychology—emphasizing the "whole child" and the "entire situation" with which he interacts—interest in developmentalism has been revived.

The developmental psychology stresses the continuity of a child's growth. It emphasizes the fact that education is a natural process, that it is a development which may be helped or hindered by influences from the environment, but that it is dependent upon the working of a person's natural powers and interests. Studying the child as a developing personality, watching his growth and development as he interacts with his environment, discovering the activities and experiences suited to each level of his maturity, and learning how to utilize his developing physical, emotional, intellectual, and social powers constitute the chief emphases.

Gestalt psychology has been, since early in the thirties, the most influential variety of several schools of psychology. While Gestalt psychology is probably not the last word in that field, it seems to have contributed some sound and helpful viewpoints.

The gestaltists tell teachers that, whatever the method used, it is a mistake to teach isolated details; that facts ought always to be related to a larger context into which they fit; that one should not attempt to teach facts about India, for example, without teaching the relations of India to the rest of the world; that every experience and every idea should be related to a larger setting. It is important, say they, to work for understandings in terms of concepts and generalizations; one should concentrate on essentials and not on details; and they believe that children cannot be understood or helped except as teachers know the environment out of which they have come. Learning takes place in a situation when there is a need felt by an individual and an obstacle to the satisfaction of that need. Many of these ideas are, of course, old in educational theory.

The father of modern educational psychology was John Frederick Herbart (1776–1841). Herbart succeeded Kant in the chair of philosophy at the University of Königsberg. Although primarily a philosopher, he early recognized the connection between philosophy and education and turned his attention to founding a science of education. He established at Königsberg a model school which served as an experimental and training center for secondary-school teachers. His ideas about method became influential in Germany and were extended to the United States through a number of teachers who studied at Jena—where Dr. Wilhelm Rein, a student and follower of Herbart, was located—as well as at other German universities.

From the period of 1887 to 1900, Illinois State Normal University, at Normal, Illinois, was the principal center of Herbartianism in the United States. Twenty-one members of the faculty and student body studied in German universities[16] and, returning to this country, taught the Herbartian method far and wide. Among these men were Charles De Garmo, who becme the president of Swarthmore College: Charles and Frank McMurray, who wrote *The Method of the Recitation*, an exposition of Herbartianism; and Charles Van Liew, closely identified with the "child study" movement of the day.[17] There were many other noted men and women who contributed to education theory and practice.

Herbart's influence is still strong, although his name is seldom mentioned outside classes in history of education, and will probably continue because the method he advocated was based on the way man thinks. It is a general method, appropriate to all teaching but particularly useful where books are used and ideas taught. It is a general method because it is the method of inductive-deductive thinking.

For classroom use Herbart advocated four steps, calling them, rather awkwardly: (1) clearness, (2) association, (3) system, and (4) method. Some of his followers redivided and renamed the steps:

16. Charles Harper, *The Teachers College*, p. 199.
17. *Ibid.*, p. 211.

(1) preparation, (2) presentation, (3) comparison, (4) generalization, and (5) application.

Like so many "methods," Herbartianism was misused; it became formalized and thereby deadened. Many teachers think that it is no longer in use, but wherever learning begins with ideas, with principles, with generalizations, if the teaching is effective, the Herbartian method is used, whether the teacher knows it or not. The "Morrison plan" of teaching is a refurbished and modernized Herbartianism, as is much of the unit-assignment method used in upper grades and high schools. Also, the "problem project" of the 1920's was an outgrowth of the fifth step, that of application; and "projects" had had a long genealogy of forebears by other names but of similar extraction.

Herbart and his followers advocated the unification and correlation of all school subjects around a central core, a forerunner of the present "integration" movement, and advocated that either literature or literature and history be made that core; they made the child the center of educational study and endeavor; they used the principle of apperception—the assimilation of new ideas by means of ideas already acquired—as their basic psychological principle; and they founded a scientific psychology of education, the details of which are no longer accepted by psychologists but the foundations of which are still in use. And while Herbart used the term "interest" with a slightly different connotation from that in use today, his teachings were probably more in harmony with sound pedagogical principles than is the popular interpretation of the modern doctrine.

Whatever the method used by the teacher, it should assist the pupil in the development of his abilities; it should help him to think more clearly and to become increasingly independent in his thought; it must stimulate thought and be based upon the way man thinks. Any method that accomplishes this is a good method. An application of this principle will mean different *special* methods with different levels of maturity and ability, with different subjects, and with different teachers.

DISCIPLINE IN THE GOOD SCHOOL

The way in which children are managed affects their development as well as does the method used and the curriculum taught

Many a teacher has failed because, as the superintendent said, he could not "discipline" his group or maintain "discipline." Some of the teacher's difficulties may have come from a misunderstanding of the meaning of this word. Too many teachers think of discipline as synonymous with compulsion or even punishment. That is a deplorable misconception. The word comes from *disco-didici*, which means "to learn." A disciple is a learner; discipline is the treatment suitable to a learner. Here is the key to pupil control. When children are interested and busy with learning, there is no difficulty with their behavior. The problem of discipline is solved by good teaching.

To decide on how we shall manage our pupils, we again need to ask: What do we want to accomplish by "discipline"? We want, of course, conditions conducive to learning; we want, also, self-controlled, independent young people, sensitive to the welfare of others as well as to their own needs, responsive to the call of duty.[18] Effective persuasion will sometimes be necessary; with some children punishment may have to be used. But if, through its use, children do not themselves redirect their behavior so that compulsion and punishment become increasingly less necessary, there is something the matter with the way it has been used and with the management of the youngsters.

We should make partners of our pupils as nearly as possible. If we can gain their co-operation and build a feeling of "togetherness," we will not have many problems of control. Children need opportunity to direct themselves if they are to grow in ability to control themselves. The wise teacher, like the wise parent, will give children more freedom gradually as they show that they know how to use it.

But every teacher, particularly the beginning teacher, should be under no illusions concerning the necessity for control. He cannot teach if he cannot control, and he must establish control at once. If possible, he should do it through interest in the ongoing work of the school and through gaining the pupils' co-operation and respect. But establish control he must. A teacher should not aim for popularity or for gaining affection. He should aim at obtaining respect. Once the teacher has the respect of his pupils, popularity and affection will take care of themselves. The majority of children are easily man-

18. Connect this with the discussion in chaps. vi, vii, and viii.

aged, but sometimes, because of the unfortunate conditions under which they have grown up, schools have to deal with lawless, hard-to-manage youngsters, too. It is important that such children learn of law and order at school if nowhere else.

Teachers should not forget, however, why they are in a position of authority. They are there not to enhance their own self-importance by exercising power over those less strong than they but to help children grow into self-directing human beings and to see that conditions under which learning can go on prevail in the classroom. Occasionally there is a teacher who forgets the purposes of classroom control and so exercises the wrong kind of control. He should exercise authority only to achieve the conditions suited to an immature learner. A learner in the first grade needs different conditions from those needed by a high-school Sophomore. A learner in a laboratory needs different conditions from those needed in a literature class. Forty people need different conditions from those needed by three. The conditions vary with the maturity of the learner, with the type of school activity in which the group is engaged, and with the size of the group.

It is probably true that the older traditional school was too severe in its disciplinary measures. Some of this was caused by beliefs concerning the natural depravity of human nature; some of it was probably inevitable because teachers were so poorly prepared and their schoolrooms were such uninteresting places. Any enterprising child, bored with dulness and quiet, would rebel. When the reaction of Progressive education came, with its emphasis first on child nature as inherently good and, second, upon activity and firsthand experience, children were often given too much freedom. There was both more play than was conducive to learning and a lack of consideration for other people's rights. John Dewey has often called the attention of his followers to the fact that their schools were weak in control.[19] In one of his more recent books he says that, while self-control is a proper aim, "the mere removal of external control is no guarantee for the production of self-control."[20] All schools of educational philosophy agree that they wish to develop men and women capable of self-control. But they differ on how much control from adults is necessary for achieving that end.

19. *Experience and Education*, p. 63.   20. *Ibid.*, p. 75.

A teacher whose fundamental tenet is respect for human personality will, in all his management, endeavor to build self-respect and independence in his pupils and to give them increasing opportunity for managing their own affairs, for making their own choices, and for assuming responsibility. But neither will he forget that he is the adult and that they are immature and that the immature have a right to expect the wise and kind guidance from adults. Children must not be left, like Topsy, just to grow.

THE PHYSICAL PLANT OF THE GOOD SCHOOL

A good school needs an adequate physical plant. It helps teachers and pupils to do their work better if their surroundings are cheerful, convenient, and comfortable. Beauty in classrooms helps to develop a sensitiveness to beauty elsewhere, and schools should be as beautiful as they can be made. This does not mean that the expenditure of a great deal of money is necessary. It is doubtful whether the approach to the palatial exhibited in the schools of a few communities is necessary or wise. The simple can be beautiful. Some of the money expended for elaborate buildings might better be used for obtaining superior teachers. Schools need more than the log on which Mark Hopkins and his student traditionally sat, but it will always be more important to have teachers approaching Mark Hopkins in professional ability than to have elaborate physical equipment and buildings.

CHANGE AND THE GOOD SCHOOL

One of the criteria by which the excellence of a school is often judged is that of constant change in its arrangements. Because of the emphasis in Progressive philosophy on the reality of change, many administrators and teachers have felt that, unless they were constantly altering curriculums and methods, they were not respectable. One writer has said: "American education is like a man who continuously builds himself new homes and never lives in one. He perishes running here and there with his stones and his new blueprints."[21]

It is not easy to strike a balance between the factors of perma-

21. Quoted by I. Kandel from T. S. Stribling, *These Bars of Flesh*, in "The Fantasia of Current Education," *American Scholar*, X (1941), 295.

nence and change. There is no doubt but that this is a world of change. It always has been. But, so far as man is concerned, there is permanence also. His nature remains fundamentally the same. Therefore his needs are fundamentally the same. The demands of the good life were the same for the man of ancient Greece and China as they are for the man of today. We have made some progress in meeting those needs. There are more changes that will be necessary before all man's needs can be adequately met. Change is necessary for progress, as has been frequently pointed out.

But because a thing is old, it does not follow that it should be discarded. The science of mathematics is very old, but we still need it and always shall. Concern with ethics is as old as man; Plato, Buddha, and Confucius can give us pointers on the subject; their advice is as pertinent today as it was two thousand and more years ago.

Proposed changes for our schools should always be referred to a a constant criterion: Will they promote the realization of educational aims? It is a mistake to change merely for the sake of changing; it is likewise a mistake to hold on to the old merely because it is old. There is no virtue in mere hoary tradition; but neither is there necessary merit in alteration. We should hold fast to that which is good, i.e., to that which promotes educational aims. And we should discard and change that which retards or does not promote such ends.

In many ways schools are better than they were fifty years or more ago. In other ways they are, perhaps, not so good as the best of the older schools. There has been a loss in thoroughness. The spirit of scholarship is not so pervading. But teachers are generally better prepared; they know more about child nature and child growth; they understand better how human beings learn, and they direct the learning process more successfully. Schools have a friendlier, more co-operative spirit in them. Sarcasm, abuse of power, brutality, are met less often—though still too often.

Some faults to be found with our schools come from crowded conditions and from the fact that we have not yet learned how to teach a group of children with widely varying abilities and capacities according to their individual needs. Vested interests in both the community and the school system sometimes prevent the institution from doing its best work. Some defects have come from the inadequate preparation of too many teachers and especially from the neglect of philosophy of education in their preparation. Education has been treated too much as only a science. It is that. But it is more than that, too.

PHILOSOPHY OF EDUCATION AND THE GOOD SCHOOL

Even though these difficulties were corrected, the millennium would not arrive. Beginning teachers usually start their work with high ideals and enthusiasm. They hope to accomplish so much through their influence and their instruction. Then they discover that teaching is much more difficult than they anticipated. They become discouraged, even cynical. They lose their educational ideals and either leave the profession or become the kind of teacher who teaches only for a pay check.

It is a mistake to expect to accomplish a great deal or to accomplish anything easily. Human nature is a strange mixture of selfishness, greed, and cruelty and of kindness, co-operativeness, and concern for others. Even idealistic Kant said that, because of human nature, we cannot expect too much of man. He wrote: "Hence it is that this problem [the establishment of world justice] is the most difficult of any; nay, its perfect solution is impossible: out of wood so crooked and perverse as that which man is made of, nothing absolutely straight can ever be wrought."[22]

Man is fundamentally an animal with an animal nature; it is a constant struggle for everyone to keep his higher nature, those elements which seem to us divine, in the ascendancy. For some, the struggle is doubtless more difficult than for others. So teachers should not become discouraged. It is perhaps even more serious for the best development of mankind to deny that human nature contains elements that are God-like than it is to forget man's animal ancestry.

William Ellery Channing, the noted New England minister, wrote:

I see the marks of God in the heavens and the earth; but how much more in a liberal intellect, in magnanimity, in unconquerable rectitude, in

22. Immanuel Kant, *The Idea of a Universal History* (trans. Thomas de Quincy), p. 8.

a philanthropy which forgives every wrong, and which never despairs of the cause of Christ and human virtue. I do and I must reverence human nature. I bless it for its kind affections. I honor it for its achievements in science and art, and still more for its examples of heroic and saintly virtue. These are marks of a divine origin and the pledges of a celestial inheritance, and I thank God that my own lot is bound up with that of the human race.[23]

A teacher's attitude toward his pupils' misbehavior should be like that of the physician toward his patient. Not shock, not indignation, not irritation, not disgust, but a determination to understand, to heal, to help. How to do this is the study of a lifetime. The greatest reward that a teacher can hope for is to see boys and girls improving a *little* and growing somewhat in self-discipline, in thoughtfulness for others, in unselfishness, in intelligence, and in strength. Adults cannot expect children to realize what a teacher is trying to do for them and to be grateful. If a teacher does for his pupils what he should, they will probably be far from grateful some of the time. It is only as they approach adulthood and look back upon the influences that have helped them develop as they should that gratitude may appear.

A sense of humor helps a teacher keep his balance. We need not take ourselves too seriously. After all, it has been only a few hundred years since our ancestors were complete savages. The educative process is a slow one. There is much to contend with in trying to develop human excellence. But let us keep our faith in the possibilities of human nature. In our Library of Congress, high on a wall, appears the motto: "The highest motive is the public good." There is no better guiding principle for teachers.

SUMMARY

A school is good in the degree to which it contributes toward the realization of educational objectives. The aim of education is to promote the general welfare through developing intelligent, creative, social-minded young people, able and willing to work toward an improved democratic society.

The teacher is the most important factor in securing a good school. It is important to attract to teaching young people more nearly on a par with those who enter other professions. Teaching needs more men of a

23. William Ellery Channing, inscription from his writings, on Channing Memorial, Public Garden, Boston.

high caliber. Improved salaries and greater prestige in the eyes of the public are greatly needed as incentives.

The materials and experiences for the curriculum should be selected with the requirements for the good life, in so far as we understand them, in mind. Since democracy is necessary for the good life and democracy demands co-operation and communication from its members, the content of *general* education, that which all citizens need, is an important problem. The search for unity seems to center about determining the respective places of the cultural heritage and the scientific method in the curriculum. It would seem that one without the other is incomplete. A related problem is that of how to use curricular materials so as to produce more integration in the learner. Subject matter has been so highly compartmentalized that learners often fail to see relationships. Except perhaps with very small children, less compartmentalization should not mean doing away entirely with subject divisions.

The method used should be one which enables the learner to obtain whatever he needs to know in order to become intelligent, creative, and morally sensitive. The problem-solving method is valuable. It can be used both in firsthand and in vicarious experience. A general method is general because it is in harmony with the way man thinks. Much of modern methodology goes back to Herbart, the father of educational psychology. Educational method is influenced today by two important psychological points of view: developmentalism and gestaltism. The central thesis of developmentalism is that education results from utilizing the child's inner development rather than by imposing adult standards. Gestaltists emphasize that learning is best where details are always related to wholes; where the child is considered as a whole, interacting with his total environment; where relationships of facts to a larger context are stressed.

Discipline is best thought of as the treatment suitable to a learner; it is good discipline when it results in progressive ability on the part of the learner to control himself in the interests of all. Teachers who cannot establish effective measures of control cannot teach. The best way to control children is through having them engage in activities of such interest that their energies and attentions are entirely absorbed by the work at hand. Few teachers are ever able to depend entirely upon this method for control of all the pupils in their groups. It is more effective to be the kind of teacher who commands respect than the kind who seeks popularity and affection. The principle of respect for human personality is always the best one on which to act.

A school needs a physical plant which furnishes surroundings of convenience, comfort, and some measure of beauty. A school need not be a palace. Money had better be spent on salaries for able teachers than on luxuries and elaborate buildings.

Education needs to strike a balance between permanence and change.

Change is necessary for progress, but there is no virtue in mere change. Proposed changes should be tested by the principle of necessity for achieving educational aims.

The educative process is slow, and it is easy for a teacher to become discouraged. This is particularly true with the idealistic teacher who hopes to accomplish much. Few of us do accomplish much. Teachers need historical perspective, a sense of humor, and a faith in human nature based on a realistic understanding of its limitations and possibilities. Then one can keep one's determination to serve the public good.

QUESTIONS TO AID STUDY

1. When is a school a *good* school?
2. Think of some of your outstanding teachers. What personal characteristics did they have which contributed to their superiority?
3. Why is one of the outstanding problems of teacher preparation that of attracting suitable men and women to its ranks?
4. How can superior young people be drawn into the teaching profession?
5. What is meant by the word "curriculum"? How can the content of the curriculum be decided upon? Enumerate the phases of human life for which it must provide. What connection is there between the good life and the curriculum?
6. Give arguments for and against the elective system. In what way was youth robbed of its cultural heritage by the institution of the elective system?
7. What are the two most important present-day problems in connection with the curriculum?
8. How does Chancellor Hutchins advocate that the problem of attaining unity be solved? How would John Dewey solve it?
9. What recommendations for the solution of this problem are made by the Harvard report?
10. Compare the proposals of the Harvard report with those of *Education for All American Youth*. Which would you rather see put into effect? Why?
11. On what grounds is the Harvard report criticized? Why would a pragmatist not approve it?
12. What is meant by the term "integration"? How has this concept affected curriculum organization on the elementary level? On the secondary level?
13. Should the curriculum be planned in advance of its teaching, or should it develop out of the growing and changing interests of the children as they work together? Explain.
14. What attitude toward truth should teachers seek to develop in pupils?

15. How can you tell whether a method is a "good" one?
16. Should school method simulate play or work? Be aimed at teaching children *how* to think or *what* to think? Explain.
17. Is extrinsic motivation justifiable? Explain. Did you ever become vitally interested in something which you would never have studied through an intrinsic interest? Recount your experience.
18. For what and how should school marks be used?
19. Show how two psychological points of view are important in determining modern methods. Be specific.
20. Who is known as the father of modern educational method? Is there such a thing as a general method? What makes it a *general* method? What is the relation of special methods to a general method?
21. When is "discipline" good? What is the key to effective discipline? Discuss the important factors in successful pupil control.
22. Discuss the relation between change and obtaining good schools. What criterion for deciding on proposed changes should be used?
23. How does it happen that some teachers lose their youthful idealism? How can one guard against this?
24. Around what principal idea or ideas would you say that this book is organized? Show how.
25. Suppose that a superintendent of schools to whom you were applying for a position asked you to state briefly your philosophy of education? What would you say? Now suppose that he asked you to illustrate how you would use that philosophy in: (a) organizing and managing your classroom, (b) selecting materials for instruction, (c) working with a child inclined to cheat, (d) helping a child who shuns responsibility and makes excuses for himself, (e) deciding whether to promote a pupil who is doing the best he can but still "fails." How would you reply?

SUGGESTED REFERENCES

BODE, BOYD. "Harvard Report," *Journal of Higher Education*, XVII (January, 1946), 1–8.

COMMITTEE ON THE OBJECTIVES OF A GENERAL EDUCATION. *General Education in a Free Society* (Cambridge, Mass.: Harvard University, 1945), especially chaps. ii and iv.

DASHIELL, JOHN FREDERICK. "Survey and Synthesis of Learning Theories," *Psychological Bulletin*, XXXII (1936), 26–75.

DE GARMO, CHARLES. *Herbart and the Herbartians* (New York: Charles Scribner's Sons, 1895), chap. iii.

DEMOS, RAPHAEL. "Mr. Bode and the Harvard Report," *Journal of Higher Education*, XVII (February, 1946), 57–62.

"Dreaming a Dream for Our Children," *Progressive Education*, XIX (1942), 243–77.

EDUCATIONAL POLICIES COMMISSION. *Education for All American Youth.* Washington, D.C.: Educational Policies Commission, National Education Association, 1944.

HORNE, HERMAN HARRELL. *A Democratic Philosophy of Education* (New York: Macmillan Co., 1932), chaps. x, xii, and xiv.

JAMES, WILLIAM. *Habit* (reprinted from his *Principles of Psychology*). New York: Henry Holt & Co., 1918.

KILPATRICK, WILLIAM H. *Remaking the Curriculum* (New York: Newson & Co., 1936), chaps. iv–v and vii (chap. vii for secondary-school teachers).

MILLER, FRANK B. "The Nature of the Individual and the Learning Process," *School and Society,* LII (December 14, 1940), 629.

REDDEN, JOHN D., and RYAN, FRANCIS A. *A Catholic Philosophy of Education* (Milwaukee: Bruce Pub. Co., 1942), chaps. v and xi–xii.

SPEARS, HAROLD. *The Emerging High School Curriculum* (New York: American Book Co., 1940), especially chap. iii.

STODDARD, GEORGE. *Frontiers in Education.* Stanford University: Stanford University Press, 1946.

THORNTON, J. W. "Gestalt Psychology," *Educational Administration and Supervision,* XXIV (1938), 177.

WASHBURNE, CARLETON W. *A Living Philosophy of Education* (New York: John Day Co., 1940), especially chap. i.

WRIGHTSTONE, JACOB WAYNE. *Appraisal of Experimental High School Practices.* New York: Teachers College, Columbia University, 1936.

———. *Appraisal of Newer Practices in Elementary Education.* New York: Teachers College, Columbia University, 1938.

GLOSSARY OF PHILOSOPHICAL TERMS

A POSTERIORI.—Refers to knowledge attained through experience; such reasoning is inductive.

A PRIORI.—Refers to knowledge attained independent of experience, at least as far as the conclusion is concerned; knowledge gained through deduction from principles; also that aspect of knowledge due to the native constitution of the mind; the ground or form which makes experience rational.

ABSOLUTE.—That which is autonomous and not dependent upon anything else; not relative or conditioned. Moral principles are considered absolutes when they are universally valid.

AESTHETICS.—That division of philosophy which deals with the nature of beauty, defined in the broadest sense, and also with standards for judging that beauty.

ANTHROPOMORPHISM.—The conception of God or gods in terms of man's nature.

BEHAVIORISM.—The school of psychology which, ignoring mind and consciousness, studies only animal and human behavior.

BEING.—Existing as an entity; having reality.

CATALYST.—An agent, which by its presence accelerates positively or negatively a chemical change, though it does not itself enter into that change but remains stable.

CATEGORICAL.—Admitting of no exceptions; unconditioned and absolute.

CHARACTER.—That quality of human nature which renders man consistent, dependable, and steadfast. A man of character is a man of principle.

CONCEPT.—An apprehended universal as distinguished from the percepts or particulars which it unifies.

DETERMINISM.—The teaching that every event, including human choice between alternative courses of conduct, has its cause and could not have been, under those circumstances, otherwise than it was.

DUALISM.—Any recognition of two irreducible and eternally coexistent principles or substances.

ECLECTICISM.—The practice of selecting what "seems best" in opposing schools of thought, frequently with insufficient attention to the consistency of the resulting product.

"ÉLAN VITAL."—A term used by the French philosopher, Bergson, to indicate a vital force within nature which is the source of evolutionary changes and of causation.

EMERGENCE.—The doctrine that, though evolutionary changes reveal continuity, these changes are never merely the mechanical product of a simpler level of existence. Because new relations result from new organizations of the previously existent constituents, these new organizations exhibit novel characteristics and cannot be understood in terms of the laws applicable to the simpler level; neither could their properties and characteristics have been predicted from the properties and characteristics of the constituents.

EMPIRICISM.—The theory which teaches that our knowledge comes from experience, usually from sense-experience.

ENTELECHY.—A term adopted from Aristotle and used to mean the power to realize actuality as opposed to potentiality.

EPICUREANISM.—The doctrine that happiness can be attained only through avoiding pain; pleasure is the highest good; but to avoid pain and attain pleasure, life must be lived with prudence and moderation.

EPIPHENOMENON.—A by-product of a process, to which it is secondary, incidental, and of no significance in the development of the process.

EPISTEMOLOGY.—The division of philosophy which deals with problems of knowledge.

ETHICS.—The division of philosophy which deals with the ideal in human character and conduct.

EUDAEMONISM.—The theory that happiness is the chief good for man.

FATALISM.—The belief that all man's acts are inevitably predetermined by external circumstances or by fate, independent of his own volition.

FORM.—The structure or pattern of anything that exists, as distinguished from the matter in which the structure is embodied; the "how" of anything, as matter or content is the "what."

FREE WILL.—The belief that man can choose freely between alternative courses of action.

GESTALT.—A German word which means any experienced whole or configuration. The word is used to describe a school of psychology whose central teaching is that wholes are more than the sum of parts and that parts derive their character from the whole.

HEDONISM.—The teaching that pleasure is man's chief good; that which gives personal pleasure is good, and that which gives the opposite of personal pleasure is bad.

HYLOMORPHISM.—The theory, Aristotelian in origin, that all physical objects are composed of two principles, matter and form.

IDEA.—An object of mental apprehension in the widest sense; in Plato's philosophy, universals or archetypes, of which sense objects were imperfect copies.

IDEAL.—A standard of excellence or perfection, functioning as a goal or object of desire.

IDEALISM.—In metaphysics, the theory that ultimate reality is spiritual or mental in nature; that the universe is the embodiment of mind. In epistemology, the theory that all that we know are mental processes or ideas.

IMMANENT.—Indwelling, inherent; an intrinsic part of.

IMPERATIVE.—A command; a categorical imperative is a command which admits of no exceptions; a hypothetical imperative is a command which is relative to some further end.

INDETERMINISM.—The belief that the connection between cause and event is not complete and that chance may enter into human decisions. The term is often used as synonymous with free will.

INSTRUMENTALISM.—The theory that knowledge is an instrument to be used for ends outside itself.

INTELLIGENCE.—The ability to discover and solve problems successfully and to meet new situations with competence.

KARMA.—In Hindu philosophy, the principle that from the sum of a man's moral merit or demerit comes fatalistically the determination of the nature and circumstances of his next reincarnation.

KISMET.—Mohammedan concept of destiny or fate.

LOGOS.—Literally, "word" or "reason"; used to denote a cosmic principle which gives order and intelligibility to the universe. Later, used to mean that which links God and man.

MATERIALISM.—The theory that ultimate reality is matter, whatever physicists may discover that to be; denies the existence of any spiritual substance.

MECHANISM.—The theory that all existence operates as a machine and can be understood in terms of a few principles of motion; ultimate reality is matter in motion.

METAPHYSICS.—The division in philosophy which is concerned with the ultimate nature of existence; often used as synonymous with ontology.

MONISM.—The teaching that there is but one substance at the basis of all reality and that the whole of reality is qualitatively or quantitatively one.

NATURALISM.—The theory that whatever nature may be, it is the whole of reality and is self-existent, self-explanatory, and self-operating. Denies the necessity for the supernatural as an explanatory principle.

NOUMENON.—The object of knowledge as apprehended by reason.

ONTOLOGY.—That division of philosophy which deals with the essence of things; with the nature of being; often used as synonymous with metaphysics.

ORGANISMIC.—A term used to describe a system of psychology which is opposed to a mechanistic conception of man; central teaching seems to be that a human being reacts as a whole and that the whole is more than the sum of its parts. Gestalt psychology is organismic.

PERCEPT.—A mental apprehension of an object presented to the senses.

PERSON.—A being who is conscious of self and capable of reasoning, of creative thought, of making moral distinctions; man, as distinguished from animals.

PERSONALITY.—The totality of mental traits resulting from the exercise of those capabilities which distinguish man from animals; a man has personality to the extent that he approaches the ideal in man.

PHENOMENON.—The object of knowledge as given through sense-experience.

PHILOSOPHY.—Literally, "the love of wisdom"; a systematic attempt to understand the nature of the universe and man's place in it.

PLURALISM.—The teaching that there is more than one ultimate substance; usually interpreted as many rather than as two.

POSITIVISM.—The doctrine that the only knowledge man can obtain is of sensory phenomena.

PRAGMATISM.—The theory that practical consequences determine truth; if a proposition works, it is true.

PREDESTINATION.—The teaching that all the events of man's life, including his eternal destiny, are determined from all eternity by God.

PSYCHOPHYSICAL PARALLELISM.—The theory concerning the body-mind relationship which holds that for every mental process there is a correlated bodily process but that there is no causal connection between the two.

RATIONALISM.—The theory that knowledge comes through the use of reason rather than from sense-experience.

REALISM.—Applied today to several schools of thought, all of which unite in ascribing independent reality to the experienced world; the realist holds that the material universe is not dependent for its existence upon mind and that we know that world directly.

REALITY.—That which has a wholly independent being and does not owe this being to anything else; absoluteness of being.

REASONING.—Thinking logically so as to draw inferences and to reach conclusions from a consideration of propositions known or held to be true. All reasoning is reducible to deduction and induction.

SELF.—The subject and object of individual consciousness; the bearer of subjective experience, as well as the contents of that experience, organized into a whole. "A self is a subject which is its own object."

SKEPTICISM.—The idea, in the field under discussion, that absolute and complete knowledge cannot be attained by man.

SPIRITUALISM.—Synonymous with metaphysical idealism; ultimate reality is spiritual in nature.

STOICISM.—A school of Greek and Roman philosophy which taught that virtue is the highest good; it is to be attained by living in accord with a rational world order. A virtuous man does his duty and finds serenity within himself, independent of anything in the external world.

SUBSTANCE.—That which constitutes ultimate reality; that which is independent, self-sustaining, irreducible, and fundamental.

SYNOPTIC.—Viewed as a whole; taken together; unified.

TELEOLOGY.—The theory that purposes, ends, goals, operate in nature; opposed to a mechanistic interpretation of the universe or of man.

UTILITARIANISM.—The doctrine that the good is that which promotes the happiness of the greatest number of persons.

UTOPIA.—Literally, "the land of nowhere"; used to denote an ideal society.

VITALISM.—The theory that living material contains a "vital principle" as well as physicochemical material; opposed to the mechanistic conception that the phenomena of life can be explained entirely in physicochemical terms.

In formulating these definitions of philosophical terms the author has consulted the following: James Mark Baldwin (ed.), *Dictionary of Philosophy and Psychology* (New York: Macmillan Co., 1901–2); and Dagobert D. Runes (ed.), *The Dictionary of Philosophy* (New York: Philosophical Library, 1942).

ACKNOWLEDGMENTS

I AM grateful to the following publishers for permission to quote from the designated books published by them:

George Allen and Unwin, Limited (London): Julian Huxley, *Evolution: The Modern Synthesis.*

American Book Company: George Hartmann, *Educational Psychology;* Robert Ulich, *Fundamentals of Democratic Education.*

D. Appleton–Century Company: J. A. Leighton, *Social Philosophies in Conflict.*

Geoffrey Bles, Centenary Press, Limited (London): Jacques Maritain, *Science and Wisdom.*

Bruce Publishing Company: John D. Redden and Francis A. Ryan, *A Catholic Philosophy of Education.*

Columbia University Press: Immanuel Kant, *Perpetual Peace;* Y. H. Krikorian, *Naturalism and the Human Spirit.*

Doubleday and Company: Hughes Mearns, *Creative Youth;* Ruth Noble, *Nature of the Beast;* Woodrow Wilson, *The New Freedom.*

E. P. Dutton and Company, Incorporated: John and Evelyn Dewey, *Schools of Tomorrow;* Radoslav Tsanoff, *Moral Ideals of Our Civilization.*

Educational Policies Commission: *Purposes of Education in American Democracy; Unique Function of Education in American Democracy.*

Ginn and Company: William G. Sumner, *Folkways;* William Turner, *History of Philosophy.*

E. M. Hale and Company: Gertrude Hartman and Ann Shumaker, *Creative Expression.*

Harcourt, Brace and Company, Incorporated: June Downey, *Creative Imagination;* Vernon L. Parrington, *Main Currents in American Thought,* Vol. III.

McGraw-Hill Book Company, Incorporated: Ellsworth Faris, *The Nature of Human Nature;* Robert Nathan, *Mobilizing for Abundance.*

The Macmillan Company: Boyd Bode, *Democracy as a Way of Life;* John Boodin, *God and Creation;* Thomas H. Briggs, *Secondary Education;* Lewis Browne, *Something Went Wrong;* Sir William Dampier, *History of Science;* John Dewey, *Experience and Education;* Dostoevsky, *The Brothers Karamazov;* Durant Drake, *The New Morality;* Sir Arthur Eddington, *New Pathways in Science;* George Hartmann, *Ethics;* C. B. Hoover, *Dictators and Democracies;* Herman Harrell Horne, *Democratic Philosophy of Education;* Harold Laski on "Liberty" in *Encyclopaedia of the Social Sciences;* Paul Monroe, *History of Educa-*

tion; George D. Stoddard, *The Meaning of Intelligence;* Alfred North Whitehead, *Religion in the Making.*

National Society for the Study of Education: *Philosophies of Education,* Forty-first Yearbook, Part I. (By permission of the secretary of the Society, Dr. Nelson B. Henry.)

Newson and Company: Boyd Bode, *Progressive Education at the Crossroads.*

W. W. Norton and Company, Incorporated: Lancelot Hogben, *Author in Transit;* José Ortega y Gasset, *The Revolt of the Masses;* James L. Mursell, *The Psychology of Secondary School Teaching;* H. A. Overstreet, *Our Free Minds;* Bertrand Russell, *An Inquiry into Meaning and Truth.*

The Odyssey Press, Incorporated: David R. Major, *An Introduction to Philosophy.*

Oxford University Press: Aristotle, *De anima, Metaphysics, Nicomachean Ethics, Politics;* J. S. Haldane, *The Philosophy of a Biologist;* W. F. Jones, *Morality and Freedom in the Philosophy of Immanuel Kant;* J. C. Meredith (trans.), Kant, *Critique of Aesthetic Judgement;* Bertrand Russell, *Problems of Philosophy.*

Pantheon Books, Incorporated: Erich Kahler, *Man the Measure.*

Philosophical Library: John Dewey, *Problems of Men;* D. D. Runes (ed.), *The Dictionary of Philosophy.*

Prentice-Hall, Incorporated: Eby and Arrowood, *Development of Modern Education;* W. A. Lay, *Experimental Pedagogy;* William P. Montague, *Ways of Things.*

Public School Publishing Company: H. H. Schroeder, *Legal Opinion on the Public School as a State Institution.*

G. P. Putnam's Sons: John Dewey, *Art as Experience; Freedom and Culture;* W. R. Wright, *General Introduction to Ethics.*

Random House, Incorporated: *The Philosophy of Spinoza* ("Modern Library").

Reynal and Hitchcock: Raoul de Roussy de Sales, *Making of Tomorrow;* William T. Stace, *The Destiny of Western Man.*

Row, Peterson and Company: H. H. Schroeder, *The Psychology of Conduct.*

Charles Scribner's Sons: Charles Bakewell, *Source Book in Ancient Philosophy;* James Breasted, *Dawn of Conscience;* J. W. Burgess, *Reconciliation of Government with Liberty;* Herbert Hoover, *The Challenge to Liberty;* John Locke, *Essay Concerning Human Understanding;* Jacques Maritain, *Art and Scholasticism; Freedom in the Modern World;* George Santayana, *The Sense of Beauty;* Alfred Weber, *History of Philosophy.*

Simon and Schuster, Incorporated: Mortimer Adler, *How To Think about War and Peace;* Albert Einstein and Leopold Infeld, *The Evolution of*

Physics; Bertrand Russell, *History of Western Philosophy;* Leo Tolstoy, *War and Peace.*

Sociological Press: Thomas de Quincy (trans.), Kant, *Idea of a Universal History.*

Stanford University Press: George Stoddard, *Frontiers in Education.*

Teachers College, Columbia University, Bureau of Publications: Frances V. Markey, *Imaginative Behavior of Preschool Children; Readings in the Foundations of Education,* Vol. I.

University of Chicago Press: Theodore B. Soares, *Religious Education.*

Yale University Press: Ernst Cassirer, *An Essay on Man;* J. Haldane, *Organism and Environment;* R. M. Hutchins, *The Higher Learning in America.*

I am grateful to the editors of the following magazines for permission to quote from the designated articles:

American Scholar: Walter Lippmann, "Education vs. Western Civilization." (Permission also secured from the author.)

Educational Administration and Supervision: T. H. Briggs, "Should Education Indoctrinate?"

Educational Record: George D. Stoddard, "The I.Q.: Its Ups and Downs."

Frontiers of Democracy: Will French, "Propaganda."

Journal of the National Education Association: Carleton Washburne, "The Case for Subjects in the Curriculum."

Philosophical Review: J. W. Hudson, "Teleology in Ethics"; H. H. Schroeder, "Some Common Misinterpretations of the Kantian Ethics."

School and Society: Hall-Quest, "Three Educational Theories: Traditionalism, Progressivism, Essentialism." (Permission also secured from the author.)

Vital Speeches: Arthur Compton, "Destiny of Man", "Science in a War Stricken World."

My thanks are also due to the Estate of William Lyon Phelps for permission to quote from his book, *Teaching in Schools and Colleges.*

SELECTED BIBLIOGRAPHY OF PHILOSOPHICAL FICTION

ANDERSON, SHERWOOD. *Dark Laughter; Winesburg, Ohio*
BELLAMY, EDWARD. *Looking Backward*
BOJER, JOHAN. *The Great Hunger; The New Temple*
BRITTAIN, VERA. *Testament of Youth*
BROMFIELD, LOUIS. *Twenty-four Hours*
BUTLER, SAMUEL. *The Way of All Flesh*
CABELL, JAMES BRANCH. *The Cream of the Jest; Jurgen; The Rivet in Grandfather's Neck*
CATHER, WILLA. *Death Comes for the Archbishop*
CERVANTES, MIGUEL DE. *Don Quixote*
CONRAD, JOSEPH. *Lord Jim*
CRANE, STEPHEN. *The Red Badge of Courage*
DE LA MARE, WALTER. *The Return: Memoirs of a Midget*
DOS PASSOS, JOHN. *One Man's Initiation*
DOSTOEVSKI, FEODOR M. *Crime and Punishment; The Brothers Karamazov; The Idiot*
DOUGLAS, NORMAN. *South Wind*
DREISER, THEODORE. *An American Tragedy; Jennie Gerhardt*
ELIOT, GEORGE. *Adam Bede; Middlemarch; Romola*
FLAUBERT, GUSTAVE. *Madame Bovary*
FORSTER, EDWARD MORGAN. *A Passage to India*
FRANCE, ANATOLE. *Thaïs*
GLICK, CARL. *Three Times I Bow*
GOETHE, JOHANN. *Faust*
GORKY, MAXIM. *The Bystander; The Magnet*
HARDY, THOMAS. *Jude the Obscure; Tess of the D'Urbervilles; The Return of the Native*
HEMINGWAY, ERNEST. *A Farewell to Arms; For Whom the Bell Tolls*
HERGESHEIMER, JOSEPH. *Java Head*
HUXLEY, ALDOUS. *After Many a Summer Dies the Swan; Brave New World; Time Must Have a Stop*
JAMES, HENRY. *Daisy Miller; The American*
KINGSLEY, CHARLES. *Hypatia*
LAGERLÖF, SELMA. *The Ring of the Löwenskölds*
LEWIS, SINCLAIR. *Arrowsmith; Babbitt*
LONDON, JACK. *Martin Eden; The Sea Wolf*
MANN, THOMAS. *Buddenbrooks; The Magic Mountain*
MASEFIELD, JOHN. *Multitude and Solitude*

MAUGHAM, W. SOMERSET. *Of Human Bondage; The Moon and Sixpence; The Razor's Edge*

MEREDITH, GEORGE. *The Egoist*

MEREZHKOVSKI, DMITRI. *Julian the Apostate; Peter and Alexis; Romance of Leonardo da Vinci*

MORGAN, CHARLES. *Sparkenbroke; The Fountain*

MORRIS, WILLIAM. *News from Nowhere*

NATHAN, ROBERT. *Autumn; Road of Ages*

NORRIS, FRANK. *McTeague; Vandover and the Brute*

PATER, WALTER H. *Marius, the Epicurean*

PIRANDELLO, LUIGI. *The Late Mattia Pascal*

POOLE, ERNEST. *The Harbor*

PROUST, MARCEL. *Remembrance of Things Past*

RABELAIS, FRANÇOIS. *Gargantua and Pantagruel*

ROLLAND, ROMAIN. *Jean Christophe*

SANTAYANA, GEORGE. *The Last Puritan*

SCHREINER, OLIVE. *The Story of an African Farm*

SEGHERS, ANNA. *The Seventh Cross*

SINCLAIR, MAY. *Mary Olivier: A Life*

STEVENSON, ROBERT LOUIS. *Dr. Jekyll and Mr. Hyde*

TOLSTOY, LEO. *Anna Karenina; Resurrection; War and Peace*

TURGENEV, IVAN. *Fathers and Sons; Rudin*

UNDSET, SIGRID. *Kristin Lavransdatter; The Master of Hestviken*

VOLTAIRE. *Candide*

WALPOLE, HUGH. *Fortitude*

WASSERMANN, JAKOB. *The World's Illusion*

WELLS, HERBERT GEORGE. *A Modern Utopia; Mr. Britling Sees It Through; Tono-Bungay*

WERFEL, FRANZ. *Embezzled Heaven; Star of the Unborn*

WHARTON, EDITH. *Ethan Frome*

WILDE, OSCAR. *The Picture of Dorian Gray*

WILDER, THORNTON. *Bridge of San Luis Rey; Heaven's My Destination; Woman of Andros*

WOLFE, THOMAS. *Look Homeward, Angel; Of Time and the River; You Can't Go Home Again*

ZOLA, ÉMILE. *Germinal*

INDEX

Activity: basic tenet of, the movement in education, 284; and development of creative ability, 315; and development of intelligence, 283–88; differences among advocates of, 287; mental, 284, 286, 287–88; movement, beginnings of, 283–86; philosophy of proponents of, 287; school, tenets of, 287

Adler, Mortimer: criticism of positivism of, 10; on educational philosophy, 242–43; on world government, 179

Aesthetics: defined, 300; Dewey's conception of, 308–9; education in field of, 305, 309–20; problems in, 300–306

Aggressiveness, cause of undue, 76

Alexander, Samuel, on nature of beauty, 303–4

Allen, Richard D., case-conference plan of, in character education, 330

American dream, and democratic principles, 148, 257

American Education Fellowship, 250–51

Aquinas, Thomas, 57; on beauty, nature of, 301; on body-mind problem, 205; on ends and means, 62; hylomorphism of, 205; on moral freedom, 130; philosopher of Catholicism, 205; on source of knowledge, 217; as student, 274

Aristides the Just, banished from Athens, 171

Aristotle: aesthetics of, 301; on causes of revolutions, 78; and change, 173; on character development, 329; concept of forms of, 204; and democracy, 144; on function of the state, 165; on happiness as the highest good, 62–63; hylomorphism of, 204; on man as a rational animal, 294; on man's desire for knowledge, 190; mean of, 63, 281; naturalism in, 196; on Platonic ideas, 197–99; on pleasure in beauty, 304; psychical determinism in, 122; on relation of the

what to the why, 38; on slavery, attitude of, 81; on source of knowledge, 216–17; theory of ultimate reality of, 191, 204

Arts: as communication, 311; creative imagination and, 300–306; developing appreciation of, 305–11; developing creative ability in, 312–15; Dewey's conception of, 308–9; nature of beauty in, 301–5; philosophies of education and, 309–12; power of, 305–6; purpose of, 300; standards for excellence in, 300–305; see also Creativeness

Atlantic Charter, freedoms of, 134

Atomic energy; control of, 180; war and peace and, 180

Atomic theory of matter, 193–94

Augustine: on nature of man, 39, 59; on predestination, 123–24; on problem of evil, 124; and use of term "character," 325

Bagley, William Chandler: as critic of Progressives, 252; as Essentialist, 252

Barzun, Jacques, on source of good citizenship, 183

Basedow, Johann: and activity movement, 284–85; and the Philanthropinum, a child-centered school, 31

Beard, Charles: on educating for democracy, 181; on solving problems of democracy, 154

Beauty: nature of, 300–306; sensitiveness to, 305

Behaviorism: as based on materialism, 202, 240; useful concepts in, 240

Bentham, Jeremy: on national co-operation for peace, 178; as a utilitarian, 65

Berkeley, George, as an idealist, 220

Biological factors: in Dewey's theory of art, 308–9; in man's nature, 23–24; in man's needs, 75–78

Bobbitt, Franklin, on relation of man's needs to the curriculum, 74

Gestalt psychology: body-mind problem in, 205–6; and curriculum, 359; insight in, 267; as Kantian, 205; and method, 366–67

Golden Rule: of education, 89; inadequacies in statement of, 102; spirit of, as basic in morality, 102

Good life: basic problem in, 73, 75–78; components of, 74–75; and curriculum, 355–56; human personality and, 183; relation of duty to, 112; relation of freedom to, 84; relation of interests to, 84–86; relation of marriage to, 79–80; relation of morality to, 99–102; relation of, to philosophy of education, 238; relation of talents to, 84; relation of work to, 81–82; religion in the, 86–88; success and failure in, 83; totalitarianism and, 153

Government: conflict between freedom and, 149–50; democratic, 149–50; as distinguished from the state, 164; leadership in, 167–70; policy formation and administration in, 167–68; as servant of people, 164–65; world, 178–80

Growth: in creative activity, 314; as educational aim, 30, 247; measuring value of educational experience in terms of, 278–79

Haldane, J. S.: and emergent evolution, 22–23; on life and conscious behavior, 25

Happiness: attainment of, 67; Christianity and, 67; making one's self worthy of, 67; theories of, as supreme value, 62–65

Harris, W. T., as leader of educational idealism, 240–41, 278

Hartmann, Nicolai, happiness as a value, 65

Harvard report on general education: criticized by Progressives, 358; program of, 356–58

Health: importance of, for the good life, 75–76; need of, by teacher, 351

Hebrew influence upon the Western tradition, 2, 357

Hedonist: beauty as pleasure, 302; happiness as pleasure, 64

Hegel, G. W. F.: influence of, on education, 240–41; on nature of beauty,

301–2; theory of, of ultimate reality, 199

Heisenberg's "principle of uncertainty," moral freedom and, 121

Heraclitus: influence of, on Plato, 198; influence of, on Sophists, 215; Logos of, 194; on permanence and change, 191–92

Herbart, Johann Friedrich: on aim of education, 326; as contributor to developmental approach to child-study, 366; as father of educational psychology, 367–68; influence of, on Henry Morrison, 368; method of, 367–68

Herbartianism, and Illinois State Normal University, 367

Heredity: and intelligence, 270–72; and the self, 33

Hobbes, Thomas: justification of totalitarianism by, 145–46; materialism of, 195

Hobhouse, L. T., on general welfare and the individual, 135

Home: and character development, 331–32, 346; developing intelligence in, 275–77; freedom in, 132; importance of, in the good life, 79–80; indoctrination in, 175; informal education and, 35–37; religious instruction in, 345

Honors courses for superior students, 317

Hoover, Herbert, on rugged individualism, 161

Horne, Herman Harrell: on developing appreciation, 310; on religion and the teacher, 342–43; as spokesman for idealism in education, 241; summary by, of Dewey's views on education as transmission of social heritage, 37–38

Human conduct: the artist and, 294, 305–6; emotions as determiners of, 109–10; relation of, to character, 326; source of, 25, 36

Human excellence: attainment of, as highest good, 60; and Christianity, 60; components of, 60; development of, 61, 373–74; and education, 255–61, 329–37, 339, 355; and educational method, 363; and morality, 99–102; relation of the good life to, 47; and the teacher, 327, 350–51

Human nature: as above animal na-

149–52; education for, 181–83; freedom in, 131–35; human, as different from animal, 55; loss to, through inferior teachers, 350; man's need for, 26, 32–33, 78–80; Rousseau's indictment of, 31; and the self, 32, 33, 47, 331–33; technological, and creative powers, 316

Socrates: on building a Parthenon, 151; on democracy, 158–60; meeting of, with Plato, 197; on moral choice, 136; moral theory of, 94–95; on morality and knowledge, 58, 324; opposition of, to Sophists, 215

Sophists: as empiricists, 215; as pragmatists, 225

Spearman, Charles, on nature of creative thought, 297

Spengler, Oswald, the cyclic theory of history of, 39, 40

Spinoza, Baruch de: determinism of, 120; identity theory of, 202–3; naturalism of, 196; rationalism of, 216

Spiritualism; *see* Idealism, metaphysical

Stace, W. T.: argument of, against moral skepticism, 114; on man's worth, 103; on morality as objective, 101

State, the: defined, 164; totalitarianism and, 152–53

Stoddard, George D.: on constancy of intelligence quotient, 271; on nature of intelligence, 268; on two basic problems of education today, 356

Stoics: democratic ideas of, 144–45; and duty, 111; fatalism of, 123; highest good of, 66; law of nature of, and natural rights, 146; Logos of, 194; nobility of, 66; progress and, 40; self-centeredness of, 66

Sumner, William G., on source of morality, 94

Symbols: relation of, to development of creative imagination, 311–12; relation of, to development of intelligence, 278, 282–88; use of, as man's distinctive characteristic, 54–56, 70, 282; and vicarious experience, 282

Synthesis of opposing views: in aesthetics, 302–6, 318; and body-mind problem in metaphysics, 203; in education, 33, 44–45, 281–82, 289–91, 312–20, 345–47, 349–76; in

epistemology, 217–18; in ethics, 67–68

Teachers: adequate salaries for, 352–53; and celibacy, 327; character of, 327, 352; and development of creative imagination, 313–17; and discipline, 369–71; and discouragement and philosophy of education, 373–74; dramatic ability in, 282; educating, for democracy, 180–83; and formulating an educational philosophy, 254–55; and furthering democracy, 153–55; and the good life, 89; for the good school, 350–54; importance of health to, 351; importance of mental hygiene to, 338; importance of philosophy of education to, 15, 238–39, 373–74; intelligence, failure of, to recognize, 274–75; men needed as, 353; need of, for tact, 291; practical imperative and, 112–13; raising standards for, 353; and religion, 342–43; responsibility of, with respect to man's chief end, 68; and social improvements, 327; use of experimentalism by, 248

Technology, creative powers in a, 316

Teleology; *see* Purpose

Tests: for intelligence, 272–73; short-answer, 273

Thales: on basic substance, 191; father of Western philosophy, 1–3; primary interest of, 5, 8

Thorndike, Edward: dictum on measurement, 13–14; on man's failure to use reason, 54; on requirements for the good life, 74

Thought: creative, 297–300; criticism of Dewey's analysis, of, 308; Dewey's analysis of, 279; inductive-deductive, as furnishing basis for a general method, 367

Tolerance, in a free society, 259–60

Totalitarianism: as contrary to human nature and needs, 141; Hobbes and, 145–46; ideology of, 152–53

Traditionalists: and development of ability to reason, 281–83; and development of creative imagination, 311–12; educational tenets of, 254; and knowledge and character, 341; as having a partial view of education, 349; philosophy of, 254; views of, as to nature of education, 19–20